ME 'N' PAUL

ME 'N' PAUL

The Legend of Dizzy and Daffy

CARL DUNCAN

iUniverse

ME 'N' PAUL
THE LEGEND OF DIZZY AND DAFFY

Copyright © 2020 Carl Duncan.

All rights reserved. No part of this book may be used or reproduced by any means, graphic, electronic, or mechanical, including photocopying, recording, taping or by any information storage retrieval system without the written permission of the author except in the case of brief quotations embodied in critical articles and reviews.

iUniverse books may be ordered through booksellers or by contacting:

iUniverse
1663 Liberty Drive
Bloomington, IN 47403
www.iuniverse.com
844-349-9409

Because of the dynamic nature of the Internet, any web addresses or links contained in this book may have changed since publication and may no longer be valid. The views expressed in this work are solely those of the author and do not necessarily reflect the views of the publisher, and the publisher hereby disclaims any responsibility for them.

Any people depicted in stock imagery provided by Getty Images are models, and such images are being used for illustrative purposes only.
Certain stock imagery © Getty Images.

ISBN: 978-1-6632-1232-0 (sc)
ISBN: 978-1-6632-1233-7 (e)

Print information available on the last page.

iUniverse rev. date: 11/20/2020

This book is dedicated to Woodrow Wilson Duncan and to John David Duncan. My uncle Woody taught me to play baseball and to love the game. My son, Johnny D had the talent but not the desire.

Acknowledgements

I want to thank my University of Plano teammates Gary Reneau, Larry Goldsmith and Tommy Ragan for contributing their memories. Every ball hit to Reneau, my shortstop, was an adventure. He made the hard ones look easy and the easy ones look hard. Goldsmith was my leftfielder for 15 years. The Dan-Dees in Little League, the Franklin Falcons in Junior High, the Hillcrest Panthers in High School, and finally the University of Plano Pirates in college. A flyball to left field was and automatic out. Tommy Ragan helped recruit me for the University of Plano and played second base. He was a smart ballplayer, taking advantage of any mistake, the opposition made. If an opposing third baseman played back Tommy would lay down a perfect bunt for a hit. Rest in peace old friend.

Rick Blair also shared his memories for this book. Rick was our University of Plano batboy then and now he is my best friend. In addition to his batboy duties Rick was coach Dean's personal gopher. Coach never could seem to make it through a game without running out of chewing tobacco. One of Rick's many duties were going through the stands till he found a fan who was willing to share his tobacco with coach Dean.

Last, I want to thank my wife, Myra for her encouragement and help. She made this book and everything else possible.

Foreword

I grew up hearing stories about Dizzy and Paul Dean. My dad and uncles were contemporaries of the Dean Brothers. Like the Deans, my folks were sharecroppers who grew up farming land they didn't own. My dad was a great storyteller like Dizzy and like Diz he never let the truth get in the way of a good story.

The Dean's story was inspirational to many poor farm boys growing up during the Great Depression. Baseball lifted Dizzy and Paul from obscure poverty to fame & wealth, from migrant farm workers to major league heroes who were two of the most famous men in America.

Paul was always in Dizzy's shadow because Dizzy was more outspoken and flamboyant. Also, Paul's career was cut short by arm problems that kept him from becoming a Hall of Fame pitcher like Dizzy. Dizzy became a famous sportscaster while Paul became a college and minor league manager and coach.

Paul Dean became the baseball coach and athletic director at the University of Plano in 1966.

He fielded his first baseball team in 1967. I was a pitcher on that team. I played for Coach Dean all three years he coached at the University of Plano and listened to his many stories about his remarkable life.

Many books have been written about Dizzy, but none about Paul. Although their lives were intertwined, Dizzy's life has been well chronicled but not much has been written about Paul after his glory days with the Cardinals. Paul intended to write a book entitled "Me 'N' Diz" because he was "fed up with all the hooey written about the Dean family".[1] He said writers usually talked to Dizzy and "Diz gets a little careless with the truth"[2], so Paul wanted to "set the record straight".[3] Paul never wrote his book. This book attempts to tell Paul Dean's story.

CHAPTER 1

Goober, Dizzy and Daffy

Life was hard for Albert Dean on that cold March day in 1917. His wife Alma had just died of tuberculosis after a long illness. Dean was a sharecropper in Lucas, Arkansas and his future appeared bleak as he was left with three small boys to raise.

Elmer was the oldest, born March 11, 1908, he was physically strong but mentally challenged. Elmer was a good ballplayer but often held up games by falling into laughing fits after a batter struck out. That than other peculiarities earned him the nickname goofy. Writers later called him Goober because he sold peanuts at the Houston Buffs stadium. Jay Hannah, later called Jerome Herman and famously "Dizzy" was seven when his mother died. He was born January 16, 1910 although he gave sportswriters several different dates and places of birth. Paul was the youngest born August 14, 1913, sportswriter's first dubbed him Harpo (after the silent Marx brother) because he talked less than Dizzy, and finally Daffy for no apparent reason other than it sounded good with Dizzy, as in sports page headlines heralding victories for Dizzy and Daffy.

Albert and Alma Dean's first two children, Charles Monroe Dean and Sarah May Dean failed to survive childhood.

War was raging in Europe and America was about to be drawn into World War I, President Woodrow Wilson tried for two years to keep the US neutral but when German U-boat started sinking American ships in the North Atlantic Wilson asked Congress for a "war to end all wars." United States declared war on Germany on April 6, 1917 and on to the Austro-Hungarian Empire on December 7, 1917. Although America was only in the war two years it had a profound effect on baseball and was a catalyst for changing Babe Ruth from pitcher to an everyday player in the outfield.

When the 1918 baseball season started the director of the military draft decreed that by July 1 all draft eligible men employed in "nonessential jobs" must apply for work directly related to the war or risk being drafted to fight on the front lines in Europe. Many players chose to enlist or find essential jobs. This decimated most major league teams (an average of 15 players per team). Most Minor League teams closed down in 1917 but the Major Leagues played a full schedule. This draft eventually included all men age 18 – 45 unless exempted due to extreme hardship.

A young pitcher on the Boston Red Sox decided to play the 1917 season rather than enlist or find essential work. George Herman Ruth was a 23-year-old left-handed pitcher who in the last three years had become one of the best pitchers in the American League. He also showed promise as a power hitter. While pitching every fourth day Ruth averaged a homer every 38 at-bats, his teammates averaged a home run every 457 at-bats. Because of the shortage of experienced players Ruth did double duty pitching every fourth day playing outfield when he didn't pitch. After being traded to the Yankees he left the mound completely and became the greatest home run hitter of his era.

When the war ended in 1918 five men with major-league experience had died in battle three future hall of famers Pete Alexander, Ty Cobb, and Christy Mathewson were also in the war. Alexander, the best pitcher in the Majors, fought on the front lines in France.

He suffered from shell shock, loss of hearing and symptoms of epilepsy that would eventually drive him to alcohol abuse. Cobb and Mathewson took part in a poison gas defense drill that went horribly wrong. Cobb escaped unharmed but Mathewson inhaled some of the poison gas. He gradually deteriorated and died seven years later at the age of 45. Another veteran of World War I was branch Rickey, a man who would change the lives of the Dean boys and in fact all of baseball. Albert Dean didn't have to worry about being drafted (he was exempted due to extreme hardship) he had to worry about feeding his family.

Alma Nelson and Albert Monroe Dean married in 1904. Albert was 32 years old; Alma was 8 years younger. Raising their three surviving children in Lucas, Arkansas. During the early years of the 20th century was a struggle.

Diz liked to tell how poor they were. "I was choppin' cotton down in Arkansas' and because of floods, drought, and the weevils we sure was pore. So, Pa used to send me out huntin' squirrel in the woods for our supper. Since we didn't have enough money to buy no ammunition until the cotton was sold at market, I had to throw rocks at the squirrels to kill 'm, that's how I got such a blazin' fast ball by throwin' rocks at them squirrels, and I got good control too because if I missed 'em, we didn't have no supper, and just had to eat black-eyed peas, and dunk our corn pone in the pot likker from the peas."[1] Paul said later "if Diz threw a million times, he might've hit one. Nah, we never went squirrel hunting with rocks. We had a shotgun and a .22 and traps."[2]

It was while the Deans lived in Lucas that Diz said he changed his name from Jay Hannah Dean to Jerome Herman Dean. Ray Stockton of the St. Louis post-dispatch asked Diz about the name change. "I just can't help doin' favors for people," Diz said. "Sometimes I'm afraid this heart is gonna bust right through this sweater. Always been that way. You know how people follow me around now; when I couldn't see over a cotton field, it was the same way. I was very popular with the neighbors, and especially with a man who had a little boy about my age-six or seven, I guess. I often wondered whether that man thought more of me or his own boy. Then all of a sudden the boy took sick. My name, in the first place, was Jay Hanna Dean and this boy was Jerome Herman something or other. I was named after some big shot in Wall Street, or he was named after me, I don't know which. Anyhow, this boy Jerome Herman took sick and died, and we sure did feel sorry for his dad. He just moped around and didn't care for nothin' no more. So, I went to him and told him I thought so much of him that

I was goin' to take the name of Jerome Herman, and I've been Jerome Herman ever since. He perked up right away, and I guess wherever he is he's mighty proud."[3]

After Alma Dean's untimely death at age 37 Albert and his three boys did not stay in Lucas, Ark. Albert, called AB, was not from the Lucas area. AB was born in Rolla, Missouri in 1872. He lived there until he was about fifteen, then moved to Oklahoma with his family. Later AB moved to Arkansas working on the railroad, hauling logs and working in sawmills. He was working in the Lucas area when he met Alma Nelson.

Elmer was ten, Jay seven and Paul four when their mother died. In a poignant moment later in life Dizzy recalled his mother. "I don't remember much about my mother, except sometimes I can remember how she looked. She died of tuberculosis. Sara May? Well, I don't know what took her away. I know my brother Charlie died 'cause he wasn't able to get proper food and medicine. If we had them things maybe my mother wouldn't have died either."[4]

With no ties to Lucas, no mother to keep them grounded or make a home, the Dean's left Lucas. The Deans were sharecroppers, a truly miserable occupation. The rural south in the 1920's was largely agricultural; most people made their living farming. Farmers who didn't own land often became sharecroppers. Under the system of sharecropping a poor farmer would work a plot belonging to a landowner. The farmer would receive a share of the harvest as payment. Poor crops and unscrupulous landowners often left sharecroppers in debt after working a full growing season. Sharecropping doomed generations of southerners to poverty.

Pa and the boys lived on farms they didn't own growing mostly cotton which was a cash crop. They had to share the proceeds of their labor with the landowners. The boys attended school when they could which wasn't often. Diz often said, "I only went to second grade and I didn't do so good in the first."[5]

Paul disputed this claim. "Diz left school in 1926, while he was in the seventh reader at Spaulding, Okla. Now, some folks might think that there isn't much difference in those two statements, but I think there is. There are a good many people in this country who didn't get past the seventh grade, but there aren't so many who didn't finish the second. If you stop to think about it, there's a big difference between the two. By the time a person gets to the seventh grade, he has the groundwork for a pretty good education – he can read, write, spell and figure."[6]

By the early 1920's the Deans were in Oklahoma living in Purcell, Holdenville, Spaulding and other farming communities around Oklahoma City. It was in Spaulding that the Dean Brothers played their first "organized' Baseball. They played on school teams with real bats and balls. Back in Lucas there were pick-up games with other farm boys. No one had money for equipment, so the bats, balls and gloves were homemade.

Diz said his father made bats out of hickory limbs and turned worn out work gloves into mitts. "He could make the best darn baseball you ever seen. He could make a baseball outta almost anything, just scraps of stuff, like an ol' shoe tongue, a hunk of innertube for insides, a piece of sock and mebbe some twine. He could make a mighty lively ball."[7]

When Paul Dean was coaching the University of Plano in the late sixties, the players were griping about the condition of an opponent's field they had to play on. Coach told his players, "you boys are so spoiled. You don't know how lucky you are. When I was growin' up we played wearing bibbed overalls and barefooted. We played in a cotton patch and the only ones who had mitts was the catcher and first baseman. I never had a pair of spikes 'til I signed with the Cardinals. They gave me a pair and I couldn't wear 'um. I had to put gravel in 'um so I felt like I wuz playin' barefooted."[8]

In the Spaulding school 12 yr. old Paul was assigned to fifth grade and 15 yr. old Jay to the seventh. Elmer did not go to school. On the school team Paul played shortstop, Jay pitched. Even though it was "organized" baseball the fields were still primitive. Homeplate was a shingle, the bases empty feed sacks and the backstop chicken wire. Seats were anything the farmers could find, from milk pails to crates. Paul and Jay still played in overalls and barefoot.

It was at the Spaulding school that Jay first received recognition for his pitching. Ornie Mayfield, one of Jay and Paul's teammates said."

"Oh, was that Jay something." You couldn't believe how hard that boy could throw. He was as strong as he ever was, I guess just a big old country boy who would scare you to death with that speed. I played in every game he pitched that year, and when he started that motion, it was like winding up a slingshot, and when he unwound, and that thing came flying out of there, you didn't hardly know where it was coming from. Fast? God almighty, what a sight he was."[9]

Later in life Paul reminisced "Baseball just came natural for us, like puttin' on our pants and we knew the rules when we were too young to read a rulebook."[10]

CHAPTER 2

"Why you Dizzy son-of-a-bitch"

Pa Dean, a stone-faced, unsmiling man bent by tragedy and poverty, finally realized that sharecropping was a losing proposition. He abandoned that pursuit for the more nomadic life of the migrant farm worker. By the end of 1926, the Dean family, Pa, Elmer, Jay and Paul, had left Oklahoma and were living in south Texas.

One Dizzy Dean biographer, Curt Smith wrote that a child-hood friend of the Dean's told him Pa Dean married "A woman named Parham"[1] several years after his first wife, Alma, died. A second biographer, Vince Staten, wrote that he married Cora Parham, a widow with three children. Yet a third biographer, Robert Gregory, does not mention a wife after Alma. Mr. Dean's obituary in the April 4, 1956 Dallas morning news names two wives. Alma, the mother of Elmer, Jay and Paul. Also, a second wife, Mattie Sandifer, whom he married in 1939 while living in Garland, Texas. If indeed Pa Dean married while in Arkansas or Oklahoma it must have been short-lived because by the time the Deans were living in Texas it was just Pa Dean and his three boys.

South Texas in the twenties was the perfect place for the Deans to use their only skill: picking cotton. In Texas cotton was king and south Texas offered more cotton fields than Arkansas or Oklahoma because of a warmer, longer growing season.

Even with the longer harvest season, it was still hard to earn enough money to last through the fall and winter. Somebody in the family needed to find full-time employment to tide the family over from harvest to harvest. Pa Dean had no marketable skills, Elmer was slightly retarded and in 1926 Paul was just thirteen years old.

Fort Sam Houston was located on the outskirts of San Antonio and it was decided that Jay should join the Army. Although he was only sixteen years old, he was a big boy and could easily pass for eighteen, the minimum age to enlist. America was between wars, WWI and WWII, so there was no draft. Volunteers were needed to staff the Army so big able-bodied boys could enlist without any problems. Birth certificates weren't required since so many boys, like Jay, were born on the farm with no hospital records.

"I didn't figure on spendin' my life pickin' cotton," said Dizzy much later, "so I joined the Army. You got your shoes free and all the grub you wanted and the pay was $19 a month and that was more money than I'd ever seen or was gonna make on a farm somewhere, and I heard they could use smart fellas like me."[2]

Diz often said he never had a pair of shoes until he joined the Army. This was, however just another one of his many exaggerations. Dizzy told author Jack Sher "we, Paul, Elmer and me, had one pair of shoes each. They was our winter shoes, and we took 'em off in the summer to save the leather. That didn't hurt us none. It was warm in the summer, hell it was downright hot. What sometimes hurt us was the way Pa looked when the food was skimpy. We knowed how hard he worked and there never seemed to be enough. When I look back on it now, I sometimes wonder how we all went through it."[3]

However, Diz never blamed his father for their poor circumstances. "My dad did the best he could. I never knowed a man who had it tougher. He was a regular pal to us kids and he hadda be a mother, too."[4]

So, on November 15, 1926, at the age of sixteen, Jay Dean enlisted for a four-year term in the United States Army. He was assigned to the third wagon company. On the base were 60 wagons and stalls for 240 mules and horses. Jay said he was ordered to clean the stables by shoveling out the manure "like that Hercules fella."[5]

In their spare time the soldiers in Jay's unit often played baseball. Jay's ability to throw a baseball attracted the attention of Sgt. James Brought, who managed the twelfth field artillery company team. Jay was in the third wagon company and this presented a problem, he would have to play on their team.

Sgt. Brought told Jay he could get him transferred to the twelfth artillery where he could play more ball and shovel less horseshit. Jay later said, "I was in trouble anyhow with an officer. This here officer had called up and asked me when I was going to haul over some manure to put on the flower beds at his quarters. And I answered "right soon, sir, you are number two on my manure list. He figured I was getting smart with him. My chances of getting promoted to PFC in the third wagon company wasn't too good."[6] Jay transferred to twelfth artillery and became a star pitcher for their team.

While Jay was in the Army Pa, Elmer and Paul stayed close to San Antonio, picking cotton all-around south-central Texas. Paul began playing baseball on local semi-pro teams. Many companies had teams and most small towns fielded baseball teams. These teams usually consisted of boys and men who had played baseball in high school or college. Many were ex-professional players.

In south central Texas such towns as Comfort, Boerne, Kerrville, Fredericksburg, Hondo, Weimar, Utopia and Uvalde all had good teams. Local teams often traveled to Old Mexico to play against Mexican teams and they also played against local college teams.

Paul Dean told Sam Blair, a columnist for the Dallas Morning News, that he pitched for a San Antonio semi-pro team against the University of Texas in 1928 when he was just 15 yrs. old. Wearing bib overalls and playing barefoot, Paul shut them out 2 – 0, just grinning bearing down with his fastball the more they razzed him about being a country bumpkin. The San Antonio team then went south of the border and Paul beat the pride of Torreon, Mexico. The locals were so impressed they asked Paul to stay over and pitch for them three days later when their hated rivals came to town. "They offered me $200 in American money and a bullet-proof hotel room," Paul said. "The money was good, but they scared me off with that bullet-proof room".[7]

While Jay was in the Army, Pa, Elmer, and Paul lived around San Antonio during the winter, but during harvest season they joined other migrant workers traveling from place to place picking cotton. It was during this time that Elmer became "lost."

As Paul said Diz never let the truth spoil a good story. So naturally Dizzy couldn't resist inserting himself into the middle of the tale about "losing" Elmer. "It was back there about '24 or '25," Diz began, "and we was travelin' around from field to field huntin' for work. Dad an' Paul and me was ridin' in one car and Ol' Elmer, he was ridin' in a car behind us with some friends of ours. Well, we crossed some railroad tracks jest as an ol' freight is comin'. This cotton-pickin' feller drivin' the car Elmer is in; he's held up by the train. We was supposed to all meet in Dallas that night. We wait an' we wait, but they don't show up. Well, now, we had to hustle us up some work before we go to starvin', so we drive someplace else and get us a job".[8] The truth that Diz was careless with this time was the fact that he was in the Army when Elmer became separated from Pa and Paul.

Pa, Elmer and Paul were driving through central Texas from Waco to Austin following other workers from one cotton farm to another, harvesting the cotton. The migrant workers often caravanned together, driving old jalopies and pick-up trucks, so they could camp together and help each other if someone had car trouble.

The Deans had a flat tire and one of the other cotton pickers stopped to help. Elmer was hungry, so while Pa and Paul stayed to change the tire, Elmer went with one of the other workers to get food. They agreed to meet at the next store up the road. "We caught 'em just on the other side of Austin." Said Paul later. "But they run a red light and turned off a side street and that's when we lost 'em. We kept goin' for a mile or so, nearly out to the University, and went up and down all the streets but couldn't find 'em. Not a trace. We headed back out to the Waco highway and camped there for two days and we didn't see them. This fella Elmer was with had been goin' place to place with us and we knew he'd be tryin' to run into us again and drop Elmer off."[9]

They didn't find Elmer. With no cell phones, and no permanent address they couldn't expect Elmer to write or phone. Elmer was 21 but he was slightly retarded and had never been on his own. Pa wasn't worried, because Elmer knew how to work, and he figured he would stay with the other migrant workers and that he would show up someday. They wouldn't see Elmer again for four years.

Early in his army hitch Dizzy acquired his famous nickname. Private Dean was on K.P. Duty when Sergeant Brought entered the mess hall. He heard a loud clanging noise coming from the kitchen. Investigating the clamor, Brought discovered Private Dean throwing potatoes at garbage can lids. The Sergeant inadvertently gave Diz the nickname that lasted a lifetime when he yelled "why, you Dizzy son of a bitch."[10]

CHAPTER 3

"I gave him $120 I'd made pickin' cotton, and then he lost all but $40 in a crap game"

In 1929 Diz had been in the service for over 3 years, and he was sick of the Army. Diz said later "I was the worst soldier in God's livin' world!"[1] Diz had a tendency to be undisciplined, lazy and careless, traits that did not fit well in the regimentation of the army. Even Sgt Brought who loved him like a son said, "he was the laziest and most irresponsible soldier in the history of the U.S. Army and the biggest liar from here to the Rio Grande. There were times I know if that .45 I was wearing had ammo I would've shot the son-of-a-bitch full of holes even if he was the greatest pitcher I ever saw."[2]

Diz was attracting a lot of attention pitching for the twelfth field artillery baseball team. The twelfth played other Army company teams but also played semi-pro teams from San Antonio and the small towns around south central Texas. One of the teams they played was the San Antonio public service company. Diz pitched against the electric company team and their manager was so impressed he said, "we got to get that son of a bitch on our team."[3]

Word got around to Diz that if he could get out of the Army the San Antonio Electric Co would pay him more, doing an easier job and he could still play baseball. Dizzy Dean biographer Vince Staten wrote that the San Antonio Electric Co. bought Diz out of the Army. Since the U.S. was not at war buyouts were permissible, and since Diz had only eight months left in his hitch he could 'buyout' for $120. But Paul said he, not the San Antonio Utility Co. paid for Diz to leave the Army early on March 15, 1929. "I gave him $120 I'd made pickin' cotton" said Paul "and then he lost all but $40 of it in a crap game.

So, I told him he might as well try to win it back and he ended up with $140 and that's what got him out."[4]

Despite his poor record as a soldier, a few years later the U.S Armed Forces took advantage of Dizzy's celebrated Major League exploits. Ironically, the Army produced a recruiting poster with Diz's smiling face and the proud caption "THE ARMY TRAINED HIM!"[5]

Since Dizzy was getting out of the Army with a good job lined up, 1929 was shaping up to be a good year for the Dean family, however, by the end of the year the rest of America would be in deep trouble. On October 24, 1929 the stock market crashed. Called "Black Thursday," panic ensued and over the next four days stock prices fell 23%. The Great Depression began.

The depression caused many farmers to lose their land. At the same time years of overcultivation and drought caused the "Dust Bowl." Thousands of farmers, sharecroppers and migrant workers in North Texas, Oklahoma, and Kansas left formerly fertile land and headed west to California to find work and a new life.

Unemployment soared to 25 percent and many people ended up living as homeless "Hobos". Others moved to shanty towns called "Hooverville" a rebuke of sitting President Herbert Hoover.

Baseball did not escape the decade long effects of the "Great Depression". Attendance fell and by 1933 the average major league crowd declined to less than 5,000, a 15 percent decrease from the 1920's. Players pay was cut by 25%, but they were lucky. The average wage of the American worker fell 50% during the depression. A player making $3,000 a year was still making twice as much as the average industrial worker.

The Dean family was better off than many people, even though Pa Dean had hurt his back and was unable to work. Dizzy was working and playing ball for the San Antonio Utility Company. He was making $3.50 a day, almost twice what he earned in the army. Paul was working part time at a service station earning about $6.00 a week. He was also playing baseball for a semi-pro team, the Pierce Tire and Bicycle shop. They still had no news of Elmer.

CHAPTER 4

"I throwed four balls and the guy sez that's enuff. That ended my career as assistant-meter-reader"

When Diz left the Army in 1929 he went straight to work for the San Antonio public service company, just as the company's semi-pro baseball team started their season. He told about going to work for the Utility co. "I was way ahead of them Army sergeants. I started lookin' for some kinda easier job. After several months I heard about a soft job in San Antonio in the meter readin department of the Public Service Company. A fellar tole me that readin meters was the easiest work a man could do without actually bein unemployed. After talkin to the boss at the company I figgered maybe meter readin was just about the easiest job I knowed anything about. The only bad thing about it was you had to bend over once in a while. Finally, I ask the boss if he was sure they ain't got a easier job than meter readin. Well, he said there was only one job any easier. That was assistant to a meter reader. That's the job I took."[1]

Diz quickly attracted attention by winning games and striking out batters. Before the season was over a St. Louis Cardinal scout, Don Curtis, took notice of the 19-yr. old fire balling right hander. "After seeing Dizzy throw less than a dozen fastballs," said Curtis,

"I knew he had what it takes. We met and before I left, Dizzy signed a contract with the Cardinals' Houston Farm Club in the Texas League for a salary of $300 a month and no bonus."[2]

Dizzy told the story of his signing this way: "A friend of a Big-League scout seen me on the mound one day and started burnin' up the telephone lines between San Antonio and St. Louis. The Cardinals number one scout came down to Texas and ask me to throw a few balls. I throwed four balls and the guy sez that's enuff. That ended my career as assistant-meter-reader. They signed me up to a contract for three hundred bucks a month."[3]

After Diz signed with St. Louis he became the property and the headache of Sam Breadon, owner of the Cardinals, and his general manager, Branch Rickey.

Sam Breadon was a self-made man. Born in a poor part of New York city in 1876, he was one of eight children whose father died when Sam was young. By 1900 he was living in St. Louis and working at an automobile dealership and garage.

In 1904 St. Louis hosted the World's Fair. The fair, also known as the Louisiana Purchase Exposition (because it marked the 100th anniversary of the Louisiana Purchase) displayed new scientific advances, products and ideas. Hundreds of thousands of visitors viewed scientific discoveries introduced for the first time. Among them were the x-ray machine, baby incubator, electric typewriter, and the telautograph (an early version of the fax machine).

The World's Fair also introduced many new food and drink items, such as Dr. Pepper (named after a Waco, Texas pharmacist), cotton candy, popsicles, and the ice cream cone. Breadon took advantage of the new snack food craze and ran a concession stand at the fair.

With profits made from his concession stand, Breadon opened his own automobile dealership. The auto industry was new, dynamic, and expanding, Sam prospered, eventually owning successful Pierce-Arrow dealerships and became a millionaire.

Me 'N' Paul

In 1917 Breadon invested $2,000 in the St. Louis Cardinals baseball team, then a struggling second-division Major League team constantly strapped for money and resources. By 1919 he was able to purchase enough stock to get controlling interest in the club. Breadon was a rabid baseball fan and he planned to run the team, not just serve on the board. He inherited Branch Rickey who was both field manager and business manager.

Branch Rickey went on to achieve the two most significant changes to baseball in the 20th century. He was the driving force behind the implementation of the Farm System and the integration of the Major Leagues.

Rickey had been a Major League catcher, Albeit a sorry one. After a college career at Ohio Wesleyan, he played in 1905 – 1906 for the St. Louis Browns and 1907 with the New York Highlanders. He did establish one dubious record: allowing 13 stolen bases in one game. After his playing days he returned to college, earning a law degree, and then served in WWI. After the war Rickey went to work for the Cardinals.

When Breadon gained control of the St. Louis Cardinals, he realized that Rickey was overstretching himself by trying to run the front office and manage the team on the field simultaneously. Early in the 1925 season Breadon replaced him, hiring Rogers Hornsby to be the field manager. Breadon told a disappointed Rickey "in time, Branch, you will see I am doing you a great favor".[4] Freed from his duties as field manager, Rickey was able to devote all his time, energy and intelligence to the job of building the Cardinals into a perennial power.

Rickey quickly realized that the Cardinals were at a disadvantage when it came to acquiring players. Before the farm system, Minor League teams were independent of the Major League clubs. Most players reached the big leagues after their Minor League owners sold their contracts for money and/or players. The Minor League players were auctioned off to the highest Major League bidders. In this system the rich clubs had a tremendous advantage over the teams with fewer assets. Rickey was searching for a way to even the playing field with the wealthier teams.

Rickey came up with a plan to develop players through a chain of Cardinal-owned teams in various levels of Minor Leagues. He was convinced the Cardinals could save money by signing and developing players on Cardinal owned Minor League teams rather than bidding against wealthier teams for players.

Breadon was able to finance Rickey's plan by selling the Cardinal's home ballpark, Robinson field, for $275,000. He had signed a lease for the Cardinals to play in Sportsman's Park, home of the St. Louis Browns of the American League. Rickey used this money to start purchasing Minor League clubs to begin building the Cardinals Farm Team system.

Rickey's Farm System spawned the iconic baseball scout. Termed 'Bird Dogs' or 'Ivory Hunters' by sports writers, these scouts traveled all over the country searching for amateur prospects. The Ivory Hunters scouted college teams, rural town teams, semi- pro sandlot teams, and mill town teams, always searching for "the arm behind the barn."[5] Don Curtis, the man who signed Dizzy Dean was one of these scouts.

CHAPTER 5

"I got a l'il brother back home that throws harder'n me."

Dizzy Dean reported to the Houston Buffalos, a Cardinal Farm team, at the start of the 1930 season to begin his professional baseball career. Dizzy said, "man, can you imagine getting money to pitch?"[1] At $300 a month it wasn't too much of a raise over the Utility Company, but at least he just played ball and didn't have to do no meter readin'.

Pa Dean and Paul stayed in San Antonio, living in a two-room house at the southern edge of Fort Sam Houston, Elmer was still missing. The Deans had neither seen nor heard from Elmer since they were separated somewhere around Austin in 1927. 16 yr. old Paul still worked at a service station and pitched for the pierce tire and bicycle shop. Diz had promised to send some of his ball playin' pay when he could.

The Houston Buffalos played in the class A Texas league. Since Dizzy had no professional experience he was not expected to play at this level. The Texas League was the next to highest rung of the Minor Leagues.

Double A was the highest as there were no triple A until 1946. Most players were Major League veterans trying to make it back to the Majors and highly rated players with experience in the lower Minor Leagues. The lower leagues were in descending order, B, C and D leagues.

Newly signed players in the Cardinal chain were sent to Houston to be evaluated and then sent to the league commisserant with their skill. Most players with no professional experience were sent to class D, the lowest Minor League. Diz was expected to be sent to the Cardinals class D team or at best farmed out to Shawnee in the Class C Western Association.

Dizzy impressed everyone with his raw talent. The Houston Post reported: (3/18/30) *ROOKIES SHOW PROMISE. The practice ball game of this afternoon indicated the Houston Buffs have a couple of young right-hand chunkers of real promise. Dizzy Dean, a rawboned youth from San Antonio, and Roger Traweek, a big boy from Mexia, are the lads. Both are green, but each has a fast ball that bops. Dean has a bit more polish than traweek. Both likely will be farmed out to a Class C or Class D club. With any luck both will be outstanding applicants for Buff training jobs in 1931.*[2]

Diz, however, was not sent to Class C or D. He was assigned to the St. Joseph Saints of the Class B Western League. St. Joe had just started spring training at Shawnee, Oklahoma. Dizzy was given a train ticket to Shawnee and told to go to the Aldridge Hotel where the players were staying. Dizzy was familiar with the area since he had lived around that part of Oklahoma when he was growing up.

"Peaches" Davis, a Saints player, told about meeting Diz for the first time. He said he answered the door at the Aldridge where he and two other players were staying and saw a guy with dirty face and filthy clothes. He thought a hobo had just jumped off a freight train.

"Goddamn' said Peaches "I'll never forget him coming in that night. I thought he was a colored boy he was so black. I was going to tell him he had the wrong room, but then he said, "I'm Dizzy Dean." So, I let him in and asked how'd you get here? "Caught a ride with somebody," and that's all he said. Not another word about how dirty he was of if he'd crawled off a freight car, but we guessed that's what he'd done, the son of a bitch had cashed in his ticket down there and come in on the rails. I said where's your bags? And he said, "there's on the way." We showed him the shower, got him cleaned up and gave him some clothes. Then he wouldn't go to bed. He wanted to tell us what a great pitcher he was that's when I knew why thy called him "Dizzy." The next morning, he was out there throwing the fastest Goddamn ball I'd ever seen."[3]

Peaches wasn't the only one impressed by Dizzy's fastball. Veteran catcher Charles Abbott caught Dizzy at the St. Joe's training camp, saying Dean "has more stuff than any pitcher I've ever caught."[4]

Diz pitched in two games at the spring training camp. The first was on April 6, 1930 against Shawnee, the Card's Class C Farm Club. He went six innings, allowing five runs on ten hits. Diz came back in a relief appearance four days later giving up three runs on six hits in just three innings of work.

In spite of these lackluster pitching performances, the coaches thought Diz had tremendous potential. He headed North with the Saints when they broke camp on April 14th, heading home to St. Joseph, Missouri. Diz was scheduled to start the second game of the Saints upcoming season.

Dizzy Dean started his first professional game on April 30, 1930 against the Denver Bears. The first batter he faced was Jimmy Adair (Adair's son Steve Adair succeeded Paul Dean as Head Coach and Athletic director at the University of Plano in 1970). The game was tied 2 – 2 after nine innings. The Adair hit a solo homer off Diz in the top of the 10th but St. Joe scored 2 runs in the bottom of that frame giving Diz a 4 – 3 win, his first professional victory.

While at St. Joseph Diz became well-known not only for his pitching, but also his eccentric behavior. Local automobile dealers would loan him a car which he drove until he got tired of it, then he parked the car somewhere until he needed another which a different dealer would provide.

Diz didn't understand hotel procedures, because the club always handled accommodations as the players traveled. When in St. Joseph he simply went into the nearest hotel when he was ready to sleep. Never bothering to check out, he was registered at the YMCA, St. Francis hotel, and the Rubidoux Hotel all at the same time. When billed for an entire month, Dizzy told the proprietors "bill it to them Saints. There're good for it."[5]

As sports columnist Roy Stockton wrote "Nobody had ever taken the time to explain the banking system to Jerome Herman Dean, the cotton picker. Who thought it would be of importance?"[6] Diz soon learned that all he had to do to obtain goods and services with the local merchants of St. Joseph was to sign his name to a piece of paper. These pieces of paper invariably found their way to Branch Rickey, and just as Diz figured, Rickey took care of all of them. Rickey tired of this quickly and told merchants the Cardinals would no longer honor anymore of Dizzy's I.O. U's.

Diz also took advantage of his newfound celebrity status to date as many of the local ladies as possible. The St. Louis star reported "Dizzy will take three girls out in the same evening and go home engaged to all of them."[7]

Rusty Lyons, a pitcher for the Des Moines Demons, said "Diz didn't care what girl he was with or what she might have. Dean caught "The Clap" in early summer. Everybody knew it."[8] Diz was admitted to the Missouri Methodist Hospital for an "ankle infection". When he left the hospital, he brought his nurse with him, parking down the right field line and smooching between innings.

It was about this time when Dizzy first met Branch Rickey, a man destined to have a great influence on his life, Diz tells about that first meeting.

"One day in the lobby of the hotel I was talking to a girl. Some man came up to me and asked me my name. "Huh, you must be a stranger, here aren't you?" I said. "I'm Dizzy Dean, the pitcher." "Oh!" he said. "So, you're Mr. Dean." "Nope," I answered, "not Mr. Dean or Dean or J. H. dean, but just Dizzy Dean." "Think you'll ever get to the majors?" this chap asked. "Well," said I, "if this guy Branch Rickey ever wakes up to the fact that he has a real pitcher down here I'll get there mighty quick." "You don't think much of Mr. Rickey's judgment, do you?" "Well, someday I'll meet him and tell him what I think," I said. The man spoke up and says, "Well, you've met him now. I am Branch Rickey." "Huh!" I said. "So, you're the man who shunted me up to this bush league, are you?" Branch said, "Yeh, what of it?" Then I said, "Well, you're a darn smart baseball man."[9]

Dizzy kept winning games and by early August he had won 17 games, lost 8, while striking out 125 batters in 217 innings. Elated by his success Diz started calling himself "The Great Dean". The only thing Diz liked better than talking about himself was talking about his brother Paul. From the time he signed with the Cardinals Diz was telling anybody who would listen "I got a l'il brother back home that throws harder'n me."[10]

The Cardinals made it a practice not to promote players to another Farm Team if their current team was in a pennant race. St. Joseph however was in the cellar, so Diz was called up to Houston in the Class A Texas League.

CHAPTER 6

"What do they call this league? It sure is soft"

Dizzy Dean joined the Houston Buffs on August 5, 1930. Ironically, he was scheduled to pitch that very night against his hometown's Texas league team, the San Antonio Indians.

Apparently unconcerned about pitching against his hometown team or facing Texas league hitters for the first time, Diz hurled the Buffs to a 12-1 victory. He struck out 14 while allowing only six hits, all singles.

The Eagle (Bryan, TX Newspaper) reported:

Dizzy Dean is getting a lot of publicity lately over his achievements in the pitching department of organized ball. Dean had the pleasure of striking out nearly all the semi- pros around San Antonio. The San Antonio team did not even notice him. Houston did not fail to watch this lad. He was sent to Joplin, MO., and now he is with the Buffs and according to all reports he is going to set the Texas League on fire. That is the way with us all, we never appreciate what we have at home and never give it a thought until somebody else steps in and shows you up. That is exactly what Houston did to San Antonio."[1]

On August 13 Diz pitched in Ft. Worth against the Ft. Worth Panthers. Again, he had no trouble against the Texas League batters. Stopping the "Cats" on seven hits and only one run. Wins over the Beaumont Exporters and the Wichita Falls Spudders quickly followed.

Dizzy was starting to get more of the publicity he craved. An article in the Amarillo Times read: *"The feat of Dizzy Dean, former San Antonio Sandlotter, in winning his first six starts for Houston, stamped the youngster the reigning sensation among Texas League pitchers."*[2]

After winning his first six starts, Dizzy lost games to the Ft. Worth "Cats" and the Shreveport Sports. He then beat Beaumont 8-1 before closing the season beating Wichita Falls. The Brownsville Herald wrote *"Dizzy Dean turned in a hurling masterpiece as the Buffs squared their final series with Wichita Falls 3-0. The rookie star gave up only three hits, widely scattered and whiffed nine."*[3]

At the end of the Texas League season Dizzy had won 8 games and lost only 2. He was named to the League's All-Star team, just as he had earlier that year when he pitched for St. Joseph in the Western League. The 20-yr. old phenom proved he could succeed at a high rung of the Minor League ladder by striking out ninety-five batters in only eighty-five innings.

In 1930, just as today, Major League teams were allowed to expand their rosters in September. After the Minor League seasons ended promising young players were called up to the Majors. Management wanted young players to be exposed to the Big-League play.

On September 10, 1930 Dizzy Dean was called up to the St. Louis Cardinals who were playing the Giants in New York City. Diz had never been to New York City and he had some wardrobe concerns. *"When Dean was informed at Houston towards the close of the season that he was to report to the Cardinals in New York, he sought to route himself through his home city of San Antonio, explaining that he needed several shirts before going to the big town. So sincere was he about his preparedness that it was only after Dizzy had become thoroughly convinced that shirts could be purchased and washed in New York, that he was persuaded to forgo his trip to San Antonio and report the Cards in the East, promptly."*[4]

Me 'N' Paul

When Diz joined the Cardinals, they were in a tight race, trying to win a third pennant in five years. A .500 team as late as mid-August the Cards were in second place when Dizzy arrived in New York. He took one look at the third-place Giants and said, "I can beat them clowns"[5] Charles "Gabby" Street, the Cardinal manager, was not about to let a raw 20 yr. old rookie pitch in this tight, tense, pressure packed pennant race, especially in 1930, the year of the hitter.

The 1919 Black Sox scandal hurt baseball attendance; owners had been looking for ways to make the game more popular. Fans loved high scoring games, so many changes were made to help hitters. The spitball was outlawed, although pitchers who relied primarily on the spitball were "grandfathered" by allowing them to use the outlawed pitch legally until the end of their careers. Baseballs were wound tighter, thus travelling further when hit. Also, balls were replaced more frequently during games giving the batters an advantage over the pitchers.

Those changes helped Babe Ruth become a prodigious home run hitter and changed the game. Managers started relying more on the long ball rather than the traditional bunt, steal hit and run and slapping singles. These changes added up to unparalleled offense in the 1920's never before seen in baseball history. More and more Big-League managers were beginning to agree with what Ruth said "I ain't got time to mess with them little singles."[6]

But in 1920's hitting paled in comparison to the outrageous offensive statistics of 1930. Both the American and National Leagues set records for home runs and runs scored. The New York Yankees became the first team in history to score over 1,000 runs, averaging almost seven runs a game. Nine of the sixteen Major Leagues clubs batting averages were above .300 while the National League as a whole averaged .303.

Hack Wilson, Chicago Cub outfielder, shattered the National League home run and RBI records. He hit 56 homers and drove in 191 runs. His RBI record has never been broken. The Giants, Bill Terry became the last NL player to hit over .400. The Giants as a team hit .319, the highest ever recorded by any one team in modern Major League history.

The Philadelphia Phillies led the National League's offensive insanity. The Phillies team batting average was .315, second behind the Giants .319. Outfielder, Chuck Klein hit .386 with 170 RBI's. Lefty, O'Doul hit .383

and third baseman, Pinky Whitney hit .342. Every other player hit close to or over .300. All this firepower and the Phillies lost 102 games!

The Phillies pitching, if it could be called pitching, led to the teams' downfall and re- wrote the record books. Two of the dubious records remain unbroken today, opposing teams hit .346 against the Phillies and the teams ERA was 6.71.

This is the offensive-minded league, styled to favor the hitters that Diz would make his Big-League debut provided the Cards could clinch the pennant, with games left to play.

The Cardinal's manager at the time was Charles "Gabby" Street, also nicknamed "The Old Sarge" because of his service in World War I. Gabby had been a Major League catcher with the Cincinnati Reds, Boston Bean eaters, Washington Senators and the New York Highlanders. When he was playing for Washington, Gabby pulled-off one of the most publicized baseball stunts of the early 1900's.

On August 21, 1908 Street caught a baseball thrown from on top of the Washington Monument, a distance of 555 ft. Gabby missed the first twelve baseballs thrown by journalist Preston Gibson. The "Old Sarge" made a clean catch on the thirteenth ball thrown. "It didn't strike with terrific force as one might expect." The Old Sarge said "just about like stopping a fast one from a pitcher with plenty of steam."[7]

Gabby Street knew a lot about catching pitchers with "plenty of steam." His battery mate on the Washington Senators was the legendary Walter "Big Train" Johnson, said to have possessed the fastest fast ball of his generation.

In 1924, after pitching 18 years and winning 354 games, Walter Johnson finally got a chance to pitch for his Washington Senators in a World Series. Johnson was a great player for a losing franchise. 'Washington, first in war, first in peace and last in the American League' was a popular slogan. Washington was facing the New York Giants, a perineal powerhouse who had won four straight National League pennants.

Walter Johnson started the first game and lost a heartbreaker, pitching 12 innings and losing 4-3. He was roughed up in game 5, losing 6-2. Washington was able to hang on and tie the series at 3 games.

Game 7 was one of the all-time great World Series games. The Giants led 3-1 in the 8th and appeared to have the World Series wrapped up. Washington player-manager Bucky Harris came to bat with the bases loaded and 2 outs. He hit an easy grounder to third baseman Freddie Lindstrom. As the 18-year-old started to make the play, the ball took a bad hop over his head, driving in 2 runs tying the game.

Walter Johnson came in to pitch in the 9th inning on one days' rest. Inning after inning Johnson shut out the Giants. In the 12th inning Washington's Muddy Ruel lifted an easy pop foul behind home plate. New York catcher Hank Gowdy tripped over his own mask and failed to make the catch. Reprieved, Ruel got a hit. Walter Johnson then hit an easy grounder to shortstop. Travis Jackson, a future Hall of Famer, bobbled the ball putting runners on 1st and 2nd. The next batter, Earl McNeeley, hit another routine grounder to Lindstrom. Again, the ball inexplicable bounced over his head. Ruel scored and Washington won its first and only World Series.

No one begrudged Johnson his victory. Even Jack Bently, the losing pitcher was cheerful about it. "I guess the good Lord couldn't stand to see a fine fellow like Walter Johnson lose again."[8]

Diz kept begging manager Street to let him pitch. Gabby later said, "I admired his confidence and told him to save some of it for 1931, and you know what that S.O.B said to me?" He said, "don't you wanna win that pennant this year, Sarge?"[9]

Dizzy wasn't the only "character" the "Old Sarge" had to deal with during that late season pennant drive. Flint Rhem, a hard-throwing, hard-drinking, right-handed pitcher from South Carolina, was being counted on to win games during the stretch drive. Winner of six straight games Rhem was scheduled to pitch the first game of a crucial series against the Brooklyn Robins.

Flint didn't show up for the game. He had disappeared. The Cards proceeded to sweep the series without their errant pitcher. Flint straggled in after being gone for two days. Disheveled, bedraggled, and reeking of whiskey, he told a harrowing tale of bandits, guns, kidnapping and forced alcohol consumption.

Flint's story fell apart when he said he was forced to drink whiskey. Anyone who knew him would not believe Flint would ever have to be forced to consume liquor.

The Cardinals managed to clinch the pennant without Flint or Dizzy's help. On September 27th Jesse Haines pitched the Cards past the Pirates winning the pennant with one regular season game left to be played.

Since the last game of the season against the Pittsburgh Pirates was meaningless, manager "Gabby" street decided to let his brash, loud-mouthed rookie hurler start the game. Dizzy Dean was about to make his Major League debut.

Dizzy Dean started his first Major League game on September 28, 1930 against the Pittsburgh Pirates in St. Louis' Sportsman's Park. Diz remembered his first game this way, "by this time the eyes of the folks in St. Louis was weak from readin' so many headlines about me so I figgered it was easier on the eye doctors if they brung me to the Cardinals in person on the last day of the season. As I'm warmin' up before the game, the Pirate players think they are goin' to have an easy time of it, since I'm a rookie.

Larry French, who has 17 wins to his credit, is their pitcher and he gets a bonus of $1,000 if he wins 18 games. Larry probably thought that bonus was in the bag for sure when he learned he's opposin' a ganglin' kid like me."[10]

With an extra $1,000 on the line Pirates pitcher French had extra incentive to win this otherwise meaningless game. The average Big-League salary in 1930 was $7,000. The highest paid player was Babe Ruth at $80,000. When told his salary was higher than the beleaguered American President, Herbert Hoover, The Babe famously responded "why not? I had a better year than he did."[11]

Facing a potent Pirate line-up that featured future hall of famers Paul "Big Poison" Waner and Pie Traynor, Diz was masterful. After a shaky first inning where he gave up two walks and a run-scoring single, Diz settled down and by the seventh inning he was coasting. Walking to the dugout after the seventh Diz asked "what do they call this league? It sure is soft."[12]

Veteran pitcher Burleigh Grimes was impressed by the cool demeanor of the rookie pitcher he said, "We were sitting side by side in the 8th inning of Sunday's ball game. He was as unconcerned as if he was tossing rocks at a mud turtle on a log in the Meramec River. Suddenly he turned to me and said: "The Cardinal business office thinks I'm a dumb guy. My salary stops today, and that fellow Clarence Lloyd had the nerve to ask me if I wanted to make the trip to Philadelphia for the World Series. Said the club would pay my expenses. I asked him would I draw dough for going and he said no. Thought he could put that over on me. I may be dumb, but I'm not that dumb and I'm going home tonight." "He went home, too." Chimed in Flint Rhem.[13]

Diz won his first Major League victory by pitching a complete game three hitter while giving up a single run. The St. Louis Star reported:

> *The Youngster showed burning speed, a wide, sweeping curve, a clever change of pace and, best of all, unusual control for a rookie. One flash of wildness in the first inning, which might have been the result of facing the largest crowd he ever saw at one of his own ball games, cost him a shutout victory, but he redeemed that minor lapse with a heady piece of baseball that resulted in a Cardinal victory and his pitching after that opening frame was a caution.*[14]

Dizzy's success in his first professional season only confirmed what he already believed that he was the greatest pitcher alive. He became borderline insufferable after the season, but the sportswriter's loved him. Diz was always ready to give them great quotes.

Asked why St. Louis didn't bring him up earlier in the season, Diz replied "The Cardinals didn't want to shatter the other clubs hopes of winning a pennant. You know this Major League stuff is a lot easier than the Western League. Why, next year I'll just breeze through twenty or thirty games for the Cards. In fact, I don't know if any team in the National League that can beat me."[15]

Asked about his arm, Dean said "well sir, I've been trying for a long time to think of a better arm in baseball that I'd like to trade mine for and I simply can't locate one."[16]

Dizzy's braggadocios self-promotion wasn't limited to talking to sportswriters, he even wrote letters to them. The sports editor of the St. Joseph Gazette received the following letter from "The Great Dean" as Diz was now calling himself.

"Show me another pitcher in the majors who has never been defeated. I didn't go to the series. Sure, they begged me to come along. I told Mr.

Rickey I would wait until next year and win him three games in the World Series."[17]

The Philadelphia Athletics won the American League pennant for the second straight year. They would be St. Louis' opponent in the 1930 World Series. The A's were led by hitters Jimmie Foxx, Al Simmons and Mickey Cuchrane. Lefty Grove and George Earnshaw were the leading pitchers, having paired up for 50 wins during the regular season.

The A's defeated the Cards in six games to win their second straight World championship. Grove and Earnshaw were the pitching stars of the series. They had a combined ERA of 1.02 and allowed only 28 hits and 10 walks, while striking out 29 in the 44 innings they pitched.

Despite Earnshaw's brilliant pitching in the World Series and the A's victory over the Cardinals, Diz was not impressed. Dizzy said he could have won the 1930 World Series had the Cards made him eligible. "I told Earnshaw that I couldn't understand why he beat the Cards in the Series. I told him that while he might be considered a good pitcher, I was disappointed with his showing. I really expected him to have a lot more stuff than he showed me."[18]

CHAPTER 7

"I wasn't too scared of the Ivory Hunter lookin' at me"

Paul Dean signed with the St. Louis Cardinals at the end of the 1930 season. Since the baseball season was almost over, he was to report to the Houston Buffaloes for spring training in March of 1931. Paul was determined to "Make good playin' ball so I didn't have to go back to pickin' cotton and pumpin' gas"[1]

Dizzy liked to tell how he was instrumental in getting St. Louis to sign Paul. "Just after I broke into the Majors, Pa and Paul were pickin' cotton down in El Campo, TX. I take a scout with me and we go to see 'em. Do you know where Paul signed his Cardinal contract? He signed right down there in the middle of a cotton field at El Campo."[2]

Paul was actually signed by Don Curtis, the same scout who signed Dizzy, after seeing him pitch semi-pro game in San Antonio, TX. "I wasn't too scared of the Ivory Hunter lookin' at me," Paul said of the day Curtis signed him "but I wanted to show him some good pitchin' and with the bases loaded I put so much on the ball it sailed over the grandstand."[3] Paul later said, "I signed for $100 and a bus ticket to Houston."[4]

Later in life Paul talked about Dizzy's influence on his baseball career. "You know, Diz never has had as much to do with my career as most people think. That 'Me 'n' Paul' stuff makes it sound as though I've always been tied to his coattails. But I never was, and I'm not now," he said emphatically. "Diz didn't have anything to do with getting me to sign with the Cardinals because I thought it was the best thing for me to do, not because of Diz' influence. "What's more, Diz didn't help me get into the big leagues. There was just one reason that I got to the majors-I pitched my way there. That's the only way anyone ever gets to the top in baseball."[5]

Paul was only partially correct in this assessment. While it's true nobody makes it to the Majors without talent, it is also true that everyone with talent doesn't make it to the Majors. During the 1930's thousands upon thousands of young men and boys were desperate to play professional baseball to escape the throes of the Depression.

Without Dizzy constantly talking about his 16-yr. old brother who was possibly better than himself, Paul might not have been scouted by the 'Ivory Hunters'. Also, when Paul started his rookie season with the Cardinals by pitching poorly, he almost surely would have been sent back to the Minors if not for Dizzy. St. Louis Post-Dispatch Sports editor Bob Broeg said "Paul almost got sent down in '34. I think if he hadn't been Paul Dean, he would have been gone. But they stayed with him – they wanted the box office appeal of a brother act- and Paul finally came around. He was in deep trouble before that, though, and I'm sure he knew it."[6]

Dizzy did play a big role in Paul's discovery and development, but most importantly Diz promoted the Dizzy and Daffy brand. Diz was a natural showman, a brilliant self-promoter who dominated the headlines. Making Dizzy and Daffy the biggest baseball box office draw since Babe Ruth. This translated into thousands of dollars for endorsements, advertisements and personal appearances.

Sportswriter J. Frank Stockton said "Paul Dean was not like Dizzy, except in appearance and pitching skill. Dizzy talked. Paul listened. Dizzy wisecracked. Paul laughed. Dizzy was a great comedian. Paul was his best audience. Each was the other's hero. It was fortunate for Paul that nature gave him a great pitching arm. Dizzy would have made good anyhow. He was a genius with an education he would have been a shining light in any field."[7] Paul sometimes tried bragging, popping-off like Diz, but it wasn't natural, always forced. Diz was unfiltered, said the first thing that came to mine, but somehow it came out funny without offending anyone. It was Dizzy being Dizzy.

The St. Louis Cardinals held spring training in Bradenton, Florida for their Major League players and experienced Minor League players who might be able to play at the Big-League level. Since Dizzy had pitched so well at St. Joe, Houston and St. Louis he was invited to the Major League camp at Bradenton.

Paul, like all players with no professional experience was sent to Houston to be evaluated and assigned to the appropriate Minor League classification. While Paul was riding a bus from San Antonio to Houston, Diz was on a train traveling south to the Cards spring training in Bradenton, Florida. He was confident, assured he would take the Majors by storm because "he had everything it takes to be a great star."[8]

He engaged other passengers and let them know he was indeed the Great Dean they had been reading about and yes, he was on his way to lead the Cardinals to the World Championship they could not win without him last year. Waiters and bellhops were rewarded not with tips but with the Great One's autograph.

Once Diz arrived in Bradenton he was shown the stadium and told his guide "she looks fine, boy, you know, I'll kinda be glad to get back on the ol' diamond and show the people my pitchin' wares."[9]

Before Dizzy got around to showing his pitchin' wares he was displaying the same behavior that landed him in trouble when in St. Joseph, charging all his bills to 'them Cardinals'. Calling himself 'Dizzy the Great' he paraded around town buying the latest fashions in clothes, baseball gloves and golf clubs, also treating himself and his pals to meals in the best restaurants. All of this paid for with I.O.U's, which always bounced back to the Cardinals. He may have been 'Dizzy the Great' in St. Joe and Houston but to the 1931 St. Louis Cardinals he was only 21 yr. old rookie Jerome Dean.

Club officials instructed the entire town that the team would not pay anymore of Dizzy's I.O.U's and his credit quickly dried up. The Cardinals then made Dizzy the Dollar-A-Day rookie. Each morning Dizzy called upon Clarence Loyd, the team secretary and received $1.00 after he signed the following: received today - $1.00 – Dizzy Dean.

In addition to having to live on an allowance of one dollar a day Diz also had medical problems. After talking to a fellow pitcher, Cardinal Badboy Flint Rhem, Diz decided he had bad tonsils. Flint told Diz he cured his sore pitching arm by having a tonsillectomy. Diz figured if bad tonsils could affect a man's pitching why wait until the ol' wing started hurting before taking action. Not wanting to take any chances with his "meal ticket" (slang for pitching arm) Diz demanded that his tonsils be removed.

"There was a tendency to laugh last week when Dizzy Dean sought out Sam Breadon and told the Cardinal President he'd like to have his tonsils removed, and several persons remarked it was just another "Dizzy whim."[10] Much to everyone's surprise and Dizzy's delight team physician Dr. Stanley Burns agreed to be proactive and he removed Dizzy's tonsils.

Diz recovered in time to suit up for the Cardinal's exhibition game against the World Champion Philadelphia Athletics. The A's were leading after six innings 5-4. Diz was sitting on the bench, antsy and anxious to get into the game. Manager Gabby Street said "Diz was muttering 'I just wish ol' Diz was a-pitchin' I just wish ol' Diz was a-pitchin', just loud enough so that I could hear." Finally, I looked at him and screamed, "So get in there and pitch, and I hope they beat your brains out." Street continued "so what's he do? He ambles out there to the mound, a big smile over his face and strikes out three legends at bat."[11]

The three "legends" Diz struck out were not the A's big guns and future hall-of-famers Al Simmons, Jimmy Foxx and Miche Cochrane, as later writers and Dizzy himself claimed. They were in fact "center fielder Mule Haas, catcher Johnny Heving and left fielder Bob Johnson,"[12] not exactly legends of the game.

Nevertheless, Diz was still impressed with himself, as he sauntered to the bench he said to his manager "just a breeze sarge. Them A's can't hit."[13]

Diz loved basking in the publicity his spring training debut brought him. Sid Keener of the St. Louis Star walked around Bradenton with Diz while interviewing him.

"Dean strolled up fourth avenue. He came to the corner of Main Street. He stood in front of Doc Thomas' drug store. He glanced to his right and

then to his left. Those who passed did not realize they were gazing at "Dizzy the Great." Dizzy puffed out his chest. He proceeded a block to the north. He now was at third avenue, with its billiard halls and haberdashery stores, where the town fans congregate. He heard: "there's Dizzy." "There's the guy who struck out three in a row yesterday." "There's the fellow who saved the game for Gabby Street's Cardinals." "There he is." "Dizzy" adjusted his coat collar. He smoothed his hair. He took a sneaking glance over his right shoulder. He had been discovered. I finished the morning's stroll with him. "Those Athletics weren't they a lot of bushers?" he asked. "I didn't have my real fast ball yesterday. I gave them my No. 2 – the medium fast ball, and they couldn't touch me. I'm saving my real fooler-the No. 1, filled with smoke, for the Reds, the Cubs and the other National League clubs. If Gabby Street will let me alone and give me enough rope to enjoy myself off the ball field, I'll show him he has the greatest pitcher that ever came into the National League." I bowed my way out of the walk. I gave the kid the double-OO and was willing to admit he's the fanciest piece of pitching timber I have seen in many years." [14]

Dizzy's next appearance was against the Cincinnati Reds, it did not go as well as his debut against the A's. He lost the game by giving up a home run to light hitting Frankie Sigafoos. Unperturbed, Diz said "I don't mind the boys scorin' occasionally." [15]

By now Diz's outrageous behavior was starting to irritate some of his teammates. Others were jealous of all the publicity he received. Manager Street was also tiring of Dizzy's antics. The St. Louis Star reported; "Another chapter in the story of Dizzy Dean's eccentricities was added by Gabby Street today when the Cardinal's manager ordered the 21-year-old pitcher to keep away from the ballpark." [16]

Gabby said Dizzy would not obey club regulations, he neglected to report for morning practice, and he missed curfew at the hotel most nights. The final straw was when Dizzy went fishing instead of reporting for an afternoon practice. Street said "unless he changes his attitude, I don't want him on the club. While he is fishing, playing golf and roaming the streets, fellows like Grimes, Haines, Hallahan, Rhem and other pitchers are trying to get into condition for the opening of the season." [17]

Street was ready to send Dizzy back to the Minors at the end of training camp. Branch Rickey, however wanted Dizzy on the Big-League club. Rickey, an astute judge of baseball talent considered Diz "The best pitcher on his staff"[18] and wanted him with the Cardinals. Also, it didn't hurt that Diz was a tremendous drawing card. Rickey prevailed, and Dizzy opened the season as a member of the St. Louis Cardinals. The Cards got off to a good start and by the end of April were in first place. Diz stewed on the bench and hadn't played in a single regular season game. Seeing that Street was not going to play Diz, Rickey decided he would be better off getting regular work in the Minors, so on May 2, 1931 Dizzy was demoted.

When the decision was made to send Dizzy back to the Minors, logic dictated he should be sent to the Columbus Red Birds. Columbus was the St. Louis Cardinals Class AA Farm Club, the highest rung on the Minor League ladder. Having proved himself at Class A Houston, there was no need to return. However, Fred Ankerman, Houston Buff president, wanted Diz back in Houston. Ankerman wanted Diz back not only for his pitching prowess but also because he was a favorite of the fans and sportswriters. This translated into great publicity and even better attendance. Rickey relented he said, "we sent Dean to Houston because Joe Schultz (Houston Manager) knows how to handle him."[19]

This was great news for Diz. If he had to be sent down, he was elated to return to Houston. Diz immediately sent a telegram to manager Joe Schultz. Collect of course. "I'm leaving here today, will arrive Sunday morning. Pitch me Sunday afternoon and it's a cinch I'll win."[20]

The return to Houston offered Diz the chance to pitch regularly in a city where the fans and writers appreciated his eccentric personality. Also, he would be reunited with his brother Paul, who was starting his pro career with the Buffs. They would be teammates for the first time since they were kids. Unfortunately, their reunion would be short lived.

CHAPTER 8

"New York Giants given thoro beating by Red Bird slab star of 17"

The 1931 Houston Buffaloes was one of the greatest Minor League teams in baseball history. The Buffs featured two future hall of famers in Joe "Ducky" Medwick and Dizzy Dean. They won 108 games while losing only 51. Paul Dean spent spring training with this team and made the opening day roster. Ironically, Dizzy would take Paul's place on the roster.

When Paul arrived in Houston for spring training he was 6'2" and weighed 170lbs. Right-handed, he was a "natural side-arm pitcher reminiscent of Walter Johnson and Grover Alexander."[1] Everyone knew who he was, Dizzy Dean's little brother. He had an overpowering fastball and little else. Scouts, coaches and the Cardinal's front office considered him an excellent prospect. Some thought Paul had more potential than Dizzy.

When camp opened on March 1, 1931, Paul was one of 11 pitchers, along with 4 catchers, 11 infielders and 7 outfielders. Texas League rules allowed only 18 of these 33 players on the opening day roster Joe Schultz was manager of the Buffs, he had been a journeyman outfielder with seven different teams. During his 13-yr. playing career, he played for every National League team, except the New York Giants.

Schultz talked to a reporter for St. Louis Sporting News about Paul "of course, he's very green but he has an abundance of talent. However, I shouldn't be greatly surprised if he stayed with us all season."[2] Of course Diz put in his two cents worth "if you think I'm a pitcher, you ought to see Paul. There's a boy who is going to do big things in baseball."[3]

After only a week in camp Schultz started Paul in an exhibition game against the Chicago White Sox on Mar. 8, 1931. A 17-yr. old kid, who the previous summer was playing amateur ball in San Antonio, against a Major League team could prove to be brutal.

Paul, however, pitched well giving up five hits and three runs in 5 1/3 innings, while striking out five batters. The weather was cold, Paul complained that he never really "got warmed-up good."

After the regular season started Paul saw only limited action. When Dizzy joined the Buffs on May 2nd, after being demoted from the Cardinals, Paul had appeared in two games pitching only three innings and being charged with one loss. With Dizzy added to an already crowded pitching staff it became clear Paul wasn't needed.

He would be assigned to a team in the Cardinals vast chain Store Farm System. In 1931 this system consisted of over 200 players on eight teams in different leagues stretching from Texas all the way to New York. Two teams in Class AA, Columbus in the American Association and Rochester in the International League. One team in the Class A Texas League, the Houston Buffs. There were three teams in the Class B Leagues, Danville, Ill, Elmira, N.Y, and Greensville, N.C, Scottsdale, PA in the middle Atlantic League and finally Springfield Mo in the Western Association. The AAA classification would not come to baseball until 1946.

Two days after Paul and Dizzy's reunion, Paul was reassigned. Much to everyone's surprise Paul was not sent to the lower Minors, inexplicably Paul was sent to the Columbus Red Birds, St. Louis' AA Farm Club. Dizzy with two years Major and Minor League experience plus being three years older would be playing Class A ball while rookie Paul pitched at the top Minor League level. As usual even newspaper articles concerning Paul were publicity for Dizzy. Stories in both the St. Louis Post-Dispatch and St. Louis Star were captioned "Dizzy Dean's brother is sold to Columbus"[4] the Star went on to report "Paul Dean, 17-year-old brother of Dizzy Dean has been sold to Columbus by Houston, Paul, like his better-known brother is a right-handed pitcher with a lot of stuff, but possesses none of his brother's braggart tendencies. This is his first year in organized ball."[5]

The Cleveland Plain Dealer had a caption that read "two Deans on team too much.

Houston sells Paul Dean to Columbus when Dizzy arrives."[6]

Columbus, Ohio had Minor League baseball since 1888. A member of the American Association since 1902, the team was independently owned and operated as the Columbus Senators. However, by 1930 The Great Depression had wreaked havoc on the owners, and they wanted to sell. Larry Macphail, a Columbus attorney, obtained an option to buy the struggling baseball club.

Unable to raise the necessary funds to purchase the team, Macphail turned to his friend from law school, Branch Rickey. Rickey was always looking for teams to buy for the Cardinals ever expanding Farm System. The St. Louis Cardinals purchased the Columbus Senators and renamed them the Red Birds, a popular nickname for the Big-League Club.

As part of the deal, Larry Macphail was named general manager of the team. Macphail, a World War I veteran, was a bold innovator, known for his unpredictable behavior and heavy drinking. His grandson said, "my grandfather was bombastic, flamboyant, a genius when sober, brilliant when he had one drink and a raving lunatic when he had too many."[7] Whatever his faults, Macphail proved to be a successful general manager for Columbus. He supervised the building of the new Red Bird Stadium, brought in night baseball and made the games more fan friendly. While he ran the Red Birds from 1930 – 1932 attendance tripled.

Paul Dean joined the Columbus Red Birds in early May 1931. The Red Bird manager at the time was Harry "Nemo" Leibold. Leibold played 13 Major league seasons winning World Championships with the 1917 Chicago White Sox and the 1924 Washington Senators. The speedy outfielder was perfectly suited for the dead ball era. A solid slap hitter and good bunter who played all three outfield positions, drew walks and stole bases. At 5'6" Leibold was the smallest man in the Majors, nicknamed Nemo after the popular comic strip of the time "Little Nemo".

Unfortunately, he is best remembered as one of only three players to endure the infamous "1919 Black Sox scandal" with his honor and reputation intact. "It was a reeling blow to us when the investigations proved the 1919 series had been fixed" Leibold recalled "we could not believe that eight of our teammates let us down."[8]

The so called "Black Sox scandal" took place during the 1919 World Series between the Chicago White Sox and the Cincinnati Reds. The Sox were heavily favored in the nine- game series. Suspicions were raised when the Reds easily won the series in eight games. Even during the series rumors had begun to circulate that gamblers had paid several White Sox players to intentionally lose games.

Eight players – including a sure Hall of Famer, The Great "Shoeless" Joe Jackson – were later put on trial for conspiracy to throw games. Even though the eight players were found not guilty on all charges, most fans feared Major League baseball was being controlled by gamblers and gangsters.

In an effort to save the game and restore the fans confidence the owners created the office of baseball commissioner. They hired a federal judge, Kenesaw Mountain Landis, to be baseball's first commissioner. Judge Landis whose father named him Kenesaw Mountain after the Civil War battle in which he was wounded, was given unlimited authority over every person employed in the Major or Minor Leagues, from owners to batboys.

Judge Landis quickly took action against the eight "Black Sox" players. One day after a jury found them not guilty, Landis banned the eight players from baseball for life.

Perhaps the saddest story of the scandal was that of "Shoeless" Joe Jackson. Jackson was a poor boy from Greensville, South Carolina who never learned to read or write. His involvement in the plot was marginal and if he did try to throw the Series, he did a lousy job. "Shoeless" played errorless ball, collected 12 hits (a World Series record that stood until 1964) for a .375 average. The highest on either team.

Columbus manager "Nemo" Leibold played along-side Joe Jackson in the Sox outfield. He was never implicated in the scandal although he had only one hit in 18 at-bats.

Paul Dean saw his first action as a Columbus Red Bird on June 1, 1931. Just as in Houston his debut was against a Major League team in an exhibition game. Paul pitched brilliantly, going the distance and beating the New York Giants 3-2 allowing them only five hits. An Ohio sports page caption proclaimed "New York Giants given thoro beating by Red Bird slab star of 17" the story continued "Paul Dean 17-year-old brother of Dizzy Dean, the 1931 publicity champion, set the Giants back on their cauliflowers yesterday, pitching the Columbus Red Birds to a 3-2 victory. The Major Leaguers were able to collect only five hits and except in the third inning the child wonder kept the sophisticates runless."[9]

Reporters wanted to talk to Paul after such an auspicious debut. Since most newspaper articles referred to him as Dizzy Dean's little brother Paul said, "give me another year in baseball and they'll be calling that Dizzy so and so Paul Dean's brother."[10]

After Paul's promising debut against the Giants he started to struggle. Opponents soon learned Paul threw his fastball almost exclusively, so there was no need to worry about changeups or breaking pitches. High level professional hitters can hit a fastball, no matter how fast if they know it's coming. The Cardinal management decided it was time their prize rookie learned to pitch.

The Cardinals had the right man for the job, Eddie Dyer, manager of St. Louis' Class C Farm Club in Springfield, Missouri. Dyer had pitched in the Majors for the St. Louis Cardinals from 1922 – 1927. He was player-manager for the Springfield Red Wings, only 31 yrs. Old he still pitched. Before professional baseball Dyer was a three-sport star at Rice Institute in Houston, Texas. He won the Southwest Conference Championship in the broad jump and he was All-SWC in football and baseball. Dyer pitched a no-hitter against Baylor's Ted Lyons, later a hall of fame pitcher for the Chicago White Sox. Eddie Dyer was the perfect choice to teach Paul the finer points of pitching.

On June 22, 1931 newspapers reported the transaction again referring to Paul as Dizzy Deans brother. "Paul Dean, 17-year-old righthand pitcher from the Columbus American Association club and brother of the famous Dizzy Dean, today became a member of the Springfield Western Association Club."[11]

With only a week of Dyer's tutoring Paul made his Red Wing debut the St. Louis Star reported under the caption "DIZZY DEANS' BROTHER FANS TEN BATTERS" the story followed "Paul Dean, 17-year-old brother of the famous Dizzy of St. Louis Cardinal and Houston, TX. Fame, made his debut as a Springfield Red Wing last night by fanning ten Bartlesville Broncs and winning 5-4 except for one bad inning, Paul breezed the ball past the Broncs."[12]

Paul continued to pitch good ball for the Red Wings and by the first week in August he had won 7 games and lost only one. The St. Louis post dispatch reported on Paul's progress and potential under the caption "PAUL DEAN, NOT YET 18, BETTER PROSPECT THAN BROTHER "DIZZY" the article continued, "Dizzy Dean's kid brother, Paul, is going to be a greater pitcher than the Houston Storm Center himself, in the opinion of nearly a dozen scouts who have seen the two this season."[13] Paul averaged a strikeout an inning winning seven in a row before losing to the league leading Fort Smith Twins, partly due to errors by his teammates.

Paul finished the Springfield Red Wing season with 11 wins and 3 losses. The Red Wings won the Western Association Championship and Paul was named to the All-Star team. Johnny Potewitz, Paul's Springfield teammate said "Paul is destined for big things in baseball and no one realizes the fact better than the Cardinal owners. He's just a kid and a fine one at that. Sometimes he tires in the late innings but after he matures, he will be one of the greatest in the game. He's got a fast ball that sizzles. Once he learns to slow it up and develops the curve, he started working on this season he'll be plenty hard for anybody to beat. Young Dean isn't as eccentric as his brother. He's more reserved and seldom criticizes. Often, when a good play helps him win his game he goes to the player and thanks him personally."[14]

Paul's season wasn't over, when Springfield's season ended, he was recalled to Columbus. Although Paul was used sparingly, he finished the season with the Red Birds.

Paul's first year in professional baseball was an unqualified success. Not counting exhibition games Paul pitched 175 innings in 33 games in Class A, AA and C Leagues winning 11 games and losing 6. The scouts agreed Paul Dean was an excellent prospect with a bright future.

CHAPTER 9

"He never did go to talkin' and I never got so tired of being knocked down"

Meanwhile back in Houston, Dizzy was quickly becoming the sensation of the Texas League, the same day he arrived in Houston from Bradenton, Florida he shut out the Wichita Falls Spudders on three hits, winning 6-0.

By the end of the month Diz had recorded 5 wins against no losses. The only thing he lost in May was a fight against Dallas Steer Catcher Al Todd. A Dallas morning news article captioned "Dizzy Dean holds locals to five hits but takes licking in one-round bout with Todd."[1]

Diz took exception to Todd tripling in the seventh and called him "A Lucky Bastard." When Todd came up again in the ninth Diz buzzed his head with a high hard one. Todd charged the mound and preceded to pound the crap out of Dizzy. "Under instructions from League President Alvin Gardner, players were permitted to battle each other to their heart's content so long as they laid off umpires and spectators so both remained in the fray until players finally separated the combatants."[2] Diz wiped the blood off his face, threw three wide pitches to walk Todd, then struck out a pinch hitter finishing off a 7 – 1 Buff victory.

The beating was a small price to pay for the story that Diz told on radio, T.V. and in print for years to come.

"This here Todd," Diz relates, "gets a hit off'n me, which makes me mad. So, the next time he comes up I chuck a ball at his bean, this makes him mad an' he drops his bat and comes out to the mound toward me. I get all ready to do some jawin' with him. I got a dandy wise crack already for him. But he fools me. He hauls off and whacks me one on the whiskers. Down I go. I get up figurin' that he is sure to go to talkin' now, but he lets me have another one and down I go again, a-seein' stars up there in the sun. Well, he never did go to talking' and I never got so tired of being knocked down. Ol' Diz sure lost that one."[3]

The Texas League season was divided into two parts with the first half ending June 30. The Buffs were in a tight race with Beaumont for the first half title when Dizzy pitched a two-hit shutout against the San Antonio Indians on June 3rd. After the game he told sportswriters he had a special announcement.

"Boy's" he said "Ol' Diz is a-getting hitched."[4]

This was not good news for the Houston baseball club. They did not need the distraction of their star pitcher getting married in the heat of a pennant race. Club President Frank Ahkenman and Branch Rickey, himself, were strongly opposed to the marriage. They tried to talk Dizzy out of it, saying he was just a kid and should wait several years before taking such a serious step, as it might hurt his career. They also worried that the bride to be, Pat Nash, might not be the right choice.

Pat Nash was four years older than Dizzy, much more mature and experienced. She had been married twice before and had the reputation of being a "Party Girl". A teammate asked Diz if he had heard the rumor that Patricia Nash had screwed half the men in town. Diz replied "Sure, I heard it. I'm one of 'em. That's why I want to marry her."[5]

The wedding took place in Houston on June 15, 1931. Neither Pat nor Dizzy had any family in attendance. There was a small crowd of sportswriters and friends. Before the ceremony "Diz went around to everyone with his hand on his heart, asking each one to feel. 'Boy ain't she poundin', he would say grinning from ear to ear."[6]

The marriage which everyone thought was another impetuous act on the part of their "Dizzy" pitcher turned out to be a successful lifelong union. Even Pa Dean approved "Jay Hanna was the troublest boy I had until he married Pat. He ain't give no trouble much since."[7]

On June 28th the Buffs rolled into Ft. Worth for the final series of the first half of the Texas League season. Houston was tied with Beaumont for the first half title Dizzy pitched and won the first game of the Sunday double-header. Manager Joe Schultz recalled "he didn't have his stuff at the start of the first game, but he won it, 12 – 3 and allowed only seven hits in nine innings. He got better as he went along and when he asked for the assignment in the second game, I gave it to him."[8] Diz said "If I beat 'em in the first game, I might as well go ahead and pitch the second."[9] Incredibly Diz pitched all nine innings in the nightcap shutting out the "Cats" with a three-hitter beating them 3-0.

Monday was an off day, and on Tuesday June 30th Houston faced Ft. Worth on the final day of the first half. The game had added significance because the Buffs had to win just to tie Beaumont for the title. Tex Carlton, a future teammate of Diz and Paul on the Cardinals, started the game. He quickly ran into trouble, giving up runs and leaving the bases loaded. Who came in from the bullpen? Who else? The Great Dean. Dizzy worked nine more innings allowing seven hits beating the "Cats" again 10 - 9.

Manager Schultz summed up this unbelievable performance. "He pitched and won three games in three days. Think of that! I would say this is Dizzy's masterpiece. It proves that he not only is a great pitcher but a remarkable character."[10]

Although Beaumont and Houston ended the first half of the Texas League season tied for first place, there would not be a play-off. The Championship would be decided by the head to head regularly scheduled games between Houston and Beaumont in the second half of the season.

When Dizzy joined Houston back on May 5th the Buffs were six games out of first place. He said "I'll lead 'em to the top, and he did, the team finishing in a tie for first in the first half of the season."[11]

As Dizzy continued to win games and draw large crowds his fame grew. The Dallas morning news reported on Dizzy's popularity "The records show receipts have picked up perceptibly both at Houston and on the road when the fans were advised in advance that Dizzy would be on the mound. This has been true regardless whether the Buffs were meeting a last-place club or a team that was close to them in the standings. Dizzy, no doubt, has been the best single gate attraction the league has had in several seasons.

His name on the program has helped to lure fans in added numbers through the turnstiles."[12]

The fans wanted more of Dizzy and the newspapers took notice. Ralph A. Anderson of the Houston Press was the ghostwriter for a series of syndicated stories about Dizzy's life entitled "They Call Me Dizzy." The newspaper columns began appearing in papers across the country in mid-august 1931.

A promo in the August 18, 1931 St. Louis Star read:

> *You've read about baseball heroes – and seen them. But here's the prize package of them all – the rookie egotist of baseball. They call him DIZZY DEAN. He brags continually. Usually he does what he says he will do. He's a pitcher – and a good one. Has a record of 23 victories this season. Belongs to the St. Louis Cardinals. Pitches for their Houston team in the Texas League. BUT HE WILL BE BACK WITH THE CARDINALS SOON. He says he will! The first of a series of true stories of "Dizzy" Dean begins on the sports page Thursday. The whole story is "Dizzy." Dean wrote it. Rather, he dictated it, and it was set down in type. But IT'S DIZZY'S STORY. And what a story!*[13]

This is where the Dizzy Dean legend really began, with Diz mixing a few facts with a lot of fiction to tell a great story. In this fiction the missing brother Elmer is a banker and the deceased sister Evelyn is a nurse in San Antonio. "I am one of three boys – Paul, 17 years old now with the Columbus team and watch his smoke and Elmer, 22. Elmer never took much interest in baseball. He is a banker, but I guess Paul and I need a banker in the family to handle some of this big money we will make out of baseball. Evelyn, a nurse in San Antonio, was the only other child."[14]

Diz kept winning games as the Buffs ran away with the second half pennant. In the process they bested Beaumont in the "designated regular season play-off games" to become undisputed champions of the 1931 Texas League season. Dizzy finished the regular season with 26 wins against 10 losses, an era of 1.57 with 303 strikeouts in 304 innings. He also hurled 11 shutouts.

This outstanding season performance was rewarded with Dizzy being named the Texas League's most valuable player. Derrill Pratt, Galveston manager, said "it isn't easy for a pitcher to win the MVP award over a regular who plays every play, but Dean is an exceptional man. Look at the number of wins he has after a late start, the strikeouts he has hung up, the shutouts to his credit, his popularity and drawing power, consider that the Houston club wasn't going so good until he reported and lifted the Buffs right out of the rut and bear in mind that he almost single handed gave them the championship. In my opinion Dizzy is the only logical man for the award."[15]

The Texas League champion Houston Buffs now moved on to post season play in the Dixie series, a Minor League version of the World Series. Their opponents, Southern Association champion Birmington Barons, was a powerhouse team that had won the Southern Association title by 10 ½ games.

The Barons didn't impress Diz. He boasted that he would beat "them Barons" every time he pitched against them. "If they beat me, I'll grow a beard and join the house of David Barnstormin' baseball team. That beard would help me hide my blushes of shame."[16]

The house of David was a Christian Commune founded in Michigan by Benjamin Franklin Purnell, a self-proclaimed messenger of God. It was an apocalyptic cult awaiting the return of Jesus Christ. Members gave all their worldly possessions to the commune and also gave up sex, alcohol, tobacco and meat. The men were forbidden to shave or cut their hair. The cult members saw their beards and long hair as a way to live in the likeness of Jesus and His Apostles.

Founder Purnell was a sports enthusiast and soon formed a baseball team. In the 1920's, a clean-shaven era, the bearded, long-haired players were an oddity. So many fans showed up for their games that Purnell decided to take his show on the road. Barnstorming provided an avenue to preach to potential members and earn money for the cult.

The House of David Barnstorming baseball teams proved to be so popular and lucrative that by the 1930's they began to hire professional players such as future hall of famer Grover Cleveland Alexander. These ringers were not required to be converts but there was a requirement, a huge beard either real or fake.

The House of David also aligned themselves with another group of baseball outcasts. They often invited negro league teams to travel with them. The House of David team would travel in one bus with the negro league team following in their own bus. Satchel Page was one of the negro league stars who played in these games. The House of David also carried their own portable lighting system to stage night games.

Page, legendary pitcher/philosopher gave his opinion on playing under the artificial lighting.

"I done some extra special figurin' for night games. When I was with the Monarchs, we carried our own lights and poles. I was one of the first pitchers that throwed at night. When the sun is shinin' the light bounces 'round and brightens all sides. But the night game lamps shine only straight down. They light up only the top of a baseball. The bottom is dark. I throws 'em low at night. That shows the batter less top. The less top I shows the less is lit. The less is lit the less he sees. The less he sees, the less he hits. If at all."[17]

Although baseball wasn't integrated until 1946, Satchel played many barnstorming games against Dizzy and Paul and he later coached with Paul at Tulsa.

The format for the Dixie series called for the best four out of seven games played in Birmingham and Houston with the players traveling between the cities by train. This was like the World Series to fans in the south because most of the Big-League teams were in the north and the closest a World Series came was in St. Louis.

The first game took place in Birmingham with Diz on the mound for Houston. Pitching for the Barons was 43-year-old grandfather, Ray Caldwell. Caldwell's best years were behind him having pitched in the Majors 11 yrs. winning 133 games with the Yankees, Red Sox, and Indians. All he had left was control. He threw off speed breaking balls that shaved the corners of the plate for strikes. He planned to "subdue those Houston hitters with deception."[18] In a classic pitching duel old Ray beat Diz 1-0.

The second game, also in Birmingham, featured another shutout. This time Dick McCabe, Houston Hurler, pitched and gave up only 4 hits. Houston fans were not familiar with McCabe because during the regular season he had played for the Ft. Worth Panthers. A special Texas League rule allowed Houston to replace the injured Tex Carlton who won 20 games for the Buffs during the regular season was sidelined by a sore finger on his pitching hand.

The series returned to Houston for game three, each team with one win. Houston pitcher George Washington Payne, who had won 23 regular season games for the Buffs started the Saturday night game. Leadoff Baron batter Billy Bancroft singled sharply past third to start the game. That was the only hit Birmingham managed in the game. Houston pushed across one run in the bottom of the sixth to win the game 1 – 0.

Dizzy got his chance for redemption in game four Sunday in Houston. In a rematch of game one Diz faced Ray Caldwell again. Caldwell again pitched brilliantly giving up but two runs. Diz was better, shutting out the Barons, allowing only three hits. "An unusual and remarkable thing with reference to the first four games of the series is the fact that the losing club has been shut out in each game. Birmingham won the first 1 – 0, and Houston has won the next three, 3 – 0, 1 – 0, and 2 – 0."[19]

The Buffs returned to Birmingham needing only one victory to wrap up the Dixie Series Championship. That one victory proved elusive as the Barons won game five 3 – 1 and game six 13 -11. The teams scored more runs in game six than the first five games combined.

The seventh and deciding game of the Dixie Series would take place Friday night in Houston, Texas, at Buff stadium. The Barons were confident, after all they had won two straight games, blasting out twenty-three hits in the game six slugfest.

Houston was equally confident with the "Great Dean" taking the mound. In the series so far Diz had pitched 18 innings against the Barons allowing only eight hits and one run.

The deciding game would have an added advantage for Houston, in addition to filling their home stadium with rabid Buff fans, the Barons would have to face Diz for the first time under the lights. During the regular season some of Dizzy's best performances were at night. Dean said, "them Barons didn't see me at my best in the daytime, no foolin'. Nighttime is my time to shine."[20]

Through six innings Diz was breezing along and the game was tied 1 -1, but he was running out of gas as the Barons scored in the seventh, eighth, and ninth to take a 6 – 2 lead. Facing elimination in the bottom of the ninth, the Buffs scored one run and had two on, one out with the tying run coming to the plate. The Barons went to the bullpen bringing in game one hero, Ray Caldwell. As Caldwell's young bride of two weeks, watched Ray calmly struck out Houston's two best hitters, "Ducky" Medwick and Homer Peel.

After Birmingham beat Diz two out of three times he didn't grow a beard and join the House of David, but he did go Barnstorming.

Barnstorming was a popular way for professional players to make money during the off season. Towns without their own Major League teams were glad to stage exhibition games featuring Big League ballplayers. These exhibitions were popular with the fans and money makers for the players.

Small towns and cities without Major League teams were eager to host these events because they were popular with fans and usually some of the proceeds went to local charities. Players that didn't Barnstorm usually had to work in the off season at regular jobs.

Until 1947 players were only paid during the regular season, and even during the season many every day expenses came out of the players pockets. Even the best paid players played these out of season games to make ends meet. Since most Major League teams were in the northeast and mid-west fans in the west and south could only read about the players in newspapers and listen to games on the radio. Barnstorming provided a way to see the Big Leaguers in person.

After exhibition games in Columbus, Ohio Dizzy and Paul headed to Missouri. Most games featured Dizzy pitching for one team and Paul pitching for the other one. The teams were made up of local Minor Leaguers, former Major Leaguers and Semi-pro players, a typical advertisement in a local newspaper read:

CHARLESTON CARDINALS VS DEXTER

"Dizzy" Dean will pitch for Charleston Paul Dean, 18-year-old brother of "Dizzy" for Dexter.

Paul Dean, in his first year in Professional ball, won 16 and lost three games for Springfield in the Western Association. He also won three games for Columbus, Ohio, in the American Association. In early spring, pitching for Columbus in an exhibition game, he beat the New York Giants 3 – 1 and allowed them three hits. In another exhibition game at Columbus on October 4th, Paul lost to his brother Dizzy 8 – 5 so he is out to get revenge in this game.[21]

Paul's record was exaggerated to make him worthy to face Dizzy "The Great Dean" as it turned out the game was scoreless at the end of the fifth inning when Dizzy pitching for Charleston and Paul pitching for Dexter ended their day. Dizzy and Paul each gave up 2 hits, Diz fanned six and Paul nine. Charleston went on to beat Dexter 2 -1.

By Oct 20, 1931 Dizzy and Paul were through Barnstorming and planned to spend the winter in Dardanelle, Arkansas, a town close to Lucas, where they were born.

Pat Dean, Dizzy's new wife, joined Diz and Paul in Dardanelle and they settled in for the winter. Unexpectedly, Dizzy received a letter from a pharmacist in Plummerville, a town only about 25 miles away. The pharmacist, Hobbs Horton wrote that a local farm worker had seen Dizzy's picture in the newspaper during the Dixie Series and told everyone that he was Dizzy Dean's brother. Horton knew Dizzy was in nearby Dardanelle because newspapers across Arkansas reported two of state's favorite sons had returned home for the winter.

'DIZZY' DEAN AND BROTHER, PAUL, TO LIVE AT DARDANELLE

Dardanelle, Ark Oct 20. Jerome ("Dizzy") Dean, pitcher for the Houston club of the Texas League, Mrs. Dean and his brother Paul, a pitcher for the Columbus (O.) club of the American Association arrived here today to make their home for the winter. Dean who has achieved prominence in baseball circles was born near here.[22]

Dizzy and Paul hurried to Plummerville hoping they would finally find the long-lost Elmer. On a farm a few miles outside of Plummerville they found Elmer working for a man named Bill Stobaugh. Paul told about the reunion. "We liked to never get Elmer to go. He said he had to work. But we got him in the car, and he had a old pasteboard suitcase and he wore overalls. Diz had a little money in his pocket, so we started up the highway and I was drivin' and Diz was sittin' back there with Elmer – he was glad to see ol' Elmer – and Diz took that suitcase and just throwed it out of the back of the car, and Elmer said 'hellfire, Jay, them was my clothes. Them was all the clothes I got.' So, we got to town and Diz buys Elmer some new overalls and things."[23]

CHAPTER 10

"Ah've always wanted to pitch against this heah Ruth fellah"

For the Dean family, at the beginning of 1932, all roads led to Houston. Pat Dean had lived in Houston for several years before meeting Dizzy and getting married. Dizzy lived in Houston while pitching for the Houston Buffs in 1931. The Cardinals told Paul he was to report to Houston for the 1932 Minor League spring training camp. Dizzy wanted Elmer in Houston so Cardinal Scouts could evaluate him to see if he had a future in professional baseball. Pa Dean had nothing in San Antonio to keep him there, so he was eager to move to Houston.

Paul reported to the spring training camp in Houston just as he had the year before. The coaches were impressed with the new additions to his pitching arsenal. With the help of Eddie Dyer at Springfield, Paul had developed a curve and change-up to go with his outstanding fastball. Hitters could no longer sit on his fastball; they had to be ready for breaking pitches and changeups, which disrupted their timing.

The Cardinal front office agreed with coaches who believed he was ready for the highest Minor League level, and assigned Paul to Double A Columbus, but this time around he had experience, new pitches and the confidence gained by winning 11 games for Springfield. He was determined to carry over this success to Columbus.

Elmer did not fare as well. As it turned out he did not have the temperament nor the talent for professional baseball. The Cardinals would have loved the publicity of three Dean brothers playing for St. Louis, but it was not to be. Elmer was already 25 years old, late in life to be starting in pro baseball, also while Paul and Dizzy were honing their skills playing ball and being tutored by professional coaches, Elmer had been doing back- breaking work as a farm laborer.

Diz later said of Elmer, "Gol' darnit, the trouble was that Elmer hadda work too hard and never got no chance to show what he could do until it was too late. Why, that boy was a great catcher and outfielder, he could whip that ol' ball around like any Dean. He just got his chance too late, that's all, when he was too old."[1]

Although he failed as a baseball player, Fred Ankenman, Houston Buffaloes President, believed Elmer had publicity value simply being Dizzy Dean's brother. He wanted Elmer to have a visible presence at Buff Stadium, so he offered him a job as Buff's batboy.

Elmer was insulted, "Batboy he snorted. "Me who taught my kid brother Dizzy how to pitch. You know Dizzy – he works for the St. Louis Cardinals. And my brother Paul – he works for Columbus. I helped Paul make the grade, too."[2]

Elmer finally accepted a job selling peanuts at Buff Stadium. He became a star yelling "Get your goobers here and I'll tell you how I taught Dizzy Dean to pitch. He's my brother."[3] Elmer was forever after known as "Goober".

The 1932 spring training camp in Houston included not only the Class A Houston Buffs of the Texas League but also the Class AA Columbus Red Birds of the American Association and the Class AA Rochester Red Wings. These three teams were the top farm teams in the St. Louis Cardinal system.

Branch Rickey, ever the entrepreneur, arranged a round robin tournament pitting the Buffs, Red Birds and Red Wings against each other. Billed as the St. Louis Cardinal Minor League Championship, the winner would receive the Branch Rickey trophy. This tournament accomplished two of Rickey's objectives, getting his Minor League teams ready for the regular season and putting money in the Cardinal Coffers through enhanced gate receipts.

Paul, a member of the Columbus team played for them in pursuit of the St. Louis Cardinal Minor League Championship. An unusual March snowfall in Houston hampered training and Columbus resorted to practicing at the Rice institute gym. Finally, the weather warmed up and the tournament began on March 16th.

After two weeks of play it came down to the last game on March 29th with Houston playing Rochester. A victory would give the Buffs possession of the Brach Rickey trophy, a loss would mean a tie with Rochester. Columbus had been eliminated losing nine games and winning none. Paul appeared in two games during the tournament and pitched well. He started against Rochester, pitched five innings and gave up only one hit, but Columbus lost 5 to 4. Paul put in a relief appearance against Houston, taking over in the sixth after Fred Blake had given up 10 runs. Paul gave up three over the final three frames. Columbus lost 13 to 6.

Houston fell to Rochester in the final game of the tournament on March 29th creating an anti-climactic ending to the bally-hooed tournament. Houston and Rochester tied for first place. There was no play-off game since both Rochester and Columbus broke camp on March 30th and headed home.

When the Red Birds arrived back in Columbus there were two games remaining on their preseason schedule. The New York Yankees were coming to Columbus for games on April 6th and 7th.

Paul asked his manager, "Nemo" Liebold if he could pitch against the Yankees "if it's jest the same to you, ah'd like it if you would let me pitch against those Yankees. Ah've always wanted to pitch against this heah Ruth fellah."[4]

"Nemo" admired the youngster's confidence and gave him the starting assignment for the second game on April 7th against the Yankees. Starting for the Yanks was their ace "Lefty" Gomez. Vernon Louis "Lefty" Gomez was one of the premier pitchers of the 1930's. He was a 20-game winner

Carl Duncan

four times, an all-star in the inaugural game in 1933 and seven more. He was inducted into the hall of fame in 1972.

Nicknamed "El Goofo", "Lefty" was known for his quirky behavior both on and off the diamond. In one game the Yankees were playing Cleveland in Yankee stadium, the grandstands were casting shadows on the field and a twilight fog had rolled in limiting visibility. Bob Feller's fastball, hard to see under the best of conditions, the foggy twilight made it almost invisible. As he stepped into the batters' box to face Feller, "El Goofo" struck a match. Knowing Lefty was a bit of an oddball, the ump asked, "think that will help you see Feller's fastball?" "I don't give a damn about seeing Feller's fastball" Lefty replied, "I want Feller to see me."[5]

Another time with "El Goofo" on the mound and a runner of first, the left-handed batter hit a hard grounder back to Lefty. Phil Ruzzuto, the Yankee shortstop, had the coverage and raced for second base to take the throw to start the easy double play. "El Goofo" fielded the ball cleanly and promptly pegged it to startled second sacker, Frankie Crosetti. Instead of an easy double play, both runners were safe.

Enraged manager, Joe McCarthy stormed to the mound and demanded an explanation. Lefty answered, "well, you got to many Romans on this team and I got confused." McCarthy, dropped his head and sadly shook it, "thank God you didn't throw it to DiMaggio in center."[6]

It was a thrill for Paul Dean last year when he pitched against the New York Giants, however it couldn't compare to pitching against the legendary Yankees of Baby Ruth and Lou Gehrig. These Yankees would go on to win the 1932 World Championship by sweeping the Chicago Cubs four games to none in the World Series where Babe Ruth called his shot.

The "called shot" is one of the most memorable and controversial events in baseball history. The Yankees won the first two games of the series in New York. The third game was in Chicago. The score was tied 4 – 4 as the "Bambino" stepped to the plate to face Cub hurler Charlie Root. Ruth took a strike and raised one finger in the air, Ruth took another strike with his bat on his shoulder and raids two fingers. As the Cub fans went berserk the Babe calmly pointed his bat at the centerfield stands. This gesture silenced the rabid Cub fans as Root delivered the 2 – 2 pitch Ruth slammed the ball over the centerfield fence for the go ahead run.

Cubs pitcher Charlie Root claimed Ruth didn't call his shot. "If he had, I would have knocked him down with the next pitch."[7] Gehrig who was on deck at the time- maintained Ruth definitely "called his shot." Gehrig said later "what do you think of the nerve of that big monkey calling his shot and getting away with it."[8] Ruth, for his part, never confirmed nor denied he called his shot.

If 18-year-old Paul Dean was nervous about pitching against the mighty Yankees, he didn't let it affect his performance. He matched the Great Gomez pitch for pitch and at the end of six innings Columbus led New York 2 – 1. Paul had not gone the distance in any game that spring and after giving up one run in the seventh it was clear he was out of gas. In seven innings of work Paul gave up five hits and two runs leaving the game with the score tied 2 – 2. The Yankees scored two runs in the eighth off Columbus reliever Bill Beckmann, but the Red Birds got to Gomez for three runs in the ninth to win the game 5 – 4.

Paul faced Babe Ruth four times in the game. The first time up the Babe fouled out, next at bat he hit an easy roller to first and in his third at bat Babe drew a walk. His fourth time up resulted in a high fly to left center that was misplayed and fell in for a double.

Paul's outstanding outing against the New York Yankees helped earn him a spot in the starting rotation with the Columbus Red Birds as they began the 1932 season. The Red Birds were projected to have a great hitting team. "If ever a "murders row" was assembled the Columbus officials have done that since the close of last season."[9]

All eight of the position players on the Columbus Red Bird opening day line-up April 12, 1932 had a batting average of .300 or better in 1931. Paul should have plenty of run support when he was on the mound.

Paul's first starting assignment of the regular season took place on Saturday April 15, 1932. In Columbus, Ohio, on a warm, clear afternoon, 1200 fans showed up to watch the Red Birds play the Milwaukee Brewers.

All the promised run production of the Red Bird's "Murders Row" failed to materialize in Paul's first start, Paul had a rough first inning, an error, a wild pitch, three hits and a walk led to three runs. Settling down he pitched the rest of the game only giving up one additional run. However, the "Murders Row" could manage only one lone run, that on a wild pitch by Brewer right-hander Jack Knott. The first inning trouble cost Paul the game losing by a score of 4 to 1.

Paul had the chance to redeem himself in his next start on April 22nd against the St. Paul Saints. Red Bird hitters lived up to their publicity scoring 13 runs as Paul pitched a shut-out.

Back at the hotel Paul was discussing the game with his catcher, Tony Rensa. Tony told Paul he had only given up one hit. Surprised, Paul said "Aw, I did not." Paul didn't believe he only allowed the Saints one hit until he read the morning newspaper. A headline confirmed what his catcher told him "Columbus Red Bird kid pitches one-hit game beats champ Saints 13 – 0." The article read "in the American Association record book one measly single stood between 18-year old Paul Dean of Columbus and no-hit fame."[10]

The best outing of Paul's professional career was followed quickly by one of his worst. Paul's next start after his one-hit shut-out over the St. Paul Saints was against the Minneapolis Millers. He was chased from the mound in the second inning when the Millers started their vicious assault with a seven-run rally. Paul's replacement, Ed Chapman, didn't escape the punishment as the Red Birds lost to the Millers 18 – 0.

Paul's next start was on May 2nd and once again he faced the St. Paul Saints. He evidently had the Saints number because this time Paul stopped them on a five-hit shut-out, 4 – 0.

After the season's first month, Paul had two wins and two losses. His wins were a 1-hit shut-out, and a 5-hit shut-out. The Kansas Star reported on Paul's progress "Paul Dean younger brother of Dizzy Dean, who is with the Cardinals, has been pitching brilliantly and his mates say he is a better hurling prospect than his brother, whose unusual ability is somewhat offset by his eccentricities."[11] Paul, perhaps tired of constantly being referred to as Dizzy Dean's brother said, "next to me, Dizzy Dean is the greatest pitcher in baseball."[12]

Paul's next two starts resulted in no decisions. Against Kansas City on May 12th he started but went only four innings giving up three runs. Columbus ended up winning the game 6 – 3. On May 17th Paul pitched against Indianapolis leaving after the eighth inning with the game tied at ten. Columbus pushed across a run in the tenth to win 11 – 10.

Me 'N' Paul

The first night game of the 1932 American Association season took place in Indianapolis, Indiana on May 23rd, 1932. Columbus played Indianapolis with Paul Dean pitching for the Red Birds.

Night baseball was in its infancy. The first professional baseball game under permanently installed lights took place only two years before on April 28, 1930, in Independence, Kansas. The Independence Producers lost to the Muskogee Chiefs in a Class C Minor League game.

The depression caused great suffering on both Major and Minor League baseball attendance, the Lifeblood of baseball revenue was dangerously low, and teams were losing money. Minor League teams, more innovative than the Majors, tried different promotions and were quicker to try new innovations to attract ticket buying fans. Night baseball proved particularly effective at drawing larger crowds.

Baseball depended on attendance for their main revenue stream; gate receipts, concessions and the sale of game programs all needed fans in the seats. Advertising dollars were secondary with no television and radio not yet broadcasting games. Ads were limited to signs at the stadiums and in the game programs.

Night baseball allowed working fans to see games during the week and not just on the weekends. Anxious to provide entertainment for working people during the week to increase revenue, Minor League night games spread like wildfire and by the end of the 1934 season there were sixty-five Minor League teams with permanent installed lights on their fields.

The Major Leagues, ever slow to try new innovations, would not introduce night games until 1935. Proven to increase attendance in the Minors, night baseball finally debuted in Cincinnati, Ohio on May 24, 1935. The Cincinnati Reds beat the Philadelphia Phillies 2 – 1 on that night in Major League's first ever night game, played courtesy of recently installed lights at Crosley field in Cincinnati. The game drew 25,000 fans. This success encouraged the Reds and they played a night game that year against every National League team. Despite Cincinnati's wretched record of 68 wins and 85 losses, paid attendance rose 117 percent.

Needing to benefit their bottom line most Big-League teams followed suit. Teams upgraded their stadiums to included lights throughout the 1930's and 1940's until most Major League teams included night games on their schedules. One lone holdout, the Chicago Cubs, didn't host night games until 1988.

Ironically, Branch Rickey, the Great Innovator, who pioneered the Farm System and had the foresight to integrate the Major Leagues turned a blind eye to night baseball. He told the St. Louis Post dispatch in 1932.

"I have no reason to speak in any official capacity on this subject, but it is my personal judgment that the Major Leagues will not adopt night baseball at all. If they take notice of it, it will be as a mere novelty, with very limited exploitation."

"It is possible that the heads of Major League baseball will grant limited permission to try night games just as a novelty or experiment. But I feel sure they will never gain a place as part of Major League Championship schedules. Night baseball is not normal, even though the lighting systems be well-nigh perfect. Night games are highly entertaining to view, now and then, but are not good for a steady diet."[13]

On the other hand, Rickey's boss, Sam Breadon was enthusiastic about night baseball. "At Columbus where we have the latest thing in floodlights." He said, "there is not a shadow or a dark spot. In some respects, the visibility is greater than by daylight. The ball is highly illuminated by the lights, and really is more easily followed." The Cardinal owner was convinced that night baseball had a future in Major League baseball "A far greater number of persons are able and eager to attend ball games at night than is the case in the daytime."[14]

9,284 fans turned out at the Indianapolis Indian's home stadium for the first night game of the American Association season. 29,000,000 candle power of light shining down from six tall steel towers illuminated the field as Paul faced the first place Indians. After an early wild streak, he settled down striking out 12 in seven innings and beating the tribe 6 – 4.

Night baseball continued to make news as fans flocked to Minor League parks to observe the novelty. Columbus played Louisville on May 25th, the first night game in league history of Louisville which dated back to 1876. The average attendance for Louisville games stood at 1,000, that night's game drew 5,063 cash fans.

Although Paul had pitched seven innings only two nights before at Indianapolis, he was summoned to pitch in a high leverage situation against Louisville in the eighth with the score tied 4 – 4, two on and one out. Paul retired the two hitters he faced ending the threat with the score still tied at 4.

Columbus failed to score in the top of the ninth and Paul took the mound for the bottom of the final frame. Surely fatigued by pitching on two days' rest, Paul walked the first batter. A sacrifice bunt and infield hit left men on first and third with one out. Manager "Nemo" Liebold replaced Paul with lefty Pete Fowler who promptly gave up a sacrifice fly that scored the winning run. Since Paul was responsible for the men on base he was charged with the loss.

Paul next pitched in a game against the Toledo Mud Hens. He started and went seven innings giving up seven hits and losing 5 – 4 to the Mud Hens. Paul ended May with a record of three wins and four losses, but led the League in strikeouts with 51 in 58 innings.

June started with another tough loss for Paul. Things started well for Columbus as they scored 6 runs in the bottom of the first. However, the lead was short lived as Columbus pitchers Bill Lee and Jesse Fowler could not tame the tribe and after three innings the Indians had tied the Red Birds 7 – 7. Paul took over, pitched six innings and gave up 2 runs, leaving the game with one out in the ninth. Indianapolis ending up winning 12 – 9. Paul's record fell to 3 wins and 5 losses.

Paul picked up a win by pitching 3 2/3 inning in a relief role against Kansas City. He gave up 3 hits and 1 run. On June 12th Paul's next outing was his best of June and also his last. He started against St. Paul, pitched eight innings giving up 3 runs on 3 hits. Paul was lifted for a pinch hitter in the eighth with the score St. Paul 3, Columbus 2. Columbus won the game in eleven innings, resulting in a no-decision for Paul. Unfortunately, he was injured shortly thereafter. The Courier-Journal reported that Paul would be unavailable for a series against the Louisville Colonals "Paul Dean, Dizzy's sensational brother, crashed into the stands at Columbus a few days ago while chasing a fly ball in practice and will not be able to compete in this series."[15]

Paul was unable to pitch again until July 10th. Columbus had just lost the first three games of a four game series to last place St. Paul. Paul was being called upon to stop the bleeding. He had already beaten St. Paul twice, once on a 1-hit shutout. While Paul was out the Red Birds lost the Leagues lead and were now in danger of dropping deeper in the standings.

Rusty from the layoff Paul was chased in the third giving up 5 runs on 5 hits. His control was so erratic he hit two batters. Despite the rocky start, Columbus took the lead before St. Paul scored twice in the bottom of the ninth for the win.

The misery continued as Minneapolis beat Columbus in the first game of a Twin Bill. On July 12th Jesse Fowler started the second game for the Red Birds, but by the fourth inning, he was in deep trouble giving up 7 hits and 7 runs. Paul relieved with one out in the fourth and got out of the inning without further damage. Paul held the Millers scoreless for the next two innings. As he took the mound for the bottom of the eighth Columbus held an 8 – 7 lead, and Paul had a chance to end the Red Birds free fall.

It didn't happen, Paul gave up 3 runs in the bottom of the eighth and lost the game with a final score of 10 – 9. As it turned out the games were not the only losses Columbus suffered, they lost their manager longtime Skipper "Nemo" Liebold was fired.

"With Columbus in a current slump and dissension cropping out among its players, Liebold was removed" for the best interests of the club," MacPhail said. "Despite their terrific batting punch, they lost the League lead a week ago by dropping a four-game series to the last place St. Paul Saints. The crisis came when Minneapolis followed with a double licking."[16]

Billy Southworth, Rochester manager, was summoned to take the reins of the Columbus club. Rochester was a Class AA Farm team in the extensive Cardinal system, playing in the International League. Billy had managed Rochester for 5 years and won four championships.

Billy was born William Harold Southworth on March 9, 1893, near the Hamlet of Harvard, Nebraska. William "Buffalo Bill" Cody, a family friend, nicknamed him "Billy the Kid" after the gunfighter."[17] By 1902 the Southworth family had moved to Columbus, Ohio. A neighborhood boy who was friends with Billy and his brothers was Eddie Rikenbacker, the future World War I Flying Ace.

Southworth started playing pro baseball at age 19 and ended up having a decent Major League career. However, he had a hall of fame managerial career. Billy the Kid played for five big league teams, the Cleveland Indians, Pittsburgh Pirates, Boston Braves, New York Giants and St. Louis Cardinals. He managed the Cardinals in 1929 and 1940 – 45, winning three pennants and two World Series. He also managed the Boston Braves from 1946 – 1951 winning one pennant. Billy Southworth was elected to the hall of fame in 2007.

Billy the Kid would need all his managerial skills to right the ship at Columbus. The Red Birds had nose-dived from a tie for first place to fourth in the standings. Amid reports of dissension on the team, Southworth would have his hands full.

Paul impressed Billy the Kid in his first start of the new regime. He pitched against Kansas City on July 15th and pitched brilliantly, going the full nine innings giving up 4 hits and beating the Blues 5 – 2, for his fifth win of the season.

Showing his confidence in Paul, Southworth sent him to the mound in a pressure situation three days later in Milwaukee. Columbus led the Brewers 9 – 8 in the bottom of the ninth. Paul relieved Bill Lee with one out and the tying and winning runs on base. He retired the next two batters to preserve the Red Bird victory. Today Paul would have been awarded a save, but that statistic did not exist in 1932. The save became an official Major League baseball statistic in 1969.

Billy the Kid continued to ride the strong right arm of Paul Dean, starting him the next day against Milwaukee. Paul responded by pitching the full nine innings, winning 8 – 4, evening his record at 6 wins and 6 losses.

Winners of their last four games, Southworth had quelled the dissention among the players and again had them playing good baseball. President Larry MacPhail, smelling a pennant race with the accompanying spike in attendance, dealt for two pitchers, Phil Weinert and Bob Osborne. The Star Tribune reported on the deal "Possessing plenty of punch and a fair defense, the Red Birds have needed only pitching assistance to become a dangerous pennant threat. With Weinert and Osborne added to the staff that already includes Bill Lee, Sheriff Blake, Ken Ash, Lefty Wysong, and Paul Dean, the Birds are prepared to resume their bid for the League title."[18]

Paul went seven innings in his next start giving up 8 hits and 4 runs. Indianapolis beat Columbus 6 – 4 and Paul suffered his first loss since Southworth took over management of the club.

In his next starting assignment Paul pitched against Indianapolis again on Aug 2nd. He pitched a good game and in the seventh he had given up 4 hits and the score was knotted 2 – 2. Paul was lifted for a pinch hitter in the eighth. Columbus scored 1 run in the top of the ninth and Roy Parmelee picked up the victory in relief.

Paul's next start on Aug 5th had the same result as his last, he pitched good ball for seven innings, giving up 5 hits and 3 runs, leaving for a pinch hitter with the score of 3 – 3. Parmelee again received and picked up the win when Columbus scored 1 run in the twelfth to win the game 3 – 2.

Wallowing in fourth place and mired in a slump when Billy the Kid took over less than a month ago, Columbus had clawed its way into a tie with Indianapolis for second place, each having won 66 and lost 52. Minneapolis remained in first place at 67 won and 48 lost.

Paul continued his fine pitching over his next three appearances, but like his last two games he didn't figure in the decision. Columbus continued to play well and on Aug 22nd they were alone in second place 5 ½ games behind Minneapolis. Paul's record remained at 6 wins and 7 losses. He was leading the League in strikeouts with 124.

Paul finally had a bad outing in his next game. He relieved Ken Ash, pitched six innings giving up 8 runs on 9 hits. He was tagged with the loss as first place Minneapolis beat Columbus 13 – 7 and increased their lead over the Red Birds to 6 ½ games. Reporters took note of Paul's strikeouts and his seemingly inability to win games.

"Paul Dean, younger brother of the St. Louis Cardinals famous Dizzy, is running up an impressive list of strikeouts, but is having trouble winning games for Columbus. He fanned five Minneapolis batsmen yesterday, after replacing Al Grabowski, but in between strikeouts he was slapped with 9 hits. His total for the season today was around 130 whiffs, but his record showed a preponderance of defeats."[19]

It must be pointed out that pitcher's performances in the 1930's was judged primarily on their won, lost record, whereas in today's game it is not as important. Advanced statistics such as K/9IP (strikeouts per nine innings), K/BB (strikeouts per walk), HR/9 (Home runs per nine innings) WHIP (walks plus hits per innings pitched) and OOPS (opponent on-base plus slugging) are more important than won/loss record in evaluating pitching performance.

Paul rebounded with a good game in his next start. Against Milwaukee he led 3 – 2 in the bottom of the ninth having allowed 2 runs on 4 hits. Only three outs away from victory Paul ran into trouble. An error and a walk put the tying and winning runs on base. Phil Weinert relieved Paul and was unable to save the game. He gave up a game tying double, then his wild pitch scored the winning run for the Brewers. Paul was saddled with the loss, dropping his record to six won and nine lost.

August was shaping up to be a bad month for Paul. Although he had pitched well, with only one bad outing, he had five no decisions and two losses to show for his work. Paul had one more start in August and he needed to right the ship.

Paul's last start of August was in Kansas City. The Kansas City Blues were in fourth place, four games behind the second place Columbus Red Birds. It was a night game and Paul's mound opponent was Lou Fette.

Paul and Fette locked up in a classic pitcher's duel. There was no score in the game as Paul came to bat in the top of the fifth with teammate Pat Crawford in scoring position on second. Paul, who always fancied himself a good hitter, singled sending Crawford home with the first run of the game.

After seven innings the Red Birds led the Blues 3 – 0 and Paul noticed something strange. The bench was suspiciously calm, and his teammates were saying nothing to him. That's when it dawned on him, the Blues hadn't had a base hit all night. Paul was six outs away from a no-hitter.

As he took the mound in bottom of the eighth Paul knew he was working on a no-hitter. First up for the Blues was Pat Collins. He slammed a line drive down the third base line for what looked like extra bases and the end of Paul's no-hit bid. Red Bird third sacker Lew Riggs lunged toward the line and stuck out his glove, to Paul's relief, the ball stuck.

After that scare, Paul settled back down. "Not another ball was hit hard and in the ninth Blue's batsmen Tredaway, Kelly and Pick went down easily." The Kansas City Star reported "The last hitter, Pick, graciously swinging quickly and none to resolutely."[20]

Baseball etiquette, so called unwritten rules, frowned upon a hitter ruining a pitcher's no-hitter late in the game if there was little chance of victory. In one often told story, Yogi Berra was catching for the Yankees and Allie Reynolds had a no-hitter going against Boston with two outs in the ninth. The batter, Ted Williams, hit a pop foul behind home plate,

Carl Duncan

a sure out to end the game, but Yogi dropped it giving Williams another shot.

Yogi, was sweating, thinking he might have cost Reynolds a no-hitter crouched down for the next pitch. "Teddy ball game" took his stance at the plate and said, "don't worry, Yogi, I won't ruin it for him." And he didn't.

The next day's newspapers proclaimed Paul's great game, a headline read:

"AT 18, PAUL DEAN PITCHES FIRST NO-HIT GAME IN NIGHT BASEBALL."

The story followed "The name of Paul Dean today was written into baseball's record books in the exclusive section reserved for pitchers of no-hit and no-run games, Dean, younger brother of Dizzy of the St. Louis Cardinals, last night ascended to the high place by stopping the Kansas City Blues 3 – 0 and in doing it he established a record that can never be broken, for it was the first no-hit game achieved under artificial lighting."[21]

Not that it erases any luster from Paul's gem, but he wasn't 18 years old. He had just turned 19 two weeks before on August 14th. One might have some sympathy for Kansas City and especially losing pitcher Lou Fette. Back in May "Slim" Harris St. Paul right- hander pitched a no-hitter against the Blues, and ironically Fette was on the losing end of that tilt also.

Amidst all the publicity of Paul's no-hitter and rampart speculation that he would probably join Dizzy on the Cardinal staff next year. Branch Rickey weighted in on the subject. "He's still a very young man and has much to learn before he'll be ready for the majors," said Rickey when asked if the no-hit game performance might result in the younger Dean being called by the Cardinals from their Columbus farm next year. "At the present we do not plan to have him with the Cardinals in 1933."[22]

Paul had narrowly missed a perfect game because he issued four walks. In retrospect the walks may have been beneficial because his wildness kept the Kansas City hitters off balance, they couldn't dig in and get into the rhythm. Paul's record now stood at 7 wins and 9 losses.

Billy the kid had the Red Birds ready for the stretch run in the upcoming last month of the season. Columbus was 7 games behind league leading Minneapolis, so they still had a shot at the title, and President Larry McPhail's much anticipated pennant race was at hand.

Minneapolis limped to the finish winning 16 and losing 14 in the final month. Columbus however folded winning just 10 of their final 25 games, ending up in second place 10 ½ games behind Minneapolis.

Paul was not much help in September's pennant race. He lost 4 games and had one no decision. He ended the year with 7 wins and 13 losses. (Some sources put Paul's record at 7 wins and 16 losses. My research couldn't account for the three extra losses.) Paul was a workhorse for Columbus. Despite missing a couple of weeks with an injury, he pitched 212 innings, second only to Bill Lee's 255. He averaged 8 hits and 5 walks per game. Paul led the league in strikeouts with 156 while walking 113. He also led the league in hit batsmen. He plunked 17 batters; no wonder hitters were afraid to dig in on him. Overall, it was a successful year for Paul. He showed he had the tools to dominate, he just needed to refine his pitching skills.

Billy Southworth brought the Red Birds from fourth to second place, but it wasn't good enough. He was fired at the end of the season. Paul's season was not over, he joined Dizzy and three other Cardinals for some barnstorming.

These exhibition games were special events for fans in small towns. The fans could see Major Leaguers playing with and against their local baseball players. Professional ball players in the 1930's were paid only during the regular season, when the season ended so did their paychecks. Barnstorming was an easy way to keep making money from their baseball skills and notoriety. Of course, Dizzy's pay, like everything else about him, was different. He had a special arrangement with the Cardinals that spread out his baseball salary through the entire year. This was necessitated because Diz couldn't manage his money. He lived like a king during the season but when the paychecks stopped Dizzy was broke and borrowed money from the Cardinals to survive often using up the next year's salary.

This barnstorming tour was three weeks in duration with fourteen games to be played in Missouri, Kansas, and Oklahoma. Paul and Dizzy Dean were joined by St. Louis Cardinals Pepper Martin, Paul Derringer and Jimmy Wilson.

A typical game was like the one played in Jefferson Missouri on Sept. 22, 1932 The Jefferson City Post advertised *"Four Cardinal stars will join the Jefferson City Senators at Whiteway Park Monday night and help them* *in their efforts to beat the strong Fulton Stars. Admission will be $.75 and valuable prizes also will be given away to lucky fans. A dozen baseball bats, three Pepper Martin $8.50 baseball gloves, four baseballs autographed by the whole St. Louis Cardinal team and one pair of $16.50 baseball spikes."*[23] This was great entertainment in depression era America and often several thousand fans filled the local parks.

After the tour was over Paul and Dizzy went back to their home state of Arkansas. They spent the winter visiting relatives, hunting and getting ready for the 1933 baseball season.

CHAPTER 11

"Babe Ruth is worth $80,000 a year. So am I."

Dizzy Dean is arguably the most famous Minor League player in baseball history. In 1932 he had only pitched one meaningless Major League game, yet he had a 10-part syndicated newspaper column, sportswriters wrote poems about him, reporters wanted interviews in every city and town where he showed up, and when Paul pitched a good game the article usually identified him as brother of the "Famous" Dizzy Dean. Dizzy was the master of self-promotion.

Diz was again going to Bradenton, Florida for spring training with the Cardinals, the World Champion St. Louis Cardinals. 1931 has been a magical year for the Red Birds. They won the National League pennant by 13 games, outfielder Chuck Hafley won the batting title with a .349 batting average, and second baseman Frankie Frisch won the first modern-day N.L. MVP award. All these superlatives earned St. Louis a return bout with the American League winner and defending World Champion Philadelphia Athletics.

Manager Connie Mack's A's easily won the A.L. crown besting the second place New York Giants by 13 ½ games. Led by five future hall of famers, Mickey Cochran, Jimmie Fox, Lefty Grove, Waite Hoyt, and All Simmons, the Athletics were heavily favored to win their third consecutive World Series title. However, a dynasty was not in the cards. Pepper Martin made sure of that. St. Louis won the series four games to three.

Johnny Leonard Roosevelt "Pepper" Martin's 1931 World Series play was described as "The greatest individual performance in the history of the World Series" by hall of fame manager John McGraw. He set a World Series record with 12 hits, including 4 doubles and a home run. He stole 5 bases and had a .500 B.A. for the series. Pepper's daring base running and aggressive headfirst slides earned him the nickname "Wild Horse of the Osage." Unshaven, dirty from headfirst slides, playing Sans Jockey Strap or any underwear, knocking down grounders with his barrel chest, Pepper epitomized and was the prototype for the famous, roguish gas house gang that followed in the later 1930's.

After their World Series loss to the Cards the A's succumbed to the realities of the Great Depression. Like all Major League clubs, dwindling revenues from declining attendance made it difficult to stay in business. Much to the dismay of Philadelphia fans the Athletics resorted to selling off their star players.

Teams that had wealthy owners such as the Boston Red Sox, New York Yankees, Detroit Tigers and Cincinnati Reds were able and willing to buy players to stay competitive. St. Louis did not have a super-rich owner, but the Red Birds had their Farm System. The Cardinals sold star players to rich teams but unlike other teams they had a better farm hand experienced and ready to take the stars place.

The 1932 Cardinals were stacked with experienced talent and they did not seem to need the services of eccentric Minor League hurler Dizzy Dean. That changed when Branch Rickey traded away veteran pitcher Burleigh Grimes. Grimes had a great year in 1931 leading the National League in wins with 19 and followed that with two victories over the A's in the World Series. Rickey always said, "I would rather trade a player a year too early than a year too late." Grimes was sent to the Chicago Cubs for Hack Wilson and Bud Teachout. This trade left an opening on the St. Louis pitching staff and the Cardinal Brass wanted Diz to be the pitcher to fill it.

Branch Rickey wanted to talk to Dizzy to see if he had matured enough to be counted on to take Grimes' place on the Cardinals staff to defend their World Series title. Also, if Diz was ready for a Major League roster he needed to be signed to a new contract. To accomplish these goals Rickey summoned Diz to St. Louis in January 1932.

Dizzy breezed into St. Louis mid-February and immediately started talking to reporters. Yes, he was here to negotiate his 1932 contract with Branch Rickey, and if a satisfactory deal could be struck, he would be ready to win 20 to 25 games for the Cards to defend their World Series Championship. And, of course he was in great shape since he had spent much of the winter hunting with his brother, Paul near Russellville, Ark.

"You ought to see my brother" Diz exclaimed. "He is as tall as I am and weighs more than 200 pounds. What a pitcher he is going to be."[1] With that said, he disappeared into Rickey's office. Emerging from Branch Rickey's office almost five hours later, Diz seemed repentant almost humble.

"I was a fool last year" Dean remarked revealing a hitherto unsuspected capacity for penitence. "I realize that now. I had my chance but threw it away by playing around too much. But this year I'm going to buckle down." "I was surprised at the way Mr. Rickey treated me after the way I acted last year. He sure treated me fine."[2]

The humility vanished when a reporter asked, "Do you think you'll be more effective as a result of your year in the Texas League?" "No sir" Diz replied, "I couldn't be any better. I'd have been a winner for the Cards last year. But they'll be glad they've got me the coming season. I'll see that they win another pennant."[3]

Warming to the reporter's attention Diz allowed that he was a "one-man prosperity wave. They'll pay to see me play. I'll put more people in parks than any other National League player in ten years."[4]

Branch Rickey didn't think Diz would single-handedly abolish the depression. But he knew Dizzy Dean was a tremendous drawing card. He had seen how attendance spiked on the days Diz pitched at Houston and the publicity Dizzy generated with his cocky, boasting, colorful personality.

Rickey wanted Dizzy happy, but he didn't want to overplay him. Although Rickey refused to divulge Diz's 1932 salary, owner Sam Breadon revealed after the season how much Diz made. Dizzy was paid the usual rookie salary of $3,500, but to sweeten the pot and make Diz happy the Cardinals agreed to wipe out $4,000 in debts Dizzy owed the Cards.

During the marathon five-hour contract negotiations Branch Rickey noticed Dizzy couldn't sit still and seemed to be in some discomfort. Rickey suggested a visit to team doctor, Robert Hyland, and Dizzy agreed. After an examination it was determined that Dizzy needed and operation.

The St. Louis Post-Dispatch reported, "Jerome Herman "Dizzy" Dean, who signed a Cardinal contract Friday and announced that the 1932 pennant was safe for the Red Birds, will remain in St. Louis for a few days, to undergo a minor operation."[5]

The nature of Dizzy's surgery remained a mystery as newspapers only reported the surgery as a "minor operation."

For Dizzy's part he apparently enjoyed his hospital stay. A picture in the St. Louis Star showed a smiling Dizzy in his hospital bed and a pretty nurse checking his pulse. Diz said, "this is the life. I'm enjoying the rest, get fine food and the club is paying all of the bills."[6]

A cryptic clue as to the true reason for Dizzy's "minor operation" was provided in a sporting news article, "Dizzy Dean, all other things being equal, is now eligible for membership in B'Nai B'rith, as a result of the operation he underwent recently."[7]

Family newspapers could not print the reason for the "minor operation." Circumcision was not a subject that could be discussed in 1930 news media.

After being released from the hospital, Dizzy decided to stay a few more days in St. Louis to enjoy his celebrity. Along with World Series hero, Pepper Martin, he attended local sporting events. They were introduced and spoke over loudspeakers to the fans.

Pepper enjoyed the limelight almost as much as Diz.

Dizzy was mystified and intrigued by hockey. He had never seen or even heard of a game called hockey. "Addressing the 7,500 fans attending the game between the St. Louis Flyers and the Kansas City Pla-Mors Dizzy couldn't remember the name of the sport, so he named it "sockey".

With hockey sticks flying and players fighting, the fans gave Dean credit for giving the game a name more appropriate than the one it now bears."[8]

In early February Dizzy headed to Arkansas, after all he had hometown fans to regale with stories, insights, and predictions about Major League baseball. Holding court in Russellville, Arkansas Diz leaned against a lamp post in the town square and discoursed on baseball to his adoring fans.

"Babe Ruth is worth $80,000 a year. So am I."

"Pepper Martin will be the second most valuable player to the Cardinals next season.

I'm first."

"Lefty O'Doul, Brooklyn outfielder, is the most dangerous batter in the league. He won't get a loud foul against me."

"Big league batters will be easier for me than Minor Leaguers. Big Leaguers won't touch me."[9]

Attending a rotary club meeting Dizzy invited all Russellville Rotarians to the first game of the 1932 World Series. "Of course, it's going to be the St. Louis Cardinals and Naturally it's going to be Ol' Diz pitching. So, I want you all to be my guests."[10]

Not wanting to neglect the youngsters, Dizzy became a full-fledged member of the Arkansas boy scouts. After being sworn in by troop number 3, Diz said for his first good deed he would send them the baseball "that I fan Babe Ruth with."[11]

In order to fulfill his prophecies Diz had to do one thing first; he had to win a spot on the Big-League roster something he failed to do the year before. Although Branch Rickey wanted Dizzy to take the departed Grimes's place, Cardinal manager Gabby Street had two other pitching prospects he wanted to compete with Dizzy. "Tex" Carlton, Dizzy's teammate at Houston last year, and Ray Starr who had a good year with Rochester in 1931.

Gabby said Dizzy was not assured a place on the Cardinals in 1932. "Last spring when he joined us, he thought he had his job clinched without getting out and working for it. The boy will start from scratch with me."[12]

Dizzy left Arkansas in mid-February. He and his wife Pat drove to Gulfport, Mississippi to visit her relatives, before Diz had to report for spring training in Florida. Pat became ill while in Gulfport, so she stayed with her folks while Dizzy motored on to Bradenton, Florida arriving on February 22, 1932.

Upon arriving Dizzy assured reporters that he was in excellent shape, even though he appeared frail after losing 15 lbs., because of the same flu bug that his wife was now battling. Diz said he was a changed man; he now knew the behavior required of a Big Leaguer. He realized that practice was more important than sleeping late, golfing and fishing. He vowed to keep his mouth shut and work hard.

As usual keeping his mouth shut proved to be the difficult part. Diz just had to remind everyone that he was a great pitcher. "I don't think it will be any tougher pitching in this league than it was in Texas. I don't worry about control, because I have it. I don't mind admitting I have a high hard one that I can buzz through there, and I don't think too many of the boys will like tryin' to hit my curve.

Perhaps grasping the reality of his situation; a rookie vying for a spot on a World Championship team against two rivals who each had won 20 games last year at Houston and Rochester, Diz tossed the Cards a bone. "Of course, it doesn't cramp my style any to be with the best club in the Big Leagues."[13]

The "changed man" didn't stay changed for long. The first crisis came when the Cardinals refused to allow Dizzy's wife to join him for spring training. "My wife is ill in Gulfport, Mississippi" Dizzy explained "and the Cardinal club won't let me have her come to training camp. If they insist on that order, I may pick up and leave. I can't go on worrying like this. They tell me it don't look right for a young fellow trying to make a place on the ball club to have his wife down here, but I don't like that. I'd rather dig ditches and be happy than be on this ball club and be unhappy."[14]

Still intrigued by Dizzy's potential and searching for a way to end the impasse, the Cardinals turned to Joe Schultz for advice. Schultz, who managed Dizzy to his best season ever at Houston last year, knew how to handle him.

"You have to lead him, kid him along, pat him on the back and tell him how good he is" Joe explained. "If you drive him or discipline him as you would most other players he'll fold up and be worthless."[15]

Me 'N' Paul

Hoping Dizzy's wife could provide the coddling and encouragement he needed the Cardinals relented and allowed Pat Dean to join her husband in Bradenton, Florida.

Pat proved to be a good influence on her husband, Diz settled in, quieted down and concentrated on making the team. He worked hard, listened to his coaches, was punctual to practice and didn't cause any trouble.

Dizzy's efforts were not rewarded in his spring debut. Pitching in the "Spring World Series" a rematch against the Philadelphia Athletics Diz was bombed for 6 runs, including 4 home runs, in the first and only inning he lasted. After the game, a 14 – 12 loss, manager Street defended Dizzy. "I instructed Dean to use nothing but fastballs and warned him not to try to throw curves, even if the enemy hit him."[16] Gabby didn't want Diz to risk arm injury in a meaningless spring game.

Dizzy's next spring start was not any better. The Cincinnati Reds lit him up for 5 runs in 3 innings. Again, Gabby had Dizzy's back declaring the cold windy weather contributed to Dizzy's poor outing. Gabby still had confidence in Dizzy's ability saying "there is no question in my mind he has the real stuff. I have seen him work and I know what he can do."[17]

Sill Dizzy's first two starts were ugly, he had yielded 12 hits and 11 runs in 4 innings. Tex Carlton had been much more effective than Diz or Ray Starr, many writers following the team predicted Tex would be the best of the three-ballyhooed rookie pitching prospects.

After those two sorry outings fans and sportswriters were asking what's wrong with Dizzy? United Press staff correspondent Henry Mclemore went so far as to suggest "Dean's pitching apparently suffering from overdose of virtue. Pointing out that last year Diz spent more time talking, fishing, golfing, and carousing around at night than he did practicing baseball, yet enemy batters couldn't hit his pitches with a canoe paddle. Then having stood the hitters on their collective ears, the Dizzy one would proceed to make merry at a very fast pace."[18]

While this year Diz had been quiet, obedient, and working hard at practice to hone his craft. Instead of carousing he stayed home at night with his wife. However, the docile, virtuous Diz seemed to have lost his pitching prowess.

Not wanting Dizzy to "fold up and become worthless" as Buff manager Schultz said would happen if Diz was handled improperly, Gabby took him aside and had a talk with him. "Don't get downhearted about those two games you pitched," Gabby told Dizzy.

"I believe in you and I'll string along with you. You've shown an inclination to work and play fair with me and I am convinced that if you go along that way, you'll win some games for me this year."[19]

Three relief innings of 1-hit shout-out ball against the Boston Braves earned Diz a start versus the Bronx Bombers. On March 21st Dizzy started when the New York Yankees came to Bradenton, Florida.

Dizzy started strong retiring the first six batters he faced including Babe Ruth on a pop fly to Frankie Frisch at second. The Russellville boy scouts would have to wait for their "Bambino" strikeout ball.

Trouble arrived after Diz retired the first man in the third. After walking a batter, Dizzy induced pitcher "El Goofo" Gomez to hit a slow roller to second, a late throw failed to get the lead runner. Two on, one down and the score still tied at zero. Tough spot, but manageable. Catcher Jimmy Wilson went to the mound to calm Diz down. "Coupla good pitches, double play ball we're out of the inning."[20] Wilson encouraged.

Diz didn't settle down, he promptly gave up two doubles, a walk, and then a towering home run to Lou Gehrig. Just like that, six Yankee runs and an early shower for Diz. Final score New York 11, St. Louis 3. Ironically, just two weeks later Paul Dean pitched eight innings against these same Yankees and Columbus won 5 – 4.

Giving Diz a break from Major League hitters, Gabby started him when St. Louis played the bearded barnstorming House of David team. Player/manager for the House of David was old St. Louis Cardinal hero, Grover Cleveland Alexander.

Less than six years ago "Old Pete", as his teammates called him ambled to the mound at Yankee Stadium in the seventh game of the 1926 World Series. It was the seventh inning, bases loaded, 2 outs and the Cards leading by a single run.

"Old Pete", one of the original "Bad Boys" of baseball had a well-deserved reputation for extending himself under the neons. Usually hung over from a night of partying, he had been known to keep a flask of whiskey in the bullpen. He had surely been partying the night before, celebrating the Cardinal victory that forced the deciding game. Facing elimination Alexander had pitched the full nine innings beating the Yankees 10 – 2, his second victory of the series.

Rogers Hornsby, Cardinal player/manager, told about summoning Alexander from the bullpen that cool, drizzly October afternoon in New York.

"People always ask me what I said to Alex when I went out to meet him," Hornsby explains. "I left my position and met him halfway between the bull pen and the infield. I wanted to find out if he could see. He recognized me all right, which was encouraging. He had been dozing in the bull pen, but his eyes were about open when he met me. So, I told him we were ahead, but that the bases were filled, two out in the seventh inning, with Lazzeri at bat. I had told him he was our best bet and that if we needed help, I'd call him.

"'Don't worry, Rog,' Ales said to me. 'I guess there's nothing to do but give Lazzeri a lot of trouble.' And so, after I saw that he could see and walk and didn't have anything in his hip pocket, I told him to go in and pitch."[21]

Alexander took five warm-up pitches, proceeded to strike out Tony Lazzeri, Leaving the bases loaded and the Cardinal lead intact. The drama, however, was far from over. "Alexander the Great" still had to face the soon to be named "Murderer's Row" for two more innings.

'Old Pete' survived the eighth and had two outs in the ninth, but the Yankees were still in good shape as the greatest slugger in baseball strode to the plate. Babe Ruth had homered earlier in the game and could now tie the game with one swing. Pitching carefully Alexander wisely walked the Babe. Yankee fans, smelling blood cheered wildly as slugger Bob Meusel stood in the batter's box representing the winning run. To the surprise and amazement of Meusel and 40,000 fans the slow footed, spindly-legged Bambino decided he could steal second base! Catcher Bob O'Farrell's throw to Hornsby easily nailed the Babe ending the fall classic, making the underdog St. Louis Cardinals World Champions.

Dizzy had no trouble with the House of David's bearded batters. He and fellow rookie Ray Starr allowed the Barnstormers only one run on three hits. Despite the two rookies' dominance of the House of David team, St. Louis sportswriters agreed that Tex Carlton would win a spot on the Major League staff while Dizzy and Starr fought it out to see who would be the ninth and final pitcher on the Cardinal team.

The St. Louis Cardinals opened the regular season on April 12, 1932. Dizzy is on the opening day roster; however, his spot is far from secure, having been regulated to the bullpen. Use of the bullpen in the 1930's was much different than in today's game. Modern day starters are only expected to pitch five or six innings, then a middle reliever works, and finally a closer finishes the game. Starters in the 1930's pitched the full nine innings unless they started giving up too many runs.

Dizzy was still in danger of being sent back to Houston for more seasoning. Owner Sam Breadon said "Dean has not shown that he has the strength to last for nine innings in the Majors. Another year of development in the Minors might make a star of him."[22]

Most sportswriters expected the Cardinals to repeat as National League Champs. Odds- makers had the Cards as 8 – 5 favorites for the flag and the New York Giants second at 2 – 1 odds. It was a surprise when St. Louis started the season by losing five of their first seven games.

A major reason for the Cards slow start was absence of Charles James "Chick" Hafey, the 1931 National League batting champion. Chick was often at odds with Branch Rickey over salary disputes. Hafey held out for more money in 1931, not only was he denied a raise, Rickey fined him for being late to training camp. Coming off his batting title, Chick demanded that the previous year's fine be added to his 1932 salary. Rickey refused so Hafey left training camp. Rickey responded by sending Chick to the last-place Cincinnati Reds for cash and obscure pitcher Benny Frey.

Dizzy responded well to bullpen duty, by April 23rd he had relieved in five games, pitching seven innings giving up only three hits and one run. Unfortunately, the one run was a walk-off home run to Pirate slugger, Gussy Suhr. Since he was pitching so well, Gabby gave Diz his first start when Pitcher Paul Derringer went down with Ptomaine poisoning.

Dizzy started against the Chicago Cubs on Thursday, April 28th he shut the Cubbies out for the first three innings before Chicago knocked him out of the game by scoring five runs in the fourth. Chicago won the game 12 to 7.

Gabby Street needed starting pitching and still believing in Dizzy's talent sent him to the mound against the Cincinnati Reds on May 3rd. Diz rewarded his manager's confidence by whitewashing the Reds 9 – 0.

Buoyed by his first win of the year, Diz sauntered into the Cardinal's home office the day after the victory. He asked the ladies working there for his fan mail. Diz was somewhat taken back when informed he had none. "What! No fan mail? He thought a moment and said "well, I should'ave pitched a better game. I didn't have nothing but my glove yesterday. If I'd had my stuff I woulda showed everybody a real ball game."[23]

Dizzy's next start came five days later in the second game of a doubleheader against the New York Giants. The Giants skippered by hall of fame manager John J McGraw, won the opener 4 – 1, leaving the hometown fans disappointed and unhappy. Leave it to Diz to charge up the fans and liven-up game two with exploits rarely seen on a Major League diamond.

Poor bunting, baserunning uncharacteristic of a pitcher combined with sloppy fielding and wild throws by the Giants enabled Dizzy to bunt a homerun.

Diz came to bat in the fourth with no outs and teammate Charley Gelbert on first. He tried to sacrifice but his bunt was a pop fly that flew over the head of the third baseman, who like the other infielders had come in to play the expected bunt. The left fielder finally corralled the "bunt", and unable to get Gelbert at home threw wildly to second trying to nail the hard-charging Diz when the ball sailed into right field Diz was up and on the move again. One more wild throw, this time from the right fielder to home, enabled Dizzy to score.

This escapade became another story Diz loved to tell, with some embellishment of course, how he bunted a homerun that drove New York Giant manager John J McGraw into retirement.

"Since I'm a rookie they haven't learned yet what a great hitter and daring base Runner I am. So, I lays down a bunt, and beats it out at first. From the corner of my eye, I see Bill Terry jugglin' the ball, and so I break for second. He's so surprised that he throws wide to the second baseman and it gets by him. So, I just keep right on tearin' for third, and I'm goin' so fast I lose my cap. The shortstop's throw to third is ahead of me, but I slide in hard and upset the third baseman. Before they know what's happened, I'm up and a chargin' for home. As I cross the plate one of my socks has fell down over my shoe, and all the fans is cheerin' wild, because it's the winnin' run.

"The great John J McGraw, who's only been managin' ball clubs for 33 years, retires as manager of the Giants that night. When he sees a pitcher get a home run on a bunt, that's just too much for him, and he makes Terry the new manager."[24]

Diz did win the game 6 – 2 and McGraw did retire. However, McGraw's retirement was three weeks later and was more the result of the Giants poor record (17 – 23, in last place) and a serious sinus infection than Dizzy's improbable homerun.

With consecutive victories under his belt Dizzy figured he was qualified to tell the Cardinals why they were floundering under .500. Gabby Street wasn't letting him pitch often enough. Diz was convinced the Cards only pitched him once a week, on Sunday, to draw larger crowds.

"It ain't fair to work me just once a week," the Dizzy one protested. *"I know it's nice to pack the park every Sunday and I realize that I have tremendous advertising and box office value. But I want to win a flock of pennants and when they pitch me only once a week, they're hurting my future and the club's pennant chances."*[25]

Dizzy did get to pitch more often, however, he was erratic and inconsistent. By the end of May Diz had won 4 and lost 2. Especially troubling was two outings against Pittsburgh when the Pirates punished Diz for 13 runs.

Persistent speculation still had Dizzy headed back to Houston before a Major League mandated final roster limit of 23 players by June 15th. Owner Breadon said cuts would have to be made and one casualty would be a pitcher. Some of Dizzy's teammates were tired of Diz popping off. Sick of hearing Diz tell everyone he can "stop any team in the league from hitting".[26] This bravado was seen as disrespectful to opponents serving only as incentive to beat the rookie's brains out. Dizzy was admonished by manager Gabby Street to either shape up or get ready for a trip to Houston.

Two things saved Diz from another year as a Houston Buffalo. First, he pitched a rain- shortened seven-inning shut-out, beating the Cubs 1 -0. Next Branch Rickey sold three Cardinal players for cash. Pitcher Flint Rhem and infielder Eddie Delker went to the Phillies and utility man Harvey Hendrick was sold to the Reds. Sam Breadon said, "we had to cut our roster to twenty-three players by June 15th, so we sold our excess players

Me 'N' Paul

to the highest bidder."[27] Disposing of veteran pitcher Rhem assured Dizzy Major League playing time.

Selling Flint Rhem was a classic Rickey deal. He reduced payroll by replacing an expensive veteran star with a lower salaried rookie, plus he added the proceeds of the sale to the Cardinal bottom line.

Most writers agreed that Dizzy deserved a Major League berth. "Dizzy Dean has qualified as one of the regulars. He has won four games for the World Champions and is surpassed by only one other member of the staff. Bill Hallahan pocketing five victories."[28] His spot on the staff secure, Diz happily boarded the train as the Cardinals departed for a road trip through the east hoping to improve on their dismal 20 – 24 record.

While in Philadelphia to play the Phillies Diz received a letter from his wife who was back in St. Louis. She said she was mistreated by the Cardinals front office. "I got a letter from my wife and she told me they'd insulted her in the Cardinal office. They can't do that and get away with it. We were going to move to an apartment in St. Louis and she went over to get the money to pay our hotel bill. They said things to her that embarrassed her. I won't stand for that. I hope I fall out this hotel window and die if I ever throw another pitch for them."[29]

"I'm through with the Cardinals and I'm going home," Dizzy declared. *I've been fed up on the mistreatment that has been given me, ever since I joined this here ball club and I ain't going to stand it no longer. I'm underpaid and that's bad enough and I'm embarrassed to death every time I want to get a few dollars and that's pretty tough."*[30]

Dizzy also said he planned to get out of his St. Louis contract and play for a team that appreciated him. When reporters asked how he proposed the break the contract. Dizzy informed them that his contract was invalid.

"I'm going to get my outright release" Diz said "I'm underage and won't be 21 until the middle of August. (Actually, Diz turned 22 back in January). "My father didn't sign the contract although he did sign for Paul. Therefore, my contract ain't binding. You see I know all about this legal business for I'm pretty smart along those lines."[31] With that Diz left the team and boarded a train back to St. Louis.

After much publicity, wasted time, animosity toward Dizzy by his manager and teammates the matter was resolved. The Cardinal's proved they gave Pat Dean the $100 in question and had shown her no disrespect.

This made Dizzy appear henpecked. Rickey also proved Dizzy was 22 years old when he signed his 1932 contract, making Diz look foolish for lying about his age or worse an idiot for not knowing his own age. The club did make once concession in a spirit of friendship, understanding, and reconciliation. The Cardinals agreed to pay Diz $225, which had been paid to his father last year by the club and deducted from Dizzy's salary.

As far as Dizzy was concerned everything was fine and he was ready to start pitching again. He sent a telegram to manager Gabby Street.

Manager Charles Street
Ben Franklin Hotel
Philadelphia

I am sorry I left the club like I did, and if you will give me a chance to pitch in Philadelphia tomorrow and again in New York Wednesday I will show you how games should be pitched.

Dizzy Dean[32]

When Gabby received the telegram, he was not amused.

"Pitch him today huh?" Gabby growled. *"not for a million dollars I got fellows on this club who've been keeping in shape. I got pitchers who've been throwing in batting practice and shagging flies. Do you think I am going to shove them back out of turn to use some bird that hasn't worked in ten days? Not on your life."*[33]

The Cardinal players, Dizzy's teammates were also disgusted with his behavior, they had no use for a player who would quit, when the team needed him. In spite of his teammates disdain, a depleted pitching staff and Rickey mandates assured Dizzy a continued spot in the pitching rotation.

Dizzy started on June 21st against the New York Giants. He silenced his critics by beating the New Yorkers 5 – 1, stopping them on six hits and striking out eight. He missed a shut-out when the Giants scored a meaningless run in the bottom of the ninth.

As the Cardinals prepared to leave New York for their next series in Cincinnati, Dizzy started complaining of stomach pains. He was taken to

Me 'N' Paul

St. John's hospital where he was diagnosed as having an indigestion attack. After being discharged from the hospital Dizzy said he was still hurting and couldn't possibly make the trip to Cincinnati. He was sent home to St. Louis.

Turns out it was more than indigestion that kept Dizzy from making the trip to Cincy. In the middle of the first game of the Cardinal-Reds series a deputy sheriff showed up in the Red Bird dugout. The lawman explained he had a writ to be served on Jerome H. Dean.

Evidently on his last trip to Cincinnati Diz had purchased a new suit and neglected to pay for it. The writ was served to garnish Dizzy's wages in the amount of $75. The payment had to be made before the Cardinals left town or the St. Louis share of the gate receipts would be withheld. Cardinal secretary Clarence Lloyd had no choice but to pay the bill.

Back in St. Louis Diz found out about the payment and the news revived him. Still wanting to avoid Cincinnati Diz was eager to join is team in Pittsburgh. The St. Louis dispatch reported.

Dizzy Dean, who has been sick in bed for three days surprised the Cardinal office by appearing all diked out today.

"I understand they need me over there in Pittsburgh and I'd like to join the club and stop them Pirates," he said.

The club officials were mildly surprised and expressed the thought that he was too sick to pitch.

"I'll not only pitch, but I'll beat that Pittsburgh club sure. When can I leave?"

Branch Rickey thought such devotion worthy of recognition and ordered Dean to depart today. He will leave at 6 o'clock.[34]

Diz rejoined the Cardinals and actually behaved himself for the remainder of the season. He succeeded in regaining the respect of his teammates by playing hard, hustling, pitching both in starting and relieving assignments, and volunteering to pitch everyday if necessary.

He still popped-off: "I'm a star. I got color. I'm stopping the rival clubs in their tracks. I'll win that flag for us."[35] He told catcher Jimmy Wilson

He continued to brag about how he would win games. "Come out and see me beat the Giants." Diz told fans and reporters. "I'm going to bear down from start to finish and I am sure I'll win."[36]

Reporters asked Diz if he thought his teammates could get him some runs off Giants starter Bill Walker, who held the Red Birds to a pair of hits the last time he faced them.

"I don't know if they can" Dizzy replied. "But don't worry about that, I can. I'll win my own game if necessary."[37]

The great Dean proceeded to stop the New Yorkers on five hits and two runs, also he provided all the runs he needed by hitting a home run and a single for four R.B.I's. As Dizzy always said "It ain't bragging if you do it."

The 1932 season established Dizzy as a Major Leaguer. He was a workhorse, an iron man who won three games in one five-day stretch. He finished the season with 18 wins, 15 losses and led the National League in strikeouts as well as innings pitched. The Cardinals, however, were a major disappointment. The World Champion St. Louis Cardinals finished the 1932 season a dismal seventh in the National League.

Sam Breadon was disappointed with the collapsing Cards, but he was optimistic about the 1933 season and he was very high on Dizzy. "Never saw such a fellow in my life. Spirit like his is hard to find. He has natural baseball sense. He has the makings of a great pitcher and he will be one if he only can learn to hold down his occasional outbreaks."[38]

Evidently, the praise was more than mere words with Sam, the next day the club announced the signing of Dizzy to a 1933 contract. The St. Louis star reported, "Dizzy Dean has consented to grace the Cardinals" lineup with his name and presence next season. He signed his 1933 contract today, Branch Rickey announced."

"How many games did he promise to win next year." Rickey was asked. "He started with twenty-five and wound up with forty." was the reply.[39]

CHAPTER 12

"I can make them colonels look sick"

Paul Dean's success at Columbus in 1932 assured him a spot on the 1933 Red Bird roster. Instead of going to Houston as he had the past two years, Paul reported to Spartanburg, South Carolina where Columbus held their spring training camp beginning in early March 1933.

Larry MacPhail, Columbus Red Bird President, had the determination and the dollars to make the 1933 Red Birds champions of the American Association. Housed in a new stadium and backed by the St. Louis Cardinals, the Columbus club finished 1932 in excellent financial condition. MacPhail plowed much of the 1932 profits back into the club, buying and paying players to strengthen the Red Birds, he believed money invested in improving the team was money wisely spent.

MacPhail, the so-called "Boy Wonder", was a great innovator and promoter. He was a proponent of night baseball which was a huge success in Columbus and the rest of the league. He held many fan-friendly promotions, such as ladies' night, that increased attendance. The "Boy Wonder" also helped institute a play-off system in the American Association. Under this plan, the team with the highest winning percentage in the east and the leading team in the west met in a post season seven game series to determine the American Association champion. The winner of that series then advanced to the Junior World Series to play the champion of the Double A International League. Since the American Association and the International League were the top level of Minor League teams the Junior World Series was the de facto Minor League Championship.

This was a brilliant innovation, attendance increased, and fan interest skyrocketed because now instead of one pennant race there were two races in the same league. The eastern division consisted of the following four teams: Columbus Red Birds, Indianapolis Indians, Toledo Mud hens and Louisville Colonels. The Western Division were St. Paul Saints, Minneapolis Millers, Milwaukee Brewers and Kansas City Blues.

MacPhail also had no tolerance for failure. If a player or manager failed to provide value to the Red Birds he was dismissed. Midway through the prior season manager "Nemo" Liebold was fired and Billy Southworth was hired. In spite of a second-place finish Southworth was not retained.

MacPhail's managerial search focused on two current St. Louis Cardinal players, the "Boy Wonder" considered managerial timber. The candidates were catcher Bob O'Farrell and outfielder Ray Blades. O'Farrell, a former Major League player/manager was not ready to give up his Major League catching job for a Minor League managing gig, so MacPhail zeroed in on Blades. Ray Blades was at the end of a solid if unspectacular Major League career, and he was eager to try his hand at managing.

MacPhail's boss, Branch Rickey, approved of the choice. Rickey had a long history with Ray Blades having scouted and signed him for the Cards in 1920. Blades spent his entire career with St. Louis appearing in three World Series, 1928, 1930, and 1931. Like Rickey, Blades was a teetotaler and later in his managerial career he prohibited alcohol consumption among his players.

Although small at 5'7" and 160lbs, Blades was a fierce competitor with a titanic temper.

A lifetime .300 hitter Ray would be player/manager for the 1933 Red Birds.

Player/managers gained popularity during the depression. Owners loved the concept filling two positions for one salary. Even though there are no player/managers today, the tradition of baseball managers wearing uniforms continues.

Ray Blades told the Louisville Courier-Journal how he intended to manage.

"I'm going to have a fighting ball club." "There will be no handshaking with players of other teams. We are out to win the pennant and any player who won't fight to win every game will have to earn his bread and butter elsewhere. I am extremely well pleased over the prospects."[1]

Paul Dean, the 1932 American Association strike-out king, and no-hit pitcher was not considered the ace of the 1933 Columbus Red Birds, Columbus was loaded with pitching talent and Paul would have to earn his innings. He needed to prove his value and garner the confidence of his new manager.

Paul saw his first regular season action in the second game of the season. On April 14th he pitched in relief against Minneapolis, last year's American Association Champions. Paul took the mound in the eighth inning with the Millers ahead 8 – 2. He finished the game pitching 1 2/3 innings giving up no hits and no runs. Columbus didn't score again, so the final score was Minneapolis-8 Columbus-2.

Paul's first start came on April 23rd against the Milwaukee Brewers. He pitched well giving up 4 hits and 2 runs in seven innings. He was lifted for a pinch hitter after striking out 7 and walking 3, with the Brewers ahead 2 – 1. Columbus ended up winning the game in ten innings by a score of 3 – 2, saving Paul from a loss.

Manager Ray Blades was starting to have confidence in Paul as evidenced in a game against the St. Paul Saints, Paul was called on in the seventh to preserve a 3 run Red Bird lead. Things were fine until the ninth when the Saints loaded the bases. Instead of relieving Paul, Blades left him in, and Paul halted the Saint uprising to save the game.

Blades rewarded Paul with a start against the Saints two days later. On a cool, rainy day Paul was breezing along with a 6 – 0 lead in the fourth when he had a fist fight with Saints pitcher Les Munns. Paul was returning from first base after a ground-out when he passed the St. Paul dugout, Munns made a remark Paul resented so he punched him. Unlike Diz, Paul liked to fight. When trouble brewed Dizzy would start talking on the other hand, Paul would start swinging. Neither player was ejected, and the game continued until it was rained out after 8 innings. That constituted an official game and Paul won 10 – 4 for his first victory of the season.

Rosters had to be cut to 18 players by May 1st and Ray Blades announced he had pruned the Red Bird roster to within the player limit. The Columbus roster included seven pitchers, two catchers, five infielders and four outfielders. Paul's teammates included one player who was every bit as colorful and "eccentric" as Dizzy, Art "What-A-Man" Shires.

Charles Arthur Shires, a boisterous, boozing, brawling, Texan, was born August 13, 1906 in Italy, Texas. He attended Waxahachie High School, where his teammates included future Major Leaguers, Paul Richards and Jimmie Adair.

Shires began his professional baseball career at age 19 with the Waco clubs of the Texas League. While playing for Waco his hair-trigger temper landed him in serious trouble. During a game between Waco and Shreveport, Shires became incensed at heckling fans. He angrily threw a baseball into the stands, hitting an unsuspecting Louisiana man in the head. The unlucky fan, Walter Lawson, died as a result of the injury inflicted by Shires.

The fact that Lawson was a "negro" made the case very controversial and a grand jury exonerated Shire. Lawson's widow sued him for $25,000. But ended up settling for $500. A black man's life was not worth much in the segregated south during the 1920's.

By the time Shires made it to the Majors with the Chicago White Sox in 1928 he was calling himself "Art the Great". He was adept at self-promotion, well endowed with showmanship and totally shameless in his self-praise.

While with the White Sox "Art the Great" was interviewed on radio. He told listeners "no use of a great hitter like me getting a flock of skimpy singles. You never get your name in the headlines with singles. It's distance the public wants. From now on I'm aiming for the next county. I'm going out for home runs, come on out and razz me; you'll go away cheering me when I slam them against the bleachers. I sure can hit that ball and I'm not so bad around first base either."[2]

Shires was a good player for the White Sox; however alcoholism and insubordination made his stay in the windy city turbulent and short-lived.

Me 'N' Paul

"Art the Great" hit .341 his rookie year with the Chicago White Sox in 1928. This was a small sample size since he wasn't called up to the Majors until August. However, Chisox management was impressed with the performance and named Shires Captain for the upcoming season. "Art the Great" turned out to be a poor choice for Captain.

Chicago manager, Russell "Lena" Blackburne, had an inkling that their new captain might be trouble when he showed up at the team's spring training hotel after curfew and blind drunk. "Art the Great" was so soused he didn't recognize his manager, walked right past him on out to the courtyard and preceded to howl at the moon. Blackburne stripped him of the captaincy and fined him $100.

Blackburne and Shires co-existed in an uneasy truce through spring training and into May until an incident in batting practice shattered the peace. "Art the Great" stepped into the batters' box wearing what he considered a stylish red felt hat. A livid Blackburne ranted that Shires did not take practice seriously and was making a mockery of the game. The fight was on. Fists were flying until the Chisox players separated the combatants.

The next day Blackburne suspended Shires and told White Sox owner Charles Comiskey to please trade the uncontrollable showboat. Evidently Comiskey considered a .300 hitting first baseman more valuable than a manager whose current record was 16 wins and 30 losses. "Art the Great" was reinstated.

Through the summer the Sox kept losing, Shires kept hitting and managed to keep his temper and drinking under control. That control dissipated during a September road trip to Philadelphia. Blackburne was walking past Shire's hotel room, heard a commotion and looked inside, "Art the Great" was stacking empty beer bottles and shouting for more liquor. Blackburne accused him of being drunk, again. The Great one did on appreciate the accusation. He knocked the Sox manager down and began to bounce his head up and down on the floor. Fearing for Blackburne's life Lou Barbour, the White Sox travel secretary, pulled Shires off his manager. "Art the Great" turned his wrath on Barbour, biting and snarling like a rabid dog he nearly bit Barbour's finger off. Finally, the police arrived and took Shires into custody. Unbelievable Blackburne and Barbour refused to press charges.

Unchastised, the Great one said he was tired of being spied on by Blackburne and Barbour. "They came gumshoeing into my room with their chests sticking out. Can you imagine those two stool pigeons trying to scare me? I just started swinging. Frankly, I was glad to have the opportunity to thrash the hell out of the pair of them."[3]

Shires was suspended for the remainder of the season, not much punishment since the season was almost over and the White Sox were going nowhere. Cominskey did not retain the services of manger Lena Blackburne for the upcoming season, incredibly he did re-sign "Art the Great" Shires.

After he was let go as manager of the Chisox Blackburne made an unusual, significant and long-lasting contribution to the game of baseball. While fishing a tributary of the Delaware river near his home in Palmyra, New Jersey, he made an important discovery. Blackburne stepped into some mud and while cleaning it off his boots realized the mud might be the solution to a long-standing problem in baseball.

The shine on new baseballs made it difficult for pitchers to grip and control the ball. In an effort to reduce the shine, new baseballs were rubbed with a variety of substances. Shoe polish, tobacco juice, and infield dirt were among remedies used, but none were satisfactory and the search for an effective rub continued.

The mud on Blackburne's boots proved perfect for rubbing the sheen from new baseballs. He wisely kept the location of the special mud secret and formed a company to market the rubbing compound.

Today all Major and Minor league baseball teams use Blackburne's baseball rubbing mud. Before each game dozens of baseballs are mud rubbed in preparation for the contest.

Blackburne left the business to a friend, John Hass, whose family currently operates the company. The location of the valuable mud is a closely guarded corporate secret.

Perhaps encouraged by his pugilistic success against little Lena Blackburne, Shires became convinced he had a future in boxing. In December 1929 he entered the ring with "Arthur the Great Shires" emblazoned on the back of his boxing robe. He knocked out "Dangerous Dan Daley" in the first round and sportswriters dubbed him "What-A-Man" Shires. His boxing career was cut short when baseball commissioner

Kennesaw Mountain Landis ruled that any baseball player participating in boxing matches would be banned from baseball.

Continued alcohol abuse and a serious knee injury derailed What-A-Man's Major League career. He was traded three times in a two-year period. First from the White Sox to the Washington Senators, then from the Senators to the Boston Braves and finally from the Braves to the St. Louis Cardinals. Shires didn't appear in any games for the Cards and in 1933 he was sent down to the Minors. "Art the Great" along with Gordon Slade, Charley Wilson and Jim Lindsey were sent to Columbus when Burgess Whitehead was promoted to the St. Louis Cardinals.

Of course, "What-A-Man" had plenty to say about his demotion. "The Major Leagues will realize once again, just as they did two years ago, that they have made a mistake in waiving the Great Shires out the big show. I am a Major League ball player and I'll prove it before I hang up my glove. Columbus is all set now with me holding down first base.

It will be just a romp the rest of the way."[4] Columbus was in seventh place at the time.

Paul was not at his best in his next start, May 4th against Minneapolis. He pitched 5 2/3 innings giving up eight hits and six runs, however, the Red Bird bats bailed him out and Paul received credit for an 8 – 7 win raising his record to two wins and no losses.

By May 18, Columbus had clawed their way to a tie for first place with the Milwaukee Brewers. The Louisville Colonels came to town and Southpaw Clarence Heise was scheduled to pitch against the predominately left handing hitting line-up. The Louisville Courier-Journal reported "Ray Blades, skipper of the Birds, listened to the pleas of Paul Dean, brother of the Great Dizzy, who insisted he could make them Colonels look sick, and switched to Dean at the last minute."[5]

The switch to Paul paid off as he went the distance giving up 6 hits while striking out 7. The Red Birds won 5 – 3, coupled with Milwaukee's loss to St. Paul, Columbus ascended to first place for the first time that season. An associated press story reported on the Red Birds progress "For a while at the start of the season it looked as though the St. Louis Cardinals' Association branch was going to be a big disappointment. However, with transfusions of new and apparently more capable workmen - Art Shires,

Charlie Wilson and Gordon Slade – they started to improve on the recent road trip and yesterday took over first place."[6]

Paul's next appearance was against the Toledo Mud Hens in a tough save situation. The Red Birds took a 5 – 4 lead in the seventh on some smart base running by player/manager Ray Blades. Ray was on third, one out, score tied at four. As the Mud Hen pitcher began his wind-up, Blades broke for home. Surprised, the Hen hurler stopped mid wind-up, the umpire called a balk, so Blades walked home giving Columbus a 5 – 4 lead. Paul was called from the bullpen to get the final six outs. The first two men he faced in the eighth singled, the third batter tried to lay down a bunt to advance the runners but popped it up for out number one. Paul walked the next batter. Bases loaded, one out. The tall right-hander responded by striking out the next two batters. Two of the three batters who faced Paul in the ninth fanned to end the game making Columbus a 5 – 4 winner.

Shortly after the victory over the Mud Hens on May 20th the Columbus Red Birds received shocking news. Their president, Larry MacPhail had been fired. Sportswriters as well as the entire American Association were equally shocked and surprised.

The Cardinals gave no reason for MacPhail's dismissal and sportswriters struggled to understand the move and explain it to their readers.

"The secrecy surrounding MacPhail's dismissal has baseball men of the American Association guessing. Insofar as they knew, he was an efficient club leader. Even those who regarded Larry as too fresh and outspoken when he was first appointed as president of the Red Birds, came to like and admire him upon longer acquaintance. They found in him, an aggressive, virile young man who bubbled over with excellent ideas for baseball's good."[7]

The mystery wouldn't be solved until almost a month later.

Branch Rickey and new Columbus president George Troutman were on hand May 23rd when Paul Dean faced the Indianapolis Indians. Rickey and Troutman had followed the Red Birds from Columbus to Indianapolis in the wake of the dismissal of popular president MacPhail Paul didn't disappoint. He whiffed nine Hoosiers, won the game 6 – 2 and raised his record to 4 wins and 0 losses.

The Red Bird road trip continued and while in Louisville What-A-Man Shires again found trouble. Playing for Louisville was "Art the Great's" old high school teammate, Jimmy Adair. Shires and Adair reunited and decided to go out for a night of fun. Fun for What- A-Man usually included whiskey, women, and fighting. That night was no different.

The high school teammates were patronizing a local brothel when a fracas started. Adair accused one of the "ladies" of stealing $125 from his pants while he was otherwise occupied. The proprietor of the establishment, Jack Deacon, supported his employee and began to forcibly evict Adair. What-A-Man intervened and flung Dawson down a flight of stairs. The brawl continued out of the house and into the street eventually involving another man and two women. The police arrived, and peace was finally restored.

Jack Deacon, who ended up with a broken leg, was charged with malicious assault and operating a "disorderly house." Deacon's employee's Robert Armstrong, Carrie Potts and Ruth Carson along with Shires and Adair were also charged with malicious assault.

Of course, What-A-Man contended the fight wasn't his fault. "I am in the right this time.

I was only protecting myself after Deacon hit me with a club."[8]

Hard to believe but neither Columbus nor Louisville disciplined their players. Accordingly, American Association president, Thomas J Hickey, said the affair was regrettable but that he planned no action against the ballplayers.

Despite the distractions of a fired president and a brawling first baseman, Columbus continued to win. Paul was a big part of their success and by the end of May he had won six games without being charged with a loss. The Red Birds were perched atop the American Association standings with a slim one game lead over Minneapolis.

Paul won his seventh game of the season by pitching two innings of relief against Louisville. He came in with the score tied at three, top of the eighth. Paul faced six batters, struck out three, gave up no hits or walks. The Red Birds scored one run to win the game.

After the Louisville series, Minneapolis arrived in Columbus for four games with the American Association lead on the line. Columbus won the first two games pushing them into first place, one game ahead of the Millers.

The next day 9,000 fans showed up for the Sunday doubleheader.

The first game saw the Millers bombard Red Bird hurlers lefty Heise and Bud Teachout for a 7 – 0 lead going into the seventh. What looked like a blow-out turned interesting when the Red Birds staged an eight-run rally in the bottom of that frame. Paul was called from the bullpen to protect the 8 – 7 lead he responded by getting through the eighth unscathed.

Paul gave up one hit and a walk to go along with two outs in the ninth. Miller slugger Jack Holland faced Paul two on two out. Holland won the battle driving fastball over the left field fence for a three-run homer. Columbus failed to score in the bottom of the ninth tagging Paul with his first defeat of the season.

With Columbus and Minneapolis now tied for first place, Red Bird pitcher Jim Lindsey started and pitched eight innings before running out of gas. Although he had pitched two tough innings in game one, Paul was called on to get the three outs needed to protect the Red Bird 9 – 7 lead. He struck out two of the four batters he faced to save the game and move Columbus back into first.

After pitching in both ends of the doubleheader against Minneapolis, Paul was given a full four days rest before his next assignment: starting the first night game of the season. Four days rest combined with Paul's continued brilliance under the lights led to a lop-sided 10 – 1 victory over the St. Paul Saints. "Under the incandescent Dean was invincible, fanning five, giving up two hits and one unearned run."[9]

Manager Ray Blades again rested Paul for four days before sending him to the mound against Milwaukee. Paul was superb, he recorded his first shut-out of the young season, beating the Brewers 5 – 0. Paul gave up only four hits while striking out ten and walking four. The win against Milwaukee was his ninth triumph against only one loss.

Paul's tenth victory and one of his most impressive was turned in on June 14th as he blanked Kansas City 10 – 0. His success in night games continued as he struck out 12 and gave up only five scattered singles. Paul was on quite a roll; eleven hits and one run in the last 28 innings, nineteen consecutive scoreless innings, and twenty-two strikeouts in his last two complete games.

The win at Kansas City gave Columbus a 2.5 game lead over their American Association rivals. With a juggernaut line-up it looked like a Red

Bird runaway for the pennant. However, things went south on June 15th when the Columbus Red Bird's lost almost half of their starting line-up.

Art Shires, Gordon Slade, Charley Wilson and Jim Lindsey were banished from the American Association. Turns out former Columbus president Larry MacPhail was paying these four players more than the maximum allowed by league rules. The violations had cost MacPhail his job and left the Red Bird roster in shambles.

Once again What-A-Man's mouth had caused trouble. His bragging instigated the investigation that uncovered the violations. "Shires had been telling other players in the American Association that he was drawing a Major League salary for playing in the Minors."[10]

It's unlikely Rickey did not know the four players were being paid over the allowable amount and MacPhail was probably a scapegoat. However, there seemed to be no animosity between the two men. Rickey actually recommended MacPhail for a front office position with the Cincinnati Reds and MacPhail later became the president of that organization.

Losing four of their star players gutted Columbus. At the time they were barred from the American Association, second baseman Wilson was hitting .356, shortstop Slade .353 and first baseman Shires .313. Pitcher Jim Lindsey was 7 – 2 with an ERA of 3.69.

Mike Kelley, president of the second place Minneapolis Millers was ecstatic "these four boys made the Red Birds. Now the fight for first place is wide open again and that will mean new interest throughout the league."[11] A season so full of promise was suddenly unraveling.

CHAPTER 13

"Hello, Boy, this is The Great Dean speakin'" "Oh, No! You are talkin' to The Great Dean"

The genius of Branch Rickey and his farm system once again saved the St. Louis Cardinal organization. Like a chess master, Rickey began to move his pieces. Although American Association president Thomas Hickey had banned the four players from the league he presided over, Hickey had no authority over other leagues.

One of the Cardinal farm clubs was Rochester of the International league. The Rochester Red Wings were a Double A team same as Columbus. Rickey sent What-A- Man Shires, Charley Wilson and Jim Lindsey to Rochester.

Rochester players, first baseman Mickey Heath, shortstop Bennie Bergmann along with pitchers Jim Winford and Ed Heueser were assigned to Columbus. In effect for these seven players it was a lateral move.

Shortstop Gordon Slade was promoted to the St. Louis Cardinals to take the place of Burgess Whitehead who was demoted to Columbus. Chess master Rickey had made his moves, it remained to be seen if they were the right ones.

Jim Lindsey's departure left Paul the ace and workhorse of the Columbus pitching staff.

The last two weeks of June he pitched five different times.

Paul started his first game with the new Red Bird infield on June 17th against Indianapolis. He picked up his 11th victory beating them 5 – 2, while giving up 8 hits and striking out seven.

Louisville handed Paul his second loss of the season. Despite a well-pitched game, he only gave up three runs on eight hits. Unfortunately, his teammates only scored one run.

For the first time that season Paul lost consecutive starts. The Toledo Mud Hens knocked him out in the fifth inning. He gave up 7 runs in his short stint and Columbus lost 10 – 1.

Manager Ray Blades had not lost confidence in Paul. He sent him in the next day against the Mud Hens in a pressure packed situation. Toledo was leading 4 – 1 in the eighth only to have the Red Birds rally for four runs in the bottom of the frame to take the lead 5 – 4. Paul pitched a perfect ninth striking out two of the three batters he faced. Since Paul came into the game with the lead, starting pitcher Lefty Heise was credited with the win.

The last day of June brought another close game. Columbus led Indianapolis 5 – 4 going into the final frame. The Indians had one on and one out when Paul was sent in to put out the fire, however his misery continued. Two singles, a walk and a wild pitch tagged Paul with his third loss in his last three decisions. His record now stood at 11 wins and 4 losses.

Paul didn't have to wait long for a chance at redemption. Manager Ray Blades started him the next day against those same Indianapolis Indians. He gave up a run in the first inning but settled down whitewashing the Indians the rest of the way for a 3 – 1 victory. He gave up only four hits and struck out nine.

Columbus spent the next week in Minnesota playing the St. Paul Saints and Minneapolis Millers. The trip did not go well for Paul. He started three games in Minnesota, two against the Saints and one against the Millers. Paul didn't make it past the sixth inning in any of the three contests.

The first game of the St. Paul series, pitted Paul against Saint pitcher Les Munns. For the first three innings neither pitcher gave up a run, Paul faltered first giving up two runs in the fourth and two runs in the fifth. He was replaced by Ralph Judd in the sixth with the score 4 – 1. The Red Birds scored two more runs off Munns, but ended up losing 4 – 3, Paul was saddled with his fifth loss of the season after giving up four runs and six hits, he walked two and struck out four.

Three days later Paul again started against the Saints. The results mirrored his previous start. Six innings, four runs, eight hits, four strike outs and three walks. Paul left the game behind 4 – 2 but this time the Red Birds rallied to win the game 5 – 4, saving Paul from another loss.

A four-game series at Minneapolis was next on the Red Bird Minnesota tour. In spite of Paul's recent troubles Columbus had strengthened their hold on first place since losing their four-star players. Sadly, they were about to lose another star player.

This was an important series. The Millers, last year's American Association Champions, were in second place six games behind the league leading Red Birds. The first game was close. After six innings Columbus was leading 6 – 4. Minneapolis rallied for four runs to win the game 8 – 6 to pull within five games of the Red Birds.

The second game of the series was continuous from the beginning. Manager Ray Blades and Red Bird catcher Bill Delancey were unhappy with home plate umpire Joe McLaughlin's strike zone and both complained. The score was tied 6 – 6 after only three innings. The Miller's broke it wide open with five runs in the bottom of the fourth for a 11 – 6 lead. During the five-run outburst, McLaughlin finally tired of Blade's constant complaining and ejected him from the game.

In the top of the fifth McLaughlin called a third strike on Bill Delancey, that was the last straw for the Red Bird catcher. Seething with anger he slung his bat into the grandstands. The bat flew through a screen narrowly missing spectators sitting in a box near the Columbus dugout. Umpire McLaughlin immediately ordered Delancey out of the game, which Minneapolis ended up winning 14 – 6.

American Association president Thomas Hickey who less than a month earlier had banished Cardinal stars Art Shires, Gordon Slade, Charley Wilson and Jim Linsey now suspended Bill Delancey indefinitely. Hickey said, "baseball is a clean game and it's going to be clean in the American Association as long as I'm president". "Naturally, excited players always will argue decisions with the umpires, but there's a breaking point. We will not tolerate rowdyism or swearing by players at all. Furthermore, if a rule isn't good it should be erased from the books. Until it is, it must be enforced."[1]

Paul started the last game of the series, and he needed to stop the bleeding. Paul missed pitching to his roommate and longtime battery mate, Bill Delancey. He was apprehensive about pitching to Delancey's replacement, Al Funk. Funk had recently been called up from the low minors and had never played at the Double A level.

After giving up one run in the first, Paul settled down and pitched three scoreless innings. He took the mound in the bottom of the fifth with a 4 – 1 lead. He couldn't hold it as Minneapolis scored three runs to tie the game. The next inning the Millers buried Paul with a five-run barrage and once again he failed to survive the sixth. Minneapolis went on to win the game 10 – 9.

Sportswriters continued to portray Paul as a pitcher who excelled at night but had trouble winning day games. "This boy Paul Dean has as much speed as any pitcher in the American Association, but he has to depend on night baseball to gain most of his victories. For some unknown reason, he's wild in the daytime. He was that yesterday and the Millers finally shelled him from the box in the sixth. He was charged with the defeat to make his record stand at 12 and 6 for the season."[2]

Bill Delancey's "indefinite suspension" ended up being three games. He was back in the line-up for Paul's next start July 17th in Kansas City. The combination of his catcher's return and a night game helped Paul break out of his mini slump.

Paul locked up in a classic pitcher's duel with the Blue's Bill Shores. In the top of the ninth the score was Columbus Red Birds one Kansas City Blues one. Bill Delancey stepped to the plate with one on and two out. He slammed a home run giving the Red Birds a two-run lead. Paul shut out the Blues in the bottom of the ninth for a 3 – 1 win, his thirteenth of the season.

In addition to taking his regular turn in the starting rotation, manager Ray Blades used Paul out of the bullpen to stop rallies and save games. Red Bird starter Jim Winford was cruising along with a 10 – 4 lead over Louisville through seven innings. When Winford gave up three runs in the eighth without recording an out, Paul was sent to the rescue.

Paul responded by shutting down the Colonels with no hits and no runs, saving a 10 – 7 Columbus win.

Paul won his next start beating Indianapolis 9 – 3. He gave up seven hits and three walks while striking out five. It was his fourteenth victory of the year.

The Toledo Mud Hens came to Columbus and Paul engaged Mud Hen hurler Thornton Lee in a torrid pitching duel. Paul pitched a shutout except for a solo Hen homer in the fifth. He left the game after nine innings with the score knotted 1 – 1. Paul gave up seven hits and struck out nine. The Red Birds finally pushed across a single run in the bottom of the twelfth for the win, and a no decision for Paul.

Despite the turmoil of losing star players and a president, Columbus was still playing good baseball. At the end of July, the Red Birds were in first place by 4.5 games. Paul's record was 14 – 6 and he led the league in strikeouts.

Dizzy Dean and the St. Louis Cardinals arrived in Columbus on August 1st for an exhibition game against their top farm club. The game was billed as Dean vs Dean as Diz started for the Cards and Paul started for the Red Birds.

Paul's telephone rang, and a voice said, "Hello boy, this is the Great Dean speakin'" Oh, NO! shouted Paul, "you are talkin' to the Great Dean."[3]

In this game Paul was indeed "The Great Dean", easily outpitching Dizzy. Both pitched two innings; Paul gave up no hits, no runs and struck out two. Diz was nicked for two runs on three hits, one by brother Paul. Dizzy said, "Paul told me before the game that he was going to knock one down my throat. Believe me, he did. When he connected with that speed ball of mine, I mean I actually ducked when the ball whizzed past my ear."[4] The Cards won the game however 4 – 3. St. Louis moved on to Pittsburgh for their next series against the Pirates and the Milwaukee Brewers arrived in Columbus to play the Red Birds.

Columbus played spectacular baseball the remainder of the regular season. With the four new players successfully integrated into the line-up and Paul Dean seemingly unbeatable the Red Birds began to run roughshod over the rest of the league.

Paul picked up his 15th win on August 3rd against Milwaukee. Despite walking a mind- boggling 14 Brewers he managed to hang on for a 9 – 7 victory. In addition to the 14 bases on balls Paul gave up 6 hits and struck out five.

Paul's next start was against Kansas City. He bested Blues hurler Hobo Carson winning 5-1. This game Paul walked only three batters while registering his 16th victory. He struck out 11 opposing batsmen to move closer to another American Association strike- out Championship. Last year Paul fanned 169 to win the honors. Already his total was 164 strikeouts for the year, almost assuring himself the title for the second straight year.

National newspapers took notice, an Associated Press article under the headline "Dizzy and Paul Dean are in strikeout contest." Read "The Dean Boys, Dizzy of the St. Louis Cardinals, and his younger brother Paul of the Columbus club of the American Association, a Cardinal Junior Varsity outfit, are waging a strikeout contest by remote control. Each is the leader in his league. Dizzy has 152 to lead the National League. Paul, who, like Dizzy, has been in thirty-five games, has fanned 164 in his circuit."[5]

Paul decorated his 17th victory with 14 strikeouts. His victims were the second place Minneapolis Millers. The Columbus win, their third straight over the Millers. Opened up a 14.5 game lead. Paul's 14 strikeouts brought his total for the campaign to 178. The Miller's had eight hits and five walks in their 7-2 loss.

Paul had to pitch 12 grueling innings to secure his 18th win. Player/manager Ray Blades smashed a walk-off double with two outs in the bottom of the 12th making Columbus winners for the 15th time in 16 contests. St. Paul had scored only one run on eight hits and six walks. Paul had struck out nine Saints in the 2-1 victory.

Perhaps feeling the strain of toiling 12 innings his last time on the mound, Paul wasn't sharp when he started in Milwaukee against the

Brewers. He struggled for seven innings, the Brewers bashing him for six runs on nine hits and four walks. He left the game with one out in the seventh holding a 9-6 lead having added five strikeouts to his league leading total. Paul was credited with his 19th win when Bill Lee relieved and shut down Milwaukee preserving a 9-6 Red Bird win.

The next day in Kansas City Ralph Judd, Columbus mounds man, was on the hill and Paul was in the bullpen available for relief duty after pitching "only" seven innings the day before.

After seven innings Columbus led Kansas City 4-3. Paul was sent to the mound to start the eighth charged with holding the slim one run lead. He promptly walked the first three batters he faced. Paul had dug himself into a huge hole, no outs, bases full of Blues. Any sacrifice hit, or walk would swing the game in Kansas City's favor. Paul fanned the next three Blues batters! Unbelievably he had loaded the bases on walks and against all odds prevented the Blues from scoring by striking out the side. Paul pitched a perfect ninth to save the game.

Ten days after he turned 20 years old, Paul became a 20-game winner. It wasn't easy, the Saints were ahead 4-2 after seven innings. In the top of the eighth Paul's battery mate Bill Delancey delivered a late birthday present, he hammered a three run inside- the-park homerun giving Paul a 5-4 lead. He made it hold up shutting out the Saints in the eighth and ninth frames for the 5-4 win. Paul added seven strikeouts to his league leading total while giving the Saints eight hits and four walks.

After the dramatic win Paul's record stood at 20 wins and 6 losses. He was the leading pitcher in the American Association and sportswriters were taking notice. They kept searching for a nickname, first falling him "Dizzier" Dean, but after discovering he was more level-headed than his brother, Dizzy, they began calling him "Not so Dizzy" Dean.

Since he was leading the league in strikeouts Paul asked about the all-time strikeout record for the American Association.

"Informed it is 264, and that it was set by Heinie Berger back in 1906 while pitching with Columbus, 'Not so Dizzy" said: "I'll beat that easy. I'll beat it if they let me pitch four more night games, because strike-outs are duck soup for that fast ball at night, the way I throw it."[6]

Kansas City's Duster Mails agreed that Paul was tough at night. "He is a Bear at night under the lights. His speed is simply blinding in the night games."[7]

Major League teams started bidding on Minor League talent in August and September. Double A stars were the most coveted since they were usually Major League ready. Again, Branch Rickey's farm system gave the St. Louis Cardinals an advantage.

Minor League owners routinely sold their best players to Major League teams for cash to keep their clubs solvent. This infusion of cash was especially crucial during these dark days of the depression.

The St. Louis Cardinals did not need to buy players, they had great players on their farm teams to elevate to the parent team when needed. The Cards even had a surplus of star Minor Leaguers to sell.

Scouts agreed that Paul Dean was the best young prospect in the American Association. New York Yankee owner, Colonel Jacob Ruppert offered the St. Louis Cardinals $50,000 for the 20-year-old fireball artist.

The Cardinals also owned the second-best Minor-League prospect, Paul's teammate, Bill Lee, the other Red Bird Ace. Bill Lee and Paul Dean were almost identical pitchers, both were 6'3" 190lb fire balling right-handers. When Paul won his 20th game Bill Lee had won 19. Scouts liked Lee's natural pitching ability and agreed he was ready for the Majors. They considered Paul the better prospect because of intangibles.

"Scouts regard Bill Lee as lacking in "Moxie", meaning that he lacks courage under pressure. For this reason, the scouts have advised their bosses not to offer as much money for Lee as they are willing to dig up for Dean."[8]

Paul Dean and Bill Lee were not the only Cardinal properties Major League teams coveted. Columbus Red Birds Bill Delancy, Jack Rothrock, Burgess Whitehead, Jim Winford and Lou Riggs were also targeted by Major League owners.

The $50,000 Yankee offer for Paul Dean had to be tempting in those desperate depression days. Finally, Rickey and Breadon decided to sell Lee and others to keep Paul and pair him with Dizzy for the 1934 season. It proved to be a fortuitous decision.

Laying the foundation for one of the most famous teams in Major League history, the Gashouse Gang.

Me 'N' Paul

"We've had a number of glittering offers for Paul," Rickey said. "Some of them were hard to turn down. One of the best offers was from the Red Sox. Another came from the Yankees. The Cubs also were willing to talk, but we turned them all down, for Paul not only is a great Major League prospect, but naturally fitted to belong to the Cardinals."[9]

When the Cardinals announced Paul was coming to St. Louis for the 1934 season, he was interviewed by the international news service. When asked how he felt about being called up to St. Louis. Paul replied "I'm goin' out there next year and win twenty games for 'em." His statement was serious, confident, not boastful. Paul was being interviewed in the hotel lobby where the Red Birds were staying, and he was uncomfortable. "Let's go up to my room people might think I'm getting high hat if they heard me talking about myself." After retiring to his room Paul told the reporter. "You see, no one knows any better than I do that I need experience. I never did any pitching until a year before I played pro ball. Out in Holdenville and Spaulding, Oklahoma, Diz always pitched and I played infield."

"But I'll be breezing 'em right past 'em up there in the big-time after I've had a chance to look the boys over a little bit. Me and Diz are going to work together this winter and he'll help me a lot then. He's a great guy."[10]

Amidst all the publicity and excitement of going to the Cardinals, Paul was tagged with his seventh loss of the year. In a ragged game against Louisville, he lost 9 – 7 despite six Colonel Errors. Louisville reached Paul for 13 hits and 6 walks. He struck out six.

In pursuit of his 21st victory, Paul took the mound in Toledo, Ohio against the Mud Hens. He breezed through the first five innings striking out five Hens and guarding a 5 – 4 advantage. A hard smash toward the mound threatened to tie the game. Paul stopped the line-drive with his bare right hand, picked up the ball and retired the batter to protect the precarious lead.

Paul was able to complete the fifth frame, but his pitching hand became so swollen he was unable to answer the bell for the sixth. Ralph Judd took over, held the lead and Paul was credited with the win.

Columbus had already clinched the pennant, but if Paul's injury was serious it would severely damage Red Bird fortunes in the upcoming championship series against the Minneapolis Millers. The Minneapolis Star reported.

> "Paul Dean, Columbus' right-handed pitching ace, injured his hurling mitt last night when he tried to stop a line drive through the box. While reports from the Ohio capital today stated that it wasn't serious, X-rays are being taken to determine whether any bones were broken. If Dean shouldn't be able to work in the playoff against the Millers, it would be a serious blow to the Red Birds' chances. They are depending on him to beat the 1932 champions in one of the probable two-night games and if he can't work, the Red Birds will have something to worry about."[11]

X-rays proved Paul's hand was bruised, not broken. He was able to start one more game in the regular season. Paul beat Louisville 9 – 6 for his 22nd victory.

He pitched a steady game with the exception of the ninth when he eased up with the Birds in a commanding lead. Paul gave up 10 hits, struck out 5 and walked 5.

Paul finished the 1933 regular season with some impressive pitching statistics. For the second straight year Paul led the league in strikeouts. He fanned 222 batters, won 22 games, lost 7 and had a league leading era of 3.15. Paul was a work horse, he pitched 254 innings in 43 games while giving up 228 hits and 117 walks.

Columbus finished the regular season with 101 victories against only 51 defeats, an astounding 50 games over .500. The Red Birds ran away with the American Association pennant finishing 15.5 games ahead of second place Minneapolis. The play-off system devised by the departed Larry MacPhail pitted the team with the highest winning percentage in the Eastern Division team in a best of seven series for the league championship. It turned out to be a good system because the two best teams, Columbus and Minneapolis, played for the championship.

Columbus was favored to win the seven-game series. The Red Birds had beaten the Minneapolis Millers thirteen times while losing only nine during the regular season. Columbus also featured three of the best pitchers ever produced by the American Association; Paul Dean (22-7), Bill Lee (21-9), and Clarence "Lefty" Heise (17-5). Minneapolis was the better hitting club boasting a team batting average of .303, Columbus hit .292 for the season.

The series promised to be a classic match-up of great pitching versus great hitting. The Millers big bats going up against the Red Bird's shut down arms. The winner advancing to the Junior World Series against the International league champions.

The series started in Columbus, one day game and two-night games, the series would continue in Minneapolis until one team had four victories. Red Bird manager, Ray Blades told writers he would start Bill Lee in the opener and follow with Paul and Lefty Heise in the night contests. "Playing two games at night will be to the Red Birds advantage because of their corking corps of hurlers. Dean, with his fast ball, and Heise with his baffling curves, are especially effective when pitching under artificial lights."[12] wrote Minneapolis Star Tribune sports editor George Barton.

A crowd of only 4,000 fans turned out for the first game of the championship series. Cool, rainy weather kept attendance down from the 15,000 predicted earlier in the week. Big Bill Lee beat the Millers 6 – 2. He gave up only seven hits to stake Columbus to a one game to none lead in the series.

Paul was scheduled to pitch the next game, but the continuing cold rainy weather combined with a threatening forecast changed manager Ray Blade's mind. Apparently, he thought Lefty Heise would be a better choice in case the game was interrupted by rain. Lefty was a junk ball pitcher and would be less disrupted by delays than the fire balling Dean. Blades was not taking any chances with his ace. A sloppy field and rain delays were not conducive to the health of Paul Dean, the prized pitcher St. Louis was counting on for the 1934 season.

It kept raining, the field was muddy, and finally a heavy downpour forced a 53- minute delay in the eighth inning. Minneapolis finally prevailed beating Lefty Heise 5 – 3. The messy, cold, rain delayed Miller victory tied the series at one apiece.

Paul was well rested and ready to pitch under the lights; however, the weather did not cooperate and the next game as postponed. Finally, skies cleared and in view of the weatherman's promise of fair skies and warmer weather a capacity crowd of 16,000 was expected for the 8:00pm start.

On a nice night before a near capacity hometown crowd, Paul was confident as he walked to the hill. His confidence ebbed slightly when he gave up solo home runs in the first and second innings. Paul came to bat in the bottom of the third with teammate Mickey Heath perched on first. Paul crashed a double that platted Heath and cut the Millers lead in half, they now led 2 – 1.

Paul posted goose eggs after the second inning, at one point striking out the side in consecutive innings. He was lifted for a pinch hitter after working eight innings. He struck out ten and gave up six hits, two of which were the damaging solo homeruns. The Red Birds managed to push across a run in their half of the eighth, so the score was tied at two going into the ninth.

Jim Winford relieved Paul and pitched a perfect ninth. Columbus desperately needed this game, going to the foreign fields of Minneapolis for the remainder of the seven-game battle needing to win three of four was a scenario for disaster.

Player/manager Ray Blades was well aware of the Red Bird situation as he stepped to the plate in the bottom of the ninth. There were two outs and the winning run was at second base. The old warhorse swatted a walk-off single giving Columbus a 3 – 2 win and a 2 – 1 lead in the series.

The battle moved to Minneapolis and Blades came back with game one winner Bill Lee. The big right hander was ineffective this time out and the Millers won 6 - 4, knotting the series at two all.

Lefty Heise started game five but faltered early. Paul relieved in the second and pitched brilliantly over the next seven innings giving up only one run on six hits.

Paul went out for the bottom of the ninth with a 5 – 2 lead needing only three outs to secure the important win. The first two hitters singled before Paul settled down and struck out the next two Millers. He was one out away from victory when Minneapolis catcher Joe Glenn caught up with a fastball and parked it over the center field fence for a game tying three run homer. Paul finally snuffed the rally by striking out the next Miller batter.

Bill Delancey led a two run Red Bird rally with a home run in the top of the tenth. Paul retired the Millers in order for a 7 – 5 win and a 3 – 2 lead in the seven-game series. Columbus needed one win in the next two games to punch out the Millers and secure a berth in the Junior World Series.

Me 'N' Paul

The next day in a tense ten inning game, Columbus prevailed in a slugfest. Paul pitched three innings in relief, but he was ineffective giving up five runs, surely fatigued by working eight innings the day before. The Red Bird heroes were second sacker Lew Riggs and pitcher Ralph Judd.

It was a game of wild hitting, the Birds collecting 18 and the Millers 14. The Red Birds also slugged six home runs, the two biggest blows were Riggs' solo shot with two outs in the ninth to stave off defeat and Judd's 3 run blast in the tenth.

The tenth belonged to Ralph Judd. With the score tied the first two Red Bird batters were retired. Burgess Whitehead kept Columbus afloat with a two out single. Minneapolis intentionally passed Mickey Heath to get to Red Bird pitcher Judd. The strategy backfired when Judd lifted a three-run homer over the right field screen. He then took the mound and closed out the Minneapolis Millers, winning the game 14 – 11.

For the first time in 26 years the Columbus Red Birds were American Association champions. They now moved on to the Junior World Series. Their opponent was the International League champion Buffalo Bisons. The format for the Junior World Series was the best five of nine. The first four games would be played in Columbus and the necessary remaining games in Buffalo.

The series opener went to the visitors. The Bisons beat Big Bill Lee 7 – 4.

Paul started the next game and a barrage of Red Bird hits in the fourth inning, including two home runs, a double and two singles propelled Paul to an easy victory. He pitched six innings gave up three runs on four hits and struck out four. Catcher/assistant manager Mike Gonzales said that Paul was only allowed to pitch six innings because the Red Birds wanted him available for the next two games in Columbus, both under the lights. Ray Blades said Paul would see more work than any other Red Bird pitcher, in both starting and relief roles.

"Dean can stand a lot of work," Blades explained. "His blinding speed makes him and ideal pitcher to toss into a game in the late innings. He's almost unbeatable at night. As we have two nocturnal contests here and possibly the same number in Buffalo, you can see how much good a pitcher with Dean's ability can do for a ball club."[13]

Carl Duncan

Cold weather, rain and wet grounds postponed the Junior World Series two days. The two-day delay enabled Paul to start the third game, with the series tied at one apiece.

Paul was a bit shaky at the start of the game and three walks coupled with a pair of singles gave the Bison's a two-run lead in the top of the first frame. In their half of the inning the Red Birds roared back with four runs, after the eventful first, Paul was in complete control of the game. Shutting out Buffalo until he gave up three meaningless runs in the ninth. He struck out twelve Bisons in route to an 8 – 5 win, his second straight victory of the series.

In the fourth and final game in Columbus, Lefty Heise and Bill Lee pitched Columbus to an 11 – 5 victory over Buffalo. That brought the count to three victories for the Red Birds and one for the Bisons. The two teams boarded a special train that would take them to Buffalo, New York where the battle would continue until one of the teams won five games.

On the train trip north, Paul and his teammates were in fine spirits, exuding confidence, buoyed by a three game to one advantage. That lead vanished quickly as Buffalo won the next two games to knot the series at three games each.

In the pivotal seventh game Columbus turned to Paul Dean to stop the slide and regain the momentum. He didn't disappoint. Paul completely silenced the Bison's big bats as he allowed only four scattered hits and fanned 11 batters. The 7 – 2 win gave the Red Birds a 4 – 3 advantage in the five out of nine series. Paul had won three of the four victories.

In an anticlimactic finish to the series, Columbus completely overwhelmed Buffalo 10 – 2 to win the Junior World Series five games to three. The Red Birds rapped out 13 hits and Jim Winford went the distance on the mound for the win.

Paul finished the season as the American Association's top pitcher. He was in the most games – 43. He won 22 and lost 7 to lead the league. He also led the league with 222 strikeouts.

A season that started with Larry MacPhail's vision of a championship, endured scandal and adversity, ended with the 1933 Columbus Red Birds crowned champions of the Minor Leagues. Paul validated scouts' expectations and punched his ticket to the Majors.

CHAPTER 14

"Ain't enough dough there to mess with."

Dizzy Dean had signed his 1933 contract at the end of the 1932 season, yet by February 1933 he was already lobbying for more money. Following is an excerpt from a letter to Cardinal secretary Bill Dewitt. "Am in Gulfport, Mississippi and working out today. Believe me, Bill the old soup bone feels great. Honestly, I don't see how any club in the National League can beat me. I think I will be able to call in all the outfielders and then win the game. I intend to do both the hitting and pitching in my games this year. So, by being bother hitter and pitcher, don't you think the club can let some of the other players go and raise my salary accordingly?"[1]

Sincerely,

Jerome Herman Dizzy Dean, The Great

Dizzy arrived in Bradenton, Florida on March 1, 1933 for the start of the St. Louis Cardinal spring training camp. He was in much better shape than the year before when he showed up for camp racked by the flu and weighing only 165lbs.

He now weighed a robust 190lbs and was healthy, strong and anxious to get down to business. He told reporters, "no fooling, I believe I could whip any team without having to use the outfield. And if I'm half as good as I feel, I don't see how the Cardinals can miss winning that pennant."[2]

Most sportswriters did not share Dizzy's pennant prediction of a Cardinal championship.

The consensus was a third-place finish.

The pitching promised to be strong, but the infield was unsettled. Manager Gabby Street said he expected Dizzy Dean, Wild Bill Hallahan, Paul Derringer and Tex Carleton to be the mainstays of the staff. Two infield stars of 1932 were gone. First sack slugger Sunny Jim Bottomley was traded to the Cincinnati Reds and Slick Fielding shortstop Charley Gelbert had wounded his leg in a horrible hunting accident.

The depression continued to devastate the country and Major League baseball owners were losing money and insisted their players take deep pay cuts. The player hardest hit was the highest paid, Babe Ruth. It seemed inconceivable to the Babe that the Yankees would even consider cutting his salary after the year he had in 1932 - .341 batting average, 41 home runs, 137 runs batted in and then starred in winning the World Series in which he "called his shot." Yet instead of a raise the Yanks wanted to slash the Bambino's salary from $75,000 to $50,000.

Writers asked Diz how he escaped the wave of salary cuts. He said of his $3,000 salary, "ain't enough dough there to mess with."[3]

Ruth finally realized the country was hurting and the average fan had no sympathy for baseball players who received absurd pay for playing a game. He signed for $52,000. Dizzy, however, continued to bitch that the Great Dean was underpaid.

Aside from money matters, Diz had a great spring. Unlike the past two spring training sessions there were no controversies, and to everyone's surprise Diz caused no trouble. He appeared to be in good shape, healthy and happy. An established Major Leaguer he didn't have to worry about being sent down to the Minors if he had a bad outing.

Dizzy modestly related how he had been the ironman of spring training, pitching almost every day because the fans demanded to see him pitch. "Gabby told me that it would be a big boost for baseball if I'd make as many appearances as possible and give the people a chance to see me," Diz explained. "So, I hurled an inning or two every day."[4]

When Dizzy arrived in St. Louis for the start of the regular season, he took the opportunity to tell reporters the Cardinals would win the pennant. When asked how many games he would win Diz replied "twenty-four, no more, no less-providing, of course, that luck remains with me and that several of our players do not break their legs. As the club stands today, I can guarantee twenty-four victories."[5]

Dizzy Dean was the ace of the 1933 St. Louis Cardinal pitching staff, so he drew the opening day starting assignment. The Cards traveled to Wrigley Field to face the Chicago Cubs in the opener on April 12th. Diz pitched a good game giving up only three runs, but fellow Arkansan, Cub pitcher Lon Warneke pitched a shut-out and the Cubs won 3-0.

Dizzy's second start of the 1933 season was also against the Chicago Cubs. This time the Cubs came to St. Louis. Home field advantage did not propel Diz to victory. He again gave up but three runs and again he lost. This time his teammates managed only a single run.

Dizzy seemed sure to pick up his first win of the season as he took the mound against the lowly Cincinnati Reds, in his next start. However, after pitching four hit ball and giving up only one run he was lifted for a pinch hitter in the eighth. The Cards went on to win but Diz was credited with a no-decision. His record stood at zero wins and two losses. Dizzy was "0 Fer" April.

After this miserable start, Dizzy conceded it was probably his fault. Greatness after all, has a downside. His superb pitching allowed his teammates to depend too heavily on him. The Cardinal players had come to expect such brilliant pitching that they don't need to score a lot of runs. Diz said he had to wean his teammates from this great dependence on his arm, in the hope they would grab a few runs themselves.

"I've been very open and above board about my pitching," said Dean. *"I've admitted how good I was, and all the Cardinals are thinking that all we have to have is our great pitching, and it ain't so. We got to score a few runs."*

"Well from now on, or for a while, at least, I'm going to change my tack, as we nautical men say. I'll have a sore arm, or I'm not feeling good, I'll be lucky to hold the Reds or any other club to half a dozen runs, and I'll tell the

Carl Duncan

Cardinals we'd better pile up some runs in the first inning and in every inning or old Diz won't have a chance."[6]

April was as bad for the Cardinals as it was for Dizzy. After the first month of the regular season the Cards had won 5 and lost 8, they were in seventh place in the eight team National League.

The struggling Cards needed help so master trader Branch Rickey started negotiating. He knew the help he needed was not available on any of his farm teams, so he engineered a blockbuster trade with the Cincinnati Reds.

Rickey traded pitchers Paul Derringer and Allyn Stout along with infielder Sparky Adams for shortstop Leo Durocher and pitchers Frank Henry and Johnny Ogden. The deal really simmered down to Derringer for Durocher.

Paul Derringer was a valuable member of the Cardinal pitching staff. He was a legitimate Major League starting pitcher. In 1931, his rookie year, he won 18 games to help the Cardinals win the National League Pennant. Derringer lost games one and five in the World Series, but the Cardinals beat the Philadelphia A's for the championship. He slumped to 11 – 14 in 1932 and was 0 – 2 when Rickey traded him to the Reds on May 8, 1933.

St. Louis fans and sportswriters loved the trade. Sid Keener, St. Louis Star Sports columnist wrote. "The Cardinals revived pennant hopes through their unexpected trade with the Cincinnati Reds. Durocher now solves the infield problem. He's a peppy kid. A brilliant fielder, light in hitting, but a go getter. He's what they call a "Jockey." He "rides" the opposition with sarcasm and wise cracks. He loves to win."[7]

Leo Ernest Durocher nicknamed "Leo the Lip" and "Lippy" was a native of West Springfield, Mass. Growing up, Leo was a sought-after athlete. He made money playing baseball for company teams and hustling pool in local pool halls. In 1925 Durocher signed a professional baseball contract and played three years in various Minor Leagues. The "Lip" made it to the Majors in 1928 with the New York Yankees.

Leo was a starter on two World Series champion Yankee teams. Lippy was a great defensive player, he covered a lot of ground and possessed a strong, quick, accurate arm. Offensively he was a great bunter and baserunner but a poor hitter. Teammate Babe Ruth called Leo "the All-American out."

Me 'N' Paul

Yankee manager Miller Huggins, himself a little guy like Leo, loved Lippy for his competitiveness, ego, brilliant baseball mind and passion for the game. Yankee ownership however was tiring of Lippy's outspoken personality and his perchance for passing bad checks to finance his expensive tastes in clothing, nightlife and women. In addition to those vices, Ruth accused Leo of being a thief.

Leo roomed with Ruth on road trips. No one liked to share a hotel room with Ruth, because it was impossible to get any sleep with Ruth drinking, womanizing, and eating at all hours of the night. Yet, Leo did not seem to mind, and they got along well until Babe's gold watch went missing. Ruth suspected Leo was the culprit and set out to trap him.

Pitcher Elden Auker told the story "Babe planted some marked bills, supposedly $100 bills, five of them, and they turned up missing just like his gold watch that disappeared. It was in Detroit when Babe caught Durocher asleep. He went through Durocher's bag and found the $500. Babe yanked Durocher out of bed and they had to break the door down he was about to kill him." Leo was sold to Cincinnati after the 1928 season.

Leo the Lip was not exactly excited to be traded from the Reds to the Cards. Cincinnati owner Sidney Weil described Leo's reaction to the trade. "Durocher came storming in the room, shouting, 'I won't go. I won't play for that Rickey. I won't join the chain gang,' and plenty more. I said to him, 'Leo, you must be filthy rich. You can't make the money out of baseball that you do in it. In it, you can only play for the Cardinals.' He acquiesced."[8]

Again, Branch Rickey proved his eye for talent and showed he was not averse to taking on players who were considered problematic or eccentric. Durocher solidified the Cardinal infield, allowing Frankie Frisch to move from shortstop to second base to accommodate his declining coverage skills.

Leo became the Cardinal captain, he epitomized the grit, determination, and hustle that became the trademark of the gashouse gang.

The Lip told about his first encounter with fellow "eccentric" Dizzy Dean. "I played my first game as a Cardinal against the New York Giants and we were leading 4 to 3 going into the last of the ninth when Diz was sent in to pitch. Dizzy stopped on his way to the mound and asked me, 'say, kid what inning is this'? I replied, 'this is the last of the ninth, son, and all you have to do is strike out the next three batters and the Cardinals will win a ballgame.' 'Is that all' Dizzy shot back at me, then added. 'Why that'll be as easy as eatin' a juicy steak! Diz struck out the next two hitters and the third batter to face him fouled out."[9]

In early June the Cardinals played the Reds for the first time since the trade that sent Durocher to St. Louis and Paul Derringer to the Reds. Dizzy and Derringer were shagging flies in the outfield during batting practice when Derringer suddenly attacked Dizzy. Derringer said Dean had been "riding the life out of me" and demanded to know if Dizzy meant all the names, he had been calling him. When Diz said he meant every word, the big Cincy hurler uncorked a right-handed swing that may or may not have landed on Dizzy's eye depending on who tells the story.

After Derringer launched his haymaker Diz clinched him and they fell to the ground together, flailing at each other. Cardinal pitcher Dazzy Vance stopped the fight by sitting on both players until others on the two teams hauled them apart.

> Diz would claim, "I was just going after a fly when Derringer said to me, 'What's this you're saying about my courage.' I told him I meant every word of it, and he swung at me. I'm pretty clever so I ducked under the punch. Then he grabbed me and I caught him around the neck and threw him to the ground. He said that was no way to fight, so I let go right to the side of his head. By this time three fellows had hold of me-and the fight was over."[10]

There were lingering hard feelings between the two men since they barnstormed together after the 1932 season. Dizzy, Paul Dean, Pepper Martin, Jimmy Wilson and Paul Derringer played a multi-town exhibition tour and Dizzy did not want to pay Derringer his full share of the proceeds. Dizzy claimed Derringer did not play as much as the others, so he deserved less pay. The fight was a culmination of that disagreement.

Dizzy was not fined or disciplined for the fight. All the witnesses agreed Derringer jumped him. However, Diz was fined a week's pay for his next escapade.

St. Louis was scheduled to play an exhibition game in Elmira, New York. At the train station Dizzy was told which train to take, but as usual he wasn't paying any attention. He boarded a different train and promptly went to sleep. "Imagine my surprise" Diz said "when I woke up in Pittsburgh. Must have got on the wrong car."[11]

Gabby was livid when Dizzy failed to show up in Elmira. Fans were upset because they expected to see the Great Dean pitch. Street was on the hot seat anyway because of last season's sixth place finish and Dizzy's absence showed he couldn't control his players. He fined Dizzy $100, which amounted to about a week's pay.

"Hellfire" said Diz, "that ain't no way to treat a fella's mistake, sarge. It'll bust me."[12]

Gabby made a deal with Dizzy before his next start. "I told Dizzy" Street said, "that if he would shut out the Dodgers, I'd remit that fine. Winning wouldn't do him any good. It had to be a coat of whitewash."[13] Dizzy's next start would be after baseball's inaugural All-Star game.

The first official Major League All-Star game took place on July 6, 1933. It was held in Comiskey Park, home of the Chicago White Sox. Sports editor of the Chicago Tribune, Arch Ward, came up with the idea for the game after the mayor of Chicago said he would like to have a Major sporting event to be part of the 1933 Chicago World's Fair.

The All-Stars were selected by a vote of the fans, but the pitchers were selected by the managers, John McGraw for the National League and Connie Mack for the American. Many people were surprised that Dizzy was not picked by McGraw. Knowledgeable baseball men considered Dizzy the best right-hander in the National League.

Typical of scouts and coaches opinion of Diz was what Joe Sugden, a coach and scout for 40 years, said about Dizzy. "Dizzy Dean has a fast ball – fast enough to lead the league in strikeouts his first season in the majors. But he has such control wide assortment of other pitches and is so cagey about his pitching that I think he could win without his fastball. He works on the hitters with the instinct of a veteran. He fields his position like a cat, getting the lead runner almost every time. He covers first base and backs up plays. He's no pushover at the plate either, he's fast, can slide and nobody knows when he is going to steal a base. You find one man in a generation like Dean, or maybe none."[14]

Carl Duncan

When Dizzy learned that McGraw didn't select him, Diz said, "I guess Mac don't wanna win that ballgame."[15]

Even without Dizzy, the game had plenty of star power. The American League had Babe Ruth, Lou Gehrig, Charlie Gehringer, Lefty Gomez and Lefty Grove among others.

The National League featured four St. Louis Cardinals in the starting line-up. Bill Hallahan and Jimmy Wilson made up the battery. Frankie Frisch started at second and Pepper Martin held down third. Twenty of the games thirty-six All-Stars ended up in the hall of fame, along with managers John McGraw and Connie Mack.

The game itself was exciting. Chick Hafey, the former Cardinal had the first All-Star game hit, a bloop single to center to lead off the second inning. The American League scored first on an RBI single by pitcher Lefty "El Goofo" Gomez.

In the bottom of the third the Babe, fittingly, hit the first homerun in All-Star game history, a two-run shot that put the American League up 3 – 0. The Nationals game back in the sixth when Cub pitcher Lon Warneke tripled and came home on Pepper Martin's ground out. Frankie Frisch followed with a homerun to make the score 3 – 2.

Earl Averill had an RBI single in the sixth to extend the American League lead. The National League had a good chance to tie the game in the eighth. With Frisch on first and two outs, Hafey drove a ball to deep right that looked to be a homerun. The Great Babe Ruth showed he was more than a homerun hitter as he reached over the right field wall to make the catch and end the threat. The American League won the game by a score of 4 – 2.

After the All-Star game, Diz finally faced the Dodgers with the $100 fine on the line. He was well rested and almost unhittable. In the eighth inning Dizzy had given Brooklyn only four hits and no runs, but the Cards had not scored either. Finally, Frankie Frisch, Pepper Martin, and Ernie Orsatti connected on successive singles to produce the only run Diz needed to recoup his c-note. He did indeed whitewash the Dodgers, 1 – 0.

St. Louis post-dispatch sports columnist L.C. Davis was so impressed by Dizzy's feat, he penned a poem entitled <u>The Money Pitcher</u>:

> Now and then you lose your way,
>   Dizzy Dean
> And your erring footsteps stray,
>   Dizzy Dean
> You mistook your railroad track,
> And were fined a wad of jack,
> But we see you got it back,
>   Dizzy Dean.
> To escape the Sergeant's wrath,
>   Dizzy Dean,
> Take the straight and narrow path,
>   Dizzy Dean.
> You may heartily repent,
> And the loss of dough lament,
> But the boss may not relent,
>   Dizzy Dean. [16]

Dizzy's 1 – 0 shut out over Brooklyn was his third consecutive 1 – 0 game. Prior to the Dodger whitewash he beat the New York Giants 1 – 0 and lost to the Giants by the same minimum possible score, his record stood at 10 wins and 8 losses.

After Dizzy's $100 win the Cardinals were in second place 5 games behind the league leading Giants and in good position to make a surge for the pennant. Sadly, the Cards dropped eleven games over the next two weeks and fell to fifth place. Sports writers began to speculate that Gabby Street's job was in jeopardy.

During the Card free-fall Dizzy made news off the diamond. Diz and his wife, Pat, walked into a drug store in downtown St. Louis. As they entered the store, a young man suddenly appeared and stuck a gun in Dizzy's ribs. The robber ordered Pat and Diz to get in the back room and stay there.

Dizzy didn't realize they had walked into the middle of a hold-up and thought the man was joking. "I just laughed, pushed him aside and said 'quit kiddin'," Dizzy explained. "But when I realized it was a real stickup, I felt awfully weak all of a sudden."[17]

The Dean's retreated to the back room as ordered. The bandit and his accomplice cleaned out the cash register and made their getaway. After the danger had passed Diz said "I'm sure it would have been easy for me to have disarmed that guy if he hadn't had another fella along."[18]

As sportswriter's had predicted, the axe finally fell on the 'ol' Sarge. Gabby deserved better. 1930, his first year managing St. Louis he won the National League pennant. In 1931 Gabby won the World Series. Last year's sixth place finish and this year's nosedive doomed Gabby.

Many Card players, including Dizzy, wanted catcher Jimmy Wilson to be their new manager. However, owner Sam Breadon wanted Frankie Frisch. Although Frisch had managerial aspirations, he had reservations about managing his Cardinal teammates.

"Clarence Lloyd, our road secretary, told me Breadon and Rickey wanted to see me." Frisch said. "I walked into Mr. Breadon's office, and he said, 'Gabby's out, we have decided to make you manager of the Cardinals.' I was bursting with my own ideas. I longed to try them out, but not with these freewheeling Cardinals. Furthermore, Mr. Breadon demanded too much from his managers. In the past seven seasons the Cardinals had won four pennants and two World Championships, yet he had fired five managers over that period.

'Thanks just the same' I said, 'maybe in another year.'

'My dear young man,' interrupted Branch Rickey, jabbing a cigar at me. Forty minutes later he was still lecturing me, 'O.K.' I weakly agreed and signed on the dotted line."[19]

Frank Francis Frisch was a great all-around athlete. A German American born in New York City in 1898. He starred in four sports at Fordham University: baseball, basketball, football, and track. His speed earned him the nickname "The Fordham Flash."

After leaving Fordham university Frankie signed with the New York Giants. The Flash never spent a day in the minors, moving from the campus directly to Major League diamonds. Frankie played for John McGraw's Giants from 1919 to 1926 winning the World Series in 1921 and 1922 and National League pennants the following two years. After a falling out with Giant manager McGraw, the Flash was traded to the Cardinals in 1927.

Me 'N' Paul

After agreeing to manage the St. Louis Cardinals, Frankie Frisch met with reporters, telling how he planned to manage. "I won't say pointblank that my Cardinals are going to win the pennant, but I will say that from now on my club is going to be the 'fightin'est' ball club in the National League. I've come to the conclusion that you must play the driving, slashing 'Pepper Martin baseball' to be successful. And I'm sure that this will pull us out of our slump and start us on a winning streak."[20]

Frisch also told reporters that Street was too easy on the players. "I'm fed up with this team's carefree attitude and undisciplined way."[21]

However, the Ol' Flash quickly discarded a ruling put in effect by Gabby prohibiting the drinking of beer. There would be beer in the Cardinal clubhouse.

Although prohibitions was not repealed until December 5, 1933, President Franklin Roosevelt signed an amendment on March 22, 1933 allowing the sale of beer. On that occasion he famously said, "I think this would be a good time to have a beer." With America still in the grasp of the Great Depression truer words were never spoken.

Under the Ol' Flash's management the Cardinals began playing what he called Pepper Martin baseball; brash, brawling, hustling, diving headfirst into bases, and never stopping at third if home was in sight. They fought more, their uniforms became dirtier and they started winning. Reeling off six straight victories they leaped from fifth to third place.

Dizzy did not pitch in the six wins. Frisch knew that Gabby Street had pitched Dizzy to death and was determined to give Diz proper rest, so he would be more effective. Frisch said "Street depended on three pitchers, Dizzy Dean, Bill Hallahan and Tex Carleton. The burden is too heavy for three men. From now on every member of the staff will be given an opportunity to work."[22] The rest agreed with Diz, in his next start he broke a Major League record that had stood for thirty years.

Sunday in St. Louis on the last day of July Dizzy started the first game of a doubleheader against the Chicago Cubs. He proceeded to strikeout 17 Cubs in the nine-inning game, a modern Major League record. The Cards won easily 8 – 2.

After the game Diz dressed in his street clothes went into the stands to accept the accolades of his adoring fans and sign some autographs. Along about the third inning of the second game Diz returned to the clubhouse, donned his uniform and returned to the Cardinal dugout "just in case Frisch needs me to strikeout some more of them Cubbies."[23]

Diz wasn't needed to strikeout anymore Cubbies in the second game of the double-dipper. The Cardinals won anyway 6 – 5.

The day after Diz set the all-time record of 17 strikeouts, he went to see Branch Rickey with a plan that guaranteed St. Louis the National League pennant. He told Rickey, "bring my brother Paul from the Columbus Red Birds to the Cards and we'll win the pennant. Why, he's a better pitcher than I am. He'd win seven games for us yet this season. I've figured it all out, and with him here we'd be able to win the pennant."

Rickey explained that he wasn't sure Paul was ready for the Majors. "Well, he's a better pitcher than I am, and I've struck out more batters than any pitcher in history."[24] Diz replied.

Rickey did not bring Paul to the Cardinals and St. Louis did not win the 1933 National League pennant. Although they played above .500 ball during August, the Cardinals lost ground in the pennant race. By early September the Cards were running with the also-rans near the bottom of the National League.

With the Cardinals wallowing in fifth place well out of contention, Dizzy was pitching for personal glory and a bigger paycheck. Upon winning his 20th game on September 13th, Dizzy announced he was officially a star pitcher and intended to get a star's salary. He gave a warning to Cardinal management, "I want more dough."[25]

"A pitcher is considered no better than the amount of money he earns," Diz explained. "And can you show me anyone who will say Dizzy Dean's not better than a $7,500-a-year pitcher? I'm a star. I know it and now that I've set the strikeout record and won 20 games, I'm ready to ask for a star's contract. It's going to be $15,000 for Diz in 1934.

I'm going to call Mr. Rickey so that we can go over our 1934 contract affairs while my great pitching is still fresh in his mind."[26]

Even if Rickey did not pay Dizzy like a star, the fans knew he was a star and they certainly appreciated him. 18,500 fans poured into Sportsman's Park on September 17th for "Dizzy Dean appreciation day."

A picture in the St. Louis post-dispatch showed a smiling Diz in his Cardinal uniform, with one foot resting on the running board of a brand-new Buick automobile. The caption read:

> "Strikeout king gets auto Dizzy Dean, Cardinal pitching ace, with Buick coupe to be presented at Sportsman's Park this afternoon. Dean's admirers purchased the car for him."[27]

In addition to a strikeout record, 20 wins, a new Buick and an appreciation day, Diz also led the Majors in strikeouts with 199 and in complete games with twenty-six. All things considered, an excellent year for the self-styled "Great Dean."

The Cardinals however, had a very disappointing season. They finished in fifth place 9.5 games behind the New York Giants. The Giants went on to win the World Series, besting the Washington Senators four games to one.

This was the Cardinal's second straight second division finish, something that had not happened since the 1923 and 1924 seasons. Ironically, this same team with only changes in right field, behind the plate and the addition of a starting pitcher would become the iconic gashouse gang.

With the conclusion of the Cardinal season Dizzy, Pepper and Paul would once again spend the month of October barnstorming. This year their travels would take them to Utah, California and finally to Houston for a reunion with Elmer "Goober" Dean.

This tour was especially exciting for Diz, Pepper and Paul for a couple of reasons. They had never been to the west coast and never traveled by airplane. At St. Louis and Columbus, the players were able to travel by train because of the shorter distances between cities with Major League and double A teams. The west coast did not have Major League baseball until the 1950's when the Giants and the Dodgers moved to San Francisco and Los Angeles respectively.

The Salt Lake City Chamber of Commerce received the following letter:

> "I'll reach Salt Lake Friday morning with Pepper Martin and Paul Dean.

Tell your home folks I'll strike out 12 in Friday's game."[28]

Dizzy Dean

Diz did not strike out 12 hitters because he only pitched two innings. This game was typical of the games played by the Dean-Martin All-Stars on the barnstorming tour. Paul and Diz would pitch two or three innings and then play other positions. Pepper played different positions and sometimes pitched himself. Their opponents and teammates were local professional and amateur players. Fans paid to see the Great Dizzy Dean and 1931 World Series hero Pepper Martin.

Paul, of course, was not as well-known as Dizzy and Pepper. Even though Paul's Columbus Red Birds had just won the Junior World Series, he was still only a minor leaguer. Dizzy tried to remedy that situation by constantly promoting and publicizing Paul.

Diz told reporters on the west coast tour; "I'm afraid I won't be the best pitcher in the National League next year. You know I am now, but with Paul on the club I guess I'll have to be content to be the second-best pitcher. He's so good he makes my fast ball look like a change of pace compared to his fast one."[29]

After several games in Utah the Dean-Martin tour traveled on to California with games in Fresno and finally, Los Angeles. It was at a game in Los Angeles that Dizzy first played against the great black star Satchel Paige. It was the first of many games Diz and Satch would play against each other.

Dizzy and Satchel were two sides of the same coin. Both were poor southern boys, Diz from rural Arkansas and Satch from urban Alabama. Both were doomed to a life of poverty if not for their ability to throw a baseball. Their talent, personality, ego, and showmanship and self-promotion enabled them to become the dominate baseball personalities of the 1930's. Their talent made them stars; their personas elevated them from stars to legends.

Leroy Robert "Satchel" Paige was born in Mobile, Alabama sometime between 1900 to 1908. Satch, like Dizzy, gave writers several different dates of his birth. Age did not seem to matter to Satchel Paige. He famously asked, "how old would you be, if you didn't know how old you were?"

July 6, 1906 is his accepted date of birth. Paige's mother established that date because she wrote it down in her bible. Satch was still not convinced, "seems like mama's bible would know, but she ain't never showed me that bible."[30]

As a child Paige worked at any job he could to help support his poverty-stricken family. One job entailed carrying luggage for train passengers earning him the nickname "Satchel". After a stint in reform school for shoplifting Satch turned to baseball for salvation.

Satch started his professional baseball career with the Chattahooga Black Lookouts of the Negro Southern League. After becoming one of the most famous players in the Negro Leagues, he finally made it to the Majors in 1948, after Jackie Robinson broke the color barrier.

Satchel played his first Major League game for the Cleveland Indians as a 42-year-old rookie. He pitched his last Major League game for the Kansas City Athletics at age 59.

Satchel was a vagabond of the diamond playing for any team that had the money to pay him; including teams in Mexico, Cuba, and the Dominican Republic. Satch was colorful, giving his fastball different names like Bat Dodger, Midnight Rider, Midnight Creeper, Jump Ball, and Trouble Ball. He described his control as his be-ball, "cause it be where I want it to be."

On October 16th Diz, Pepper and Paul joined a team of Pacific Coast league All-Stars to play against the Philadelphia Royal Giants led by Satchel Paige. This was not a typical exhibition game; each team was stacked with high-caliber professional players.

The Pacific Coast league of the 1930's and 1940's was a premier Minor League, easily the equivalent of the Double A American Association and International Leagues. The PCL had iconic teams such as the San Francisco Seals, Oakland Oaks, Los Angeles Angels and Hollywood Stars. The league produced such Major League stars as; the DiMaggio brothers Joe, Dom and Vince, Ted Williams, Ernie Lombardi and Bobby Doerr.

Another prominent Pacific Coast alumni, Chuck Conners, spent the majority of his professional career with the Hollywood Stars. Conners made it to the Majors playing briefly for the Brooklyn Dodgers and Chicago Cubs. The 6'5" athlete also played professional basketball for the Boston Celtics. Conners finally abandoned sports, going from playing for the Hollywood Stars to be a Hollywood star. First starring in the TV's "The Rifleman" and later carving out a lucrative career in the movies. Conners credited baseball for his success. "I owe baseball all that I have and much of what I hope to have. Baseball made my entrance to the film industry immeasurable easier than I could have made it alone. To the greatest game in the world I shall be eternally grateful."[31]

The Pacific Coast League All-Stars teaming with the Dean-Martin trio included Gene Lillard, 1933 PCL homerun king and future Major Leaguers catcher Hughie McMullen, first baseman Jim Oglesby and shortstop Bill Knickerbocker.

Satchel's teammates included Major League talent that never played in the Majors because of the color of their skin Negro League stars Turkey Stearns, Cool Papa Bell, Willie Wells and Mule Suttles were anxious to get a chance to show they could compete against the white stars.

Many Major Leaguers refused to play against the negro teams. Even Commissioner Kennesaw Mountain Landis continually discouraged Major League players from "demeaning" themselves by competing against negros. Dizzy and Paul had no problem playing against blacks. They had spent years picking cotton next to blacks who worked as hard and were just as poor.

"Blacks desperate lot in life mirrored their own. Much of the racial superiority of white southerners came from a belief that downscale labor was not for white folks."[32] This experience led Diz and Paul to have great empathy toward black ballplayers.

The first game in Los Angeles was a must-see event. L.A. Times sports columnist, Bob Ray hyped the game: "Pepper Martin whose sensational exploits practically single- handed won the 1931 World Series for the St. Louis Cardinals and Dizzy Dean, a loud- mouthed hurler who can back up his remarks, make their first appearance before Los Angeles fans tonight at White Sox park, where they lead an All-Star squad against the Philadelphia Royal Giants, a strong colored outfit. Also accompanying Pepper and Dizzy will be Paul Dean, Dizzy's younger brother who led the American Association in strikeouts this year and reports to the Cardinals next spring. Satchel Paige, lean colored fire-baller who has a fast ball that sizzles on its way to the plate will twirl for the Giants."[33]

Dizzy started on the mound for the All-Stars, pitched four innings allowed two hits and one run. Paul did not play because he had injured his hand. "Paul was hit by a pitched ball and his right hand was swollen like the Mississippi in flood time. An x-ray showed that no bones were broken."[34] Pepper had an RBI triple and two stolen bases as the Dean-Martin All-Stars beat the Royal Giants 2 – 1. Satchel was limited to pitching only three innings because he had pitched a 3 – hit shutout the day before, striking out 15. One of the hits off Dizzy was a solo homerun by Royal Giant catcher, Tommy Dukes. Paul, nursing his injured hand in the dugout, just had to razz Diz when Dukes hit his homerun. Paul jumped off the bench and yelled at Diz, "What! You let those guys score off you? Why you oughta be ashamed of yourself."[35]

After their game with Satch and the Royal Giants, the Dean-Martin trio departed to Houston, Texas for a charity exhibition game and a reunion with brother Elmer and Pa Dean. Dizzy would pitch for one team and Paul the other. Elmer played on Paul's team. It must have been a proud moment for Pa Dean, seeing all three of his boys on the diamond at Houston Buff Stadium.

Despite Paul's injured hand he started the game, but after only one inning he was done. It would be irresponsible to risk further injury in an exhibition game. Diz pitched three innings and his team won 9 – 1. Their highlight of the game was Elmer's triple off his brother Dizzy. Some fans suspected Diz grooved one for his brother but there was no doubt Elmer had crushed the ball.

After the game Dizzy revealed he was on his way to St. Louis to negotiate his 1934 contract. "Instead of the $15,000 I demanded after my 20th win, I've thought it over and now I want $20,000 instead of $15,000."[36]

Dizzy met with Cardinal owner Sam Breadon in St. Louis on October 25, 1933. After huddling behind closed doors for close to two hours the Card hurler and the Red Bird magnate emerged smiling, although neither would disclose terms of Dizzy's 1934 contract. "I've promised to be silent about the matter," the pitcher admitted.[37] Of course Dizzy could not remain completely silent, less than a week later he told reporters, "I was given increased salary that didn't like so much of meeting my demands for $20,000 a year."[38] Actually, Dizzy had signed his 1934 contract for $7,500.

Carl Duncan

Ever the publicity hound Dizzy had agreed to be a celebrity chef at a St. Louis culinary school. Dizzy was on stage with 500 spectators in attendance when he suddenly whirled around and started hurling eggs into the audience.

"Watch out! Duck! He's gone crazy! Came cries form the crowd. A mad scramble to get under seats and behind posts followed until the "eggs" started bouncing they were made of rubber! The Dizzy one got a big hand."[39]

Dizzy and his wife Pat left St. Louis and traveled to Bradenton, Florida to spend the remainder of the winter. It promised to be a Merry Christmas with a fat new contract and the prospect of brother Paul joining him on the Cardinals for the 1934 season, life was good.

If you were fortunate enough to be on Dizzy's Christmas mailing list, you would have received not one but two Christmas cards. "One shows himself holding the medal he received for fanning seventeen batsmen in one game last season and the other shows him doing the trick."[40]

CHAPTER 15

"Me 'N' Paul will be sure to win 45 games between us"

The Gashouse Gang was born in 1934 but not named until 1935. Although the 1934 St. Louis Cardinals were forever after known as the Gashouse Gang, the name was not coined until 1935. There is also controversy over the origin of the nickname.

People in the 1930's knew Gashouses were factories that turned coal into gas. The gas was used by cities for lighting and cooking. Gashouses were common in the United States before the widespread use of natural gas. These plants were usually located close to noisy railroad yards.

The process of turning coal into gas produced a foul smell and left coal dust to coat the immediate area. The neighborhoods in close proximity to the factories and railroad yards were very undesirable places to live. Only the poorest, roughest people lived in these smelly, dirty, noisy gashouse districts.

The comparison of the 1934 Cardinals to a Gashouse Gang was obvious and accurate. The Cards were dirty, smelly and loud. Even if their uniforms started out clean, their style of play soon dirtied them. Frisch encouraged his team to play "Pepper Martin baseball"; aggressive, headfirst sliding, tobacco chewing, trash-talking brawlers, who did not let rules or sportsmanship stand in the way of dismantling their opponents. As Leo the Lip Durocher said, "nice guys finish last."[1]

There are at least three plausible possibilities for the nickname's origin. Two of them involve Leo the Lip.

"Ballplayers are a superstitious breed" Leo said "while you are winning, you'd murder anybody who tried to change your sweatshirt, let alone your uniform. During a winning streak the uniforms were so filthy that we could have thrown them in a corner and they'd have stood up by themselves. The bills of our caps were all bent and creased and twisted. We looked horrible, we knew it and we gloried in it."[2]

Leo thought a newspaper cartoonist, Willard Mullins, saw them play in New York on one of the Cardinal winning streaks and drew a cartoon that appeared in the New York World-Telegram newspaper. "It showed two big gas tanks on the wrong side of the railroad track, and some ballplayers crossing over to the good part of town carrying clubs over their shoulders instead of bats. And the title read 'The Gashouse Gang'."[3]

The second scenario involving Leo the Lip took place in New York. Leo was being interviewed by sportswriter Frank Graham when Dizzy wondered by and told Graham the Cardinals could win the pennant in any league including the American League. Leo said, "Oh no, they wouldn't let us play in the American League. They'd say we were a lot of Gashouse ballplayers."[4]

Frankie Frisch gave a third explanation for the Gashouse Gang moniker. He said Chicago sportswriter Warren Brown climbed aboard the Cub's train bound for St. Louis. He noticed the curtains on the sleepers were drawn and all the Cub players had turned in for the night. "What's the matter?" Brown asked in a loud voice, "are you boys afraid that Pepper Martin is on the train? You all had better stay on your side of the tracks, or the Gashouse Gang will get you."[5]

The Cardinals would return to Bradenton, Florida for their 1934 Major League spring training camp. Thirty-four players were invited to camp but only twenty-three were allowed on the final roster.

Spring training camp opened on March 5th, but Paul and Dizzy had been in Bradenton since January. They spent the two months prior to training camp hunting, fishing and playing golf. Dizzy and his wife, Pat enjoyed Bradenton so much they bought a house there. Sportswriters and locals began calling Bradenton, Deanville.

Dizzy told reporters he believed the two Deans would lead the Cardinals to the 1934 National League pennant. "How are they going to stop us?" snapped Dizzy. "Paul's going to be a sensation in the league. He'll win 18 or 20 games. I'll count 20 to 25 games for myself. I won 20 games last season, and I know I'll pass that figure."[6]

Manager Frankie Frisch, however, refused to predict a pennant for his Cards. "Don't make me look foolish" he told reporters. "Of course, we're going to be in there fighting, and so are others. But it's nonsense to try and pick the spot where this club or that one will end up."[7]

Frisch did agree with Dizzy about Paul's potential. "Our biggest gain is the addition of Paul Dean, Dizzy's brother, to our pitching staff."[8]

One manager who would pick his own team to win the pennant was Bill Terry. Terry was player/manager of the World Champion New York Giants. "Anybody want to bet a hat that we don't win again?" he asked reporters. No one wanted to bet. "Pittsburgh, St. Louis, and Chicago will be the teams to beat." Terry said. Asked if he feared cross-town rival Brooklyn, Terry replied, "is Brooklyn still in the league?"[9] That sarcastic reply would come back to bite him in the butt.

Cuban coach/catcher Mike Gonzalez also liked the Cards chances. Mike was a player/coach for Columbus in 1933. He had coached and caught Paul at Columbus and now he was a coach under Frisch at St. Louis. Mike was telling everyone that Paul Dean was a great pitcher and he would help the Cardinals win the pennant.

"We have to win," the veteran catcher said. "If everybody she hustle, we win. Good year to win, too. I tell you, my frien' we win and St. Louis' forget we had what you call him a depression."[10]

Always butchering the English language, Gonzalez, nevertheless, made a lasting contribution to baseball terminology. The Cardinals asked Mike to scout a player in the Cuban League. Mike thought the player was outstanding defensively but a liability at the plate. He wired back a four-word scouting report: good field, no hit. The phrase is still in use today.

Branch Rickey also believed the Cardinals would win the 1934 National League pennant. Rickey offered two reasons for his pennant prediction; "those demon Dean brothers Dizzy is the greatest pitcher in the league today. I look for Paul to be even better. Between them they'll win 40 games for us this season."[11]

Hearing all this praise for Paul, Dizzy decided that his younger brother was underpaid.

The $3,000 Cardinal offer was not near enough for a pitcher of Paul's caliber.

"The club offered Paul a raise over what he got at Columbus, but it wasn't enough for a man of his skill." Diz explained. "It was the same salary the club offered other young pitchers, and Paul ain't no ordinary pitcher. He's a great pitcher. He's even greater than I am, if that's possible. Paul is willing to gamble on his ability. He told Mr. Rickey he'd pitch for nothing until he won a certain number of games, say 15, and then let the Cardinals pay him $500 for each victory. And the club turned that offer down! You can't tell what a club's going to do nowadays."[12]

Rickey did not mind praising Paul but paying him was another matter. He was willing to discuss Paul's request for $1500, more than the $3,000 the Cardinals were offering, but after two conferences, Rickey said, "we have offered young Mr. Dean a contract and it is up to him to sign it or reject it."[13]

After his last meeting with Rickey, Paul said he was leaving for Houston where he had a good job lined up in a factory. "They're making a mistake if they let Paul get away." Dizzy declared. "Me 'N' Paul can clinch the pennant for the Cardinals. It makes me sick and I've got a good notion to quit myself, if they don't give Paul a better break."[14]

"I fear Paul is being advised badly" Rickey told sportswriters. "We will not conduct any further negotiations with him. We have made our final offer."[15]

Dizzy was not convinced, he wanted Paul to continue to hold out. "That Rickey's bluffin'" he said. Paul did not want to spend another year in Columbus and he certainly did not want to work in a Houston factory.

Me 'N' Paul

"He ain't bluffin' I'm signin'" Although he signed for $3,000, both Paul & Diz deeply resented Rickey's hard-nosed bargaining tactics.

Once Paul signed and the holdout drama was over Dizzy and Paul were confident and ready to go to work. Diz said "I don't see how anybody can beat us now, with two Deans on the ball club. Me 'N' Paul will be sure to win 45 games between us and if we have six other pitchers, they ought to account for about 50 more games on the right side of the ledger and that should put us in the World Series. It ought to be a breeze from now on."[16]

"It looks like a great year for the Cardinals with me in line to help Dizzy."[17] Paul said.

Leo Durocher overheard Dizzy telling reporters "Me 'N' Paul will win 45 games." Leo said sportswriters were laughing at the outrageous prediction and so were other Cardinal players. The Lip looked over at Frankie Frisch and said "well, let's go fishing for six weeks, we've got 45 won. We don't have a worry in the world." Frankie said, "let's win them first, then we'll talk about it." Dizzy did not appreciate the snickering. Undaunted, he yelled at the top of his lungs "45 Frankie, mark it down."[18]

Once he signed, Frisch and his coaches knew Paul was the real deal. An article in the St. Louis Star and Times proclaimed Paul the sensation of spring training camp.

"Paul Dean is the talk of camp. The real hot tip in camp is that Paul Dean, will be a better pitcher than his brother Dizzy. According to the inside dope, Paul will be another Walter Johnson, just as fast as the former smokeball king of the American League."[19]

Paul's success at Columbus, coaches and scouts rave reviews along with the gate attraction of having Dizzy and Paul in the Card pitching rotation, assured Paul a place on the 1934 St. Louis Cardinal roster. Manager Frisch was so convinced of Paul's talent, he only pitched him six innings in preseason games. The flash wanted to evaluate other pitchers to see if they could help the Cardinals in the upcoming season.

By the end of spring training the 1934 Cardinal roster was set, and it was not very different from the 1933 team that finished fifth in the National League. Jack Rothrock replaced George Watkins in right field, Jimmy Wilson was replaced by Spud Davis and Bill Delancey who platooned at catcher. Paul Dean was added to the pitching staff. A different right fielder, a different catcher and an additional pitcher transformed a fifth- place club into the legendary Gashouse Gang.

George Watkins and Jimmy Wilson were long time St. Louis Cardinals. Both were valuable starters on the Cards 1930 National League Championship team and the 1931 World Champion St. Louis Cardinals. Catcher Wilson was upset when Frankie Frisch replaced Gabby Street as Card manager mid-season 1933. Jimmy thought he deserved the managerial job. Rickey traded Wilson to Philadelphia where he became player/manager.

George Watkins was yet another example of Branch Rickey's classic maneuver. He traded away an expensive veteran, replacing him with a cheaper player. In this case the replacement player was former Minor League player, Jack Rothrock.

Jack Houston Rothrock was a very versatile baseball player. He could play any position on the diamond, including pitcher and catcher. In eight Major League seasons he played 639 games in the outfield, 78 games at shortstop, 63 at second base, 48 at third base and 38 at first. He caught in one game and pitched in another.

A speedy switch-hitter, Jack was born in Long Beach, California, on March 14, 1905. He played baseball for Long Beach high school. However, he received pay for playing semi- pro ball and thus was ineligible for his senior year of high school baseball and the many college scholarships he was offered. With no other amateur options, Jack signed to play professional baseball.

Jack began his professional career in 1923 and by 1925 he was in the Majors playing for the Boston Red Sox. Never a great hitter, Rothrock was nevertheless an asset to any team. He was a tremendous defensive player who could play both infield and outfield. Jack was widely considered the fastest man in baseball at the time, so he was valuable as a pinch runner and as a late inning defensive replacement.

Considered a utility man instead of a regular everyday player, Jack was traded to the Chicago White Sox and finally to the Cardinals in 1933. St. Louis demoted him to Columbus where he was a star for the 1933 Columbus Red Bird Championship team. Finally playing regularly Rothrock hit .357 and was named to the American Association All-Star team. His outstanding performance earned Jack a return to the Major Leagues with the 1934 St. Louis Cardinals.

Jimmy Wilson was replaced by Spud Davis and Bill Delancey. Spud came over from Philadelphia in the Wilson trade. Delancey had an outstanding year at Columbus in 1933 and Rickey deemed him ready for the Majors in 1934.

Virgil Lawrence "Spud" Davis was a southern boy born in Birmingham, Alabama on December 20, 1904. He grew up poor in an urban environment, raised by a single mother and sisters, Spud was a star high school athlete playing baseball and football.

An uncle called him Spud because of his fondness for potatoes. "I liked potatoes so much growing up that I was nicknamed Spud." Davis explained. "But I loved baseball more than potatoes, so I cut them out."[20] The 6'1" 200lb Alabaman constantly fought a losing battle with his weight.

Spud began his professional baseball career in 1926. He had a great year batting .356 for the Gulfport Tarpons in the Class D Cotton States League. The New York Yankees took notice and purchased his contract. Spud did not make the roster of the legendary 1927 Yankees and he was picked up by the St. Louis Cardinals. After only one more Minor League season, Spud made it to the majors with the St. Louis Cardinals.

After only two games as a Cardinal, Spud was traded to the Philadelphia Phillies for Jimmie Wilson. Davis became the Phillies primary catcher in 1930 when their other catcher was killed in a freak accident by a runaway delivery truck. Spud had four productive offensive years with the Phillies averaging over .300. Then before the 1934 season Spud was traded back to the Cardinals, ironically for Jimmie Wilson.

Davis was a good hitter with plenty of power, but he was slow afoot and a poor defensive catcher. He did not fit the image of the Gashouse Gang. A sportswriter described Spud as "The personification of the southern gentleman. The Spud does not poke his nose into an open conversation but is reserved and retiring. He does not hoard his money, dresses in the height of fashion, enjoys good shows and is fond of movies."[21]

Spud may not have fit the image of the Gashouse Gang, but he certainly contributed to the gang's reputation for being crazy. Spud was very superstitious and before every game he had pitcher Dazzy Vance recite a Seminole Indian prayer over his bat. Dazzy would stroke Spud's bat affectionately and chant the prayers of Seminole Chiefs. Spud was sure this ritual helped his hitting.

The other catcher William Delancy came from a large Irish family. One of seven brothers and six sisters, he was born on November 28, 1911 in Greensboro, North Carolina. Bill grew up playing baseball and by the time he was 18 years old he was a pro prospect.

A six-foot-tall, 185lb left-handed hitting catcher, he had a good arm and hit for power. The St. Louis Cardinals signed Delancy in 1931 and he began his journey through the Card Farm System.

Bill played for Cardinal Farm Clubs at Danville in the Class B Three-I League and Springville of the Class C Western Association. By 1933 Delancy was the starting catcher on the Class AA Columbus Red Birds. Bill and Paul Dean were good friends and Bill was the catcher for Paul's 22 wins in 1933.

Branch Rickey knew Bill Delancy was his Cardinal catcher of the future, but he could not rely solely on a rookie for his pennant contending 1934 Cardinals. Platooning Delancy with veteran Spud Davis was Rickey's solution for his catching problem.

St. Louis sportswriter Bob Broeg was impressed with rookie Delancy. "I always ranked Delancy as one of the three greatest catchers I ever watched play. He was a knock-kneed left-handed hitter, had a good throwing arm, and he was tough. He'd be catching Dean, who sometimes lost his concentration, and Bill would walk out to the mound and say 'you big cocksucker, don't you jake on me.' Diz loved it. He was like a slap in the face."[22]

Bill was respected by teammates for his "fearless nature." Bill did not back down to veterans and demonstrated his leadership with a stern gaze or a streak of curse words. Rickey called him a master with pitchers.

Dizzy liked pitching to Delany so much he refused to pitch to Spud Davis. Consequently, Frisch had to let him catch every time Diz was on the mound.

The other seven regulars were all starters on the 1933 Cardinal team. Ripper Collins played first base, player/manager Frankie Frisch still survived at second, Pepper Martin toiled at third, Leo "The Lip" still was the best defensive shortstop in the league. Joe "Ducky" Medwick and Ernie

"Hollywood" Orsatti patrolled the outfield. The main pitchers were, Dizzy Dean, Tex Carlton, Wild Bill Hallahan, Bill Walker and Jesse Haines.

James Anthony Collins was the son of a Pennsylvania coal miner. He was born on March 30, 1904 and by the time James was 13 years old he was working in the coal mines.

His father played on the coal company's baseball team and young Jimmy wanted to play baseball like his dad. Jimmy's father taught him to switch hit and to throw both right and left-handed. He attended high school at night, a common practice in coal mining towns because the boys had to work in the mines during the day.

Since there was no high school baseball Jimmy honed his skills playing on the company team alongside his dad. He acquired the nickname "Ripper" during a game with the company team. He hit a baseball so hard, it hit a nail protruding from the outfield fence ripping the cover nearly off. From that day, the rest of his life, Jimmy Collins was known as "Ripper."

Ripper knew that baseball could be his ticket out of the coal mines. "I knew I had to make the grade in baseball. Handicapped by my lack of education, I realized that if I failed as a ballplayer, my life would be a dull, pitiful existence as a coal miner."[23]

Ripper signed his first professional contract in 1922. From then until 1929 Rip bounced around the Minor Leagues and worked back in the coal mines during the off season. Finally, in 1929 Ripper made it to Double A Rochester which had been purchased by the St. Louis Cardinals the year before.

Ripper was 5 feet 9 inches tall and weighed 165lbs, not exactly a prototypical first baseman. Still the Cardinals thought he could handle the position because he had quick reflexes and an uncanny ability to pull down errant throws and scoop low ones out of the dirt.

Ripper led the Rochester Red Wings to International League pennants in 1929 and 1930.

1930 was Ripper's best season, leading the International League with 40 home runs and hitting .376. This amazing display of power and batting average led to his promotion to the Cardinals in 1931. After splitting playing time with Jim Bottomley in 1931 and 1932 Bottomley was traded and Ripper Collins became the Cardinals full-time first baseman.

At second base was Frankie Frisch, though declining defensively, he was still a feared clutch hitter. Since the Flash was also manager of the Cardinals, Branch Rickey was concerned that Frisch's managerial responsibilities combined with his defensive deficiencies would prevent the Cardinals from winning the pennant.

Rickey said to his assistant Gene Karst "I don't think I can win the pennant with Frisch at second base, he has lost a lot of speed. I should convince Sam Breadon to trade him." Rickey knew Frisch really was Breadon's pet, and after thinking it over, he dropped the idea. "I don't think I can do it."[24] His not doing it, turned out to be the right decision.

Leo "The Lip" Durocher was still the best defensive shortstop in the league and the best jockey. He continued to verbally harass opponents unmercilessly. Racial slurs and derogatory comments about wives and sisters were not off-limits for Lippy.

Off field distractions kept dogging Leo. He still haunted pool halls, association with less than desirable characters. Also, he dated a woman who became pregnant and forced Leo to marry her. A nasty divorce followed with salacious details splashed across newspapers, bringing negative publicity to the Cardinals.

A headline in the Cincinnati Enquirer read; "Leo Durocher punched her, tied her up in bed sheets, wife charges in suing baseball player for divorce."[25]

Leo's estranged wife Ruby Hartlett Durocher sued him for divorce. Ruby alleged Leo was abusive, and she sported one black eye a month while she was married to Durocher. Ruby told the court about coming home late after playing bridge with relatives when an irate Leo tied her up in bed sheets and hit her on the jaw. She displayed to the court a picture of herself with a badly distorted jaw.

Further damaging to Durocher were love letters Ruby produced from several women to Leo. "Mrs. Durocher's counsel called her to the stand and had her identify several mushy love letters and telegrams, signed Virginia, Marie and sis, addressed to Durocher. Virginia, Marie and sis wrote or wired often. One Marie letter told of being lonesome because her only chance to go out was with old fossils who were not like my loving Leo. She closed with all my love. The letters from the others were equally voluble in endearing expressions."[26]

Ruby's lawyers also contended that Leo failed to care for his elderly mother. They claimed the Ohio humane society had filed charges against him because of his neglect to provide for his aged mother. She was reduced to working as a maid at a Cincinnati hotel.

Leo cross-sued and told his side of the story. Yes, he had punched Ruby in the jaw on the night in question, but only after extreme provocation. Leo said Ruby had not been playing bridge with her relatives. She had been out drinking and who knows what else with one Charles McDonald. McDonald's wife was divorcing him for being too friendly with Ruby Durocher.

Leo contended that Ruby was drunk, screaming uncontrollably, and threatening him. "I tried to quiet her by telling her she would wake the baby, and out of the clear sky she said, 'the baby needn't concern you. It doesn't belong to you.' I said, 'what did you say?' she said, 'you heard me; the baby doesn't belong to you.' Then I struck her."[27]

Leo's attorney asked him to explain the love letters from various women. Not love letters, The Lip explained, "fan mail." And finally did Leo have any proof of Ruby being too friendly with Mr. McDonald. As a matter of fact, he did. At that point Leo's "aged" mother took the stand to tell a lurid story.

Mrs. Clara Durocher, who was indeed a maid at a downtown Cincinnati hotel, told the court she heard the voice of her son's wife coming from room 1706. She knocked on the door.

"A man came to the door and asked for some towels," she said, "he was in his shorts. I saw Ruby Durocher in a dressing gown. When the room was cleaned up there were whiskey bottles and face powder there, and lipstick on the pillow slips. The man was Mr. McDonald."[28]

The judge ruled that Ruby was guilty of gross neglect and granted Leo the divorce. Ruby was given custody of the baby, and Leo was ordered to pay child support.

Dizzy's barnstorming buddy, Pepper Martin, still toiled at third base, knocking down grounders with his barrel chest and terrorizing base runners with his errant throws. Pepper hated to field bunts. Leo The Lip said, "there was a series in Boston where Pepper's back was so sore he could hardly bend. Naturally the Braves began to bunt on him. Pepper went to the mound, called Rip Collins over and told him, 'next guy bunts on me, forget the bag and back up the runner. I'm going to bounce one off his groin.' He missed the first one, got the second one, and that ended the Brave's bunting for the day."[29] "When I bunted on Pepper" Pirate outfielder Lloyd Waner said, "I ran to first base with my hands covering my head."[30]

On the base paths Pepper was like a runaway freight train. Instead of sliding into a base the prudent way, feet first, Pepper risked life and limb by diving in headfirst. Having Pepper in a rundown was like having a wild tiger in a cage, sometimes you got him out, sometimes you got Hauled.

Pepper and Dizzy were responsible for the Gashouse Gang's reputation for fun loving mischief and practical jokes. From water bag bombs dropped from hotel windows to sneezing powder and exploding cigars, Pepper was at the center of the fun. For Pepper Martin, one of the most popular gashousers, summers were filled with fun and the miracle of getting paid to play baseball.

Joining Jack Rothrock in the Card outfield were "Ducky" Medwick and "Hollywood" Orsatti. Joe Mewick's parents were both born in Hungary. Joe's father, a carpenter, brought his family to America in 1893 looking for a better life. His fourth child, Joseph Michael Medwick was born in Carteret, New Jersey on November 24, 1911. At home his parents spoke Hungarian and Joe was fluent in the language.

When Joe started high school he was big boned, short and muscular, ideally suited for football. He won All-State honors as a high school halfback. Although he had numerous college football offers, Joe preferred baseball. He was tempted by Knute Rockne's offer to play football at Notre Dame, but he knew he could make money immediately playing professional baseball. In order to keep his amateur status, in case he decided to attend Notre Dame, Joe played pro baseball under the name Mickey King.

Before the 1970's if an athlete received pay for playing any sport, the athlete's amateur status was forfeited. Therefore, athletes who wanted to retain their amateur status played pro sports under assumed names. Two famous incidents demonstrate the wisdom of playing professional baseball under an alias.

An American Indian, Jim Thorpe, gained National recognition as an All-American football player at Carlisle college. He played a summer of professional baseball, using his real name, a mistake that cost Him greatly. At the 1912 Olympic games Jim Thorpe won the gold medal in the pentathlon and decathlon, earning him the title World's Greatest Athlete. Thorpe's Olympic heroics generated publicity and attracted attention to the Indian athlete. Unfortunately, this interest in Thorpe uncovered the fact that he had been paid to play baseball. Because of the amateurism rules in place at the time, Jim had to return the gold medal and his records and titles were erased.

While Jim Thorpe was playing football at Carlisle college one opponent was the United States Military Academy, West Point. A player on the West Point team went on to become one of the most influential men of the 20th century, Dwight D. Eisenhauer. If a young Eisenhauer had made the same mistake Jim Thorpe made, World History might have been changed.

Eisenhauer actually played a summer of pro baseball before he entered West Point, however, he knew to use an alias to preserve his amateur status, which enabled Ike to play football for West Point. Eisenhauer was the starting running back for West Point until he suffered a torn knee when tackled by Jim Thorpe.

Medwick signed with the St. Louis Cardinals in 1930 when he was 18 years old. Perhaps a big reason for Joe choosing professional baseball over Notre Dame football was the Wall Street crash the year before, signaling the onset of the great depression. Joe needed to make money to help his family who faced an uncertain future.

The Cardinals paid young Joe a $500 signing bonus and assigned him to Scottsdale, Pennsylvania of the Class C Middle Atlantic League. St. Louis considered Medwick Major League material. The Cardinal scouting report said he had "all of the requisites to a high degree – arm, speed, punch, ambition, a great athlete. Only weaknesses youth and hitting bad balls."[31]

At Scottsdale, Medwick hit .419 with 22 home runs. This outstanding performance enabled Joe to skip Class B ball entirely and go directly to the Class A Houston Buffaloes of the Texas League. Medwick spent the 1931 and 1932 with the Buffs where his teammate was Dizzy Dean.

Medwick had a good year in 1931 but the 20-year-old outfielder dominated the Texas League in 1932 with a .354 B.A. and 342 total bases. While at Houston Joe acquired a nickname he despised that followed him his entire career. A female fan wrote to a Houston sportswriter "Please tell me about Joe Medwick, he is my favorite Buff player. I have nicknamed him "Ducky" because he walks like a duck."³² When the sportswriter, Lloyd Gregory included the letter in his column, Joe's teammates picked up on it and started calling him Ducky or worse yet, Ducky Wucky.

With only three years in the minors, Ducky Medwick made his Major League debut with the St. Louis Cardinals on September 2, 1932. Still a month shy of 21st birthday, Joe was an unrepentant bad ball hitter who never met a pitch he didn't like. He was hot- tempered and quick to fight. Perhaps because of his immigrant parents Medwick harbored an inferiority complex, he carried a chip on his shoulder and felt like he had to constantly prove himself. Joe was described as surly, sulky, humorless and belligerent. He was quick-fisted and also tight-fisted. A teammate said "Joe, thinks tipping is a city in China."³³ He had some peculiar personality traits, but Ducky Wucky could hit a baseball. In 1933, his first full Major League season, he hit .306 with 18 H.R. and 98 RBI's.

Ernie Orsatti, who was born and raised in Los Angeles California, had no adolescent ambitions to play professional baseball. "My interest, as a boy, was in motion pictures and not in baseball, I wanted to be an actor, a director, a cameraman, anything that would identify me with motion pictures."³⁴

Born on September 8, 1902 to Italian immigrant parents, Ernie quit school to pursue his Hollywood aspirations. He went to work at movie studios and became a stunt man. He made his living doing death defying stunts such as diving off cliffs, walking on the wings of airplanes and crashing cars.

Ernie became a professional ballplayer in a very atypical way and at a much older age than most baseball players. In 1922 Orsatti started working as a bit player and prop man at a studio of the great silent film star, Buster Keaton.

Keaton was a rabid baseball fan and a good amateur player. Buster organized a baseball team comprised of his studio employees. Actors, stunt men, musicians, writers and cameramen were all encouraged to try out for Buster's amateur team. Keaton was also part-owner of a professional team, the Vernon (California) Tigers of the Pacific Coast League.

Orsatti played on Keaton's studio team for two years and one of his teammates was Mike Donlin, a former Major Leaguer turned Hollywood supporting actor. Donlin told Buster Keaton that Orsatti had professional potential. Keaton and Donlin convinced Ernie that he could make more money playing baseball than working for the studio. In 1925 Keaton signed Ernie Orsatti to play for the Vernon Tigers, starting his professional baseball career at age 23.

Despite his late start in baseball Orsatti made it to the Majors in 1927 with the St. Louis Cardinals. He proved he could hit Major League pitching by posting a .315 average in 92 bats, however his fielding was inadequate. He was sent back to the Minors for the 1928 season to learn the finer points of playing the outfield. Ernie spent most of the 1928 season in the AA American Association. By August 18th Ernie's defensive play had improved and he was hitting .381 with 15 homers. He was recalled to the St. Louis Cardinals for the rest of the 1928 season.

Orsatti remained with the Cardinals his entire Major League career. Ernie was a speedy baserunner who dived head-first into bases like Pepper Martin. He batted and threw left-handed, a line-drive hitter he hit .300 consistently. His uniform was constantly dirty, but once he stepped off the field, Ernie was a flashy dresser bringing Hollywood style to St. Louis. A sportswriter described Orsatti's look, "he never wears a hat, and his thick growth of well-oiled black hair is pushed back from his forehead. His flashy sweaters, golf hose, knickers and sport coats are Hollywood importations, and his wardrobe is the envy of the league."[35] No wonder his teammates called his the dashing dago.

In addition to Dizzy and Paul Dean the other main pitchers for the 1934 St. Louis Cardinals were Tex Carleton, Wild Bill Hallahan, and Bill Walker.

Although Dizzy & Paul lived in Texas for several years, James Carlson was the only native-born Texan on the 1934 Cardinals. Appropriately nicknamed Tex, he was born August 19, 1906 on a ranch near the small West Texas town of Comanche. Tex grew up working on the ranch, riding horses and herding cattle.

Carleton was a natural all-around athlete, he played basketball, football and baseball at Texas Christian University(TCU) in Fort Worth. After two years at TCU, Tex quit school to pursue a career in professional baseball. In 1925 he signed to play in the Class D East Texas League, pitching for the Marshall Indians.

Carl Duncan

After only one year with Marshall, Carleton was signed by the St. Louis Cardinals and began his trek through the extensive Cardinal Farm System. Tex pitched for the Class D Austin Senators in 1926 and won 11 games and lost 9. He then played the 1927 and 1928 seasons for the Class A Houston Buffaloes winning 10 games each year.

Tex was promoted to one of the Cardinal's top farm clubs, the Double A Rochester Red Wings for the 1929 season. He came through with his best season winning 18 and losing 7 for the International League Champions. He also won two games in the Junior World Series even through the Red Wings lost the series to the Kansas City Blues.

After his great year Tex was invited to spring training with the St. Louis Cardinals. However, the 1930 Cards were stacked with veteran pitchers, so Carleton was sent back to Rochester. Tex was a moody ballplayer and brooded when he thought he was being criticized. He did not respond well to being sent back to the Red Wings. Unhappy and sometimes belligerent Tex slumped to a 13 – 13 record, his ERA ballooned to 5.01. This sorry season resulted in a demotion back to the Class A Houston Buffs for the 1931 season.

Tex overcame his disappointing 1930 season and resurrected his career with the 1931 Buffs. Teamed with Dizzy Dean, Tex and Diz tore up the Texas League. Dizzy won 26 games and Tex won 20. Houston was upset in the Dixie series by Brimington, in part because Tex had fractured a finger on his pitching hand and could not pitch in the series.

Although Tex had proved himself in the Minor Leagues, Branch Rickey was reluctant to bring him up to the Cardinals. Despite being 6'1" and 180lbs, Tex seemed to lack stamina. In an era before relief specialists, pitchers were expected to pitch a full nine innings. However, Tex was high-strung and a worrier, prone to losing weight and strength as the long season wore on.

Finally, Cardinal team physician Dr. Hyland, found a solution to Carleton's nervous condition. In an era before tranquilizers, Dr. Hyland recommended that Tex have a few alcoholic beverages to relax him.

Tex explained how he obtained alcohol during the prohibition. "I used to get prescription whiskey – it still being prohibition – and carry it with me on the road. I'd have a couple of highballs and go around blowing my breath in the other guy's faces."[36]

Dr. Hyland's prescription must have worked, by 1933 Tex was a mainstay of the St. Louis staff. He finished the 1933 season with a record of 17 wins 11 losses and an ERA of 3.38 for the fifth place Cards.

William Anthony Hallahan's small stature belied his ability to throw a baseball harder than his peers. Born in Binghamton, New York on August 4, 1902 Bill suffered an unhappy childhood. His parents were concerned that he was left-handed and they tried to make him right-handed by tying his left arm behind his back.

It was a common practice in early 20th century America for parents to repress their children's left-handedness because of the bias against left-handers. With only 10% of people left-handed, the world is designed for right-handers. Many common every day items are designed for use by righties and are inconvenient, painful or even dangerous for left-handed use. Machinery, musical instruments, kitchen gadgets, tools from scissors to saws are designed for right-handed people. In addition there were social stigmas attached to left-handers. At different times in history left-handedness has been seen as a sign of many things; dishonesty, stupidity, rebellion, criminality, and even homosexuality. No wonder parents did not want their kids to be left-handed.

Bill was a poor student and failed several grades. Other kids teased him because of his small size and big ears. The only way Bill excelled was throwing a baseball. Sick of school he quit after eighth grade and went to work.

Bill found work at a factory that manufactured Corona typewriters and played for the company baseball team. He gained a reputation as the strikeout artist and the fastest pitcher in local semi-pro circles. This notoriety attracted the attention of professional scouts who were always interested in a southpaw who threw hard.

He signed with the Syracuse Stars for the 1923 season and began his professional career. Branch Rickey had just acquired fifty-percent interest in Syracuse for the Cardinal Farm System. Rickey was impressed with Bill and invited him to spring training with the Cardinals in 1924.

Rickey knew Bill was not ready for the Majors, he just wanted Card coaches and scouts to gauge his potential. After that first spring training, Rickey said, "he's so wild, he can barely hit the backstop, but there's a pitcher who someday will pitch and win a World Series game."[37] Intrigued by his speed Rickey sent Hallahan to Fort Smith of the Class C Western League to learn to harness his fastball.

Failure to control his blazing fastball earned Hallahan the nickname "Wild Bill". Hallahan's blazing left-handed speed earned him his first Major League action in 1925. He appeared in six games for the Cards, but his lack of control sent him back to the Minors. In 1926 Wild Bill was returned to St. Louis late in the season to help the Cards as they fought for the pennant. He pitched in 19 games and made a brief World Series appearance.

Still not Major League ready Wild Bill returned to the Minors where he spent the 1927 season with Syracuse and the 1928 season with the Houston Buffs. Finally, in 1929, he rejoined the St. Louis Cardinals for good.

Southpaw pitcher Bill Walker was a weak, sickly child who was not allowed to play sports because of a heart condition. He actually had a heart attack at age seven and doctors told his parents that Bill should refrain from physical activity for the rest of his life.

Bill loved baseball and finally convinced his parents to let him play. He became a good pitcher and was having no problems with his health until age 15 when he suffered another heart attack. Miraculously, Bill survived the second heart attack and resumed playing baseball.

A native of east St. Louis Bill attended a try out at sportsman's park, home of the Cardinals and Browns. Scouts were impressed with the frail lefty and he signed his first professional contract in 1920 at age 17.

Walker toiled for seven seasons with Minor League teams in different organizations. At one low point, thinking he was not Major League material, he decided to quit baseball. "I finally said to myself, Bill, you're through. You'll never be a Major League pitcher."[38]

Walker told his manager of his decision to give up on baseball. Informed that he had been traded to the Denver Bears, he decided to play another year.

That next year, 1927 proved to be a breakout season when he won 19 games for Denver. In September the New York Giants purchased his contract for a reported $25,000. He made his Major League debut on September 13, 1927.

Control problems plagued Walker and during the 1928 season he was sent down to the Toledo Mud Hens. By 1928 Bill was back with the Giants and found success in the Big Apple winning 17 games in 1930, followed in 1931 by a league leading 2.26 ERA and 16 wins.

His success in New York brought Bill media attention and he was considered one of baseball's most eligible bachelors. "He looks like a movie actor"[39] wrote the sporting news. Despite the media attention and his thirty suits of tailor-made clothes, Bill was shy and spurned the spotlight.

1932 proved to be the Giants worst season in 15 years as they fell to sixth place. Legendary manager John McGraw resigned mid-season and was replaced by player/manager Bill Terry. Walker was part of the problem, he lost 12 games while winning only 8 with a 4.14 ERA. A week after the 1932 season Bill was traded to the Cardinals.

His trade to the Cardinals was a homecoming for Bill who still lived with his parents in East St. Louis. 1933 was another losing season for Walker who finished with 9 wins and 10 losses for the fifth place Cardinals. Despite his 1933 record Frisch and Rickey were counting on Walker to be one of their key pitchers in 1934.

The Gashouse Gang was now assembled; however, they were not exactly a united band of brothers. There was jealousy, the players fought among themselves and the team was divided into cliques. Of course, Dizzy continued to be a thorn in Cardinal management's ass.

CHAPTER 16

"I wasn't thinkin' A nothin' out there but foggin' it through"

Teams hated to go into St. Louis to play the Cardinals in the summer of 1934. All other National League teams were north and east of St. Louis in New York, Boston, Philadelphia, Chicago, Pittsburgh, and Cincinnati, all cities with cooler summers than St. Louis, Missouri. Hall of fame catcher, Al Lopez said, "you'd come out of Boston with a cool breeze off the Charles River into the cauldron of the Mississippi valley, and the Cardinals would psyche you out. Sure, they had to be hot playing there three and four weeks at a time. Somehow, they'd get used to it or pretend they did, anyway."[1]

The summer of 1934 was especially hot, dry and dusty due to a weather phenomenon that came to be known as the dust bowl, or dirty thirties. The dust bowl was a period of severe drought that started in 1934 and continued for most of the rest of the decade.

The drought and poor farming methods turned top soil on the Great Plains into dust which winds blew away in giant clouds that blackened the skies. These choking black blizzards traveled from their origin in the Texas panhandle, Oklahoma, New Mexico, Colorado, and Kansas all the way to the east coast.

Mechanized farming equipment such as tractors and combines enabled farmers to cultivate the Great Plains. The native deep-rooted, moisture-retaining grasses were replaced by cash crops that needed more rain. When the rains did not come, the soil turned to dust and blew away.

The dust bowl devastated farm families. Because of crop failures, farmers were unable to pay mortgages, so they lost their land. Tens of thousands of displaced destitute people, now homeless, began to migrate west toward California. Unfortunately, the Great Depression had made economic conditions in western states little better than what they left behind. John Stienbeck chronicled this sad chapter of American History in his classic novel <u>The Grapes of Wrath</u>.

In addition to the miserable St. Louis weather, many Cardinal players had reputations for behavior that bordered on insanity.

Dizzy was notorious for throwing at batters. Other teams had heard about Diz hitting seven straight New York Giant batters in an exhibition game, because the Giants had scored seven runs off him in one inning. Of course, players knew better than to dig in on the old master. Leo the Lip said, "Diz would just stand there nodding his head until the batter was finished and then he'd yell, 'you all done? you comfortable? Well, send for the grounds keeper and get a shovel because that's where they're gonna bury you.' And-boom-down he'd go."[2]

Dizzy and his partner in crime Pepper Martin loved to show other teams that the Cardinals were immune to the stifling St. Louis heat. An opposing player said, "that crazy Pepper Martin and Dizzy Dean, they'd build a bonfire in front of their dugout, put Indian blankets around their shoulders, squat and rub their hands together over the fire as if they were cold."[3]

The suffocating heat, Diz beaning batters, Pepper throwing at runners, Lippy's blistering tongue, and Medwick's uncontrollable temper made St. Louis a thoroughly unpleasant place to play the Cards.

The Cardinals opened the regular season at sportsman's park in St. Louis on April 17th against the Pittsburgh Pirates. Lucky for the Pirates it

Me 'N' Paul

was spring, and the summer heat was yet to arrive. 7,500 fans showed up to watch Dizzy pitch the opener.

Opening day ceremonies included speeches, and a parade to the flagpole where Old Glory was raised as a brass band played the National Anthem. St. Louis mayor Walter Dickmann walked to the mound and borrowed Dizzy's cap and glove to throw out the first pitch. "Meanwhile Dizzy donned the mayor's derby and pranced around wearing his honor's 'iron hat'."[4]

Diz made short work of the Pirates giving them six hits and only one run. Ducky Medwick homered and Pepper Martin clouted two doubles as the Cards easily beat the Pirates 7 – 1.

"Yea, said Diz, sizing up his good beginning and puffing on a Camel, I guess the Ol' Flipper ain't changed none, but wait'll you fellas see my brother, Paul, tomorrow. He'll show 'em what this family has for breakfast."[5]

Paul Dean made his Major League debut on April 18, 1934. The visitor's dugout was occupied by the Pittsburgh Pirates, Dizzy's victims the day before. Paul talked about his first Major League action, "I wasn't nervous or nothin'. Nah, me 'n' Diz was never scared in our life. But this was my first game and I wanted to show 'em they'd have two of us to deal with. Then I heard Ol' Diz yell, 'fog one in there, boy', and that's what I reared back to do."[6]

Paul retired the first two Pirates to open the game, with two outs Paul Waner singled to center. Now only needing one out, Paul faced Buc Slugger Pie Traynor. Paul went into his stretch, held the runner at first and delivered his best fastball, Pie deposited it in the left field bleachers for a two-run homer. Paul induced the next hitter to ground out to Frisch to retire the side. The Cards failed to score in the bottom of the first and Paul took the mound to start the second inning. The first Buc batter, Gus Suhr, hit a home run into the right field pavilion. The next batter walked but was erased on a ground ball double play. A double to left field and a single to right made the score Pirates 4 Cards 0. Paul got the third out on a pop fly to the catcher. That ended Paul's Major League debut, five hits and four runs in two innings including two home runs.

The Cardinals rallied to tie the game in the seventh only to have Pirate rookie Cookie Lavagetto homer in the eighth for a 7 – 6 Buc win. Since the games was tied after Paul was pulled, he was not charged with the loss.

Manager Frankie Frisch commented on Paul's performance, "Paul was pitching them too good. He was shooting that fastball down the middle and the Pittsburgh hitters were meeting the ball. The next time he pitches I look for him to fool them."[7]

Pitchers had been complaining all spring about the new baseballs being used, calling them "rabbit" balls. Both the American and National leagues had adopted a new livelier baseball for the 1934 season. Owners were convinced that fans wanted to see more home runs and livelier baseballs would help boost attendance in those dark depression days, nine home runs on opening day and 16 on the second day seemed to show the plan was working.

Not everyone was pleased with the new power surge. New York columnist Damon Runyon wrote, "at the rate of 13 or so a day, there may be 2,000 homers hit by the end of the season, making the game more and more a matter of slug and run home. It seems as if all one has to do to hit a homer is to let the bat meet the ball."[8]

The third game of the Card-Pirate opening series saw Wild Bill Hallahan get shellacked by the Pirates 14 – 4. The Bucs left St. Louis unimpressed with Card pitching except for Dizzy Dean. The Pirates pulverized Cardinal pitchers for 21 runs in the two games that Diz did not pitch.

The Chicago Cubs came in for a two-game series and the Cardinals sent Tex Carleton to the mound for his first start of the regular season. Tex pitched a great game against Chicago, but Cub hurler Charlie Root was better, and Chicago won 2 – 1. The Cardinals had now won only one game while losing three in the new season.

The Cardinals sent Diz to the mound in the next game to stop the bleeding Chicago had been seeking revenge on Dizzy ever since he struck out 17 Cubs in one game the previous season. The single game strikeout record was humiliating enough, but then Diz went on the radio and ridiculed the entire Cub Team. "We had boys down in the Texas League better than them Cubbies taking care of our bats."[9] The Cubs were out to make Diz regret that radio interview.

The vengeful Cubs ravaged Dizzy for 6 hits and 4 runs in the first inning! Diz headed to the showers after only 3 innings, the Cubs had lit him up for 8 hits and 6 runs. Dizzy left the field to the mockery, hoots and jeers of the Chicago players, "tell them on the radio how good you are, big shot." Diz retorted, "them Cubbies can kiss my ass."[10]

Paul was called in to stop the carnage. The lust for revenge extended to any Dean, and the Cubs fell on Paul for 6 more hits and 2 more runs in only two innings. When the game was finally over Chicago had defeated St. Louis 15 – 2. The Cubs had pounded the Dean boys and two other Cards pitchers for 22 hits, while Chicago pitcher Lon Warneke allowed the Cards only one hit. With the home stand over, the Cardinals embarked on a long road trip.

The Cardinals traveled to Forbes Field in Pittsburgh for a three-game series with the Pirates. St. Louis lost the first game running their losing streak to five in a row. A game was postponed because of cold weather and finally on April 26th the Cardinals returned to the win column when Wild Bill Hallahan beat the Bucs 10 – 1. Neither Paul nor Diz pitched in that Pittsburgh series.

The Cardinals next went to Chicago for a three-game series with the Cubs. In the opener Chicago beat St. Louis 3 – 2 in 11 innings. Dizzy was rested and primed to re-establish his dominance over the hated Cubbies in the second game.

Once again, the Cubs had Dizzy's number. He was driven from the mound after only three innings after the Cubs scored 5 runs on 7 hits. Paul followed Diz into the fray but fared little better. He lasted only two innings giving up two runs on three hits, including a tremendous home run to Chuck Klien, which was almost a record breaker for distance. This was Paul's third bad outing in a row, although he still had not been charged with a loss. Paul's record was 0 – 0 with an ERA of 7.50.

After the Dean debacle, the Cardinals salvaged the last game of the Chicago series. Bill Walker tamed the Cubs 9 – 4. St. Louis' record stood at 3 wins and 7 loses, tied with Cincinnati for next to last place in the National League.

On the last day of April St Louis went to Cincinnati for a three-game series. The first game featured sorry play by both teams and the battle for sole possession of sixth place resulted in a ragged St. Louis victory. Dizzy started for the Cards and was staked to a five-run lead. He could not hold it. Diz was chased from the mound in the seventh as the Reds tied the score. Luckily, the Cardinals came back to win 10 – 6.

Carl Duncan

St. Louis beat the Reds the next two games to sweep the Cincinnati series, with no help from Paul and Dizzy. After nearly a month of the season Diz had won one game and lost two, Paul was 0 – 0, a long way from Dizzy's promised 45 wins.

Next up on the Card schedule were the Philadelphia Phillies. St. Louis beat Philadelphia 7 – 6 for their fifth consecutive victory, and Paul Dean picked up his first Major League victory. He did not deserve it. Paul relieved in the third and was cuffed around for 7 hits and 5 runs in five innings. Jess Haines had to come in to save the game. A Ducky Medwick bases loaded homer enabled Paul to leave the game with the lead and secure his first Major league win.

Paul's first four Major League appearances resulted in a truly ugly stat line; 11 innings, 21 hits, and 13 runs, including 4 home runs. These sorry performances convinced Paul's teammates he was not ready to compete against big league hitters. They thought Paul made his reputation by striking out a lot of Minor Leaguers under the lights at Columbus. Everyone seemed to agree "if he wasn't *Dizzy's* brother he would be long gone. That's the only reason they're keeping him up here."[11]

Paul stayed in the Majors but was regulated to the bullpen. Medwick's homerun helped Paul win his first big league game and ironically Ducky inadvertently helped Paul return to the starting rotation.

During batting practice, pitchers routinely shagged balls in the outfield. Southpaw starting pitcher Bill Walker suffered a broken ulna bone when struck on the forearm by a wicked line-drive off Ducky's bat during pre-game batting practice. Manager Frisch suddenly needed a starting pitcher. He turned to Paul.

"I was worried about Paul Dean." Frisch said, "the twenty-year-old boy obviously was overawed by his big brother. He was imitating Dizzy's style on the mound, but he lacked Dizzy's colossal self-confidence. I asked Paul to share a double porterhouse with me.

'When we play the Giants on our next homestand, 'I told him, 'I'm starting you in the third game. They're tough, but smart pitching can lick 'em. Let's analyze their batting form.' I was an infielder, not a pitcher, but I gave a good imitation of a pitching coach during that two-hour dinner. Dizzy's name was never mentioned. Paul listened. As I paid the check, he spoke his only words, 'thanks Mr. Frisch'."[12]

Me 'N' Paul

True to his word Frisch started Paul against the New York Giants on May 11th. In the first game of the series Diz shut-out the Giants 4 – 0. In the series' second game the Cards outlasted New York 5 – 4. The Giants sent their ace, the great Carl Hubbell, to oppose Paul in the third game.

A ladies' day crowd watched as Paul matched King Carl pitch for pitch and at the end of regulation play, the score was knotted at two apiece. In the bottom of the tenth, the Lip led off with a double. Paul came to the plate and hit a short fly to shallow right field, second sacker "Blondy" Ryan faded back and right fielder "Lefty" O'Doul thundered in after the pop-up, both yelling they had it. Neither could hear the other because of the feminine fans yelling so loud. Fearing a collision, each player slowed up and the ball fell in for a hit. "Pepper" Martin was walked to load the bases and Jack Rothbock came through with a base hit to win the game 3 – 2.

It was an improbable victory. No one, except Diz and Paul, expected a rookie to beat Carl Hubbell, the best left-handed pitcher in baseball. "I wasn't worried about me none", Paul said later, "and when me 'n' Diz saw they was warmin' up Hubbell on the other side, Diz says to me, 'beatin' him is gonna take another great pitcher and that's you, boy, so go on out there and do it,' and that's what I was a-fixin' to do."[13]

Paul had pitched his best game of the season, he went to full 10 innings allowed 9 hits, 3 walks, and struck out 5. Dizzy told reporters after the game, "them Giants don't have a pig's chance in winter of beatin' me 'n' Paul."[14]

Apparently, Frisch's two-hour steak dinner with Paul did not help because Paul said, "I wasn't thinkin' a nothin' out there but foggin' it through."[15] A victory for God-given talent over manager-given strategy.

New York avoided the Card sweep by winning game four of the series. The Giants battered Tex Carleton and Wild Bill Hallahan for a 6 – 4 win. St. Louis was now in third place with 14 wins, 9 losses and the woeful Brooklyn Dodgers coming to town.

Dizzy beat Brooklyn in the opening game 12 – 7 for his fourth win of the season and the Cardinals sixth win in the last seven games. St. Louis was winning and moving up in the standings. Just as their season was turning around, they began to fight among themselves. Predictably Ducky Medwick was the instigator.

Medwick's surly, moody personality made him unpopular with his teammates. Ducky loved to hit because that's how he made his money, more base hits, homers, and RBI's translated into bigger paychecks. Pitchers salaries were based for the most part on number of games won, and Ducky's lackadaisical sloppy outfield play sometimes cost Card pitchers wins.

St. Louis pitcher Jim Mooney said, "I used to hit fungoes to Medwick all the time, and shoot! You had to hit 'em right in his hands. He wouldn't even run to catch 'em. Medwick had a strange attitude. I never could figure him out."[16]

During the Brooklyn series in St. Louis, the Cards were taking batting practice. The pitchers were taking their turns when Medwick butted in to take extra cuts. When Tex Carleton objected, Ducky dropped his bat and threw a hard right to Tex's jaw, knocking him backwards. Carleton recovered and took several wild swings only to be punched again, causing Tex to end up with a black eye. After the fight, "both insisted the row arose on the spur of the moment and was not the aftermath of two defeats suffered by Carleton due to fielding mistakes by the man with whom he scuffled."[17]

The only Card who liked to fight more than Ducky Medwick was Paul Dean. Paul told about a run-in he had with Medwick. "Joe Medwick and me had a little scrap. I just happened to look over at him playin' cards at the table, and I was out of the pot, so I just looked at his hole card and he got mad. So, I thought I'd get up from the table and stomp the hell outta him. When I was getting' up he hit me in the eye. He hit me, and I was all over him. I was on him with my feet and everything else. They pulled me off and took me to the drawin' room and kept me there for about a hour."[18]

After the Medwick/Carleton fight, the Cards lost to Brooklyn 6 – 5 to split the series. (One game was rained out) the Cardinals left St. Louis on May 16th for a road trip, with the first stop in Boston.

At about this time sports writers finally settled on a nickname for Paul. After many failed attempts such as Harpo, Dizzier, Not So Dizzy, and Little Dizzy, they found a nickname that stuck. Red Newton, a Tampa, Florida sports columnist started referring to Paul as Daffy Dean in his columns. On May 19, 1934 Chicago sports writer Francis J Powers used

Me 'N' Paul

the nickname Daffy in an article that was picked up by the Consolidated Press Association and appeared in newspapers all across the country.

"First of all, the Cards have the Dean Boys, "Dizzy" and "Daffy". Dizzy is one of the game's best and since Daffy (Paul) received his baptism of big-league fire, he is looking like a winner and Frisch expects him to be one of the regular starters."[19]

Many years later Paul talked to Dallas morning news columnist Sam Blair about how he and Dizzy acquired their famous nicknames. "Dizzy got his nickname in the army and then some sports writer tagged me Daffy after I joined him in St. Louis, shoot, it didn't bother me. I always said it didn't matter what folks called me as long as they called me in time for supper."[20]

Paul pitched the opener in Boston, but before the game three Deans put on quite a show. Professional wrestler Man-Mountain Dean burst from the Boston Brave dugout. The gigantic bearded strongman rushed to the St. Louis dugout to confront the Cards. Dizzy produced a huge spear and he and Paul attacked the Giant to protect their teammates. "The man-mountain ended the monkey business by getting a headlock on the pitchers, one under each of his muscular arms."[21] The crowd clapped and roared their approval of the pre-game entertainment.

Paul proved his victory over the Giants was no fluke by beating the Boston Braves 5 – 3. He helped his own cause with two hits, a double and single. Paul struck out five, gave up one walk and nine hits while pitching his second consecutive complete game. It was his third straight win and the 14th for the Redbirds in the last 17 games.

Boston won the second game of the series 6 – 2 and the Cards won the rubber match behind Tex Carleton 2 – 1. St. Louis left Boston and headed to New York where Diz was scheduled to pitch the first game of the series. Paul had never been to New York City and Diz told reporters he was going to show his brother around the Big Apple, "I know that town like a chicken knows it's coop."[22]

The first game of the series was played on a sunny Sunday afternoon and 40,000 fans showed up to watch dueling aces. Fire balling Dizzy Dean for Frisch's Redbirds against screw balling Carl Hubbell for Terry's Titans. (A screwball broke the opposite way from a traditional curveball and Hubbell's was said to be almost unhittable).

Dizzy, always seeking any advantage, slit the long sleeves of his undershirt believing the flapping fabric would distract the New York hitter. Giant batters were baffled by Dizzy's fastballs shooting out from ragged sleeves and by the sixth they had only one hit. Homers by Ripper Collins and Ducky Medwick plus a bases loaded triple by Frisch sent King Carl to an early shower. With a big lead Diz eased up, clowned around and allowed the Giants some meaningless runs. The 9 – 5 final score made the game seem closer than it really was.

Fat Freddy Fitzsimmons, the second-best Giant hurler, was scheduled to pitch the next day, but a freak accident put him out of the game. "Fitzsimmons was warming up in front of the grandstand, minding his own business, when suddenly a bat flies out of the hands of Jim Mooney and cracks Fitz plunk in the kidneys. He fell like a stuck ox."[23]

Unknown and little used pitcher Joe Bowman got the start. (During the entire 1934 season Bowman won only 5 games) Wild Bill Hallahan pitched for the Cardinals but was bested by Bowman 5 – 2.

Paul was sent to the mound for the rubber match against the Giants. He pitched well and by the top of the ninth each team had scored four runs. Paul came to bat with one out and looped a single to center. Burgess Whitehead lined out and Paul was unable to advance leaving the Cards with two outs, Paul still on first. Jack Rothrock kept the inning going with a double, sending Paul to third. The Flash came to the plate needing a hit to win the game. Giant skipper, Bill Terry, knew Frisch was a seasoned clutch hitter and chose to walk Flash and pitch to Ducky Medwick. Medwick made him pay, blasting a triple chasing Paul, Rothrock and Frisch home, for a 7 – 4 lead.

Paul took the mound needing three outs. He struck out two pinch hitters, the third Giant grounded out to the Lip and Paul walked off with his fourth win and third consecutive complete game. He gave up 9 hits, while striking out 6 and walking 3.

Paul's fourth straight victory was all the leverage Diz needed to again demand more money for his little brother. He told reporters, "Paul won't pitch another ball for the St. Louis club until the team pays him a living wage."[24]

The strike ended as quickly as it started. Apparently, Frisch promised to get Paul a raise in pay when the team completed their current road trip and returned to St. Louis. Of course, the Flash had no authority to give Paul a raise, all he could do was talk to Sam Breadon and Branch Rickey on Paul's behalf. However, it placated Diz and Paul because neither missed a start.

"Let's forget it," Dizzy answered when asked about the strike. "Everything is going to be all right."[25]

"Paul also was reluctant to discuss the strike, but intimated that he had reason to suppose that a new contract would be offered."[26]

After the three game Giant series, the Cards moved across town and were beaten by the Brooklyn Dodgers 5 – 3. Tex Carleton won game two of the Dodgers series and the third game was rained out. The Cardinals traveled to Philadelphia for their next series.

Rain continued to dog the Cards as their second straight game was rained out. Diz had been scheduled to pitch the Sunday afternoon game and a large crowd was expected. Diz would now pitch the Monday game in front of a lot less fans.

The patrons who did show up certainly got their money's worth. Dizzy pitched a great game and after nine innings the score was tied 2 -2. Diz came to bat in the tenth. "He hammered out a home run, a mammoth clout into the left field bleachers against a 40- mile gale. This clinched the contest and sent the Cardinals bouncing up the ladder to second place."[27]

St. Louis made it to two wins in a row by beating the Phillies 10 – 0. Wild Bill Hallahan picked up the win and St. Louis traveled to Cincinnati for their next series.

The Cincinnati series began with a doubleheader on Memorial Day. Paul pitched the first game and after 6 innings he had a 7 – 2 lead. The Reds roared back with a 4 run seventh and as Paul toed the rubber to start the eighth his lead had shrunk to 7 – 6. The first Red batter singled and when Paul hit the next hitter Frisch had seen enough. The Flash signaled for Dizzy to finish what his brother had started. Diz stopped the Reds rally, the Cards scored 2 in the top of the ninth and Dizzy closed out Cincinnati for a 9 – 6 Card victory. Paul was credited with his 5th win, giving up 6 runs on 9 hits and 2 walks.

He struck out 5.

St. Louis won the second game of the doubleheader 9 – 2 behind Tex Carleton. Ducky Medwick did the damage ripping Cincy pitching for

5 hits in five at-bats, including a double and two triples. After the game Ducky told reporters, "I just smell the lettuce, I have two good friends in this world. Buckerinos and base hits. If I get base hits, I will get buckerinos. I smell World Series lettuce, and I'll get my two or three hits a day."[28]

Winning the Reds double dipper propelled St Louis into first place in the National League. Paul had a record of 5 wins and 0 losses and Diz was 6 – 2. St. Louis had won 24 games and lost 13.

The Cards finished the Cincy sweep with a 3 – 2 10-inning victory over the Reds. They departed for Pittsburgh for a four-game series with the Pirates at Forbes Field, with Dizzy scheduled to pitch the first game.

When the Cardinals arrived in Pittsburgh, Dizzy announced that he couldn't possibly pitch because of a sore arm. The "sore arm" was the result of a meeting in Cincinnati between Frisch and Branch Rickey. Instead of lobbying for an increase in Paul's salary, Frisch obtained Rickey's permission to take a hard line with the Dean Brothers.

Armed with Rickey's backing, Frisch met with Dizzy and laid down the law. He would not ask President Sam Breadon to give Paul a new contract and if Dizzy did not want to pitch, he could turn in his uniform. Dizzy told reporters he gave Frisch a verbal tongue lashing because of the manager's betrayal. "When me 'n' Paul went on strike in New York, Frisch promised he would plead our case to Mr. Breadon. Now Frank has turned his back on us." Diz then issued his ultimatum, "Paul must get $1,000 cash in hand, and there will be no compromising."[29]

Paul agree, "what Dizzy says is right. I was told in New York I'd be fixed up and I took that to mean I'd get me a new contract. Now, they're tellin' us to take our suits off. Goddamn, it's hard to make a dollar nowaday's."[30]

It was a classic standoff. St. Louis management seemed to hold all the cards. If Diz and Paul refused to play, they would not get paid. Also, they could not play for another Major League team because at this time there was no free agency. Players were bound to their teams until they were either sold or traded. Because of the reserve clause, players were at the mercy of the owners.

On the other hand, Paul and Diz held a pretty good hand. Frankie Frisch knew he could not win the Pennant without Dizzy, and Paul was proving irreplaceable as well. The old Flash really wanted that pennant in his first full year as Cardinal manager. Branch Rickey and Sam Breadon wanted a Pennant and they also wanted the gate attraction the Dean brothers provided.

Surely, a Pennant and World Series appearance was worth more than the $1,000 Diz demanded. Still the Cardinals did not want to renegotiate contracts mid-season, fearing a dangerous precedence that would open the floodgates for other player's demands.

Wild Bill Hallahan took the sore armed Dizzy's place and lost to the Pirates 4 – 3. Suddenly the impasse was bridged. Neither side said how the dispute was settled, but some money must have changed hands because now the Flash was Dizzy's best buddy and a great manager. Diz told sportswriters, "my arm's getting better fast. Tell Frank that I'll throw this arm off to win for old Frank and the boys. There never was a fellow like Frisch. Isn't he a pip? You know there must be something wrong with anybody who wouldn't pitch his arm off for old Frank. Show me a guy who says a word against old Frank and I'll bash his face in."[31]

It seems illogical that more promises from Cardinal management would have made Dizzy happy, and Paul did not receive a new contract. Therefore, a logical conclusion is that Paul received some sort of secret cash bonus.

Satisfied, at least for the time being, Dizzy pitched the first game of a doubleheader and the Cardinals beat the Pirates like a rabid dog winning 13 – 4. The Bucs came back to win the second game 6 – 3. Paul was called in to pitch during the eighth inning of the second game. The bases were loaded, and he gave up a triple, securing the Pirate win. Paul was not charged with the loss because he inherited the three runners that scored.

The Pirates won the third and final game of the series, beating Tex Carelton 4 – 2. The Cardinals then boarded a train back to St. Louis in first place but by the thinnest of margins, .015 of a percentage point.

First up on the Cardinal homestand, the hated Chicago Cubs. Paul took the mound eager to defend the Dean honor after the terrible shellacking the Chicagoans inflicted on him and Diz their prior meeting. The bruins continued their assault on Dean pitching with a single and homerun in the first for a 2 – 0 lead. Paul came to bat in the fourth with Leo the Lip on second and the score 2 – 1. He smashed a double scoring Durocher and tying the score 2 – 2. The Cards went on to win 6 – 3.

Paul went the distance striking out 7 and giving up 7 hits. He elevated his record to 6 – 0 and his batting average to .364.

Diz, still fuming from the humiliation dished out by the Cubs in Chicago, started the second game of the series. Paul had exacted his revenge on the Cubs, but Diz could not, the Bruins battered Dizzy for 9 hits and 5 runs in 5 innings sending him to an early shower. Jim Mooney and Jess Haines held the Cubs to only one more run, the Cards scored 6 and after nine innings the score was knotted at 6 apiece. The Cardinals were still in first place, but Chicago was only 1 game behind, so Frisch wanted this win. Although he had pitched nine full innings the day before the old Flash signaled for Paul Dean to save the game.

Paul pitched brilliantly through the tenth, eleventh and twelfth innings allowing no runs and no hits. The Cards came to bat in the bottom of the twelfth with the score still 6 – 6, then all hell broke loose.

Medwick was aboard at first with two outs, when Ripper Collins ripped a double to the wall Ducky lit out, never hesitating at second or third he thundered toward home with the winning run. Cub catcher Gabby Hartnett blocked the plate, but Ducky dove in headfirst and got a hand on the corner of the plate. Home plate umpire, Charley Rigler called Medwick out and the war was on. Frisch charged from the dugout and grabbed Rigler by the sleeve. Rigler turned around and swung his mask, which crashed against the Flash's jaw. Medwick and Coach Mike Gonzales joined the fray and the four men tussled until they were finally pulled apart.

Umpire Rigler was incensed at what he considered an attack by Frisch, Medwick and Gonzales, so he tossed them from the game. Paul was done after pitching 12 innings in two days and Tex Carleton took over in the top of the thirteenth. The mini-riot took all the fight out of St. Louis and the Cubs erupted for 7 runs to crush the Cards. The next day Chicago won the rubber match 1 – 0 as Card bats went cold.

The homestand continued as the Pirates invaded St. Louis for a three-game series. Tex Carleton pitched effectively, Medwick produced three hits and Rip Collins homered for a 6 – 2 Red Bird win.

The second Buc game was rained out, Dizzy took the mound for the series finale. Diz stopped Pittsburgh with 9 hits but only 2 runs. The Ripper had a home run and a double that powered the Cards to a 3 – 2 win.

Me 'N' Paul

Diz said after the game, "them Pirates ain't really that tough, if you know how to pitch, and us Deans know how to do it. Paul would have beaten them sure if the rain hadn't shortened the series, and from now on you can depend on the Deans winning two games of each series we play with the Pirates. Why, those Palookas are lucky whenever they get a run off me 'n' Paul."[32]

Next up on the homestand, the Boston Braves. Paul pitched a complete game giving up 13 hits and only 3 runs. He struck out 5 and walked 2. The Cards scored 7 runs as Paul picked up his seventh victory. The hitting stars were Collins Martin and Paul Dean. Ripper went 3 for 3 with a single, triple, and home run. Pepper also had a single, triple and homer in 5 at bats. Paul was 2 – 4. That victory gave the Cardinals 30 wins, the Dean brothers had accounted for half of those victories. Diz was 8 – 2 and Paul was 7 – 0.

Boston won the next two out of three games from St. Louis. Diz and Paul did not pitch in any of the three games. Leo the Lip almost single handily lost one of the games by making four errors. He redeemed himself the next dray by driving in 6 runs. Lippy Leo's best batting day of his career came just 24 hours after his all-time worst fielding performance.

Paul and Diz were rested and ready to pitch when the Philadelphia Phillies came to St. Louis on June 16th for a four-game series. Dizzy started the first game. Jimmy Wilson, Dizzy's old pal and former battery mate, now managed the Phillies. He really wanted to beat his old teammates, something he had been unable to do all season. Mission accomplished. Philadelphia plummeted Diz for 12 hits and 8 runs en route to an 8 – 2 win.

The next day brought a Sunday doubleheader with Paul starting game one and Wild Bill Hallahan starting the second. Paul pitched his best game as a Major Leaguer, registering his first shutout in a 6 – 0 victory. He held Philadelphia to 5 hits, with no Philly advancing past second base. He struck out 7 and walked only 2. Leo the Lip continued his torrid hitting driving in 3 runs with a double and 2 singles. Paul's eighth win tied him with Dizzy for most Card victories.

Philadelphia bounced back against Wild Bill in the second game and after six innings the Phillies led 5 – 3. As Wilson's boys prepared to bat in the top of the seventh, they were surprised to see Diz take the mound for the Cards. Although he pitched eight innings the day before, Diz wanted another shot at Wilson and the Phillies. He said to Frisch, "let me have 'em Frank."[33] Dizzy retired the Phil's in order and in the bottom of the seventh the Cards rallied. With men on base and Philadelphia clinging to a precarious lead, Wilson began to stall. The weather turned inclement with high winds, dark clouds and impending rain. "A storm was about to break and Jimmy Wilson decided if he could delay things the elements would come to his aid, prevent the game's completion and protect his team's lead."[34] Wilson would bring a pitcher in, let him take his warm-up pitches, pitch to one batter and then put in another pitcher to repeat the stalling maneuver. Since the rules provided that a manager could change pitchers as often as he wanted as long as each pitcher faced one batter, there was nothing the umpires could do to prevent the obvious ploy.

Wilson's delaying tactic did not work. The rain held off, the Cardinals scored four runs and won the game 7 – 5. Diz picked up an unlikely victory and moved past Paul in the win department 9 games to 8.

The two teams had Monday off after the Sunday doubleheader. Tex Carleton started Tuesday for St. Louis, but Philly battered him, Mooney and Lindsey for 8 runs. At the end of six innings the score was tied 8 – 8. The Cardinal bullpen was overworked, so Paul volunteered to pitch, despite the fact that on Sunday he had hurled a nine-inning shutout.

Paul pitched scoreless ball for five innings, five Phillies struck-out, none walked, one singled but was erased trying to steal second base. The game would have Paul's ninth victory if the Cardinals could have scored a run for him in the seventh, eighth, ninth, tenth or eleventh innings. The Cards could not and in the twelfth, it was apparent that Paul had been asked to shoulder too much of a burden. He weakened giving up 2 runs on 3 hits. The Cards did not score in the bottom of the twelfth and Paul was tagged with his first loss of the 1934 season.

Casey Stengel, a rookie Major League manager brought his Brooklyn Dodgers to St. Louis for four games. Stengel was a former Major League outfielder. He was known more for his practical jokes (once while at bat he tipped his cap to the crowd and a sparrow flew out) and his funny paradoxical statements (good pitching will always beat good hitting and vice versa) than for his playing skills. Casey went on to become a Hall of Fame manager due to his incredible success managing the New York

Yankees from 1949 – 1960. Stengel managed the Yanks to five consecutive World Series Championships, a feat unmatched in Major League history.

The Dodgers handed Wild Bill Hallahan his fourth straight beatdown in the initial contest, winning 9 – 5. The Cardinals were counting on Wild Bill to be one of the mainstays of the pitching staff. A record of 2 wins and 7 losses showed he was failing miserably. While referring to himself in the third person, Hallahan conceded he was having an off year and acknowledged he was the shortest Card pitcher, "a fellow blows himself to a bad year every now and then. Maybe this is a bad one for Little Bill."[35]

Dizzy's wife and business manager, Pat Dean, just had to point out the disparity in Cardinal contracts. Dizzy and Paul's combined contracts totaled $10,500 and they had won 17 games. Two-win Wild Bill's contract called for $12,500. "This struck Mrs. Dizzy as eminently unfair, which it may be at that."[36]

Paul kept pace with Dizzy by pinning a second straight defeat on Brooklyn. He gave up 2 runs on 8 hits and 1 walk while striking out 10 batters. St. Louis scored 7 runs led by Rip Collin's sixteenth homer and Frankie Frisch's 2 doubles and 3 singles.

This was the Dodgers first encounter with Paul and they were impressed. As good as Dizzy was against them, the Brooklyn batters judged Paul the superior pitcher. "According to the Dodgers, the kid of the family has a better fastball and better control."[37]

Brooklyn catcher Al Lopez was especially impressed, "that fellow is a real pitcher," he said "he just winds up and explodes in front of you, and don't let anybody tell you he isn't smart out there on the rubber. I don't think he made a mistake all afternoon. All of our players think he's a wow!"[38] Manager Casey Stengel said, "there's too many of those Dean boys."[39]

The fourth and final game of the series produced an odd situation with historical implications. Wild Bill Hallahan finally ended his four-game losing streak as he was credited with the win in a relief role. However, the day after the game it appeared that Dizzy might snatch Wild Bill's victory away from him.

Wild Bill entered the game in the top of the sixth with the Dodgers ahead 3 – 0. He gave up one run on two hits. Bill was lifted for a pinch hitter in the bottom of the sixth and the Cardinals went on to score five runs to take a 5 – 4 lead. Dizzy came in and saved the game by shutting out Brooklyn for the final three innings giving up only two hits.

Since Hallahan was the pitcher of record in the sixth when St. Louis took the lead he was credited with the win, just as he would under today's rules. However, at that time official scorers decided which pitcher received credit for wins and losses in games where two or more pitchers were used. There were no written rules for deciding until 1940.

Evidently the official scorer, Martin Haley, was having second thoughts about crediting Hallahan with the win. Obviously Dizzy pitched better than Wild Bill, holding on to a one run lead for three pressure packed innings to secure the Cardinal victory. Under today's rules Dizzy would be credited with a save, but that option was not available to Haley in 1934. He therefore decided to seek a second opinion.

"Dizzy Dean, who blanked Brooklyn the last three innings yesterday to protect a one-run lead, may be credited with the victory. Martin Haley, official scorer, originally named Bill Hallahan the winning pitcher, but announced that he would set forth the facts in a report to President John Heydler and ask him to make a decision."[40]

The last four games of the homestand featured the first place New York Giants. The Cardinals were in second place only two games back, nipping at the Titans tails. Temperatures, in St. Louis soared to over 100 degrees and even the umpires shed their coats and called the games in their shirtsleeves.

The Giants won the opener 9 – 7, pushing the Cards three games back of the league leaders. The stifling heat took its toll on the pitchers. Nine were used in the game, five by the Cards and four by the Giants.

The second game was not advertised as the St. Louis Cardinals vs the New York Giants. Posters and newspaper ads announced a battle between the Great Dizzy Dean against King Carl Hubbell. Baseball's best righthander vs baseball's best lefthander.

Fans were irate and Card manager Frisch was pissed when Dizzy turned up sick. Apparently, this was not another one of Dizzy's ploys to extract more money from the Cardinals as he was hospitalized to be treated for dehydration.

When Frisch learned Diz was unavailable to pitch, he vented his anger to reporters, "my gang should be pitching hay instead of baseballs. At least they'd be earning their pay. This leaves me with one pitcher, Paul Dean, and he won't be ready until tomorrow."[41]

Frisch sent Hallahan to pitch in place of the absent Dizzy. As Wild Bill went to the hill instead of Diz as advertised, the fans showed their displeasure by raining boos down upon the hapless Hallahan. Of course, the Giants bombed him en route to a 10 – 7 win.

The two consecutive Giant victories left St. Louis four games behind New York. The Cards would have to win the last two games of the series just to be back where they started. Paul was ready to get the first one and Frisch hoped Diz would recover enough to pitch the last game of the homestand.

The Cardinals gave Paul plenty of run support, after five innings St. Louis led 13 – 2. Armed with a safe lead Paul eased up and coasted to an easy 13 – 7 win; his tenth of the year with only one loss. Dizzy also had 10 wins to go with 3 losses. The Card record was 37 wins and 25 losses. Since the Dean boys were 20 – 4, the rest of the Cardinal pitchers had won 17 and lost 21.

Despite the heat wave steaming the diamond to a sizzling 115 degrees, Diz left his hospital bed ready to show the Giants two Deans were double trouble. Dizzy struggled, but going into the top of the ninth the Cards led 7 – 6. Diz retired the first two batters, but needing only one out for the win, he gave up three successive singles which erased the lead and left the score tied 7 – 7. Card catcher Bill Delancey delivered a walk-off homer in the bottom of the ninth.

Although Mooney was the pitcher of record when Delancey's homerun won the game, official scorer Martin Haley gave the victory to Dizzy. That decision did not please some of the other Cardinal pitchers, who were resentful of the Dean's publicity and the fan's adulation. One of them said, "you can bet that if the positions of Mooney and Dean had been reversed, Dizzy still would have received the credit."[42]

Ironically this was Dizzy's second controversial victory of the day. Earlier the Cardinals received news that National League President John Heydler had awarded Dizzy credit for the June 23rd victory over Brooklyn, taking the win away from the long-suffering Wild Bill Hallahan.

Carl Duncan

After their split with New York, the Cardinals departed St. Louis for an extended road trip. The first stop was in Cincinnati where the Reds ripped Tex Carleton for seven runs in a 7 – 1 romp over the Cards.

The second game in Cincy produced Paul's second loss of the season. Paul entered the game with two on and no outs in the bottom of the eighth with the Cardinals ahead 3 – 2. He retired the first two Reds batters and needed only one out to put out the fire. An infield single, a walk, another single, a double and another walk ended Paul's day still needing that elusive third out. Jim Mooney relieved Paul but was ineffective and when the inning was finally over nine Reds had scored, all after two outs. The Cards lost 11 – 4.

Again St. Louis had lost the first two games of a four-game series. Frisch turned to Dizzy to turn the series around, in the opening game of a scheduled doubleheader.

Dizzy locked up in a titanic battle with Reds pitcher Tony Freitas, nearly five hours and seventeen innings later both Dean and Freitas finally left the game with the score tied 6 – 6. Diz picked up the win when the Cards scored two runs in the eighteenth inning.

The second game of the doubleheader was essentially the third game of the day since the first game had lasted eighteen innings. The game had to be called because of darkness after five innings with the score tied 2 – 2.

The Cardinals left Cincinnati battered after losing two out of three games. With Dizzy unavailable for the up-coming Cub series after pitching 18 grueling innings against Cincy, things looked grim. The Chicago series offered a chance for third place St. Louis to gain ground on the second place Cubs. New York occupied first place in the standings. That chance now appeared slim.

Paul pitched the opening game of the Cub series on only two days rest. He put up goose eggs in the first, second, fourth, fifth and sixth innings. However, in the third he gave up three runs. The Cubs led 3 – 1 going into the bottom of the seventh when things went to hell.

The Cubs had loaded the bases with only one out when Chuck Klein lifted a high pop fly in front of home plate. The Windy City lived up to its name as a gust of wind blew the ball out of Card catcher Bill Delancey's grasp. A run scored, and Klein was safe at first. An irate Frankie Frisch went jaw to jaw with home plate ump Bill Klem demanding to know why he had not made the obvious call; batter out under the infield fly rule. (The rule is designed to prevent a defensive player from intentionally dropping a pop fly in order to get a double play) when there are men on first and second or the bases are loaded with less than two outs, a batter who hits a pop fly to the infield is automatically out.

Dizzy and Coach Mike Gonzales joined Frisch loudly demanding an explanation. Umpire Klem was not in an explaining mood, so he threw the Flash, Diz and Gonzo out of the game. Frisch would not leave and refused to let his players take the field.

Finally, Frisch agreed to continue the game but told Klem he was playing under protest and would personally inform National League President John Heydler of Klem's utter disregard for the rules of baseball.

The Cubs went on to win the game 7 – 4, with Paul absorbing his third loss of the season. This was his first defeat in a game he started, the other two losses came in games where he pitched in relief.

For his part in the fracas Frisch was fined $100. For "extremely bad conduct in defying a league umpire by repeatedly refusing to resume play." Diz was not fined, but Coach Gonzales drew a $25 fine for "unreasonable delay of game and repeated threats to punch an umpire."[43]

Frisch lashed out at President Heydler telling him, "you're making a joke of the National League by permitting your umpires to assume a belligerent attitude. I can't understand why you don't make your umpires stay awake, attend to business, and call plays right."[44] The fines stood.

With Chicago beating Paul in the first game and Dizzy unavailable, the prospect of three more games with the Cubs without the Deans appeared bleak. The next two games would have to be entrusted to Wild Bill Hallahan and Tex Carleton. This pair combined had been knocked from the mound in nine straight starts. Jim Mooney would have to be promoted from the bullpen to start the last game of the series.

Surprisingly, Wild Bill beat Chicago 7 – 3 in the second game, and Tex tamed the Cubs 6 – 2 in the third game. With a chance to win the series three games to one, Mooney pitched well for five innings. However, he folded up shortly thereafter and Chicago won the game 6 – 2.

The last series before the All-Star break was another encounter with the Cincinnati Reds. In the first game St. Louis paraded seven pitchers form the mound to the showers in a 16 – 15 loss. The next day the Cards evened the series 1 – 1 as Wild Bill Hallahan won his second straight game, beating Cincy 10 – 4.

The Cincinnati series concluded with a Sunday doubleheader featuring the Reds facing Dean and Dean. Dizzy pitched the first game, struck out ten Reds and won 6 – 1 for his fourteenth victory of the year.

Paul started the second game of the double dipper. He gave up one run in the first, pitched a perfect second and a memorable third inning.

After one out in the third, two base hits and an intentional walk loaded the bases. Paul ran the count even at two balls and two strikes. He then broke a curve across the plate for an apparent strikeout. When the ump signaled ball three, Paul objected but to no avail. With the bases juiced and the count full he had to groove one which Harlin Pool poled out of the park for a grand slam.

The episode escalated when Leo the Lip accosted the home plate umpire about that bad call. He was quickly ejected from the game. Suddenly, Paul charged the Reds dugout.

"Paul wanted to fight either the Reds as a whole or some hard-riding bench jockey or the whole wide world. He just wanted to battle, and he wasn't choosy as to the identity or the number of his opponents."[45] Dizzy and other Card players intercepted Paul before he reached the Cincy dugout. Paul continued pitching, but he was still shaking with anger and gave up two more runs before retiring the side. Cincinnati won 8 – 4.

That loss was Paul's third in a row. Frankie Frisch commented on Paul's slump, "it's too bad in a way that Paul hasn't Dizzy's happy-go-lucky disposition. Paul is more serious. Dizzy is just plain crazy."[46]

At the All-Star break St. Louis was in third place, 4 games behind the league leading New York Giants and 2 games behind the second place Chicago Cubs. The Cardinals record was 43 wins 31 losses. Dizzy had won 14 and lost 3 and Paul had 10 wins to go with 4 losses. The Dean boys had combined for over half of the Card wins and were over half way to Dizzy's predicted 45 wins.

CHAPTER 17

"I hope they pitch that Hubbell against me, I'll beat him sure."

The second annual All-Star game took place in New York City at the polo grounds on July 10, 1934. The teams were selected by fans voting. However, the American and National league managers, Joe Cronin and Bill Terry were not bound by the fans vote.

The game itself was not popular with players or managers. The players did not receive extra money for playing in the game and managers were concerned an injury to a player could cost them a pennant. The proceeds from the game went to an association devoted to the relief of sick and destitute ex-major leaguers.

Bill Terry, player/manager of the World Series Champion New York Giants, stuck to the fan voting more so than Joe Cronin, player/manager of the American League champ Washington senators. However, both All-Star managers went against the fan's wishes and chose some players for their squads who had not received the majority of votes at their positions.

"The popular poll for the All-Star teams has been rudely disregarded; that the great masses of fans have been brazenly affronted and mocked and as a result, the annual All- Star game designed to promote additional interest in the National pastime, may react with the opposite effect."[1]

Paul Dean was one of the players fans voted into the game who was left off the team by Terry. He chose instead Boston Brave's pitcher Fred Frankhouse. Otherwise National league Skipper Terry stuck with the people's choices for the remainder of the pitching staff; Giant Carl Hubbell, Card Dizzy Dean, Cub Lon Warneke, and Dodger Van Lingle Mungo. Three other Cardinals were on the National League roster, Frankie Frisch, Ducky Medwick, and Pepper Martin.

Immediately preceding the All-Star game Dizzy had pitched 28 innings in nine days. Reporters asked Diz if that heavy workload would affect his performance against the American league's slugging line-up. "Nah" he answered, "I could go a week on bread and water and still beat them American leaguers."[2]

While Diz, Ducky, Pepper, and the Ol' Flash traveled to New York City for the All-Star game, the rest of the Cardinals went to Elmira, New York to play an exhibition game. Attendance at the game between the Cardinals and Elmira Red Wings was sparse because the All-Star game was being broadcast on radio, and fans stayed home to listen. The Cards had a radio in their dugout and picked up parts of the All-Star game amidst much static.

At the polo grounds Babe Ruth and Lou Gehrig entertained 50,000 fans with pre-game batting practice by blasting balls over the fence. Both the National and American league teams consisted of 15 position players and 5 pitchers, of these 40 players, 28 would eventually be inducted into the Hall of Fame.

Home team was the National league and screw balling Carl Hubbell went to the hill to start the game. He immediately pitched himself into a jam. Detroit's Charlie Gehringer led off the game with a single. Washington Senator Heinie Manush followed with a walk. Next to face King Carl were three of the greatest sluggers of all time, Hall of Famers Babe Ruth, Lou Gehrig, and Jimmie Foxx. With two on and nobody out the situation appeared dire.

The Babe was caught looking at a third strike. Sweet Lou struck out swinging, but Gehringer and Manush pulled a double steal ending up on second and third. The crazed capacity crowd was insane with anticipation, two outs, men on second and third with the Great Jimmie Foxx batting. Double X was no match for Hubbell's screwball, he struck out swinging. "The crowd lifted the polo grounds six feet off the ground with a roar and then set it down again."[3]

First to the mound for the American league was Lefty "El Goofo" Gomez. Leading off for the Nationals Frankie Frisch drove the second pitch he saw into the left-field stands to give the senior circuit a 1 – 0 lead. El Goofo survived the first inning without further damage.

Another Hall of Famer, Al Simmons, led off the second inning. Hubbell hummed three strikes past him. Four future Cooperstown inductees, four K's. Washington player/manager Joe Cronin became King Carl's fifth straight strikeout victim. Later reporters asked Hubbell what he threw to Ruth, Gehrig, Foxx, Simmons and Cronin. "Screwballs" King Carl replied, "I figured they saw fastballs and curves every day but that they didn't see a screwball very often. So, I gave them nothing but screwballs."[4]

Hubbell's historic heroics concluded after three innings without anymore strikeouts. In the bottom of the third Card Ducky Medwick padded the National league lead to 4 – 0 with a three-run homer off Gomez, once again showing his bad ball hitting expertise, "when Joe Medwick got that homerun, he hit a ball high over his head. How anybody can get so much power on a ball at that height is a mystery."[5]

El Goofo Gomez was irate that Ducky had hit a high outside pitch over the fence. Gomez screamed at Medwick as he rounded the bases, "you no-good Hungarian bastard. I'll never give you anything you can hit again. I'll put 'em all right down the middle." Ducky replied, "I'm not worried your control ain't that good."[6]

The Americans mounted their comeback scoring two in the fourth off Lon Warneke. They scored six more in the fifth, chased Warneke and continued their onslaught on Brooklyn Stalwart Van Lingle Mungo. The Nationals countered with three runs and at the end of five innings, the American league led 8 – 7.

Enter Dizzy Dean, who upon being named to the All-Star team gave the American league some bulletin board material. Diz suggested that

Carl Duncan

American league hitters might be spooked by his pitching prowess, "where they hidin'? Prob'ly have their heads under the covers somewhere."[7]

As Diz entered the game at the start of the sixth inning Paul was in Elmira, New York listening to the All-Star game on radio in the Card dugout.

Radio – "Dizzy Dean goes in for the Nationals."
Paul Dean – "Come on Diz!"
Mike Gonzales – "Who's pitchin'?"
Paul Dean – "Diz"
Radio – "Foxx fanned."
Paul Dean – "I guess Diz is bearing down in there today."
Jim Mooney – "Who's pitching now?"
Paul Dean – "Diz is. He just fanned Foxx. Hot Dog!"
Radio – "Simmons is up."
Tex Carleton – "Well, Diz won't fan this guy."
Paul Dean – "Oh, yeh?"
Radio – "Simmons hits to right and Frisch and several others are after it. It's got away from Frisch. It will be scored as a double."
Paul Dean – "Lucky stiff."
Radio – "Joe Cronin up, Cronin doubles. Simmons scoring."
Leo Durocher – "Who's pitching?" Paul Dean – "Oh, Diz is – or was." Radio – "Dickey walked."
Paul Dean – "Nice pitchin' Diz. Two doubles and a walk. Cripe, I could do better than that. Great going, Diz!"
Jess Hanes – "Who's pitching?"
Paul Dean – "Diz and he's lousy. I'm sick of this game. That brother of mine is lousy today."[8]

Dizzy escaped the sixth with only one run scored and pitched a scoreless seventh and eighth. Frank Frankhouse closed the game without giving up a run in the ninth, but the National league was unable to score and lost the game 9 – 7.

The American league batsmen did not impress Dizzy. "Just a bunch of wild swinging sluggers,"[9] he said.

The regular season resumed on July 11th with the Cards in Philadelphia for a four-game set. The Phillies dealt the Cards a 5 – 2 loss, in the opener. Tex Carleton was the losing pitcher.

In the next game, first of a doubleheader, Paul retired Philly in order during the first and second innings. When he came to bat in the third, Paul hit a hard grounder and was safe on the second baseman's error. Pepper Martin singled, and Paul tore around second and headed for third. A moments indecision almost cost Paul a season ending injury.

As he approached third Paul appeared undecided about whether to slide or go in standing up. He elected to stay up, beat the throw but caught his cleat in the bag and went down hard. Paul had to be carried from the field by Diz and three other Cards. He was taken to the hospital for x-rays. If Paul's ankle was broken, as he feared, a brilliant rookie season was over. A potential disaster for the St. Louis Cardinals loomed.

Jim Mooney went in to pitch for the Cards in the bottom of the third with a 2 – 0 lead. He could not hold it. Dizzy was called to the rescue in the sixth inning, pitched 3 2/3 innings, struck out eight and racked up his fifteenth victory of the season.

The Cardinals lost the second game of the doubleheader behind Bill Hallahan. The Phils pelted Wild Bill for 6 runs on 7 hits in three innings and coasted to an 8 – 3 win. The fourth game of the series was rained out, but before the Cards left Philly, they received good news. Paul Dean's ankle was just sprained not fractured, he was limping badly and using a cane, but he was lost for only 10 – 14 days not the entire season.

Fortunately for the Cardinals, the pitcher whose injury gave Paul his chance to start had recovered. Southpaw Bill Walker was ready to make his first start since early May when a line-drive off Ducky's bat fractured his left arm.

Walker's long-awaited start came in Brooklyn against the Dodgers on July 14th. The lowly seventh place Dodgers mauled Walker and his fellow Card hurlers for 10 runs on 11 hits and 9 walks. The sloppy Cards also committed 3 errors. Cardinal batsmen could only get 4 hits off 22-year-old rookie Johnny Babich, who was making his first Major League start.

St. Louis exacted revenge on the Dodgers in the next day's doubleheader. Dizzy pitched the first game and shut out the Dodgers on 4 hits, winning 2 – 0. Diz helped his own cause by clouting a homerun in the eighth. Dodger catcher, Al Lopez said Diz was unhittable that day. "A combination of Ty Cobb, Napoleon Lajoie and Rogers Hornsby couldn't have hit that guy this afternoon. That ball came up there so fast if jumped like a jackrabbit when it crossed the plate."[10]

Tex Carleton was the winning pitcher in the second contest, but Ducky Medwick was the star of the game. "Medwick completely ruined the Dodgers with 2 homeruns and 5 runs batted in. The first homer he hit "off his ear." It was high and inside."[11]

After the games were over Diz dashed from the players' gate and snagged a taxi just as it was leaving the curb. When he discovered there was already a passenger occupying the backseat Diz assured the rider that today was his lucky day because he would be sharing a cab with the great one himself, Dizzy Dean.

As Diz settled in for the ride to his hotel he recognized the other passenger, St. Louis sportswriter J. Roy Stockton. Delighted, Dizzy began to spin his tales. "I sure did pour it on them Dodgers today, didn't I? Boy, did I have Casey Stengel burnin' up! But I like Brooklyn. They got good guys writin' for the papers over here. I like Tommy Holmes and Bill McCullough and that McGowan. They says nice things about me and I'm nice to them."

"I give 'em a scoop last time we're here. It's funny, but their bosses all comes up with the same idea the same day. Told 'em to get a piece about Ol' Diz. Well, Tommy come first and wanted to know where I was born, and I told him Lucas, Arkansas, January 16, 1911. Then it wasn't two minutes after he leaves that McCullough comes along, and doggone if he don't want the same piece. Now, I wasn't going to have their bosses bawl 'em out for both getting' the same story, so I told Mack I was born at Bond, Mississippi – that's where my wife comes from – and I pick February 22, which is giving George Washington a break. McGowan was next. He's with the Times. I guess me 'n' Paul has helped to get jobs for a lot of guys. McGowan wanted the same story, but I give him a break, too, and says Holdenville, Oklahoma, August 22. Now each goes back and can tell their editor they got a scoop about Ol' Diz."

"But Dizzy, which is your official birthday?" Stockton asked.

"I'll swear I'm mixed up myself now, but I believe I'll keep 'em all. Maybe I'll add Bradenton, Florida, especially if they change the name to Deanville, like they said. Four birthdays shouldn't ought to be too many for a great pitcher like me."

"Here we are at the hotel. Take care of the cab, will you, Roy? I gotta see the Ol'

secretary and get some dough. Boy, did I pour it on them Dodgers today?"[12]

When Stockton's story about Dizzy's different dates and places of birth appeared in the St. Louis Post-Dispatch, fans were confused as to where or when Diz was born. For his part Dizzy never bothered to clear up the confusion. Maybe a great pitcher did indeed need multiple birthdates and birthplaces.

No game was scheduled for July 16th, the day after St. Louis' sweep of the Dodger doubleheader. On that day off the Cardinals received some astonishing news. The controversial infield fly rule game would be replayed! National League President John Heydler ruled that the infield fly by Chuck Klein in the July 2 game between the Cards and Cubs should have been called an out.

Heydler added that the game must be replayed from the point where the dispute arose, with the same players in the same positions. The game was to be resumed in the seventh inning and played prior to the scheduled July 31 Card-Cub game.

Brooklyn and St. Louis split the remaining two games of the series. The Dodgers beat Wild Bill Hallahan and Jess Haines 7 – 6 and Bill Walker won his first game since coming back from injury, 5 – 3. Duckey Medwick was the outstanding player of the Card-Dodger series. He had 10 hits, including 4 homers, a triple, 2 doubles and 11 R.B.I.'s.

The Cardinals moved on to Boston and Diz beat the Braves 4 – 2 for his seventeenth win of the season. Tex Carleton made it two in a row over Boston beating them 5 – 1.

Wild Bill Hallahan started the third game of the series but was knocked out of the game by a line drive that dislocated his left index finger. Jim Mooney relieved and won his first game since May 10th. The Cards won 5 – 3 led by the hitting of catcher Spud Davis, who had three hits and drove in two runs. However, hitting help was provided to Spuds by a supernatural force.

The superstitious Spud liked to have teammate Dazzy Vance chant a Seminole Indian prayer over his bat before each plate appearance. The dazzler was happy to perform the chant and it was working that day because Spud singled in the second inning and again in the fourth. When he came to bat in the fifth Spud realized Dazzy had been sent to the bullpen and there would be no Seminole magic to empower his bat. With the useless lumber he weakly grounded out.

When Spud saw he was likely to get another at-bat in the seventh with the score tied, he panicked, knowing he needed that Seminole Indian prayer chant. Spud pleaded with utility infielder Pat Crawford to carry his bat to the bullpen so Dazzy could do his chanting. "Against his better judgement, Crawford carried the Davis war club out to the bullpen for the Vance Seminole medicine. Dazzy willingly quit warming up for a minute stroked the bat affectionately and muttered the words of the Seminole Chiefs."[13]

Armed with his recently blessed bat Spud strode to the plate with the bases loaded and the score tied 3 – 3. He promptly drilled a single up the middle driving in two runs, which proved to be the margin of victory.

Since Dizzy had pitched two days earlier and Paul was out with a sprained ankle, the Cards faced Boston in a Deanless doubleheader. Bill Walker won the first game 5 – 4 and the old Seminole prayer chanter, Dazzy Vance, was pressed into duty in the second contest due to Hallahan's dislocated digit. The Dazzler must have saved some Seminole magic for his aging right arm, because he beat the Braves 4 – 2.

The five-game sweep of the Boston series elevated the Cardinal's season record to 52 wins and 35 losses, third place in the National League. They were four games back of the league leading New York Giants and only one game behind the second place Chicago Cubs. With a four-game series against the Giants next on the Cards schedule, St. Louis had a good opportunity to gain some ground on the World Champs.

In game one of the Giant series Diz continued his dominance over New York, winning for the fourth straight time. It was Dizzy's eighteenth win of the year and tenth in succession. Diz did not have his best stuff in the 6 – 5 Card victory, but that did not curb his confidence.

"It doesn't look like those fellows could ever beat me, does it."[14] "Give Ol' Diz a run or two after five or six innings and the other fellows might as well fold up."[15] Diz said after the game.

New York evened the series at one apiece when Giant "Tarzan" Parmelee shut out the Cards 5 – 0. "With no Deans, Dizzy or otherwise, the Giants swung sharply back to their winning ways."[16] Tex Carleton took the loss proving a Card not named Dean could not beat the Giants.

Paul's ankle had healed enough for him to start the series third game, his first action since July 12th. Evidently Dizzy's confidence was rubbing off on Paul. He told reporters; "I hope they pitch that Hubbell against me, I'll beat him sure, and then we'll take three out of four because if we beat Hubbell the Giants ought to fold up. Sure, my ankle is all right. I can run as fast as ever. I can throw my full weight on it when I pitch without feeling any pain, and after all this rest I ought to be able to throw a ball through a brick wall."[17]

"You're right, Paul" coach Mike Gonzales agreed. "You throw him through two brick walls. I know, because I catch you in warm-up, and my hand you almost knock him off."[18]

Paul would get to face All-Star hero Hubbell, but he would have to wait one day as rain delayed the series. Since there was no game to cover, New York sportswriters had to find material to fill their columns. With Dizzy Dean in town they knew where to go. As New York World-Telegram reporter Tom Meany said. "Nobody will ever need a rubber hose to get information from Diz. He will talk about anything at any time."[19]

With sports reporters gathered, Dizzy expounded on his pitching philosophy; "Power and more power. Smart pitching, this so-called pitching to weaknesses of hitters is bunk. You finally get so that you're outsmarting yourself. I got myself in a jam trying to be smart against the Giants Monday. With a couple of men on base, Frisch, Durocher and Delancey flocked around me giving advice. I listened and tried to do as I was told. And I only got in more trouble. Then I says to myself, 'Phooey on that smart stuff', and I just reared back and let 'er go. I struck out Watkins and Critz, and we were out of that jam."[20]

On physical fitness; "I don't have to worry about weight. I'm about 180 now, and I never go above 188. I pitch best when I'm eating lightly. Light breakfast, no lunch, and then a good dinner with a nice steak. I don't drink coffee, use milk instead. Smoke cigarettes but only after meals. Don't touch liquor. Take plenty of exercise. Sleep in my pajamas, uppers and lowers, taking no chances of kicking off the clothes and catching cold."[21]

The rain-out was made up the next day as the first game of a doubleheader. The contest appeared to be a mismatch. The first place

World Champion New York Giants with ace of aces, All-Star game and World series hero, King Carl Hubbell on the mound at home against 20-year-old rookie Paul Dean and the rag-tag Cards.

As it turned out, the game was a mismatch. Paul dominated the Giants and the Cards dismantled King Carl. Seven Card runs drove Hubbell from the mound after only four innings, and Paul only gave up two runs in seven innings. He left the game with a 7 – 2 lead.

Not wanting to risk re-injuring Paul's ankle and unwilling to trust anyone but a Dean to beat the Giants, Frisch pulled Paul and sent Dizzy in to finish off New York. Diz just breezed the final two innings, no hits, no walks, and no runs. Paul was credited with his eleventh win of the season. The Dean boys had each beaten the Giants four times since opening day and not lost once.

The Giants failed to fold as Paul predicted. Giants knuckleballer, Fat Freddie Fitzsimmons, stopped the Cards 6 – 3 securing a split of the four-game series.

The Cardinal road trip continued in Pittsburgh with a three-game set. St. Louis lost the opener 4 – 0 and Diz was sent in to stop the slide in the second game.

The Pirates were led by big poison and little poison, brothers Paul and Lloyd Waner. The Waner boys poisoned Diz, Lloyd had 3 singles and 2 walks while Paul pounded Diz for a double and a home run. The result was a 5 – 4 Buc victory, breaking Dizzy's ten game winning streak.

Tex Carleton started the final game of the series. Tex exited after seven innings with the score tied 5 – 5. The Cardinals pushed across two runs in the top of the eighth and Paul was called in to save the game. He responded by shutting out the powerful Pirates the last two innings on one hit while striking out three. Paul struck out Paul Waner, who had drubbed Tex for a single, and a home run, besides drawing a walk and scoring three runs.

Paul Waner was impressed by Paul Dean. "The pitcher who has more stuff than anyone in the league? that's easy. Paul Dean of the Cardinals. If he gets proper control, he will be a greater pitcher than his brother, Dizzy. Sunday I was hot, but Paul Dean sent three fast ones over to strike me out. The ball came up with terrific speed and raised about three inches as it came across the plate."[22]

After losing two out of three in Pittsburgh, St. Louis was in third place 5 games behind New York but only 1.5 games below the second place Chicago Cubs. The Cardinals went to Chicago to play the Cubs 3 games but with a chance to gain 4 games in the standings.

This unique situation was created because veteran umpire Bill Klem failed to recognize an obvious infield fly. This grievous miscall necessitated a partial replay of the July 2nd Card/Cub game. National League President John Hedler ruled the game had to be resumed from the point of Klem's mistake with the same players in the same positions.

Paul took his position on the pitching rubber with a chance to erase a loss from his record and pick up a game on the Cubs. The replay began in the bottom of the seventh, Cubs at bat two outs, with runners on second and third. The Cubs batter, Babe Herman, was intentionally walked to load the bases. Paul then induced a groundout to end the inning. Chicago led in the game 5 – 1, with two innings to play.

St. Louis failed to score, Jim Mooney pitched the last two innings for the Cardinals and gave up 2 runs. Final score Chicago 7, St. Louis 1. The replay took only 22 minutes, the Cubs kept their win and Paul had to keep his defeat. The Cardinals fared no better in the regularly scheduled game. Chicago won 7 – 2.

The next game featured Paul Dean's second shutout of the season as the Cards dealt Chicago a 4 – 0 loss. Paul dominated the Cubs allowing only 4 hits while striking out 7 and walking 1. It was his 12th win of the year.

Card Coach Mike Gonzales explained Paul's success, in his own animatedly way, "Paul's good pitching – she is because him pitch to hitters. He pitch outside, inside, low, high, not try to blow by the pitch. Blow by the pitch is stupid when she has hitters like this Cubs. Paul smart feller. Smart dummy. Mike tell Paul how to pitch. Frank tell Paul how to pitch – Paul remember. Smart boy, great pitcher. Paul win plenty game. He can do. He can do."[23]

Paul and Dizzy both relied mainly on their blazing fastballs and they loved to talk about how they just reared back and fogged the ball across the plate. However, they learned in order to survive Major League hitters they needed control and secondary pitches.

The rubber match of the Chicago series was the end of a long St. Louis road trip. Wild Bill Hallahan faced off against Paul's former Columbus teammate Bill Lee. The Cardinals lost 6 – 2 and headed home to St. Louis.

Pittsburgh came to St. Louis for four games. In 110 heat Diz beat the Bucs 9 – 3, for his nineteenth win of the year. Tex Carleton started the next day but the frail cowboy from Comanche began to wilt in the heat. With two outs in the eighth, the Bucs had pulled to within one run of the Cards and the tying run was at second.

Frisch left his position at second and went to the mound as the crowd began to chant "we want Dean" "we want Dean." Although he had pitched nine innings the day before, Diz grabbed his glove and hurried to the mound. Frisch knew Diz gave the Cards their best chance to win, so he took the ball from Tex and handed it to Diz. Dizzy quickly struck out the Buc batter to retire the side. He blanked the Bucs in the ninth to save the game for the Cards and preserve the win for Tex.

After losing the first two games the Pirates sunk the Cards in a Sunday doubleheader. Paul lost the opener 6 – 4. "One of the many misfortunes of the game was the fifth defeat of the year for Paul Dean, who could have marched off with his thirteenth victory if the Cardinals had displayed more skill afield and had been more alert at critical times. Three Pirate runs were gifts."[24] The Pirates punished the two Card Bills, Hallahan and Walker, for seven runs to win the second game.

The next three games were against Cincinnati and Dizzy won two of them. Diz shutout the Reds 2 – 0 in the first game for his 20th victory of the year. The Reds beat Wild Bill Hallahan 9 – 2 in the second contest.

Jess Haines started the rubber match but the old veteran tired after seven innings and Frankie Frisch called on Paul to save the game. He was wild, giving up two runs in two innings before being lifted for a pinch hitter. With the score deadlocked 4 – 4 after regulation. The tireless, rubber-armed Dizzy took the hill in the tenth. Diz mowed down the Reds for three innings. Finally, the Cardinals exploded for 6 runs to give Dizzy his 21st victory.

After the game Diz puffed on a cigar and said, "this country may have needed a good five-cent cigar, but what the Cardinals need is more Deans."[25]

Me 'N' Paul

Ironically, Branch Rickey planned on getting publicity by signing a third Dean. Rickey's ploy would alienate Dizzy and his wife, Pat. Diz wanted Rickey to give his older brother Elmer a good job in St. Louis with the Cardinals. Dizzy expected Elmer to be given an easy job in the front office or clubhouse. Rickey envisioned publicity and increased concession sales.

Elmer left his job selling peanuts at Buff stadium in Houston and boarded a train bound for St. Louis. The St. Louis newspapers gave Rickey the publicity he craved.

A headline in the St. Louis Post-Dispatch read "Another Dean joins Cardinals and he's greater than Dizzy – At selling peanuts and soda pop."[26]

A St. Louis Star and Times headline declared "Cards buy a third Dean pitcher – and it's a nutty idea."[27]

Under the headlines was a picture of a smiling Elmer wearing a hat clearly inscribed, "Elmer Dean." Much to the dismay of Dizzy and Pat Dean, Elmer would be continuing his career as a peanut vendor.

Dizzy and Pat believed Branch Rickey was disrespecting the Deans. Pat Dean was incensed, "that goddamned Rickey. He arranges for his brother to be a Cardinal scout but it's peanuts for the Deans. He's trying to embarrass us when our pitching is what's keeping this club in the Pennant race."[28]

Elmer's Major League career was short-lived. Pat Dean evidently believed it was all right for Elmer to sell peanuts for the Minor League Houston Buffs, but not for the Major League Cardinals. Dizzy and Paul wanted Elmer back in Houston to help care for Pa Dean. For his part Elmer said, "the big leagues ain't what it's cracked up to be. I didn't like the looks of St. Louis."[29] He returned to selling peanuts in Houston, where he was warmly welcomed back by Buff fans and management.

The Chicago Cubs came to St. Louis on August 10th for a four-game series. They entered the inferno that was sportsman's park with a 3.5 game lead over the Cards. As thermometers on the field registered 120 degrees the Cardinals exploded for 21 hits and beat the Cubs 17 – 3 in the opening game.

On Saturday August 11th St. Louis made it two in a row over the Cubs as Bill Walker won 6 – 4. St. Louis fans were rabid with excitement about the next day's doubleheader, the Dean brothers against the hated Cubbies.

A sweep would leapfrog the Cards over the Cubs into second place. 40,000 fans braved the heat to witness the expected twin killings of the Bruins.

Paul started the first game and shutout the Cubs for four innings. With one out in the top of the fifth Paul gave up a solo homerun that tied the game 1-1. After a fly-out George Stainback singled. With two out Stainback broke for second to get into scoring position. A good throw would have nailed him, but Bill Delancey's throw was low. Leo Durocher failed to block the ball which rolled into center field, Stainback kept running and scored easily. Clearly upset with the sloppy fielding, Paul gave up another solo homerun before retiring the side.

Paul was pulled for a pinch hitter in the bottom of the fifth and was tagged with the loss although he gave up only one earned run. The final score was 7 – 2.

Dizzy started the second game but fell victim to the ragged and erratic fielding that doomed Paul. Cardinal errors led to four unearned runs and St. Louis lost 6 – 4. The series started with two Cardinal victories that left St. Louis only 1.5 games behind Chicago but ended with the Cards back to a 3.5 game deficit. To make matters worse, the Cards fell 7.5 games behind the league leading New York Giants.

Adding to the gloom of the Dean's doubleheader defeat was an exhibition game to be played in Detroit the following day. The Cardinal players were to board a train and ride all night from St. Louis to Detroit for a meaningless game.

Still stinging from, the ill-fated Elmer affair and perhaps peeved at his teammates for their poor defensive play in the doubleheader loss, Diz decided to skip the exhibition game against the Tigers. "Me 'n' Paul is tired of playin' in them games that don't count none, and besides my arms sore and Paul's ankle is still botherin' him."[30]

Paul chimed in, "my ankle has not been right since I sprained it a month ago. When we went from Philadelphia to New York, and I was hobbling on crutches, I had to get along the best I could when I got off the train. The hotel was several blocks from the station and I had to hobble all the way."[31]

In retrospect it does seem counterproductive to play an exhibition game in the midst of a Pennant race. It seems greedy owners would rather make extra money than give their exhausted players a much-needed day off.

While Dizzy and Paul were relaxing in St. Louis their teammates were in Detroit beating the Tigers 7 – 1. Wild Bill Hallahan won his first game of any kind in a month. After the game the Cardinals rode the train all night back to St. Louis arriving in time to play the next day's game against Philadelphia.

In the clubhouse before the Philly game while the Cards were putting on their uniforms, Diz was saying that he'd missed the train on purpose and he'd do it again if he felt like it. At that point Frankie Frisch told Dizzy he was fined $100 and Paul he was fined $50. Frisch said there was no excuse for the Deans missing the Tigers game when everyone else on the team had to play.

When Dizzy realized he was being fined, he told Frisch, "you'll take them fines off, or the Cardinals will finish the season without me 'n' Paul."[32]

Frisch told Dizzy the fines stuck, and he and Paul better get on the field with their teammates. "We're not a-goin' out on the field!" Dizzy hollered.

"You're not?" Frisch shouted. "Well then, take off those uniforms. You're both suspended!"

Dizzy went berserk, he began cussing and kicking over benches and chairs. He screamed he would never pitch for the Cardinals again and ripped off his uniform not bothering to unbutton it, which tore it to shreds. Diz stormed to his locker, found his other uniform and began to rip it apart. "This will be the end of my Cardinal uniforms!

In the middle of this tirade sportswriter Ray Gillespie and his photographer arrived. Gillespie told Dizzy he sure would like to get an action picture. Would Diz mind tearing up his uniform again?

"Sure, Ray", Diz replied. "Let me see if I can find a piece around here somewhere."[33]

Paul went along with Dizzy's decision to strike. The confrontation with Frisch took place on August 14th, Paul's 21st birthday. Instead of a birthday party, Paul had been hit with a $50 fine and suspended!

Dizzy told reporters, "me 'n' Paul is headed to Florida to do some fishin'."[34] With that said the brothers went to the Cardinal office to collect their semi-monthly pay checks. When Dizzy looked at his check, he was shocked. Not only was the $100 fine deducted, he was also charged $36 for the two uniforms he tore to pieces.

Diz responded to what he thought was sorry treatment from the Cardinals. "I don't think that was right. I was mad and lost my temper when I tore the uniforms, but they weren't destroyed. They could have been mended."

Me 'n' Paul was ready to accept the fines, but Frank was mad at us and came into the clubhouse where we was in uniform and told us to get out of uniform, that we was suspended. That's what made me sore. I tore up my uniform then and also ripped the gray one in my locker. I won't put on a uniform again until the fines are rescinded, and Frisch apologizes to me for popping off like that in the clubhouse."[35]

An epic season was in danger of derailment because of Dizzy's disruptions. Cardinal management and many players were weary of Dizzy's tantrums and they had little tolerance for a man who would quit on his teammates. The Cardinals wanted to prove they would win without Dizzy Dean.

CHAPTER 18

"My arm felt fine, it was working jest like a ol' slingshot. I could have gone 27 innings without gettin' tired."

Frankie Frisch did not apologize, and the fines were imposed. Diz and Paul did not go to Florida, neither did they go back to work. During the Philadelphia series Diz and Paul sat in the stands, talking to fans and signing autographs. The Cardinals swept the Phillies Sans Deans.

Diz was unfazed at the Cards beating Philadelphia without the Deans. "The Cards don't need us none now. Anybody can beat them Phillies, but the Giants are comin' in here next week and we figure Rickey will be beggin' us to let him give us our money back. It takes me 'n' Paul to stop them Giants and he knows it."[1]

Despite Dizzy's bluster, the Deans were beginning to waiver. Diz was losing $50 a day and Paul was losing $23. Despite the paychecks they just received being short because of fines and destroyed uniforms, it was as Pat Dean pointed out, their last if they continued to strike.

Dizzy and Paul capitulated. They both publicly assumed blame and promised to follow Frankie Frisch's rules. They each wrote apologetic letters which appeared in St. Louis newspapers. It was a complete and utter victory for Frisch and the Cardinals, however it was not enough for Branch Rickey and Sam Breadon.

Rickey decided to teach Dizzy a lesson. He was tired of Dizzy flaunting rules, challenging authority and generally causing trouble. Paul was welcomed back and in uniform for the fourth and final game of the Philadelphia series. However, Dizzy was told he was suspended for ten days which would cost him an additional $500.

Of course, this ruling incensed Dizzy and he came out swinging. Diz vowed to take his grievance to the Czar of baseball, Commissioner, Kennesaw Mountain Landis. Dizzy drove seven hours to Chicago and met with Commissioner Landis. Surprisingly Landis agreed to travel to St. Louis and arbitrate the dispute.

The Cardinals had won three in a row from Philly and Paul Dean was reinstated, rested and available for the series final. After making a separate peace with the Cardinals, he was anxious to get back in action. Dizzy was on his own.

Jim Mooney started but did not survive the first inning. He gave up two runs while recording only one out. Dazzy Vance relieved but the old dazzler was only good for 1 2/3 innings. Frisch turned to Paul in the third inning, desperate to complete the Philly sweep.

Paul's teammates accepted him back without fanfare or condemnation. They were sympathetic and encouraging. It was clear they blamed Dizzy for the Deans absence from the team. Everyone knew Diz was the ringleader and had influenced Paul to strike.

"I'm glad to see Paul back with us," owner Sam Breadon said. "This is the first time we have had trouble with him. Dizzy, however, has been a source of worry on each of the teams he has been with since joining our organization" asked if the Cardinals would sell Dizzy, since he was such trouble. "Hell no," Breadon replied. Not even for $500,000.[2]

Paul rewarded his forgiving teammates with seven innings of four-hit shutout ball, and the Cards pulverized Philly pitchers for 12 runs. Paul won his 13th game as St. Louis beat Philadelphia 12 – 2. At least one Dean was back.

Me 'N' Paul

The Cardinals bats continued to explode, and St. Louis beat Boston 15 – 0 in the first of a four-game series. Even Leo the Lip Durocher joined the hit parade with a homerun and two doubles prompting some teammates to give him a new nickname, "Captain Slug."

A Sunday doubleheader followed and in the first game Boston jumped all over Jesse Haines and Jim Mooney for 7 runs and had the bases loaded in the top of the fourth, with no outs. Frisch signaled the bullpen and an unexpected figure emerged to put out the fire.

Frisch figured the game was out of hand and he did not want to exhaust his depleted pitching staff in a losing cause. The second game of the doubleheader loomed and with Dizzy still suspended Frisch had no pitchers to spare. He solved this dilemma by sending in the wild horse of the Osage, Pepper Martin, to make his Major League pitching debut.

Surprisingly, Pepper retired the first Boston batter on a fly-out and induced the next Brave to ground into a double play. The Cardinals fought back and after eight innings the score was tied 9 – 9. Presented with an unexpected chance to win the game, Frisch sent Paul Dean to the mound to start the ninth.

Boston scored a solitary run on a walk, a double and a sacrifice fly. The one hit and one walk led to Paul's 7th defeat as the Cards failed to score in their half of the ninth.

Fortunately, St. Louis only needed one pitcher to win the second game. Bill Walker gave up only one run on seven scattered singles. Ducky Medwick and Ripper Collins hit homeruns in the first inning as the Cardinals won 3 – 1.

With no game scheduled for Monday, sportswriters and fans turned their attention to the St. Louis park plaza hotel where Commissioner Kennesaw Mountain Landis held a meeting to decide Dizzy Dean's fate.

Ever the publicity hound, Dizzy wanted the hearing to be made public, with reporters given access. Commissioner Landis, however, decreed a closed-door meeting. The secrecy Landis required was breeched when newspapermen were able to overhear the proceedings through an open transom above the hotel door.

The hearing lasted over four hours with Dizzy airing his grievances against the Cardinals ranging from poor pay for "me 'n' Paul" to the shoddy treatment of Elmer. "I thought you were going to give him a good job" Diz shouted at Sam Breadon, "but you had the newspaper print that he was goin' to be a peanut peddler, so Elmer went home."³

Dizzy also pointed out that he publicly apologized for not going to Detroit and was willing to pay the $100 fine, but the Cardinals insisted on ten-day suspension.

Breadon and Rickey countered by reviewing Dizzy's bad behavior ever since he was signed by the Cardinal organization. They even had some of Dizzy's teammates testify against him. Jesse Haines said, "he told us once he could get a sore arm whenever he felt like it."⁴

Leo Durocher told about Dizzy wrecking the clubhouse and tearing up his uniforms. "He came in storming, I told him he put himself in a fine mess by not going to Detroit, and I offered to bet him $20 that he would be fined."⁵

Leave it to he Lip to admit to gambling in front of Kennesaw Mountain Landis, the man who banned eight Chicago White Sox players from baseball for conspiring with gamblers to throw the 1919 World Series.

On it went until Commissioner Landis had heard enough. He ruled that the Cardinal baseball club acted within its rights in fining and suspending Dizzy Dean. Landis said the suspension and fines were not excessive.

Now that Dizzy had been chastised by Landis, Rickey was eager to have him back in uniform, so he suggested that the ten-day suspension be reduced to eight, whereupon Sam Breadon said, "I don't want to be hard on Dizzy. I'll cut it to seven and make Dean eligible to return to uniform tomorrow."⁶

Dizzy still could not believe Landis had ruled against him. "I got a raw deal. It was unfair, but what can I do? I'm whipped. I can't afford to lose any more money."⁷

Tex Carleton pitched the Cards to their seventh triumph in the last eight games beating Boston in the series finale 6 – 2. Despite the winning streak St. Louis was still mired in third place six games behind first play New York. However, the Giants were coming to St. Louis for three games and Giant killers, Paul and Dizzy Dean were waiting in sizzling Sportsman's Park.

In the first game of the series Paul faced Giant ace Carl Hubbell. The Cards lit up King Carl for 8 hits and 3 tuns, knocking him out of the

Me 'N' Paul

game after only 5 innings. After 8 frames the Cardinals led 3 – 2 and Paul needed only three outs for the crucial victory.

There was one out in the ninth when Giant catcher Harry Danning singled, but Paul seemed to be on his way out of trouble when the next Giant popped out. With two down pinch hitter Hank Leiber looped a Texas league single to center. The next hitter, Joe Moore hit one over the right field pavilion roof for a three-run homer. The Giants had won at the last possible moment, New York's first victory of the year over either of the Dean brothers.

Dizzy righted the St. Louis ship in the second game by shutting out New York 5 – 0. However, Diz took the loss in the rubber match when he was rushed to the rescue in the seventh after Bill Walker was shelled from the mound. Diz had nothing left after pitching nine innings the day before, consequently the Giants pounded him for 6 hits and 4 runs to win the game 7 – 6.

The Brooklyn Dodgers came to St. Louis for a five-game series that wrapped up the Cardinal's long homestand. St. Louis won three of the five games.

Paul pitched the fourth game of the series and shutout Brooklyn 2 – 0. He scattered 8 hits, struck out 4 and walked 2. It was his 14th victory of the year.

After the Brooklyn series the Cardinals left St. Louis heading east for a month-long road trip. St. Louis was still in third place behind New York and Chicago with time running out.

The Cardinals arrived in Chicago with a chance to catch the second place Cubs. Dizzy won the first game 3 – 1 for his 22nd victory of the year which brought the Cards even with Chicago. Both teams 5 games behind New York. Wild Bill Hallahan won the second game to move the Cards into undisputed 2nd place. The third game was rained out.

In Pittsburgh a Labor Day crowd of 20,000 turned out to see sensational St. Louis rookie Paul Dean pitch the first game of a doubleheader. The Pirates were languishing in fifth place 19.5 games behind first place New York, but they were ready for Paul. Pittsburgh loaded their line-up with left-handed hitters and the Pirates poleaxed Paul for 8 runs in only three innings, on their way to an easy 12 – 2 victory.

In the second game, with two on in the top of the ninth and the Cards trailing 3 – 2, Pepper Martin ripped a bases clearing triple to give St. Louis a 4 – 3 lead. Ducky Medwick's sacrifice fly plated Pepper with an insurance run. Frankie Frisch knew the Cardinals had to win this game to stay within shouting distance of the Giants, so he sent in the durable Dizzy to save the game.

A seemingly good choice because Diz owned the Bucs, his current record against Pittsburgh was 4 wins and 1 loss. The Flash was confident Diz would close out the Bucs, but two singles and a double sent Dizzy to the showers. Wild Bill Hallahan could not hold the Bucs who went on to win the game 6 – 5.

The devastating loss was charged to Dizzy causing fans and sportswriters to declare the Cards done in the pennant race.

Ray Gillespie wrote in the St. Louis Star-Times. "The double loss suffered in Pittsburgh virtually eliminated St. Louis from the 1934 pennant race."[8] Gillespie had good reason to believe the Redbirds were dead. St. Louis was 6 games behind New York with only three weeks left in the season. To make matters worse the Cardinals would be on the road until September 25th while the Giants would be home at the polo grounds where they had won 75% of the time.

Roy Stockton, sportswriter for the St. Louis Post-Dispatch, agreed St. Louis was out of the pennant race, "second place is still open to the Cardinals, but the Giants margin virtually silences the old pennant bee. It is practically impossible for the Cardinals to win."[9]

New York sportswriters also knew their Giants had the National League pennant wrapped up. "The Giants lead insures them fully against anything in the way of bad breaks and bad luck. The Giants can be overtaken, but it's a million-to-one shot."[10]

After the Pirates beat the Dean boys in the twin bill, a writer asked Frisch, "give up, Frankie?"

"Never, not until we're counted out officially," he fired back. "No team of mine will give up. We're in this race until we're out of it, and, believe me, we'll fight to the last pitch. When I played under John McGraw, I was taught to fight to the finish, and you can bet your last dollar that every man playing for me will do the same."[11]

Me 'N' Paul

Eerily like the situation that resulted in Dizzy and Paul's suspension, the Cardinals were scheduled to play an exhibition game the day after the Dean's doubleheader loss to Pittsburgh. However, this time Dizzy was excused from the exhibition game. Frisch instructed Diz to take a train to New York while the rest of the team stayed in Pittsburgh to play the next day's exhibition game in Greensburg Pennsylvania, about 50 miles from Pittsburgh.

Publicly Frisch said he was sending Dizzy to New York for some rest before the crucial series against Brooklyn. In reality Frankie did not want to risk upsetting his star pitcher and have him causing trouble and dissention on the team. The only calming influence on Dizzy was his wife, Pat, and Branch Rickey had learned it was worth the expense to have Pat accompany Dizzy on road trips to keep him at least semi-controlled.

Diz and Pat were supposed to be on the 11:00 p.m. train from Pittsburgh to New York, but at 10:30 Pat was frantically rushing around the hotel searching for Frankie Frisch.

"I must find Frankie," she said. "Dizzy refuses to go to New York. He's upstairs in a poker game with several players and positively won't accompany me to the station."[12]

Pat did not find Frisch and Dizzy did not leave his poker game, prompting sports reporter Roy Gillespie to ask the question, "if the Cardinals fined Dizzy $100 for failing to go to Detroit for an exhibition game, what will be the penalty – or bonus – for insisting on going to an exhibition game at Greensburg after team management had excused him from going?"[13]

As usual Dizzy had answers for everything. Diz told Frisch he didn't catch the train to New York because he didn't want special treatment. All he wanted was to be with his boys, a team united for a final push to the pennant, and besides he didn't need rest to beat "them Dodgers." The Flash accepted Dizzy's lies and neither fined nor gave him a bonus.

Diz was right about not needing rest to beat Brooklyn. He won his 24th game only allowing one run on three hits. Solo homeruns by Ripper Collins and Bill Delancey downed the Dodgers 2 – 1.

Tex Carleton made it to two in a row beating Brooklyn 7 – 5. Paul did not get his chance against the Dodgers as the next three games were rained out. The Cardinals moved on to Philadelphia.

Carl Duncan

Paul pitched the first game in Philly, hanging up his 15th conquest of the year, permitting the Phil's only four hits while fanning ten men, it was the first game of a Sunday doubleheader and St. Louis won 6 – 1. The Cards won the second game 7 – 3 behind the fine pitching of Bill Walker.

The double dipper victories left St. Louis in second place 5 games behind New York and 2.5 games ahead of third place Chicago. After the games, in the visitor's clubhouse the Cardinals celebrated Frankie Frisch's 36th birthday. The gang presented Flash with a portable radio. The gift card read:

> *"Here's to Frankie, the Fordham Flash, we offer advice instead of cash. Don't Ever take a 3 – 2 pitch but swing away, you son of a bitch."*[14]

Dizzy made it three in a row over the 7th place Phillies. His 25th victory featured only 1 Philly run on 5 hits. Dizzy, a hitter not to be trifled with, accounted for 1 of St. Louis' 4 runs. Diz loved to hit and was fast on the base paths. He smacked a single to left, Pepper followed with another single that propelled Diz to third. When Jack Rothrock sliced a single Diz dashed for home, executed a picturesque hook slide across home plate, bounded to his feet and doffed his cap to the crowd.

The slide was completely unnecessary – no play was made on him – but Dizzy always tried to put on a show for the fans. "Us stars gotta give the customers their money's worth."[15]

After winning the first three games of the six-game series, Philadelphia won two of the last three. Paul did not pitch in the final three games, but Dizzy relieved in two of the games. He saved a 6 – 4 victory for Wild Bill Hallahan relieving in the 7th with two men on and no outs. He struck out the side and finished the game unscathed.

Dazzy Vance started the final game of the Philly series, and the Old Dazzler pitched well until he tired in the 8th inning. With the bases loaded, no outs and the score tied 1 – 1, Dizzy trudged to the mound for the third time in three days. Philly Ethan Allen lifted a shallow fly to center, not deep enough for the runner on third to tag and score. Ernie Orsatti charged in to make the play but to Dizzy's dismay the ball bounced off Orsatti's glove and two runs scored. The Cards did not score in the ninth, so Philadelphia won 3 – 1. Not only was the game lost but apparently so was the pennant. The loss dropped St. Louis 5.5 games behind the New York Giants.

The Cardinals still clung to pennant possibilities by the thinnest of threads since they were not yet mathematically eliminated. The last series of the year against New York started the next day at the polo grounds. St. Louis had to take at least three out of four from the Giants to have any chance at the Pennant.

Paul started the first game of the crucial Giant series. He whitewashed New York for nine innings but the Cardinals were unable to score on Fat Freddie Fitzsimmons and the game went to extra innings. The brilliant pitching continued as neither team scored in the tenth or eleventh innings.

With one out in the top of the 12th Ducky Medwick singled to left. Ripper Collins followed with a single chasing Medwick to third. On Bill Delancey's long fly out to Mel Ott, Ducky broke for home and Ott heaved away the ball game.

Ott's throw to home sailed to the backstop letting Ducky score and Ripper advance to third. He scored on Leo the Lip's single for a 2 – 0 lead. Paul needed three outs for the biggest win of his brief Major League career.

Paul retired the first two Giants in the bottom of the twelfth, but he walked pinch hitter Lefty O'Doul. With one on and two out manager Bill Terry sent ex-Cardinal George Watkins to hit for Fitzsimmons. Watkins lined-out to Lippy Durocher ending the struggle and giving Paul his 16th victory, a masterful 12 inning, 6 hit shutout. He struck out 7.

The next day the Giants regained their 5.5 game lead over the Cards as New York beat St. Louis 4 – 1. Again New York newspapers proclaimed the Redbirds dead. "This result virtually doomed whatever lingering hopes Frankie Frisch and his crew may have entertained of snatching the Pennant from the Giants."[16]

The next day's game was rained out and New York writers again turned to Dizzy for interviews to fill the void in the sport pages. Diz was already looking ahead to next year.

"The Giants are in. There's no use kidding ourselves. Sure, me 'n' Paul will beat them tomorrow, but after that it don't matter."

"Next season the Cardinals gotta pay me. I'll have to get a lot more money or I won't pitch. Look at it this way," he said "I bring 'em into the parks, and I win games. So far, I've won 25 games and lost 7. Those 7 was unlucky. I expect to win 2 more and maybe lose 1. I can't see any chance of winning 30 with only 16 to play."[17]

Diz was asked about his relationship with Frankie Frisch since the incidents of the torn uniforms and suspension. "I think Frisch is the most wonderful manager in the world."

The reporter asked, "why, Diz?"

"Because" replied Dizzy, "he's the only man who could keep a club in a Pennant fight with only two pitchers."

"Who are the pitchers, Dizzy?" "Me 'n' Paul."[18]

Reporters loved to interview Dizzy, but some New York writers did not appreciate Dizzy's pranks. "Jerome Dean has a distorted sense of humor. On Friday, Dean invaded the Giant dugout with this cat. A particularly black and sinister beast. He added insult to injury by pointing its nose at second baseman Hughie Critz, an impressionable little fellow from Mississippi, and making all kinds of hex signs and mumbo passes in Hughie's direction.

'Cat, get Critz' said Mr. Dean, 'Critz, get jinxed. ZMMMMM!

Mr. Critz looked around for the nearest exit and vanished into the clubhouse.

Mr Dean seemed satisfied, 'that got him.' He said. 'This will get 'em all!

Then Diz proceeded to walk the cat up and down the dugout in full view of the fans.[19]

62,500 Pennant-hungry New York fans jammed the polo grounds to see the Dean brothers pitch a doubleheader against their beloved Giants. The polo grounds only had 52,000 seats which left 10,500 rabid fans jamming the aisles, clinging to rafters and standing in places with only a partial view of the diamond. An additional 15,000 people were turned away as the New York City fire department locked all the gates.

Dizzy beat the Giants 5 – 3 in the first of the two must-win games. All the pressure then descended on 21-year-old rookie Paul Dean.

Giant manager Bill Terry, anxious to drive the final nail into the Card coffin, sent his ace to the mound. Terry was confident Carl Hubbell would administer last rites to the Cardinals.

Although Paul had pitched 12 tough innings shutting out the Giants 2 – 0, Frankie Frisch had no reservations about starting him with only two days rest. Who else but a Dean could he trust to beat the Giants?

The overflow crowd witnessed an epic pitcher's duel. The Giants drew first blood in the bottom of the third on a wind-blown triple and a sacrifice fly. St. Louis tied the game on a Ripper Collins solo homer in the seventh. That was all the scoring through ten innings as King Carl and rookie Paul retired batter after batter.

Before the start of the eleventh inning the umpires consulted to consider calling the game a draw. It was getting dark and there were no stadium lights at the polo grounds. The umpires decided to allow one more inning of play.

King Carl cracked first, in the top of the eleventh Pepper Martin sent a screwball into the stands for an opposite field homerun. Jack Rothrock followed with a single, the Flash sacrificed him to second and Ducky drove him home with an insurance run.

Paul retired the Giants in order for his 17th win of the year, bringing the Cards to within 3.5 games of New York. In the space of four days Paul pitched 23 innings against the World Champions and they scored one run!

After two games in Boston were rained out the Cardinals maintained their slim mathematical possibility of winning the pennant by taking a doubleheader from the Braves. Tex Carleton and Wild Bill Hallahan executed the twin killings by beating Boston 4 – 1 and 1 – 0. Between them they allowed the Braves only 1 run on 12 hits in 18 innings. Finally, Card pitchers not named Dean were winning critical games.

St. Louis returned to New York, this time to play the Brooklyn Dodgers. The Cardinals were still 3.5 games behind the Giants, but the well-rested Deans were set to start a Friday doubleheader against the Dodgers.

When the Cardinals arrived in Brooklyn, reporters tracked Dizzy down at the hotel where the team was staying. Always eager for Dizzy's quotes and predictions the writers ask him about the upcoming doubleheader. Diz said, "Zachary and Benge (Dodger pitchers Tom Zachary and Ray Benge) will be pitching against one-hit Dean and no-hit Dean."[20]

In the visitors' clubhouse at Ebbits field before the games Frankie Frisch was going over the Dodger line-up with his assembled team. He explained each Dodger's strength, weaknesses and how to pitch to them.

Dizzy listened, somewhat intently, until he could not stand anymore. "Let's stop this silly business, Frank. Don't you think it's kind of silly for a ordinary second baseman like you to be telling a great pitcher like me how to pitch to anybody?"[21]

Dizzy went out and proved he did not need "a ordinary second baseman" telling him how to pitch. He shut-out Brooklyn 13 – 0 in the first game giving up only 3 hits, the first coming in the 8th inning, once again, the pressure of a must-win game fell on Paul Dean.

The visiting Cards batted first in the second game but failed to score. Paul started strong striking out the first batter he faced and induced the next to fly-out. He then walked Dodger center fielder Len Koenecke, a walk that would haunt him. Paul avoided further trouble when another fly-out ended the inning.

Brooklyn pitcher Ray Benge matched Paul pitch for pitch, both hurlers put up goose- eggs for five innings. Finally, in the sixth Paul doubled to left-center and Pepper followed with a double that platted Paul with the first run of the game.

The Cardinals scored two more solo runs and going into the bottom of the ninth inning St. Louis led 3 – 0. Len Koenecke, who Paul walked in the first inning, was the only Dodger baserunner of the game. Paul Dean was three outs away from a no-hitter!

Players on the Cardinal bench could be seen with their fingers crossed as Paul marched to the mound for his chance at baseball immortality. Brooklyn manager Casey Stengal was not conceding the no-hitter to Paul, he sent up two left-handed pinch hitters to face the right-handed Paul.

Jimmy Bucher batted for catcher Al Lopez, unfazed Paul struck him out. Two to go. The next pinch hitter, Johnny McCarthy, hit a fastball a mile, fortunately, straight up. Frisch camped under it for the second out. One out to go.

Buzz Boyle, who had ruined Dizzy's no-hit bid in the first game, was the third batter in the ninth. He hit a shot to short, that blasted into Durocher's glove, but Leo could not hold it. For a split-second Paul and 18,000 fans held their breath but the Lip pounced on the ball like a puma and his quick throw just beat Buzz to end the game.

Thousands of fans descended on the field engulfing Paul, but Dizzy and several park policemen finally managed to get him off the field. In the visitor's clubhouse all the Cardinals were wildly excited, except Paul.

"You see," he said, "I pitched a no-hitter once before – a night game for Columbus in Kansas City."[22]

Captain Leo Durocher was beside himself with excitement. "Last spring Dizzy said him, and Paul would win 45 games between them. We thought he was crazy. This is the 45th – Diz won his 27th. Paul won his 18th today – but even Dizzy wasn't Dizzy enough to predict that the 45th would be a no-hitter!"[23]

Frankie Frisch was jubilant, with St. Louis only 3 games behind New York the Flash declared. "We may catch those Giants yet."[24]

Dizzy was peeved, "the only thing that makes me mad is that I didn't know I hadn't given them Giants any hits in the first seven innings of the first game. I should have knowed that. Then I'd have really breezed 'em in there and we'd both have a no-hitter."[25]

Paul answered reporter's questions after his brilliant no-hitter, "I felt mighty good when I went out to pitch that second game. I always feel fine after my brother, Dizzy, wins a game. Well, he allowed them Dodgers only three hits in the opener and no runs. My arm felt fine. It was working jest like a ol' sling shot. I could have gone 27 innings without getting tired."[26]

Asked when he first knew he had a no-hitter going, Paul replied, "when did I first think about it? After the third out in the first inning. I said to myself as I went to the dugout, 'well no hits so far! And after the second I said the same thing. "Then after a couple more innings I started to talk to Delancey about it. We're roommates, and I think a lot of him, and we told each other after each inning that there wasn't no hits yet."

> "I've heard tell that you jinx a no-hit game by talking about it, but I think that's all bunk, because somebody's sure to think about it and what's going to happen is going to happen. I never was excited about nothing. But I was pouring that ball through there in the late innings. How did you like them strikes. I throwed to Bucher in the ninth inning? He ain't never saw anything I throwed."[27]

Did he have more stuff than usual?

"It wasn't just the fastball that got 'em. After a couple of steamers, I'd toss in a slow curve. They didn't know what was coming. It took a lot of practice, but I've got that change of pace down pretty good now, so that I don't telegraph what I'm goin' to throw. When the ball leaves my hand, the batter don't know whether it's a fast one or a curve."[28]

> *"What was the biggest thrill of the game?*
> *"I got the biggest kick out of my hitting. I guess those two hits I got will knock Dizz off for a while. Did I hit those or didn't I? I never hit so good in my life. That Single to right was good, but that double I larruped out there to left-center was What I got a big kick out of. Yes, sir, I guess Diz won't talk about his hittin' for a While after those two wallops."*[29]

St. Louis Post-Dispatch columnist L.C. Davis was so inspired he penned a poem:

> *The Dodgers spoiled a no- hit game*
> *for elder brother Dizzy*
> *then, peeved, his brother Paul became,*
> *and straightway he got busy.*
> *He pitched a no-hit, no-run game,*
> *and passed a single Dodger,*
> *and in the well-known Hall of Fame*
> *young Dean is now a lodger.*
>
> *This brilliant pitching feat of Paul's*
> *on magic seemed to border;*
> *excepting for one base on balls*
> *he set them down in order.*
> *With speed, control and nerve to spare,*
> *across the plate he'd stick it,*
> *but missed perfection by a hair*
> *by giving one free ticket.*[30]

Brooklyn was also impressed with Paul, both fans and players. "I'm telling ya!" shouted five hundred average fans, grabbing five hundred other average fans by the coat. "That guy'd be worth half a million to Brooklyn! They ought to buy him. They ought to get him no matter what he costs."[31]

Dodger catcher Al Lopez said, "if there is such a thing in getting a kick in losing, I got it today. I think we were all up there with our mouths open in admiration of the stuff those two were throwing at us."

"I know I was," said left fielder Johnny Frederick, "it must sound like an exaggeration, but I'll swear that Paul struck me out on a fast ball that hopped a foot."[32]

The day after Paul's no-hitter the Cards gained a half game on the Giants. The Cardinal's game in Cincinnati was rained out and New York lost to Boston, reducing its lead to 2.5 games.

Reporters wanted to know what Frankie Frisch thought about the Dean boys after their historic Dodger doubleheader. The Flash was earnest in his praise. "Some people may think these boys are a little erratic," he said, "but they are really as sincere, ambitious, and hard-working as any players I have ever known. Both would rather pitch than do anything else, and they are not only willing but anxious to go in out of turn to help out at any time. They are terribly hard losers too, and I admire them for that. Too many present-day players dig up excuses and alibis when their team loses and laugh off a defeat as if it didn't mean very much. But Dizzy and Paul would rather lose a week's salary than a ball game. If all players had their winning disposition, baseball would be even better than it is."[33]

Dizzy and Paul proved they were ready to pitch at any time in the next day's doubleheader in Cincinnati. Paul relieved in the second game and Dizzy relieved in both games.

St. Louis had a commanding 9 – 4 lead going into the bottom of the ninth in the first game. After the Reds scored two runs and had the bases loaded, Diz was called to the rescue. He put out the fire and St. Louis won 9 – 7.

Tex Carleton started the second game and pitched effectively giving up only one Reds run through five innings. In the bottom of the sixth Ripper Collins muffed a pop foul, Frisch made a wild throw to the plate and Leo Durocher missed a grounder. All this led to one run and Reds at first and second. With the score tied Frisch summoned Paul from the bullpen.

Paul stranded the two Reds runners to preserve the 2-2 tie. He retired Cincinnati in order in the seventh and eighth innings. As St. Louis came to bat in the top of the ninth, the scoreboard showed Boston had defeated New York. Grasping a chance to gain a full game on the Giants St. Louis scored a run to take a 3 – 2 advantage.

Paul faced Cincy in the bottom of the ninth determined to protect the slight one run lead. After one out, Paul ran the count to 2 – 2 on the Reds hitter, Adam Comorosky, Paul broke a curve across the plate at which Comorosky half-swung. Paul thought he had a strike-out, but the ump called it a ball. The Cards complained bitterly, and Paul became visibly upset. He walked Comorosky. With the tying run on first, Alex Kampouris pinch-hit for Cincy pitcher Paul Derringer. He bunted to sacrifice the runner to second. Easy play for Paul, but he overthrew the short-statured first baseman Ripper Collins and the ball rolled to the grandstand. Collins retrieved the ball as Comorosky rounded third and headed home. Ripper's throw was a little wide, but catcher Bill Delancey grabbed It and put the tag on Comorosky.

To the dismay of Paul and the Cards Comorosky was called safe. Without a hit Cincinnati had tied the game! After venting his rage on the home plate umpire Paul was in no condition to continue the game. Once again Dizzy was summoned to try to salvage the ragged game.

With a Red on third and one out Frisch opted for the stereotypical strategy; intentionally walking two batters to load the bases and set the stage for an inning ending double play. Cincy third baseman Mark Koenig failed to follow Frisch's script and hit a sacrifice fly to Ducky Medwick sending home the winning Reds run.

Paul took the loss hard. He thought home plate umpire, Ernest Quigley, had robbed him of the game with two bad calls. Paul was inconsolable as he sat in front of his locker with tears streaming down his face. Although the rest of the Cards put up a brave front, they knew the pennant was a distant, disappearing dream.

The Cardinals had seven games remaining while the Giants had only four. If New York went 2 – 2, St. Louis would have to win all seven of their games to capture the Pennant. A 1 – 3 break for the Giants would force the Cards to go 6 – 1 to gain the flag. If the Giants should lose four in a row, a 5 – 2 record would win it for St. Louis. Four wins for New York would mathematically eliminate Frisch's men even if they won all seven of their games.

Stanley Frank of the New York Post wrote, "although the Cardinals are the best team in the National League right now, the Giants cannot possibly blow the Pennant no matter how hard they try."[34]

The Cardinals had one game in Chicago before going back to St. Louis for the last six games of the season. The Cards prevailed 3 – 1 and picked up a half game on the idle Giants.

The Pittsburgh Pirates invaded St. Louis and Dizzy beat the Bucs 3 – 2. In the first inning an error, Frisch's double, Medwick's single, Collins' double and Spud Davis' sacrifice fly accounted for all three Card runs. Those three runs were all Diz needed to record his 28th win. In Philadelphia the Giants lost to Philly.

Unbelievably, the Giants lost again to the seventh place Phillies. With an opportunity to tie New York for fist place, the Cards continued to deal their aces. Dizzy had beat the Bucs with only one day's rest, surely Paul could win since he had not pitched in two days.

Paul's mound opponent was the ageless Waite Hoyt, who had been pitching professionally since 1916. Paul pitched his heart out, but a single, double and homer by Pirate Arkie Vaughan sunk the Cards. Old Waite pitched a two-hit shout-out while Paul gave up three runs on six hits and struck out seven, in six innings. St. Louis lost 3 – 0.

The Cardinals were one game back with four left to play, all against the Cincinnati Reds at Sportsman's Park. The Giants had only two games left on their schedule, both against cross-town rival Brooklyn. New York had owned Brooklyn all season winning 14 of 20, however the Dodgers were still smarting from Giant manager Bill Terry's springtime scornful quip about Brooklyn baseball.

Ever since Terry had sarcastically asked, "is Brooklyn still in the league?" Brooklyn fans had been seeking revenge for their beloved Dodgers, who had been disrespected by Terry. The Dodgers would get their chance.

In New York, the idle Giants waited nervously for the final score in the Card game. In St. Louis, Cincinnati battered Bill Walker, Dazzy Vance and Tex Carleton for 13 hits and 5 runs but Card bats exploded for 8 runs. The 8 – 5 win left St. Louis only .5 game behind the Giants. An excited

Frankie Frisch vowed to "pitch no one but Dizzy and Daffy until the flag is either clinched or lost."[35]

The rampaging Redbirds beat the Reds 4 – 0 behind Dizzy's seven hit shut-out elevating St. Louis into a deadlock for first place with the New York Giants. Both teams had two games left to play and the National League made contingency plans in case a play-off was needed. "Give me 'n' Paul a couple or three runs and there ain't gonna be no play- off."[36] Diz said

On a lady's day crowd of 25,000 Paul trudged to the mound, working on only two days rest. He hurled brilliantly, scattering 11 hits so effectively that Cincinnati could score but one run. A front-page headline in the Brooklyn Times screamed the news!

> "Brooklyn Dodgers 5; New York Giants 1
> St. Louis Cardinals 6' Cincinnati 1
> Yes, indeed, Mr. Terry, the Dodgers are still in the league."[37]

The victory enabled St. Louis to take over first place for the first time since June 5th. It was Paul's 19th victory against 11 losses. Finally, the Cards held their destiny in their own hands. Beat the Reds and the Pennant belonged to St. Louis no matter the outcome of the Giant-Dodger game.

A roaring crowd of 38,000 fans filled the seats and overflowed into aisles and ramps at Sportsman's Park to see Dizzy Dean bring home the flag to St. Louis. The game was decided early as the Cards scored 2 in the first and 3 in the fourth, the barrage was led by homers from Rip Collins and Bill Delancey. Diz kept putting up goose-eggs and the Cards led 9 – 0 going into the bottom of the ninth. The only question remaining was whether Dizzy's 30th victory would be a shut-out.

The first three Reds reached the base causing the fans and Dizzy's teammates to wonder, was Diz tired? Or was he toying with the Reds to add some last-minute excitement to the game? Grinning mischievously, Dizzy struck out the next two batters and the third popped up, causing most to believe he had deliberately filled the bases to heighten the drama.

Bedlam and pandemonium ensued as thousands of fans stormed the diamond shouting, whistling, and ringing cowbells. A group of policemen and firemen rushed out and hustled Diz to the clubhouse. Amidst the crazed, screaming fans a small boy emerged carrying a four-pound block of ice.

The boy carefully placed the block of ice on the pitching rubber. Asked to explain his strange behavior, the boy said "Dizzy told me this morning to put it there after the game, said it would be burning up if I didn't. Go ahead and feel it. Even the ice hasn't gotten it cooled down yet.[38]

Not that it mattered to the Cards, but New York blew a 4 – 0 lead and lost to Brooklyn for the second day in a row. St. Louis won the Pennant by 2.0 games and Casey Stengel's Dodgers had their revenge.

What a year for the Dean boys! Dizzy led the league in wins and strikeouts. He won 30 lost 7 and struck-out 194. Paul's rookie year was incredible, 19 wins 11 losses and a no- hitter! Me 'n' Paul put the Cards on their backs down the stretch and carried them to the Pennant. They pitched in five of the final six games winning four. The Cardinals finished the season with 95 wins, Diz and Paul won 49, over half of the 95 victories.

The jubilant Cards made their way to the clubhouse and the celebration began. "We're in the mon-ey! We're in the mon-ey!"[39] sang Ripper Collins. Leo the Lip burst into the dressing room shouting, "uncork the champagne!"[40] However, there was no champagne, tightfisted Card owner Sam Breadon was too tight to buy liquor for his players.

Coach Mike Gonzales was grinning and exclaiming "Mike, she tole you, we could do."[41]

Perhaps Dizzy captured the feelings of the entire Card squad when he kept hollering over and over "This is the greatest thing that has ever happened to me!"[42]

CHAPTER 19

The G-Men

The Detroit Tigers won the 1934 American League Pennant, vanquishing the mighty New York Yankees of Babe Ruth and Lou Gehrig. The Babe's career was winding down, he hit "only" .288 and 22 homers. Gehrig took up the slack winning the triple crown with a .363 B.A., 149 R.B.I's and 49 homeruns. However, it was not enough to overcome the Tigers who finished the season with 101 wins and only 53 losses. The Tigers ended up 7 games ahead of the Yankees thus ending a 25-year Detroit Pennant drought.

The 1934 Detroit Tigers fielded a powerhouse offensive line-up. They outscored opponents 958 to 708 and seven of their eight regulars hit .295 or better. The Tigers were led by player/manager Mickey Cochrane, who was named the American League's most valuable player.

Hall of Fame catcher Cochrane was nicknamed "Black Mike" because of his fiery, competitive nature. That competitive drive led the 1934 Tigers to the Pennant after being picked to finish fifth in the talented American

League. He hit .320 and won the Pennant in his first year managing a Major League team.

Black Mike was born in Bridgewater, Massachusetts and excelled in five sports at Boston University. Cochrane considered himself better at football but chose to play professional baseball because professional football was not yet well-established and Major League baseball was the most popular sport in America.

After only one year in the Minors, Mickey made his Major League debut in 1925 with the Philadelphia athletics. By 1926 Cochrane was considered the best catcher in baseball. The A's won the Pennant in 1929, 1930, and 1931 when Black Mike hit .331, .357, and .349 respectively. They won the World Series in 1929 and 1930. Cochrane was sold to Detroit in 1934 for much needed cash, by the financially strapped Athletics.

Hammering Hank Greenberg held down first base. The "Hebrew Hammer" was America's first Jewish superstar. He was born Hyman Greenberg in New York City on the first day of 1911. After high school the New York Yankees offered the 6'4" Greenberg a contract, which Hank declined. His best position was first base, and the Yankees were set at that position with Lou Gehrig in the midst of his iron man stint.

Hank eventually signed with Detroit and after three years in the Minors made it to the Tigers in 1933. In only his second Major League season Greenberg was quickly developing into the hall of fame player he would become. One of the few Jewish Major leaguers, Hank announce late in the 1934 season he would not play on Rosh Hashanah, the Jewish New Year. Disappointed Detroit fans appreciated sportswriters pointing out that Rosh Hashanah came every year, but the Tigers had not won a Pennant since 1909. After much soul searching the Hebrew Hammer decided to play.

Yankee pitcher Lefty "El Goofo" Gomez nicknamed Tiger second baseman Charlie Gehringer "The Mechanical Man" because of his consistency as a hitter and fielder. Mickey Cochrane joked, "Charlie says hello on opening day and goodbye on closing day, in between he hits .350."[1] It was no joke in 1934 as Gehringer hit .356.

Charlie Gehringer, widely considered one of the best second basemen in baseball history, was born in Flowerville, Michigan on May 11, 1903. He played basketball and baseball at the University of Michigan and

Me 'N' Paul

ironically, he lettered in the former but not in the latter. After only a year at Michigan Gehringer was given a try-out by the Detroit Tigers. Player/manager Ty Cobb was impressed and signed Charlie to his first professional contract.

By 1934 Geheringer had been a full-time Major Leaguer since 1926. He was a bonafide star chosen for the American League All-Star game in 1933 and 1934. Charlie spent his entire hall of fame career with the Detroit Tigers.

Batting fifth and playing shortstop for the 1934 Tigers was Billy Rogell. Although not as accomplished as the four-future hall of famers who surrounded him in the Tiger batting order; - Mickey Cochrane, Charlie Gehringer, Goose Goslin and Hank Greenberg – He had a Cooperstown worthy season in 1934 batting .296 and driving in 100 runs.

The Springfield, Illinois native played 14 Major League seasons and finished with a .267 lifetime batting average. He played in two World Series winning one World Championship, yet Rogell is best remembered for making one of the strangest plays in the World Series history. Of course, it involved Dizzy Dean.

Marv Owen rounded out the 1934 Detroit Tiger infield nicknamed the "Battalion of Death". He played third base and was involved in an on-field fight in the 1934 World Series that started a near-riot. Not surprising was his opponent, Ducky Medwick.

Owen was born in Agnew, California and like several of his Tiger teammates he was a multi-sport star, playing baseball and football for the Santa Clara University Broncos. Marv was a marvelous defensive third baseman with hands so large he was featured in <u>R ip le y's Believe it or Not</u> because he could hold seven baseballs in one hand. Owen had a career-best year in 1934.

Leon "Goose" Goslin, the pride Salem, New Jersey, was traded to Detroit before the 1934 season. He starred in the 1924 and 1925 World Series while playing for the Washington Senators.

In 1924 23-year-old Goose Goslin helped Washington to a 92-win season and their first World Series Championship. He hit .344 for the season and led the American League with 129 RBI's. Goslin then led the Senators past the New York Giants in the World Series with 3 homeruns and 7 runs batted in.

Carl Duncan

Washington again won the American League Pennant in 1925. Goose hit .334 to go with 113 RBI's in the regular season. His 3 homeruns and 6 RBI's were not enough to keep the Pittsburgh Pirates from defeating Washington for the 1925 World Championship.

Goose continued his torrid hitting with a .354 batting average in 1926 and .334 in 1927. He won the 1928 American League batting title barely.

Goslin led the American League in hitting for most of the 1928 season but St. Louis Brown outfielder Heinie Manush closed the gap in September and by the last day of the season they were tied for the batting championship. Washington played St. Louis in the seasons' final game, so Manush and the Goose played against each other with the batting title on the line.

It came down to Goose's last at bat, he was a fraction of a point ahead of Heinie. If he made an out, he lost the title, if he got a hit, walked or did not bat he won the championship. Senator manager Bucky Harris offered to send in a pinch hitter so Goose could clinch the title.

Goslin remembered, "well", I said "I've never won a batting title and I sure would love to, just for once in my life. So, I think I'll stay right here on the bench."[2]

Goose's teammates pointed out that people might consider him "yellow" for winning the batting crown sitting on the bench. Against his better judgement, Goslin decided to bat. He promptly regretted that decision when the ump called two quick strikes. Goose did some fast thinking and realized his best option was to get ejected from the game so the at-bat would not count. "I pretended to be mad about the strike calls" Goose said, "and I called the ump every name in the book. I stepped on his toes, I pushed him, I did everything."[3]

The umpire saw through the Goose ruse and told Goslin he was not going to eject him or walk him so he best try to get a hit. Goslin told what happened:

> "I got a lucky hit! Saved me. I guess that hit was the biggest thrill I ever got. Even Bigger than that single that won the World Series in 1924. Another lucky hit."[4]

Opposing players gave Goslin his nickname. He was a poor fielder and when he circled under a high flyball with his long arms waving he resembled a large bird flapping its wings. Since his surname was Goslin the large bird became a Goose.

Goslin patrolled left field as best he could and hit .305 with 100 RBI's for Detroit in 1934.

Pete Fox, Jo-Jo White, and Gee Walker filled out the Tiger outfield. Fox played right field, White shared Center field duty with Walker.

Ervin Fox acquired his nickname while playing for Beaumont in the Texas League. Fans impressed by his speed called him Rabbit. Rabbit evolved into Peter Cottontail and finally, Simply Pete.

Pete was born on March 8, 1909 in Evansville, Indiana. After high school he went to work in a furniture factory. While playing for the company team, he was scouted and signed to play professionally.

After three Minor League seasons Fox made it to the Majors in 1933 with Detroit. He was one of four 1933 Tiger rookies along with Hank Greenberg, Eldon Auker, and Schoolboy Rowe who became mainstays of the 1934 Pennant winning team. Fox hit .285 and scored 101 times in his sophomore campaign.

Center fielder Joyner White was a native of Red Oak, Georgia, born on the first day of June 1909. His heavy southern accent made Joyner sound like Jo-Jo, so when he introduced himself people thought his name was Jo-Jo White.

Jo-Jo began his professional baseball career in 1928 and after playing four years in the Minors made the opening day roster of the 1932 Detroit Tigers. When Hank Greenberg joined the Tigers in 1933 the Hebrew Hammer and the Georgia Redneck became roommates. This truly odd couple, a Jew from the Bronx and a small-town southern Christian were road-trip roomies for five years.

The roommate relationship helped erase White's anti-semantics. Jo-Jo said before he roomed with Greenberg he thought "all Jews had horns on their heads."[5] Greenberg said he and Jo-Jo had a great relationship and they enjoyed being on the road together.

White batted left-handed and threw right. He was a speedster who covered a lot of ground in center, stole bases and scored runs. Jo-Jo had a career year in 1934 hitting .313 with 28 stolen bases and 97 runs scored.

The "Madman from Mississippi" filled out the Tiger outfield. Gerald "Gee" Walker earned the Madman nickname for his daring, sometimes reckless exploits on the base paths. Like Black Mike Cochrane, Walker was a college baseball and football star. He is a member of the Ole Miss sports hall of fame.

Walker was born in Gulfport, Mississippi on March 19, 1908. After college and a brief Minor League stint, Walker became a Tiger regular at the start of the 1931 season. He quickly became a fan favorite because of his fearless baserunning, fiery competitiveness and zany antics.

Walker's brazen baserunning delighted Detroit fans but his inattention infuriated Mickey Cochrane. The Madman was easily distracted often listening to fans or talking with rival ballplayers instead of concentrating on the game. He once attempted to steal second base while the batter was being given an intentional walk!

On June 30, 1934 the Madman was picked off twice in one inning. With Hank Greenberg on second Walker was caught off first base by a quick throw from the catcher. Instead of tagging out Walker the alert first baseman threw out Greenberg trying to advance to third. The Madman ended up on second but was promptly picked off for the third out.

In spite of Gee Walker's occasional mental lapses, he was a valuable Tiger and an offensive force. In 1934 the Madman from Mississippi hit an even .300 and stole 20 bases.

This powerful line-up was complimented by outstanding pitching. Starters Schoolboy Row, Tommy Bridges, Eldon Auker and General Crowder along with reliever/starter Firpo Marberry formed a formidable pitching staff.

Lynwood Rowe won 16 consecutive games for the 1934 Detroit Tigers and finished the season with 24 wins and only 8 losses. Born January 11, 1910 in Waco, Texas he grew up in El Dorado, Arkansas. It was while Lynwood was a 15-year-old high school student in El Dorado that he acquired his nickname. The 6'4" Rowe played on the men's town team and since he was still in high school the other players called him "Schoolboy".

At El Dorado high school Rowe was described as a "one-man All-American athletic team" he was a track and field champion, throwing the javelin, discus, and shot put. He also excelled as a sprinter. He was a star on the basketball, football, golf and tennis teams. However, Schoolboy's best sport was baseball, unfortunately El Dorado high school did not have a baseball team.

In 1926 when Rowe was still a 16-year-old schoolboy he signed a professional baseball contract with the Detroit Tigers. He received a $250 signing bonus and was assigned to the Class C Fort Smith Twins. Unwilling to quit high school Rowe hid his professional status while continuing to star for El Dorado high.

Rowe kept refusing to play for teams assigned him by Detroit, until he was finally suspended from professional baseball. Schoolboy played semi-pro ball until 1932 when he decided to report to Beaumont, a Detroit Farm Team.

Rowe was an immediate sensation leading the Beaumont Exporters to the Texas League Championship. He won 19 games and posted a 2.30 ERA. He also blasted 10 homeruns in only 112 at-bats.

Schoolboy made his Major League debut on April 15, 1933 for the Detroit Tigers. He quickly became a fan favorite because of his quirky, eccentric behavior. Schoolboy was very superstitious always carrying different tokens for good luck and never picking up his glove with his pitching hand. He also talked to the baseball.

He called the baseball Edna, after his high school sweetheart Edna Skinner. Schoolboy described his preparation for pitching "just eat a lot of vittles, climb the mound, wrap my fingers around the ball and say to it, 'Edna, honey, let's go." His devotion to his fiancé was evident when he ended a radio interview by asking "how am I doin', Edna?"[6]

During the World Series Leo "The Lip" Durocher made Schoolboy regret that question.

Thomas Jefferson Davis Bridges was cleverly named after two Presidents. A United States President and the President of the Confederate States of America. Tommy was born in Nashville, Tennessee on December 28, 1906.

Bridges pitched for the University of Tennessee where he developed a reputation as a strike-out artist. He was small at 150 lbs., but Bridges possessed courage and a devastating curveball. After turning pro, he struck out 20 batters for the Minor League Wheeling Stogies in 1929. By 1930 Bridges was pitching for the Detroit Tigers.

On August 5, 1932 the Detroit Tigers were hammering the Washington Senators 13 – 0. Tommy Bridges had retired 26 Senators in a row, he needed only one more out to gain baseball immortality. The perfect game seemed assured as the next batter was the Washington pitcher Bob Burke, who was hitting a paltry .182. Unbelievably, Senator manager Walter Johnson, himself a hall of fame pitcher, sent up a pinch hitter.

Dave Harris who was hitting .344 singled, spoiling the perfect game, and Bridges finished with a 1-hitter. Fans and sportswriters were appalled that Walter Johnson, considered one of the finest gentlemen ever to play the game, would send up a pinch hitter when the game was surely lost.

"Dave Harris should be exiled to the North Pole. Walter Johnson doesn't deserve to see his Senators win another game. They should finish in the cellar."[7]

Three more times in his 16-year Major League career Bridges took a no-hitter into the ninth inning, but he never achieved the elusive accomplishment.

Elden Auker was yet another former multi-sport college star on the 1934 Tiger team. Elden was born on September 21, 1910 in Norcatur, a rural Kansas town with a population of about 500. After high school Elden attended Kansas State University where he earned nine varsity letters – three each in baseball, basketball and football.

he was first team All-American in baseball, second team All-American in football and All-Conference in basketball. Ironically a football injury helped Auker become an outstanding Major League player.

"We played Purdue" Auker remembered, "I tackled, and I got what they called a knockdown shoulder. I couldn't get my arm up to throw. I injured the shoulder twice more and I got to the point in baseball where I could only throw sidearm."[8]

After college Auker was offered $6,000 to play professional football for the Chicago Bears. He chose instead to play baseball and signed with the Detroit Tigers. A Minor League coach further altered Aukers delivery from sidearm to an underhanded "submarine" motion. An opposing pitcher, Virgil Trucks, remarked "Elden's knuckles used to graze the ground when he delivered the ball."[9]

This unique underhanded delivery, not seen on a Major League mound in many years, enabled "Submarine" Auker to baffle batters. The right-handed hurler pitched ten years in the Majors and won 130 games.

Although Alvin "General" Crowder served three years in the Army during World War I, he never attained the rank of General. By the time Crowder made it to the Majors in 1926 he was 27-years-old and one of the few WWI Veterans in the big leagues. The nickname "General" was a reference to his service, and from Enoch Crowder, a famous WWI General.

Alvin Floyd Crowder was born January 11, 1899 in Winston-Salem, North Carolina. He received little formal education quitting school after the fifth grade to work on his family farm. He played some sandlot baseball as did most farm boys of that era but was not enamored with the game. Crowder joined the Army when the United States entered WWI.

While in the service Crowder returned to baseball. "He reluctantly volunteered for the baseball team in order to avoid the menial, mundane tasks of an enlisted soldier. The team recognized that the hesitant ballplayer had a strong arm. They asked him to pitch, and his new career was born."[10]

After the service Crowder signed to play professional baseball, and due to his late start in pursuing a baseball career he finally made his Major League debut with the Washington Senators on July 24, 1926 as a 27-year-old rookie. At 5'10" and 170 lbs. the General was not an intimidating mound presence, but he did have a risqué' appearance. Draped over his shoulders and arms was a tattoo of a naked woman, a souvenir of his time spent overseas during the war.

After only one and a half seasons with Washington Crowder was traded to the St. Louis Browns. After three good seasons the General was traded back to Washington where he became an All-Star in 1933 when he won 24 games and led Washington to the American League Pennant. However, Crowder pitched poorly in the World series losing two games to the eventual World Champion New York Giants.

When the 35-year-old Crowder slumped to a 4 – 10 record and an era approaching 7.00 in 1934, Washington figured the General was washed up. On August 4, 1934 Crowder was sent to the Detroit Tigers. The General responded by making nine starts and compiling a 5 – 1 record helping Detroit win the American League Pennant.

Firpo Marberry is considered one of the first relief specialists in Major League baseball. However, during Firpo's career relief pitchers were undervalued, they were only used when the starter was ineffective. Pitchers were expected to finish the games they started.

Firpo was a fine pitcher and too valuable to pitch solely in relief, so managers often used him as a starter. During the 1934 season Firpo started 19 games and appeared in relief 14 times. He finished the regular season with 15 wins and 5 losses.

Frederick Marberry was a Texan, born November 30, 1898 on a farm about 75 miles south of Dallas. Marberry worked on the family farm growing up and had little time for baseball. The closest town to the Marberry farm was Streetman and like many small Texas towns of the era they had a baseball team. As a teenager Fred played for the team as an infielder. He did not start pitching until he was 21-years-old.

Mexia, a town 20 miles south of Streetman had a Minor League team and they soon became aware of the hard-throwing Marberry. Professional teams were always on the lookout for big farm boys with big fastballs. Mexia signed the 6'1" 200 lb. Marberry to his first professional contract in 1922.

Despite Marberry's late arrival on the mound, he quickly mastered his craft. After rapidly ascending through the Minors Fred pitched his first Major League game on August 11, 1923 for the Washington Senators. He was 24-years-old still having pitched for only three years.

The tall, amiably Texan was accepted early on by his Senator teammates. As the custom of the times they found him a nickname. Evidently Marberry bore a striking facial resemblance to Argentine heavyweight boxing contender, Louis Firpo.

The fighter Firpo known as "The Wild Bull of the Pampas" fought heavyweight Champion Jack Dempsey for the title in 1923. The Wild Bull knocked Dempsey completely out of the ring in the first round. Unfortunately for Firpo, Dempsey returned to the ring and in the second round knocked out Firpo to retain his Heavyweight Championship. Louis Firpo's career faded but Fred was forever after known as Firpo Marberry.

Firpo pitched for Washington from 1923 until he was traded to Detroit in 1933. He was a member of the Washington's 1924 World

Series Champions, the Senators first and only World Championship. Firpo pitched in four of the seven games finishing with an ERA of 1.12.

The press, ever eager to tag a player or a team with a moniker, decided to call Detroit the G-Men. In the midst of the Depression America was drowning in a wave of lawlessness. Some of the poor, displaced people turned to crime to sustain their lives. Bank robbing and kidnapping were crimes of choice.

Banks that had foreclosed on family farms were seen as villains and fair game for desperados such as Bonnie and Clyde, Machine Gun Kelly, Baby-Faced Nelson and John Dillinger. They became folk heroes to a down-trodden populace. Kidnapping also seemed justified to some as it was seen to be relieving rich people of ill-gotten fortunes built at the expense of the working class.

To combat the crime wave J. Edgar Hoover's Federal Bureau of Investigation came to the forefront. Criminals armed with stolen submachine guns, browning automatic rifles, and driving V-8 Fords outgunned and outdistanced local law enforcement. Worse yet, criminals were able to escape by crossing state lines where local lawmen lost authority. The FBI had Federal jurisdiction, so their reach extended across all state lines.

G-Men was short for Government Men a slang term for the FBI.

What made G-Men appropo for Detroit was three of their star players had surnames that started with G, Goslin, Greenberg and Gehringer.

On paper the match-ups appeared to favor Detroit, however, St. Louis was installed as an 8 – 5 favorite to win the series. Perhaps based on the Cards late surge to the Pennant and also the dangerous duo of Dizzy and Daffy Dean, whom Babe Ruth rated the best and third best pitchers in the series with Schoolboy Rowe sandwiched in between as the second-best series starter.

Detroit had a decisive advantage at catcher. Mickey Cochrane won the American League's most valuable player award for 1934 even though Lou Gehrig won the triple crown – most homeruns, RBI's and highest batting average. Cochrane was a terrific defensive catcher with extensive experience handling pitchers. He hit .320 with 75 RBIs.

The Cards platooned at catcher with Veteran Spud Davis and rookie Bill Delancey. They combined for a .308 batting average and an impressive

Carl Duncan

105 runs batted in. Although Spud had more experience both Dizzy and Paul preferred pitching to Delancey.

First base was a toss-up. Hammering Hank Greenberg had a sensational sophomore season for Detroit. A potent power hitter he blasted 26 homers, drove in 139 runs and had a .339 batting average. Defensively Hank was much improved over his rookie campaign and at 6'4" tall his height and reach made him adept at turning errant infielder's throws into outs.

Ripper Collins was not a prototypical first baseman, only 5'8" tall he was unable to coral high or wide throws from his infielders. What he lacked defensively he made up for with his potent bat. He led the Cards in every major offensive category; hits – 200, BA - .333, HR – 35, RBI's – 128. His 35 homeruns were the most in the National League.

Detroit held the edge at second base where the mechanical man reigned supreme. A superb defensive second baseman, Charlie Gehringer could cover ground and turn the double play. His offensive production for a second baseman was peerless. Gehringer hit .356 and led the American League in hits with 214 and runs scored with 134. He also drove in a staggering 121 runs.

At 36-years-old Frankie Frisch was still a great ballplayer. However, he was not as fast as when he earned the nickname "Fordham Flash". Not yet a liability at second base he had lost a step and was only adequate. Frisch was still a feared clutch hitter who finished the 1934 regular season with 75 RBI's and a .305 batting average.

Babe Ruth compared the two World Series shortstops, "Durocher is a more brilliant fielder than Rogell, one of the best I have ever seen. But Rogell clearly excels him as a hitter, and Rogell has developed into a high-class fielder".[11]

The Babe was right, Billy Rogell gave Detroit the nod at shortstop. He hit .296 and drove in an even 100 runs for the 1934 Tigers, while playing a flawless shortstop.

The Lip was easily the best defensive shortstop in either League, but he simply could not hit. When Leo played for the Yankees Ruth called him the "All-American out." If Lippy could have averaged only .280 at the plate he would have been one of the all-time great shortstops. Leo's leadership, baseball knowledge, bench jockeying and fine fielding made up for his .260 BA in 1934.

Career-wise Pepper Martin was a better third baseman than Detroit's Marv Owen. However, Pepper had a down year in 1934, so the Tigers had the advantage at third in the series. Owen was superior to Martin both hitting and fielding in 1934. Marv hit .317 and drove in 98 runs while playing in all 154 games.

Hampered by nagging injuries Pepper played only 110 games for the Cards while batting .289 with 49 RBI's. Always daring on the base paths, Pepper Leo the National League in stolen bases with 23. Although the 1934 season was sub-par for Pepper, Babe Ruth cautioned against underestimating Martin in the upcoming World Series.

"I can't forget that Martin is at his best when something big is at stake. As in tight finishes or World Series."[12]

The Babe was referring to the 1931 World Series when writers dubbed Pepper "The Wild Horse of the Osage" as he demolished the Philadelphia Athletics with his hitting and rampaging running of the bases. Pepper hit .500 and swiped 5 bases on his way to series M.V.P.

The two series left fielders were both future hall of famers and both had outstanding 1934 seasons, however, Detroit had the advantage. Tiger, Goose Goslin had World Series experience having played in the 1924 and 1925 fall classics, and therefore unlikely to wilt under the glare of World Series publicity. On the other hand, Ducky Medwick's hair-trigger temper made him an unknown factor. Neither Goose nor Ducky were accomplished defensive outfielders.

Tigers, JoJo White and Gee Walker shared center field duties. They contributed a combined .306 batting average 83 RBI's and 48 stolen bases to Detroit's offensive machine. Both were swift ball-hawking fielders.

Ernie "Hollywood" Orsatti was a fast, slick-fielding center fielder for the Cardinals. He batted an even .300 but had little power, driving in only 31 runs with no homeruns in the 1934 season. Advantage Detroit.

Detroit deployed Fleet Pete Fox in right field. His 25 stolen bases were second best for the Tigers behind JoJo White's 28 swipes. Pete batted .285, hit 2 homers and drove in 44 runs. He was an elite outfielder.

Jack Rothrock was rock-solid playing in all 154 Cardinal regular season games. Jack was almost as fast as Fox and he packed more power. He crashed 11 homeruns and drove in 72 runs while hitting .284. Rothrock was a steady if unspectacular outfielder. Slight edge to St. Louis.

No pitcher in Major League baseball could equal Dizzy Dean's 1934 season. He led both the National and American Leagues in three categories; wins – 30, strikeouts – 195 shutouts – 7. His 2.66 ERA was second in the National League. Dizzy was simply the best pitcher in baseball.

Detroit's ace, Schoolboy Rowe, had an outstanding 1934 regular season. He won 24 lost 8, struck out 149 and had an ERA of 3.45. Edge to St. Louis.

Number two starters, Cardinal Paul Dean and Tiger Tommy Bridges, had similar statistical seasons. Paul won 19 lost 11, struck out 150 and had a 3.43 ERA. Bridges finished 22 – 11 with 151 strikeouts and an ERA of 3.67. He was more experienced, but Paul accomplished something that forever eluded Tommy Bridges, a no-hitter. Slight edge to St. Louis.

"Submarine" Auker had a better year than Tex Carleton. Auker: 15 – 7, 3.67 ERA, 86 strikeouts Carleton: 16 – 11, 4.26 ERA, 103 strikeouts. Slight edge to Detroit.

Firpo Marberry and Wild Bill Hallahan had almost identical ERA's and strikeouts. Firpo – 4.57 ERA, 64 strikeouts. Wild Bill – 4.26 ERA, 70 strikeouts. However, Firpo went 15 – 5 while Wild Bill won only 8 and lost 12. Advantage Detroit.

Frankie Frisch and Mickey Cochrane were hall of fame players, however they both were rookie managers. Both the Fordham Flash and Black Mike piloted teams to the Pennant that were underdogs in their respective leagues. No advantage either way.

The 1934 World Series format was a best of seven series. The first two games were to be played on October 3rd and 4th at Navin Field in Detroit. The next three games were scheduled for October 5th, 6th, and 7th at Sportsman's Park in St. Louis. The teams would return to Detroit for games six and seven on October 8th and 9th if necessary. The first team to win four games would be declared World Champions.

CHAPTER 20

"Diz wasn't sayin' nothin' he was just talkin'"

After five years of playing professionally Dizzy finally arrived on sports biggest stage. That stage seemed built for Dizzy Dean. With Babe Ruth fading, Dizzy was the premier box office attraction in professional sports, and Paul was along for the ride. Dizzy and Daffy were receiving more publicity than other contemporary duos, Amos and Andy, George and Gracie, Tarzan and Jane or Bonnie and Clyde.

Before American's obsession with pro football made the Super Bowl America's ultimate sporting event, the World Series dominated the sports landscape.

On the eve of the first game of the 1934 World Series a column appeared in the St. Louis Post-Dispatch;

> Dizzy figures series "just a breeze" for him Paul and Birds
> By Jerome (Dizzy) Dean
> Leading pitcher of 1934

Some exerts from that article:

> "This may look like a tough series to some folks, but it looks like just a breeze to me, and Paul, my brother, feels the same way about it. We ought to beat them without too much trouble."
>
> "When the Detroit players see my fastball and Paul's they'll realize Schoolboy Rowe's fast one is just an ordinary change of pace."
>
> "I told Frank Frisch I was ready and that I figured I could pitch all four games, if necessary, but that wouldn't be fair for Detroit."
>
> "Me 'n' Paul are thinking of starting a school for pitchers this winter and I'd like nothing better than to have Mickey Cochrane send his whole staff to us to learn the finer points of the game."[1]

And so, it went, praising me 'n' Paul while trashing the Tigers, instead of incensing Tiger fans, the publicity only enhanced the allure of Dizzy and Daffy. When the Cardinals arrived in Detroit for the first game of the World Series, fans mobbed the streets hoping for a glimpse of the dazzling Deans. Jimmy Powers of the New York Daily News chronicled the hysteria;

"The two brothers, the most sensational adolescents to bounce into baseball headlines in this generation, literally held the sole attention of this cock-eyed village. Schoolboy Rowe? Frankie Frisch? Mickey Cochrane? You ceased to think or hear of them. The Deans were the story. Wherever they went there immediately followed a siren- shrieking squad of police cars, a clattering escort of stick-swinging mounted patrolmen, and a surging, ogling crowd of fans."

"The Deans are on every lip. Vaudeville actors insert allusions to them in impromptu acts, movie organists compose parodies of popular songs in their honor. The papers carry headlines of the size usually employed to announce a declaration of war. They tell hourly bulletin movements of the two grinning, roistering, record-breaking farmer boys."[2]

Grantland Rice described the Dean's invasion of Detroit in verse:

> "Genghis Khan left a blazing trail
>   With a killing drive as the nations fled;
> Atilla marched and the world turned pale
>   Where his thundering Huns turned the highway red;
> But hark to the rumble of poisoned hoofs
>   From out of the West, where the sun goes down –
> And machine guns wait from the city's roofs
>   As the Terrible Deans reach Tiger town.
>
> Hannibal's elephants, over the Alps,
>   Handed the jitters to ancient Rome –
> The red men struck for the pale face scalps
>   And the tomahawk fell on the white man's dome;
> And Sherman swept to the open sea,
>   Leaving a swath that was bare and brown,
> But today the women and children flee
>   As the Terrible Deans reach Tiger town.
> Step by step they are on the way,
>   Their ju-ju drums sound a deeper note –
> But the stalking Tiger still seeks his prey
>   With a snarl and a growl from his Bengal throat;
> Cochrane and Gehringer, Goslin and Rowe
>   Swarm to the ramparts with glare and frown,
> Attila, Sherman and Khan look slow
>   As the Terrible Deans reach Tigertown."[3]

Celebrities wanted to meet the dazzling Dean duo. Diz and Paul ate breakfast with Will Rogers and Damon Runyon at the Venetian Room located in the Book-Cadillac hotel.

Will Rogers was a humorist, social commentator, National newspaper columnist, radio personality and also a star of stage and screen. By 1934

Rogers was America's leading wit and Hollywood's biggest box office attraction.

Will was a poorly-educated Okie who claimed he studied the fourth reader for ten years. He felt a special kinship with Diz and Paul because of their similar backgrounds. Will picked the Cards to win the series, knowing many of the Cardinals were uneducated hard-working rural boys whose only chance of fame and fortune depended on their diamond success.

Although Damon Runyon was born in Kansas, his fame came from his stories and newspaper columns celebrating the World of Broadway and New York City. He also reported on the New York City sporting scene for William Randolf Hearst's publishing empire.

Runyon was a notorious gambler, who once paraphrased a bible verse in print' "The race is not always to the swift, nor the battle to the strong, but that's how the smart money bets."[4] Damon was not college educated, but he was betting on Detroit whose roster was laden with smart collegians.

Henry Ford hosted Diz and Paul on a tour of his automobile factory. Ford's innovative assembly line process revolutionized automobile manufacturing and made Fords affordable for most Americans.

Ford greeted the Cardinal pitchers and then said, "Dizzy, you've done more to bring the World out of the doldrums than any other man alive. I admire you and I wish you luck in the World Series."[5]

Dizzy was flattered and for once in his life, vaguely humble. "Mr. Ford, why don't you come down to St. Louis and buy the Cardinal ball club? I'd like to work for you. You see, I won thirty games for Sam Breadon, but I'm sure I could win fifty for you."[6]

After a morning of hobnobbing with Will Rogers, Damon Runyon, and Henry Ford, Diz and Paul returned to the Book-Cadillac hotel where the Cardinals were staying. In their room the Deans gave some interviews to reporters before descending to the lobby to wait for the bus that would take the team to Navin Field for an afternoon practice. All of a sudden, Diz announced "I ain't gonna ride no bus"[7]

Was Diz demanding special treatment? Did he require a limo? Had the publicity gone to his head? No, Dizzy said he was going to walk to the stadium.

Me 'N' Paul

The huge crowd gathered outside the hotel, waiting to watch the Cards board the bus, were surprised to see Dizzy Dean emerge from the hotel and start walking down Michigan Ave. Mounted policemen were immediately beside him and police cars soon joined escorting Diz and the fans with lights flashing and sirens blaring. Diz talked constantly, praising Me 'n' Paul, predicting the demise of the Tigers and signing everything thrust into his hands.

Dizzy arrived at Navin Stadium as the Tigers were wrapping up their practice. Still in his street clothes Diz walked out on the field, snagged a bat and shoved a startled Hank Greenberg out of the batter's box.

"Outta my way, Mo. I'll show you how to hit."[8]

Mo, short for Moses, is what ballplayers of the era called Jewish players. This was not an offensive racial slur, depending on who said it, and how someone chose to take it. Italian players were referred to as "Dagos". Joe DiMaggio called himself "The Big Dago" and his teammate Phil Rizzuto, "The Little Dago."

Greenberg laughed good-naturedly and let Diz hit. Diz waggled the bat and yelled to Del Baker, a Tiger coach who was pitching batting practice, "Heave me a few, fella. I ain't hittin' at no wind this series. Throw me a ball."[9]

Baker complied and Diz began lashing liners to the outfield until suddenly the bat shattered in his hands. Diz turned and dropped the bat pieces at Greenberg's feet. "That's the way to hit the ball, Mo."[10]

His hitting exhibition over, Diz headed to the visitors' clubhouse.

Intrigue continued to dog Diz. The big question before the first World Series game; who would be the starting pitchers? Fans wanted to see a duel of aces, Dizzy Dean against Schoolboy Rowe. However, that dream match-up began to seem unlikely.

Dizzy was drained after pitching nearly everyday during the Cardinals thrilling Pennant charge. Frankie Frisch was reluctant to push his ace to complete exhaustion. Frisch could rest Diz in the opener and still start him three times if the Series went the full seven games.

The decision as to the starting pitchers became a soap opera. There was speculation that Dizzy's mystique had spooked Mickey Cochrane and if Diz started, Mick would pitch General Crowder rather than risk Schoolboy against the invincible Dizzy Dean.

Diz could not believe he might be denied the spotlight of starting the first game of the World Series. He was petulant;

"Guess I won't pitch any games," moans the Dizzy one, who pitched the Cardinals to seven-hit shutouts over the Cincinnati Reds on Friday and Sunday. "Well, maybe my arm is tired, but it tells me it's ready to shoot Tigers right now."[11]

Schoolboy Rowe was confident, and he wanted to face Diz in the opener. Detroit fans and sportswriters were sure Rowe was equal to the task. The writers always touted Schoolboy's amazing athletic ability.

"Rowe was a ten-second sprinter. He was a discus thrower. He hurled the javelin beyond 200 feet. He was a crack tennis player. He won the interscholastic golf championship. He was a star basketball and football player."[12]

Dizzy, tired of hearing about Schoolboy's athletic prowess, correctly pointed out, "ain't gonna be no javelin throwin' or tennis playin' in the World Series."[13]

Detroit and all of America was infected by World series fever. Thousands of fans camped out overnight at Navin Field in order to vie for bleacher seats going on sale the morning of the first game. Ford Motor Company enabled Americans who could not attend the games to at least listen to them. Henry Ford's company paid $100,000 for radio broadcast rights to the series.

In Houston, Texas, Pa Dean boarded a Greyhound bus bound for St. Louis where he would attend World Series games three, four and five. Elmer "Goober" Dean, who lived with Pa Dean, declined a return to St. Louis where he was briefly a peanut and soda salesman at Sportsman Park.

At a stop in Dallas Pa told reporters, "If you think Dizzy is good just wait until Paul gets one more year of that Big League pitchin' and you're gonna see some pitchin'."[14]

The starting pitcher soap opera in Detroit continued and on the eve of the opener, Frankie Frisch still refused to name his starting pitcher. "I do not know right now who will pitch for us," Frisch said. "And I won't know until shortly before it is time tomorrow to give the signal for the warm-up. If Dizzy looks right to me, he will start, but he has been doing a lot of pitching, you know, and he may need an extra day."[15]

Me 'N' Paul

The 1934 World Series began on Wednesday October 3rd under sunny skies with cool temperatures. The start of the game was delayed 20 minutes to allow ticket holders time to fight their way through the throng of fans surrounding the stadium.

Henry Ford sent his limousine to pick up Dizzy's wife, Pat, who was accompanied by movie star Joe E. Brown and Dizzy's business manager, Frank Rosenthal. A motorcycle police escort led the group to Navin Field.

The overflow crowd was delighted to see Dizzy warming up. Diz had finally convinced Frisch to let him start the first game of the series. As Dizzy was warming up, he was suddenly attacked by a man wearing a Tiger costume! After several minutes of scuffling, Diz snatched the Tiger's tail and started twisting. The man wearing the Tiger costume, baseball comedian Al Schacht, surrendered as the crowd roared with laughter.

When Mickey Cochrane was sure Dizzy was starting for the Cards, he sent General Crowder to the mound to start the game, instead of his ace Schoolboy Rowe. This move contradicted what Cochrane said before the start of the series. "I will lead with my ace, if we used any but our best against their best, we'd be conceding the game and the Tigers aren't conceding anybody anything."[16]

The visiting Cards were up first, and Pepper Martin grounded out on the first pitch of the World Series. Jack Rothrock followed by flying out to JoJo White. Batting third, Frankie Frisch hit a routine grounder to third, Marv Owen bobbled the ball for the first error of the series, a sign of things to come. General Crowder avoided further trouble by inducing Ripper Collins to fly out.

Diz trudged to the mound to start his third game in six days. He escaped the first inning without giving up any runs, but he gave up one base hit and the three batters he retired each hit the ball hard. Clearly Dizzy was not as dominating as usual.

Unbelievably Detroit's famous "Battalion of Death" infield made two more errors allowing St. Louis to score two runs in the top of the second. Dizzy was scuffling, he gave up a lead-off single to Goose Goslin in the bottom of the second inning, then Dizzy ran the count full to Billy Rogell before he swung and missed for a strikeout. Goslin broke for second on the 3 – 2 pitch, Frisch took the throw from catcher Bill Delancey and the Goose was cooked. He slid hard into second and was out but so was Frisch.

The Flash was knocked out for several minutes. His Cardinal teammates rushed to his aid, but he recovered and did not have to leave the game. Dizzy fanned Marv Owen to end the inning.

Two more Tiger errors enabled the Cards to take a 3 – 0 lead into the bottom of the third. Diz was laboring mightily. He gave up a run and had Tigers aboard at second and third with two outs. Hank Greenberg came to the plate needing only a single to tie the score. Frisch, Collins, Durocher, and Martin huddled around Dizzy to discuss strategy in that crucial situation.

Leo the Lip knew what Diz should do. "Throw Mo a pork ball, the son of a bitch won't touch it."[17] Leo advised loud enough for Hammering Hank to hear. Dizzy laughed out loud and then pumped three strikes past Greenberg, the third strike was a head=high pitch that Hank swung at and missed.

The fourth was uneventful as neither team scored. Ducky Medwick took the General deep for a solo homerun to put the Cards up 4 – 1. Dizzy had a clean fifth inning as he retired the Tigers with no runs and no hits.

Relief ace Firpo Marberry replaced General Crowder to start the sixth and Dizzy greeted him with a long double to right-center. That opened the floodgates as the Cards erupted for four runs and an 8 – 1 lead. Diz coasted the rest of the way giving up two meaningless Tiger runs, one a Hammering Hank homerun.

St. Louis won game one of the 1934 World Series 8 – 3. Diz gave up 8 hits, walked 2 and struck out 6. It was the fourth time in nine days that Dizzy had pitched a full nine inning game and won. General Crowder pitched a decent game but was mauled by five Tiger errors. Ducky Medwick was the hitting star of the game with four hits, one of them a homerun.

Paul Dean critiqued his brother's performance. "He didn't have a thing out there. His curve ball was as straight as the foul lines."[18]

Dizzy agreed with Paul's assessment. After the game in the visitor's clubhouse, Diz bummed a cigarette from a reporter and announced he had pitched a terrible game.

"Boys" he said between puffs, "I'm telling you the truth when I'm telling you I was lousy out there today. That old curve ball of mine just wouldn't work. I couldn't do a thing with my fast one, as a result I had to pitch my head off."[19]

Reporters asked Dizzy how Paul would do when he started against Detroit.

"Boy" Diz said "he'll knock them silly with that fastball of his. He's really got a fast one. He can lay it in there."[20]

That night Dizzy was on a National radio broadcast. A Columbia network announcer made an introduction and explained that Diz would talk to rear Admiral Richard Byrd who was at the South Pole operating a meteorological station. Byrd was a world-famous aviator and polar explorer. He led expeditions that were the first to reach both the North and South Poles by air.

Dizzy never met a stranger, he talked to the famous explorer like he was an old friend. "Howdy there, Dick Byrd, down at the South Pole," Diz began and then told Byrd how he beat the Tigers. "Well, it was a hard-pitched game. I didn't have anything on my ball. That's why I had to work so hard. I finally staggered through, but it was a lousy, tick-flea-chigger-bit ball game. Them Tigers wasn't so good as I figured they ought to be.

Why, I could take any of four National League teams and beat 'em for a World Series – if I pitched."[21]

Mickey Cochrane was disappointed with the game one loss but said he and his team quickly put it behind them. "It's gone" he said. "Tomorrow's another day and I'll shoot Rowe at them."[22]

Frankie Frisch decided to save Paul for the opener in St. Louis. He named Wild Bill Hallahan his game two starter.

Navin Field was rocking as fans streamed into the stadium hungry for a Detroit victory. The Tigers had never won a World Series game in Detroit. Their only World Series win had been in Chicago on October 12, 1908. In a series which Detroit lost four games to one.

As the teams warmed up for the start of the game, Dizzy was restless. Diz had no need to warm up since he was not playing, so he roamed around the diamond. Bored with watching the Cards Diz wandered over to watch Detroit. He positioned himself behind Schoolboy Rowe who was warming up to start the game. Diz was giving the Schoolboy unsolicited advice on how to pitch the Cards. Mickey Cochrane complained to an ump and Diz was ordered back to the St. Louis dugout.

Carl Duncan

On the way back to his side of the field Diz stopped by Detroit's dugout, picked up a Tiger bat and walked away with it. "You fellas don't know what bats are for, anyway,"[23] Dizzy remarked.

Continuing back to the Card dugout Diz paraded in front of the box seats pausing to shake hands with Henry Ford, Will Rogers and other celebrities. He then stopped in front of a brass band that was playing the Cardinals World Series theme song "Hold that Tiger."

"Dizzy became enwrapped in a huge tuba and at least indicated that he was playing it as the crowd cheered and photographers took pictures."[24]

The game finally started with Wild Bill Hallahan pitching for the Cards and Schoolboy Rowe on the hill for Detroit. Neither team scored in the first, but the Cards drew first blood in the top of the second. Bill Delancey scratched out a single and Hollywood Orsatti tripled him home, Detroit failed to score in their half of the innings. Cardinals 1 Tigers 0.

The Cards struck again in the top of the third. Pepper Martin singled and Jack Rothrock sacrificed him to second. Ducky Medwick singled him home. Wild Bill pitched another scoreless inning. Cardinals 2 Tigers 0.

The Schoolboy settled down and started putting up goose eggs. In the fourth inning Detroit scored a controversial run. Billy Rogell doubled and took third on a groundout. Pete Fox followed with a liner down the left field line that appeared foul. The umps deemed it a fair ball and Rogell scored. The Cardinals protested vigorously but unsuccessfully. Cardinals 2 Tigers 1.

Wild Bill and the Schoolboy continued to pitch brilliantly and going into the bottom of the ninth the score remained 2 – 1 in favor of St. Louis. Wild Bill needed three outs for the win, and a two game to none lead in the World Series.

Pete Fox singled to start the bottom of the ninth and was sacrificed to second. With the tying run in scoring position Cochrane sent Gerald "The Madman from Mississippi" Walker up to pinch hit for JoJo White. The Madman popped up a puny fly between home and first base. Easy play for Ripper, but inexplicably he flinched at the last second and the ball fell harmlessly to the ground in foul territory.

Given a new reason for his existence the Madman singled in Fox to tie the game at two apiece. Frisch went to his bullpen and replaced Wild Bill with his other southpaw, Bill Walker. As usual the Madman was inattentive as he took his lead at first. Walker promptly picked him off for the second out. Cochrane, at the plate, was so exasperated by the sorry base running that he struck out sending the exciting game into extra innings.

The Schoolboy continued to school the Cards in the tenth, eleventh and twelfth giving him nine consecutive scoreless innings. Walker held Detroit scoreless in the tenth and eleventh but ran into trouble in the bottom of the twelfth. With one out Walker walked Charley Gehringer and Hank Greenberg. Goose Goslin gave the game to Detroit with a walk-off single.

It could have been the Cards game if not for Ripper's error on the pop foul in the ninth. After the game Ripper explained why he missed the pop-up. He told reporters "someone flashed a mirror in my eyes."[25]

Dan Howley, former Cincinnati Red manager, confirmed Ripper's assortations. "That was the dirtiest trick I have ever seen performed on a baseball field."[26]

Even Frank Navin, owner of the Detroit Tigers, believed Ripper. "It is a lamentable trick, and I am going to do all in my power to bring the culprit to punishment."[27]

None of this changed the outcome, the game still went to Detroit. Damon Runyon aptly summed up the game:

"The song must be of Lynwood "Schoolboy" Rowe, not of Wild Bill Hallahan, for the World does not ask how you won – but did you win? It cannot pause to listen to the sad, sad tale of a loser."[28]

There was no travel day so both teams went directly from the game to the train station. They would travel overnight to St. Louis for games three, four and five, in the Major League's southern outpost.

Pa Dean had arrived in St. Louis via Greyhound bus from Houston. Reporters were anxious to interview him about his famous boys.

"No man could ask for better sons." Pa said. "Dizzy was always a little stubborn, but if you would brag on him, he would work his head off. You couldn't, however, get anywhere with severe methods. When he was a youngster, I'd tan him until his backside was on fire, but he would just get white-mouthed and wouldn't budge. He had to be smoothed down."[29]

Asked about Paul, Pa just smiled. "Schucks, Paul never gave anyone any trouble. He was always agreeable."[30]

Three World Series games in St. Louis brought fans streaming up from southern states. Farmers, ranchers and other rural folks poured up from the cotton belt. St. Louis was the southernmost Major League city and World Series games within driving distance of Arkansas, Mississippi, Tennessee, Texas and Oklahoma were not to be missed. They came to cheer for the native sons. Twelve sons of the confederacy saw action in the 1934 World Series, six Cards and six Tigers.

The six Cards were Dizzy and Paul Dean, born in Arkansas, raised in Oklahoma and Texas. Pepper Martin, Oklahoma's contribution to Major League baseball. Tex Carleton, pride of the Lone Stare state. Catchers Spud Davis from Alabama and Bill Delancey a native of North Carolina.

Detroit also fielded six sons of the south. Georgia peach JoJo White. The Madman from Mississippi, Gerald Walker. Tennessee Tommy Bridges. North Carolinian, General Crowder. Texan Firpo Marberry and finally Schoolboy Rowe. Rowe was born in Texas, but Arkansas claimed him as one of their own after his star-studded career at El Dorado high school in Arkansas.

As thirty-four thousand fans filled Sportsman's Park, Dizzy's wife Pat sat in field level box seats along the third base line. She was joined by Pa Dean, Joe E Brown, Will Rogers and Betty Holt, a young lady from Columbus, Ohio, Paul was dating.

Sportsman Park did not have a public address system, so the starting line-ups were announced by a man with a megaphone. The hometown crowd cheered as the Cards took the field. Twenty-one-year-old rookie Paul Dean ascended the mound to start the most important game of his fledgling Major League career.

JoJo White led off and hit a long drive to left field that Ducky Medwick caught in foul territory. Mickey Cochrane struck out, but Charlie Gehringer followed with a single. Hank Greenberg fouled out to catcher Bill Delancey.

Tommy Bridges took the mound and faced Card lead-off hitter Pepper Martin. Pepper promptly hit a shot off the right field bleacher screen which would have been a double for anyone less speedy, but Pepper slid into third on his chest for a triple. Jack Rothrock flied out to centerfield which plated the first run of the game, as Pepper tagged up and scored. Frankie Frisch singled to right on Bridge's first pitch to him. Ducky fanned and Frisch was thrown out trying to steal second ending the inning.

The Goose led off the second inning by bouncing one of Paul's fastballs over Frisch's head and taking second when Rothrock juggled the ball. Billy Rogell flied out but Paul plunked Marv Owen on the thigh putting Bengals on first and second with only one out. Paul pulled himself out of trouble by popping up Fox and burning Bridges with a called third strike.

St. Louis started their half of the second with a Ripper Collins single. A Delancey double followed culminating with Cardinals perched on second and third, a Bridges fastball struck Orsatti loading the bases. Leo the Lip was loudly cheered as he stepped to the plate with an opportunity to break the game wide open. However, the All-American out popped out to Greenberg. Paul Dean was next up trying to help his own cause. He blasted a long line drive that Pete Fox was able to run down. Ripper tagged up and scored from third with the second Card run. Paul was credited with an RBI sacrifice fly. Bridges avoided further damage by inducing Pepper to fly out to center.

Trouble loomed for the Cards in the third. After JoJo flied out, Cochrane worked Paul for a walk. Charlie Gehringer hit a liner to short left-center which Ducky dove for and missed giving the Mechanical Man a double. Cochrane should have scored but he was slowed by a spike wound suffered in game two, and only made it to third. One out, Tigers on second and third with two future hall of fame sluggers, Greenberg and Goslin, coming up. Paul was in deep excrement, and as the game dangled by a thread, he called upon Dizzy's advice.

"When you get in trouble," Diz told him, "fog 'em through or plow 'em through and that's all you need."[31]

Paul fanned the Hebrew Hammer, walked the Goose and retired Rogell to extinguish the fire. St. Louis failed to score in the bottom of the third but thanks to Paul's poise under pressure the Cardinals still led 2 – 0.

Paul loaded the bases again in the fourth. Marv Owens started the inning by grounding out, Fox singled. Pitcher Tommy Bridges, up next, should have been an easy out, however, Paul walked him. JoJo fouled out but Paul continued to flirt with danger by walking Cochrane to fill the bases. Charley Gehringer, the Mechanical Man, and All-Star .350 hitter was coming to bat, and there was nowhere to put him.

Also, troubling, the Mechanical Man already had a single and double off Paul in his two previous at-bats. Ripper, Pepper, Leo and the Flash huddled around Paul and Delancey discussing strategy. The conference proved effective as Gehringer grounded to Frisch for the third out. For the second consecutive inning, Paul dodged disaster.

Bridges schuffled effortlessly through the Cards in the bottom of the fourth. Two strike-outs and a pop-up left the score St. Louis 2, Detroit 0.

Paul walked the lead-off hitter, Hank Greenberg, to start the fifth inning. After Goslin flied out, Rogell singled sending Greenberg scurrying to third. One out, Tigers on first and third, Paul was treading water trying not to drown. He survived. Paul proved he could blow the ball by the Bengals when necessary by fanning Fox and Owens.

St. Louis scored two runs in their half of the fifth on Pepper's double, Rothrock's triple and a single by the ol' Flash. After five innings Paul had yielded 5 hits, 5 walks and a hit batsman. He managed to squirm out of two bases loaded jams and strand 11 Tiger baserunners to preserve a 4 – 0 lead.

Chief Hogsett who relieved Tommy Bridges to finally fold the Cards in the fifth was the first batter in the Tiger sixth. Elton Hogsett, like Paul Dean had a nickname that did not suit him. His only connection to the Native Americans came when he played Minor League baseball in Oklahoma. "I roomed with a full-blooded Kiowa Indian and the nickname just kinda stuck."[32]

Paul promptly struck Hogsett out. JoJo singled, then Paul retired Mickey Cochrane and Charlie Gehringer. The Chief erased the Cards in order to close out the sixth.

Paul tamed the Tigers in the seventh and eighth with no runs, hits or walks, the Chief kept the Cards down and going to the ninth St. Louis still led 4 – 0. Paul was three outs away from a World Series victory!

JoJo kept the Tigers clawing with a lead-off single to start the ninth. Paul bared down, popping up Cochrane and Gehringer. One more out to go. Hank Greenberg stood in the batters' box and Paul blasted two fastball strikes past him. The third straight fastball resulted in a foul ball. When Paul attempted to force a fourth fastball past him, Hammering Hank hammered a triple off the fence scoring JoJo from third.

Goose Goslin came up with a chance to keep the Tigers alive. The infield again converged on the mound, Goose possessed power to spare and must be pitched carefully. Goslin hit a short fly into no-mans land between centerfielder Hollywood Orsatti and second sacker Frankie Frisch. Hollywood came racing in, but he was facing the setting sun making it difficult to track the ball. If it fell in for a hit Greenberg would score and the tying run would come to the plate.

At the crack of Goose's bat, the Ol' Flash turned his back to the infield and ran all the way into right center field to make the catch and save the game. Paul had his first World Series win! He gave up 1 run on 8 hits and 6 walks. He struck out 7 and stranded 13 Tigers on the base paths.

When the Cardinals reached their dressing room, they swarmed around Paul yelling and slapping him on the back, everyone was congratulating and praising Paul.

"He certainly pitched a swell game," Frisch said, "particularly in the pinches when he bore down with the bases loaded. He was as cool as ice out there all afternoon."[33]

Leo the Lip said, "Paul was faster than Dizzy today and we never had any doubt about Paul coming through even when he loaded the bases a time or two. He's the coolest kid in the Major Leagues, you know, and is never so tough as when the other team is threatening."[34]

Of course, Dizzy chimed in. "Them Tigers can't beat Me 'n' Paul. Didn't I tell you how this series would be – Me 'n' Paul – that's all."[35]

Paul was worn out but happy, "I was glad Pa was out in the stands to see me pitch. You see, Pa wasn't so awful excited about the result of today's game. He knows what the Deans can do on a mound."[36]

Asked if he was nervous since it was his first World Series game, Paul said, "no, I wasn't nervous. It seemed like just another game to me. I never get upset when there are men on bases. The more on base the harder I pitch and when I get three men on base, I know I have to get that next guy, so I bear down. Another thing, don't forget that I hadn't pitched for six days and I may have been a little bit off form."[37]

Even the opposition was impressed. Schoolboy Rowe said "I am glad the Deans aren't triplets. Two of them are trouble enough to any ball team and they strike me as being too much trouble for one Detroit team in this World Series."[38]

The Cards were home leading the series two games to one. With two more games in St. Louis they could close out Detroit without returning to Detroit.

When Diz was leaving the stadium after Paul's World Series win, he accepted a ride with two well-dressed strangers in an automobile with New York license plates. Card owner Sam Breadon witnessed the event and was horrified. He thought Dizzy was being kidnapped!

Breadon was relieved when he reached the hotel and found Diz safe and sound. He lectured Dizzy on the danger of gamblers kidnapping him in an effort to affect the outcome of the World Series. Breadon was so concerned he hired a policeman to protect his star pitcher.

"Dizzy was proud of his escort and introduced the policeman by name to all he met.

Each introduction was followed by a gesture of the thumb, and a whisper, 'he's guarding me.'"[39]

Game four featured two former college football players opposing each other on the mound. Pitching for Detroit Eldon Auker, a Jayhawker from Kansas and pitching for St. Louis Tex Carleton, a Horned Frog from Texas Christian University.

After a scoreless first inning, St. Louis pushed across a single run in the bottom of the second. The Tigers roared back in the third with three talleys driving Tex from the hill. Dazzy Vance replaced Tex. It was the first World Series appearance of the Ol' Dazzler's long career. Ripper Collins drove in a run in the Card third making the score, Detroit 3 St. Louis 2.

Detroit took a two-run lead with another run in the top of the fourth. The Cardinal fourth found Frankie Frisch making one of the biggest blunders in World Series history.

Hollywood Orsatti led off with a single and Lippy Leo reached on an error. Spud Davis pinch hit for the Ol' Dazzler and singled scoring Orsatti, Leo scurried to third. Spud's single made the score 4 – 3 and left Redbirds on first and third with no outs. At this juncture manager Frisch used "a million-dollar asset on a ten-cent errand."[40] He sent his star, irreplaceable pitcher to run for Spud.

Everyone, reporters, fans, even Tigers and Cardinals were stunned to see Diz trot out to first base. Diz to run? Why? Any reserve player or relief

Me 'N' Paul

pitcher could run. Why risk injury to the ace you were depending on to win the World Series?

Pepper Martin came to the plate and grounded to Gehringer, with no chance to nail Leo at home he threw to Rogell to start the double play. Rogell touched second base for the force out, then unleashed a throw toward first to complete the double play. Diz was sailing into second head up and erect. The ball struck him in the side of the head and bounced high into the air where Hank Greenberg caught it in shallow right field. Dizzy crumpled like a puppet whose strings suddenly snapped.

Dizzy lay prone and semi-conscious on the infield dirt between first and second as players from both teams rushed to his aid. Dizzy was carried from the field feet first by Paul and three other Cards. He was rushed to St. John's hospital for x-rays and observation.

When play resumed the score was tied at four with Pepper on first and one out. Jack Rothrock flied out and Frankie Frisch grounded out ending the bizarre fourth inning.

Dizzy's injury seemed to collapse the Cards, they failed to score the rest of the game. The Tigers mauled the Cardinals for six additional runs and won the game 10 – 4. The World Series was tied at two games apiece.

Dizzy spent the night in the hospital as a precautionary measure. X-Rays showed he was not seriously injured, and he showed no ill effects of the crushing blow to his head except a huge headache.

"You can't hurt me, hitting me in the head." Diz said. "I never knew I was hit until I woke up on the ground. I didn't see the throw. All I saw was a lot of stars and moons and dogs and cats. I didn't see no Tigers."[41]

Paul said he knew Dizzy was all right even as they carried him off the field. "Why, he talked all the way to the clubhouse."

"What was he saying?" Asked a reporter.

"He wasn't saying nothin'", Paul replied. "He was just talkin'".[42]

Frankie Frisch steadfastly defended his decision to use Diz as a pinch runner.

"I used Dizzy because I needed him, and he is an excellent base runner. This sort of accident will not happen once in the next 20,000 times, if at all. I feel that it was merely this miracle mischance and not bad judgement that resulted in his being hit on the head."[43]

The Detroit shortstop's savage shot to Dizzy's skull did not dull his confidence and enthusiasm.

"Sure, I'm gonna pitch tomorrow. I've been dying to get at them Tigers again. I'll beat 'em, too."[44]

The weather was clear and warm in St. Louis as 38,000 fans packed Sportsman's Park for game five of the 1934 World Series. The St. Louis fans were expecting to get their first look at Schoolboy Rowe. He was rested and ready to go, but Mickey Cochrane played the same hand as in the first Card game.

He was still unwilling to use his ace against Dizzy Dean. He knew if Diz was right not even the Schoolboy could defeat him. When Cochrane found out Diz was pitching he decided to use Tommy Bridges who had lost to Paul Dean in game three.

Dizzy was not exactly "right" but he was still tough. Diz kept the Cards in the game and going into the bottom of the ninth St. Louis was behind 3 – 1. Frankie Frisch led off with a single. After Medwick flied out, Ripper Collins came through with a single putting Cards on first and third with only one out. That brought Bill Delancey to the plate representing the winning run.

Delancey had accounted for the only Cardinal run with a solo homerun in the seventh inning, so things looked good for the Cards. However, umpire Brick Owens called two quick strikes on Delancey that Bill said was so far outside that "I could hardly have hit them if I'd stepped across the plate."[45]

"You'uh givin' them the fuckin' game," Delancey drawled, and Owens said that would cost him $50.

"Why don't you make it a hundred?" said Delancey. "A hundred it is," replied Owens.

"Fuck you" shouted Delancey, "make it two." "Two it is!"[46]

Delancey struck out and silently returned to the dugout, either out of cuss words or out of money. Orsatti grounded out giving Detroit the win and a 3 – 2 edge in games. The series would finish in Detroit with the Tigers only one win away from the World Championship.

Dizzy refused to blame his injury for the loss. "There's one thing about us Deans. We ain't alibi ballplayers and there ain't gonna be none about the loss today. I didn't have no headache after my accident when I

Me 'N' Paul

was skulled by that ball and the best way to tell the story is to say Tommy Bridges pitched a whale of a game."[47]

Diz did however have a warning for Detroit. "This is gonna be a bitter pill for them Tigers to swallow when we overcome their lead and take this series away from them in Detroit. Paul will take 'em tomorrow and I hope to get another crack at 'em before this thing ends. Me 'n' Paul don't want to be pigs, but we'd sure like to go down to Deanville, Florida this winter with a couple of World Series wins each."[48]

The Cardinals believed the umpires had robbed them of the game. Frankie Frisch said "that Owens is blind as a bat. He's just an American League umpire and never gave us a break all day."

Leo the Lip agreed with the Flash. "Owen ought to be in a home for the blind."[49]

Again, there was no day off for travel, the teams rode all night by rail for game number six in Detroit. Frisch had decided to start Wild Bill Hallahan, the lefty who pitched so well in game two. Frankie figured he would save Paul for game seven instead of pitching Diz on one day's rest.

When Paul arrived at Navin Field and found out Frisch planned to start Hallahan, he was irate. Paul cornered the Flash and demanded the starting assignment.

"What is this here news I hear about you using Wild Bill today?" He asked Frisch. "That's right," said Frankie. "I'm going to save you for tomorrow."

"Yeah" Paul said "you ain't gonna do no such thing. The pots out there on the table, ain't it? They slapped Diz yesterday, didn't they? They put a bump on his head so big he has to wear two caps, didn't they? There's two thousand bucks riding on every pitch today, ain't there?"

"You're right," said Frisch.

"Well, gimmie that baseball and tell Wild Bill he can pitch tomorrow. I'm going out there and fog the living daylights out of them Tigers. I ain't gonna take no chances on there being no tomorrow. I'm going out there and make a tomorrow."[50]

Paul was starting to sound like Dizzy and Frankie loved it. Frisch believed Paul could be as good as his brother if only he had Dizzy's colossal confidence. Although it made little sense to start a rookie in an elimination game when he had a veteran with World Series experience at his disposal, Frisch started Paul.

The Tigers were favored to win the game and wrap up the World Series. Detroit was holding all the cards; playing at home, coming off a road win over Card ace Dizzy Dean, their own ace, Schoolboy Rowe, rested and ready, with only a 21-year-old raw rookie standing in the way of a World Championship.

Once again Paul found himself in a pressure-packed situation, win or go home. He understood the financial ramifications of winning and losing the World Series. Since the players renumeration was calculated on the proceeds of the first four games, Paul knew the losers share was $2,000 less than the winners. Also, he agreed with Leo about not wanting the losers share, The Lip said "I'm $6,000 in debt, which is just about what the winners share is going to come to. I'm not interested in the losers share."[51]

A record crowd of 45,000 fans filled Navin Stadium and cheered as their hero, Schoolboy Rowe, strode to the mound to start the game. Amid the cheers Schoolboy could hear Lippy Leo's game-long taunt "hi, Edna, honey, how'm I doin'?"[52] Rowe regretted his shout-out to fiancé Edna Skinner during a radio interview at the start of the series.

For the fifth time in the series St. Louis scored first. The Schoolboy popped Pepper out to start the game. Jack Rothrock stretched an ordinary single into a double when right fielder Pete Fox reacted slowly. After Frisch lined out, Ducky Medwick drove Rothrock home with a solid single-his ninth base hit of the series. Ripper Collins flied to Fox for the third out. St. Louis – 1, Detroit coming to bat.

JoJo White led off for Detroit and Paul poured three strikes past him. After Mickey Cochrane singled Paul retired two of the G-Men, Gehringer and Greenberg, on grounders. After one inning St. Louis led 1 – 0.

Bill Delancey started the second inning with a long drive to left and Goslin surprised everyone with a truly outstanding defensive play. The Goose deprived Delancey of a homerun when he leaped high against the left field screen to snatch the long smash. After the scare Rowe mowed down Orsatti and Durocher for a 1-2-3 inning. Paul also had a clean inning with two strikeouts and a groundout.

St. Louis failed to score in the top of the third although Rothrock singled for his second hit of the game. Paul popped up Fox and fanned the Schoolboy for two quick outs in the bottom of the third. Before Paul could record the third out, the inning turned strange as both managers went down.

JoJo White worked Paul for a walk. Mickey Cochrane came to the plate and on Paul's first pitch JoJo tore out for second. A perfect peg by Delancey had JoJo by five feet but White went in with spikes high sending Frisch sprawling and the ball spinning away. JoJo jumped to his feet and raced for third. The Card infielders gathered around the dazed Flash who after a few minutes was able to return to his position.

When play resumed Cochrane hit a grounder to Collins which he beat out for a hit while colliding with Paul who was covering first. JoJo scored while Mickey lay prostrate with a twisted knee and a deep spike wound. Mick was able to keep playing although he limped badly. Paul was unhurt and retired Gehringer to end the weird inning. After three innings the score was tied at one apiece.

Neither team scored in an uneventful fourth. Leo the Lip led off the fifth with a scratch single off Gehringer's glove. Paul laid down a perfect sacrifice bunt putting Leo in scoring position at second. Pepper pushed a single toward Goslin in left field. The Goose grabbed the ball off the ground and came up throwing as Leo rounded third and headed home. The throw sailed over Cochrane's head sending Pepper passed second and safely into third. Pepper scored when Rothrock grounded out to shortstop. In the bottom of the inning Paul retired the Tigers in order and after five innings St. Louis led the game 3 – 1.

The Tigers roared back in the sixth. Schoolboy dealt the Cards misery in the top of the inning fanning Ducky and Ripper, then inducing Delancey to fly out. Once again JoJo White worked Paul for a walk. A limping Mickey Cochrane beat out an infield hit sending JoJo to third. Charlie Gehringer came to the plate with teammates on first and third and no outs.

Gehringer swung for the fences but only produced a puny dribbler straight to Paul. In his haste to pick up the ball for an easy out at the plate, Paul permitted the ball to roll between his legs as JoJo scored and Mick made it to second.

The Goose laid down a bunt attempting to get Cochrane to third but Mick, slowed by his bum leg, was thrown out by Card catcher Bill

Delancey. Gehringer went to second. Paul retired Rogell on a fly to center and was one out away from escaping the inning with a one run lead. That escape was foiled as Hammering Hank hit a run scoring single tying the score at three. Marv Owens grounded out to end the inning.

Schoolboy Rowe walked to the mound with momentum on his side and facing the bottom of the Cardinal's batting order-Ernie Orsatti, Leo Durocher and Paul Dean. Orsatti flied out to the Goose bringing Leo the Lip to the plate. Little Leo the weakest hitting regular Card blasted a double. Paul proved he was not only a pressure pitcher but also a clutch hitter by stroking a solid single to drive in Leo for a 4 – 3 Card lead. Rowe retired Rothrock and Martin to prevent further damage.

Paul needed nine outs without the Tigers scoring. He had a razor thin one run lead to protect so there was no room for error. Like Rowe in the top of the inning Paul faced the bottom of the Detroit batting order. Number eight hitter Pete Fox was due up followed by the Schoolboy.

Fleet Pete promptly doubled, putting the tying run in scoring position. The Schoolboy sacrificed him to third with a perfectly executed bunt. The Cardinal infield played in to cut off the run at the plate. Paul did his job getting JoJo White to hit a grounder to the drawn in infield. The Lip scooped up the ball and shot it home as Fox streaked to the plate. When the dust cleared umpire Brick Owens called him out. The Tigers howled in protest but in vain. JoJo was safe at first on the play and of course tried to steal second on Paul's first pitch. Card catcher Bill Delancey pegged perfectly to Frankie Frisch and JoJo was out retiring the side.

St. Louis failed to score in the top of the eighth and Paul ambled to the hill still nursing a one run lead. Cochrane limped to the plate and grounded out, Frisch to Collins. Gehringer beat out an infield hit, and the Goose singled to right center, with Gehringer reaching third. Paul was in another jam, Tigers on first and third, only one out.

Leo the Lip said, "I was a little afraid for the kid at that point, so I went to the mound and said 'easy, kid, we're all behind you.' All he did was look at me pityingly and say, 'we're as good as in, right now.' I thought, wow, that boy has ice water in his veins."[53]

Billy Rogell hit a lazy flyball to center, Hollywood Orsatti camped under the ball, and unleashed a throw to Delancey that discouraged Gehringer from tagging up and trying to score. He wisely stayed on third.

Hammering Hank Greenberg stood in the batter's box with a chance to put Detroit ahead. He hit a pop fly that headed into the stands foul behind first base, but Ripper reached over the rail and snatched the ball out of the air for the third out.

The Cardinals mounted another threat in the top of the ninth. After Delancey struck out, Orsatti singled. Little Leo continued his hitting spree with a single that sent Orsatti to third.

Paul came up and hit a sharp grounder to second. Orsatti broke for home and Gehringer threw him out by ten feet, however, Hollywood still barreled into Cochrane like a fullback hitting the line. The already injured catcher was knocked off his feet but held on to the ball for the second out. Pepper popped out to end the inning.

As Goose Goslin came in from the outfield with the inning ended, he passed Durocher and said, "you fellows think you're pretty tough, don't you?" No, we just play that way," replied Leo. "Well, by God, you'd better not cover if I come down to second. I'll knock you on your ass." "You come down, Goosie," Leo answered, "and I'll make you eat that goddamned ball."[54]

Paul retired the Tigers in order to finish the 4 – 3 victory and St. Louis lived to fight another day. The 1934 World Series would be decided in the seventh and final game.

Like Indians on a warpath or lunatics on the loose the Cards stormed into the visitors dressing room in a wild, frenzied celebration.

"You can have anything I got," screamed Dizzy. He hurled himself on his brother and wrestled him to the floor. "Oh, baby, what a guy you are! What a pitcher! The greatest pitcher the Dean family ever had, that kid brother of mine. Didn't he prove it? Didn't he?"[55]

The Cards flung themselves on Paul hugging and slapping him on the back with congratulations and gratitude. He had beaten the invincible Schoolboy Rowe, he had saved the Cards from elimination, tied the series and won his own game with a hit that drove in the winning run!

Paul and Dizzy wrapped their arms around each other, kissed and re-kissed the baseball Paul last threw in the game as dozens of photographers snapped pictures. Paul finally disengaged himself from Dizzy and his appreciative teammates, sat on a stool in front of his locker and talked to reporters.

"I finished strong and felt strong all the way," said Paul. "The only time I didn't feel right was when I let Gehringer's roller go through my leg's in the sixth. Then I felt foolish. I didn't work nearly as hard as I did the last time out. I didn't feel I had to. I feel right now as if I could go right back in there tomorrow and beat them again. But Dizzy will take care of that."[56]

Diz agreed "Me 'n' Paul will beat them Tigers tomorrow together or separately. This is a family matter."[57]

Leo the Lip was elated over getting three hits in the game, more than he had in the previous five games combined. "Boy, do I feel great?" he yelled. "Gosh, it feels great to be a slugger."[58]

Over in the Detroit dressing room Klieg lights, wires, camera's and other recording equipment was set up, reporters were waiting, expecting to capture for posterity Mickey Cochrane explaining how he led Detroit to the World Championship. Instead Mick was lying on a table with a doctor attending to the long spike wound inflicted in a collision with Paul Dean.

Mick did not blame Paul because he knew it was an unfortunate accident, but he was incensed at Orsatti for deliberately knocking him flat at Homeplate. He freely admitted "I would like to punch Orsatti in the jaw."

"Just think what would have happened if the crazy cave man had hit you." Goose said, referring to Pepper Martin.

"Yeh, that's right," said Mickey. Those Cards are the craziest lot of guys I've ever seen on one ball club. They're all half nuts. I don't see how the rest of them have nerve enough to call Dean Dizzy. They're dizzier than he is."[59]

Still Cochrane contented the Cards did not beat them. "St. Louis did not beat us, umpire Owens did" exclaimed Mickey. "I was safe at third in the sixth, but Owens had me out before I hit the bag. That was the turning point in the game. We had Daffy Dean on the run and would have finished him, but the umpire stopped us."

"We were beaten by an umpire and hitters like Daffy and Durocher. That's a hot one, isn't it?"[60]

Mickey was then transported to a local hospital where he received further treatment and spent the night. Doctors said Cochrane would probably be able to play in the climatic seventh game.

Me 'N' Paul

Unlike Diz and Paul, Rowe was apparently an alibi ballplayer and he had a unique alibi for the loss. Schoolboy said that before the game movie comedian, Joe E. Ross shook his hand too vigorously causing swelling and discomfort that negatively affected his pitching. However, it seemed unlikely that a short, middle-aged actor could injure a young athlete of Schoolboy's stature.

"Such an accusation is ridiculous" Brown said. "The handshake was a normal friendly one with a wish of good luck. Rowe gave no indication of any injury at the time and I don't understand how he could say that."[61]

Sportswriters praised Paul's performance. "Paul Dean was more that a pitcher for the Cardinals today. He was fortified with a strong arm and a stronger heart. When his arm failed him, he called on his heart, which beat back every challenge, every counter- thrust, every desperate drive of the Tigers."

To see him working out there in the clutches with destruction hovering around his head, you never would have known he was a 21-year-old country boy, fresh from the cotton patch, he was as cool as Christy Matthewson, smart as Chief Bender and as courageous as Walther Johnson."[62]

St. Louis fans were delirious with excitement over Paul's victory. Mrs. Clifford Wilson was in the hospital under an anesthetic as doctors delivered her baby. Her first question on returning to consciousness was who won the game?

When her physician assured Mrs. Wilson that Paul Dean had pitched the Cards to a 4 – 3 victory, she smiled and told him she would name her new baby boy Paul Dean Wilson.

Once again Frankie Frisch refused to name his starting pitcher, telling reporters he would not decide until game time. Speculation centered on whether Frisch would start Wild Bill Hallahan whom he had passed over in favor of Paul Dean or go with Dizzy on only one day's rest.

Frisch was not just refusing to name his starter to gain a tactical advantage, he seriously found himself on the horns of a dilemma. Wild Bill Hallahan was well-rested, had pitched a great eight innings in game two plus he had extensive World Series experience having defeated the Philadelphia Athletics twice in the 1931 World Series. On the other hand, Frankie knew Dizzy would push hard for the starting assignment.

However, Dizzy might not be the right choice. If Frisch gave Diz the start he would be pitching with only one day's rest. Dizzy was not his dominating self in game five and might still be suffering ill-effects from Rogell's shot to his head.

On the morning of the final game, October 9, 1934, a picture of Mickey Cochrane in a hospital bed appeared on the front page of the Detroit free press. The caption read: "Our stricken' leader." Leo the Lip had his jockeying material for game seven.

As game time neared the Tigers were taking batting practice and Frankie Frisch was holding a meeting in the Cardinal dressing to go over the game plan. Instead of attending the Card meeting Dizzy was wondering around the field watching Detroit warm up. He stood behind Tiger starting pitcher Eldon Auker, bent forward at the waist with hands clasped behind his back as if scouting Auker.

After several minutes Dizzy hollered at Mickey Cochrane, "are you gonna pitch this guy today? You must have given up."[63] Auker and Cochrane screamed for Dizzy to get off the field. Laughing, Diz retreated to the Cardinal dressing room.

All the St. Louis players were in the meeting except Dizzy and Frankie Frisch finally made his decision, "Hallahan you start, Walker you're in reserve." Diz walked in just as Frisch said that and heard for the first time he wasn't starting.

Dizzy was irate and said to Frisch, "Franko, you know what the problem is? You're going over the batting order, trying to decide who's gonna pitch. You want to win, don't you? There's only one man to pitch, an' here he is." Frisch said, "are you sure you're able to go?" Diz replied, "you let me pitch, an' you won't have anymore problem." Frisch thought a minute and said, "okay, you start, and Hallahan you're in reserve."[64]

Once Diz secured the starting assignment he ran out of the meeting to let the media, fans and Tigers know the great one would be on the mound for the crucial seventh game.

Diz bumped into Hank Greenberg and told him, "hey, I'm pitching this afternoon. You know what that means, you won't touch me."[65]

Diz told reporters, "I've got to keep up with Paul. I'd like to win anyhow-I always like to win-but I can't let Paul down. He carried us to the seventh game. It's my time now, and if I have to, I'll just throw my arm off to show the two Deans still move together. I wouldn't let Paul down for the world. A great pitcher? sure. But he's a great kid too. He's the finest kid you ever met."[66]

On the Detroit side Mickey Cochrane was out of the hospital and although hobbled vowed to fight to the end. "I may be down, but we'll be tearing apart the Cards in the Series final."[67]

Goose Goslin described the tense atmosphere surrounding the last game. "Everybody seems to be mad at everybody else in this series, with all hands sore at the umpiring, which has been terrible. So, watch out for fireworks today."[68]

40,000 fans filled the stands at Navin Field as the Tigers took the field to start the deciding game of the 1934 World Series. As Mickey Cochrane limped to his position behind Homeplate Leo the Lip yelled at him, "how's our stricken leader?"

Eldon Auker started the game by fanning Card lead-off batter Pepper Martin, Jack Rothrock followed with a double putting a Card in scoring position for Frankie Frisch and Ducky Medwick. Auker retired the Flash on an infield fly and Ducky fouled out stranding Rothrock at second.

As Dizzy walked on to the diamond no one knew what to expect. Could he really be effective after only one day's rest and also surviving a blast to the head that sent him to the hospital? JoJo White led off and grounded out. "Our stricken leader" also grounded out and Charlie Gehringer flied out to right field giving Dizzy a 1-2-3 first.

Ripper Collins opened the second with a lead-off single. Bill Delancey grounded to Marv Owen at third and the Tigers turned a double play, Owen to Gehringer to Greenberg. Ernie Orsatti continued the assault on Auker with another base hit. With Durocher at bat Orsatti attempted to steal second but Cochrane gunned him down for the third out.

Diz survived the second with only an infield error to blemish his inning. After two innings neither team had scored and Diz had not given up a hit or walk.

Lippy Leo led of the third by flying out. Dizzy came to bat anxious to show everyone both Dean's could hit. He lifted a lazy flyball over third in front of Goose Goslin for a base hit. The Goose lazed toward the ball not expecting a pitcher to try to stretch a single into a double. Goose was right, any sane pitcher would stop at first to save his energy and body for his main job pitching. But of course, Dizzy was a little crazy. He rounded first as startled first base coach Buzzy Wares held up his hands and screamed whoa, whoa! Diz paid no attention to Buzzy and evidently learning nothing from his last baserunning exploit, tore toward second.

After his slow start Goose grabbed the ball and fired to second. Gehringer caught the ball and was waiting for Dizzy two feet from the bag. Leo the Lip told what happened: "There was no way for Diz to get around him, and Gehringer, a hall of fame second baseman hadn't missed a tag in fifteen years. As Diz would say, he 'slud into second, there was a big cloud of dust, and I don't know how, why or whether Gehringer had missed him, but the umpire signaled that he was safe."[69]

Pepper Martin, up next, hit a grounder to the right of first base. Greenberg fielded the ball as Auker raced to cover first. Instead of throwing to Auker, Greenberg decided to tag first himself. Big mistake, Pepper beat him to the bag and Diz ended up on third. One out, Cards on first and third.

Jack Rothrock was the next Card batter and on Auker's first pitch Pepper stole second. Cochrane decided to walk Rothrock and pitch to Frankie Frisch. The Flash had not hit well in the series and Cochrane thought Auker could get him to hit into an inning ending double play.

Auker shot two quick strikes by Frisch to put him in a hole. Protecting the plate Frisch fouled off pitch after pitch. After seven fouls Frankie Frisch proved he was still a clutch hitter by doubling down the right field line scoring all three Card runners.

Cochrane sent Auker to the showers and summoned Schoolboy Rowe to bail out Detroit. He was greeted by calls of 'how'm I doing, Edna?" from the Cardinals bench. Ducky Medwick grounded out but Ripper Collins came through with a two-out single that scored Frisch. Delancey doubled Ripper home. The Schoolboy was replaced by Chief Hogsett who promptly walked Orsatti. Durocher singled and Delancey held at third loading the bases.

Bases loaded, two outs, Cards ahead 5 – 0 and here comes Dizzy Dean again. This time the Great One scratched out an infield single scoring Delancey and leaving the bases full. His two hits in one inning tied a World Series record.

Pepper worked the Chief for a walk forcing Orsatti home for the seventh Cardinal run of the inning. Cochrane could not tolerate a walk with the bases loaded, he pulled the Chief and called Tommy Bridges from the bullpen. Jack Rothrock, the thirteenth Card to bat in the inning, finally ended the Tiger misery by grounding out.

Diz was ecstatic with his seven-run lead. Between innings he walked up and down in the Cardinal dugout kidding and congratulating his teammates. Frisch told him to sit down, rest, and keep his arm warm. However, Dizzy could not contain his excitement.

"It's over," Diz said. "I told you, one was all I needed. They're not going to get any."[70]

Neither team scored in the fourth or fifth. The Tigers finally had their first hit in the fourth and two more in the fifth. Dizzy still had not given up a run nor a walk.

Pepper Martin started the sixth by slashing a hit to left field. The Goose was clumsy handling the ball, so Pepper flew past first and dove headfirst into second. Bridges retired Rothrock and Frisch on flies to the outfield. Ducky Medwick then hit a 1-2 Bridges pitch off the right field fence scoring Pepper.

Ducky rounded second and headed to third where Marv Owen was waiting to take the throw. Ducky slid in feet first with one leg underneath and the other spiked shoe aimed at Owen's chest. The ball never reached Owen as shortstop Rogell had cut off the throw. Ducky went in hard knocking Owen on top of him. Ducky started kicking Owen and the fight was on.

Umpires and coaches quickly separated the combatants. Ducky extended his right hand in an attempt to apologize but Owen refused. Medwick said, "he told me where I could stick my hand." Frisch added, "I thought Joe was showing unusual self-restraint, you couldn't do any talking in a row with Joe. He'd swing that right of his after very little jawing and down you'd go."[71]

The game continued and Ripper Collins connected for his fourth straight hit driving in Pepper, making the score 9 – 0. Delancey struck out ending the Card sixth. As the Cardinals took the field for the bottom of the inning, all hell broke loose.

When he took his position in left field, fans started booing and throwing debris at Ducky. The fans fired fruit, vegetables, bottles, seat cushions, and everything not nailed down. They were frustrated by the score and upset at what was perceived as Ducky's dirty playing.

Ducky retreated out of range of the garbage barrage, picked up an apple and started playing catch with Orsatti. This mockery further infuriated fans and they renewed the bombardment.

Ducky headed for the safety of the infield as groundskeepers picked up the refuse. Durocher met him and said "they can't do that to you, Joey. Don't back off. Get back out there!"

Medwick snapped back. "If you're so goddamned brave, why don't you play left field, and let me play shortstop?"[72]

Every time the field was cleared and Medwick returned to his position, the angry spectators resumed the attack throwing everything they could get their hands on and chanting, take him out! Take him out!

Finally, after a delay of nearly twenty minutes umpires sent the players to their dugouts and sought counsel from the commissioner of baseball who was standing dressed in a topcoat and hat at his box seat between home and third base.

Commissioner Kennesaw Mountain Landis took control of the situation. He summoned the combatants Marv Owen and Joe Medwick, managers, Frankie Frisch and Mickey Cochrane plus umpire Bill Klem for a conference.

After questioning Medwick and Owen, Landis issued his ruling, "Mr. Medwick you are out of the game to prevent bodily harm from the fans."[73]

Ducky was irate, he had a chance to break Pepper Martin's World Series record for hits, but now he was out of the game. Medwick was escorted off the field by four policemen to insure his safety.

Medwick was angry at Landis. "That goddamn commissioner Landis, the son of a bitch took me out of the Series. I could have broken the Series record for hits. I had 11 hits. He had no right to do that. I would have broken that record."[74]

The long delay did not bother Dizzy. He retired the Tigers in order in the bottom of the sixth. No runs, no hits, no walks, no errors.

St. Louis added two more runs to the rout in the top of the seventh. The big blows were a triple by the surprisingly slugging Leo Durocher and a double by Jack Rothrock. The Cardinals lead was increase to 11 – 0.

Billy Rogell led off in the bottom of the seventh and Diz retired him on a pop fly to Durocher. Hank Greenberg came to the plate, Delancey signaled the pitch he wanted but Diz shook him off. Delancey called for several more pitches only to have Diz shake off all of them. Having exhausted all the pitches in Dizzy's repertoire Delancey went to the mound to see what the hell Diz wanted to throw. Frisch and Durocher joined the conference.

"Frank," Diz said, "Do you think Hubbell is a better pitcher than me?"

Frisch replied, "no Diz, Hubbell's no better than you. You're a better pitcher than God. Come on, you're going great. Throw the ball and let's get this game over with."

Diz seemed to be satisfied, "well, if Hubbell's no better than me then I ought to be able to throw a screwball."[75]

A screwball, Carl Hubbell's signature pitch, which Diz had never attempted, was the pitch he wanted to throw in the seventh game of the World Series! Frisch just shook his head and returned to his position. Delancey told Diz to throw whatever he wanted, and he would catch it. Dizzy's pitch selection was evidently effective. Greenberg went down on strikes and Owen grounded out.

Neither team scored in the eighth. General Crowder came in to pitch and retired the Cards in the top of the ninth.

As Diz strolled to the mound in the bottom of the ninth, the only question remaining, would Dizzy complete the shut-out? However, Dizzy seemed unconcerned as Charley Gehringer led off with a base hit. Goose Goslin grounded into a fielder's choice and Billy Rogell blasted a single past Frisch. Two Tigers aboard, one out and one of the best hitters in baseball, Hank Greenberg, coming to bat.

Dizzy feigned surprise and yelled to Mickey Cochrane, "what, no pinch hitter?"[76]

Diz was having fun but Frisch finally had enough of Dizzy's antics. The Flash was mad as he stalked to the mound. "Quit fooling around" he told Dizzy, "we have a lot at stake here."[77]

Dizzy recalled the confrontation, "I just stood there and looked at him like he must be outta his mind. Me leadin' 11 – 0 with one out in the last of the ninth. Well, you know what Frisch told me? He said you lose this guy and you're through. Eleven-nothing and he was gonna pull me."

"That Greenberg couldn't hit my fastball if he'd started to swing when I wound up. He didn't even see the third strike an' the next guy was Owen, an' he forced Rogell an' the whole thing was over. When I had my fastball, nobody could hit me."[78]

The St. Louis Cardinals were World Champions and Dizzy and Daffy were the most celebrated stars in American sports. Columnist Grantland Rice wrote:

"As the bulky figure of Babe Ruth fades out of the picture, an old-fashioned schooner fading into the fog, two kids from the dust of the western trail take his place as the greatest sensations baseball has known-matching the glamour of Mathewson, Hans Wagner, Ty Cobb, and Babe Ruth. In one brief six months, they have called upon their strong right arms to write one of the greatest of all sporting classics."[79]

CHAPTER 21

"Paul's liable to have a bridal suite, and no bride."

The Cardinal's World Series special arrived at St. Louis' Union Station on Wednesday October 10, 1934 at 8:00a.m. The early weekday morning did not keep thousands of fans from mobbing the train station. All were eager to see their World Series heroes and to celebrate the World Championship they brought to St. Louis.

Mounted police and approximately 100 other officers struggled in vain to control the crowd. The fans cheered as Diz left the train wearing a white safari pith helmet and carrying a toy rubber tiger with four knots in its tail.

"This here's my tiger hunting hat" Diz shouted, pointing to the safari helmet, "and them knots in the tiger's tail is for Me 'n' Paul's four series wins!"[1]

The World Champion Cards disembarked from the train into cars and trucks for a victory parade through downtown St. Louis. Mayor Bernard Dickman along with Sam Breadon, Branch Rickey, and Frankie Frisch were in the lead car. Paul, Dizzy and Pat Dean rode in the second of about 25 vehicles making up the parade.

Spectators from tall downtown buildings showered the parade with improvised confetti, made from shredded toilet paper and dubbed "depression ticker tape. Dizzy stood up in a convertible, choked and abused the toy tiger as the throng of fans shrieked in delight. Kids asked Ducky if he had any fruit. Immediately following the parade, Diz, Paul and pat boarded a flight for Oklahoma City to start a barnstorming tour.

Barnstorming was only one post season revenue stream Diz and Paul planned to tap. Companies were lining up ready to pay large sums of money to have their products endorsed by Dizzy and Daffy. They were besieged with offers to advertise a wide range of products including, baseball equipment, breakfast cereal, school supplies, shirts, hats, beer and even cigarettes.

In the 1930's cigarettes were proclaimed to have medicinal value, even doctors recommended smoking as a way to relax and relieve tension. Athletes claimed tobacco gave them extra energy. Cigarette companies were quick to capitalize on the Cardinal's World Series victory. By October 12, 1934 full-page advertisements appeared in newspapers across the country. Under the headline "21 out of 23 World Champions Cardinals prefer Camels."

Ripper Collins: "Poling out home runs takes a lot of energy – a Camel has a way of turning on my energy."

Ducky Medwick: "Smoking Camels takes away the tired feeling as soon as I leave the field and turns on my pep again."

Pepper Martin: "I can smoke all the Camels I want without upsetting my nerves."

Dizzy Dean: Smoking Camels sure brings back your energy after a hard game."

Daffy Dean: "A Camel gives me the feeling of having more energy and never gives me the jumpy nerves."[2]

The movies and vaudeville offered deals and the Dean brothers were also compensated for personal appearances and banquet attendance. America was fascinated by Dizzy and Daffy. Amid this post season gold rush Paul suffered a romantic mishap.

Paul was somewhat inexperienced in the love game. Only the year before when he was pitching for Columbus, a female reporter asked Paul his views on matrimony.

"I ain't gonna get married for 10 years," he told her. "An' when I do, I'm gonna git me a gal down in Dixie."[3]

Not long after Paul exposed his theories on love and marriage, he met a pretty Ohio State University co-ed, Miss Betty Holt. They had been dating for the past year and Betty watched Paul pitch in the World Series.

After the World Series Paul expressed his desire to wed Miss Holt and took the liberty of reserving the bridal suite at a luxury hotel in Cleveland. When Betty returned home to Columbus and learned of Paul's plans she was not pleased.

"Paul's liable to have a bridal suite and no bride," Betty told reporters.[4]

When newsmen pressed her for details, Betty said "our engagement hasn't been announced, and when I get ready to announce it, I'll call you."[5]

She made it plain, however, that it was up to her, not Paul, whether they were to be married. When asked "off the record, now are you going to marry Paul?" she answered, "I haven't made up my mind."[6] Betty Holt was proving to be more troublesome to Paul than the Detroit Tigers ever were.

Diz and Paul's barnstorming tour was organized by a promoter named Ray Doan. An entrepreneur from Iowa, Doan specialized in helping athletes capitalize on their celebrity. He had a flair for showmanship and a gift for marketing unusual athletic events.

Doan promoted the house of David Baseball team, organizing their tours and publicizing their brand; beards and long hair. He contracted with Babe Didrikson to turn her Olympic success into money-making ventures, including golf, basketball and baseball. Doan also made a lot of money out of a game called donkey baseball. Hard to believe but people during the depression were so desperate for entertainment they paid to watch people play baseball while riding donkeys.

Another animal related athletic event which Doan proudly claimed to have invented was not as popular as donkey baseball. "I'm the fellow who thought up playing softball with the infielders and outfielders tied to goats," he said. "It's the funniest goddamned thing you ever saw."[7]

Diz knew Doan from a previous business association. Dizzy was an instructor at Doan's All-Star baseball school in Hot Springs, Arkansas after the 1933 baseball season. Dizzy along with other Major Leagues Rogers Hornsby, Lon Warneke and George Sisler were hired by Ray Doan to tutor young men with ambitions to play professional baseball. The aspiring ball players paid to attend the school.

Dizzy liked to tell about some of his experiences as a baseball "perfessor." "I told this one fellow to show me his wind-up and follow through" and he said, 'I don't need no wind-up but your gonna love my follow through.' "With that he showed me the worst follow through I ever saw and ended up out of position to field a ball hit back at him, so I said what would you do if a batter hit a line-drive back at you?"

"Oh, he said, "don't worry none about that. Nobody can hit a line drive when I'm pitchin'![8]

Doan decided the Dizzy and Daffy tour would be different than past barnstorming efforts. Instead of playing in small towns, Doan scheduled games in large cities, some in Major League stadiums. He planned to fill these large venues by playing interracial baseball. Ray Doan was gambling that both black and white fans would pay to see Dizzy and Daffy compete against the best black baseball players.

Doan partnered with four owners of Negro Major League teams to bring his plans to fruitions. The owners were J.L. Wilkinson (Kansas City Monarchs), Ed Boldon (Philadelphia Stars), Nat Strong (Black Yankees), and Gus Greenlee (Pittsburgh Crawfords) the tour also featured a few games against local white All-Star teams. Dizzy and Paul were to be paid $75 each per game plus 50% of the gate receipts. Doan would pay all expenses.

Paul was sick when their flight landed in Oklahoma City. Not lovesick, sick at his stomach.

"It's that egg sandwich I ate," Paul said. "Must've been tainted."[9]

The first game of the Dizzy and Daffy baseball tour was against the Kansas City Monarchs, legendary Negro Major League Champions. The game was to be played under the lights at Oklahoma City's Texas League park. Long before the 8:15 start time the stands were full and by the time stadium lights were turned on thousands of fans had pushed their way out onto the diamond.

The police were dispatched to control the crowd, but the fans refused to move away form the first and third base foul lines. They were packed

Me 'N' Paul

15 to 20 feet deep right to the edge of the playing field. Every time a ball was hit anywhere off the field fans kept it.

Paul recovered sufficiently from his 'tainted egg sandwich' to start the game. He was backed by the so-called Oklahoma All-Stars, a rag-tag collection of Minor League and amateur ball players. Paul pitched the first three innings giving up eight hits but no runs.

Dizzy followed Paul on the mound and the fans became even more excited and unruly. Every ball hit anywhere near the overflow crowd that was now encroaching on the playing field, disappeared. Diz was only able to pitch two innings because the supply of baseballs was exhausted, and the game had to be called off after only five innings. Diz gave up only one hit and no runs.

A police escort was necessary to get Diz and Paul to their hotel as hundreds of autograph seekers surrounded the pair of World Champion Cards. A long day that started with a victory parade in St. Louis, Missouri finally ended with an exhibition game in Oklahoma City. A game that saw thousands of blacks and whites interacting socially, a sight seldom seen in the segregated south of the Jim Crow era.

Dizzy, Pat, and Paul took a train from Oklahoma City to Wichita, Kansas the site of their next game. The Kansas City Monarchs, Diz and Paul's current barnstorming companions, traveled in their team bus the 150 miles to Wichita.

Dizzy and Paul played with a group of local players that included only one with Major League experience. 10,000 fans packed Lawrence stadium and cheered as Dizzy started and went the first three innings. Paul pitched the fourth and fifth. The Deans did not stay around for the game's conclusion. As soon as Paul finished his stint on the mound, they "packed up their duds and disappeared."[10]

The large crowd seemed satisfied with Diz and Paul's performance even though they left before the game was over. The Wichita Eagle estimated the Dean's share of the proceeds to be between $2,000 and $2,500.

Kansas City was the next destination on the Dizzy and Daffy traveling baseball show. Waiting for Dizzy at his hotel in Kansas City was a telegram containing an unusual offer, $500 to play quarterback for the Philadelphia Eagles.

The Philadelphia Eagles were preparing to play the Detroit Lions when reporters asked Bert Bell, Eagle President, how he planned to beat the Lions.

"The Detroit eleven is the greatest in professional football, unscored upon and leading the league with four straight triumphs." Bell said, "The only man who has a chance to beat Detroit is Dizzy Dean. If he will play quarterback for me next Sunday, I will pay him $500. I am going to wire him now."[11] Prior commitments prevented Diz from accepting Bert Bell's generous offer.

The game in Kansas City was again against the Kansas City Monarchs. Although the crowd was large, nearly 15,000, they were well-controlled staying in their seats and off the field. In fact, some fans were having trouble getting a good look at Dizzy Dean.

A young soft-drink vendor leaned his head in the dugout and said to Dizzy, "can you help me out?"

"Glad to, buddy," Diz answered, "what is it?"

"All you got to do is stand up in front of the dugout so those men in that box can get a good look at you. They said they would buy everything I have if you would."[12]

The Monarchs were a formidable opponent. Even though these games were exhibitions, they were usually competitive. The black baseballers wanted to test their talents against Major Leaguers. They were eager to prove they could play in the big leagues if given the opportunity. Also, Dizzy and Daffy's fame insured press coverage from major newspapers, recognition negro players craved.

As for Diz and Paul once the games began their competitive juices started flowing. However, games against the black pros were stacked against the two Cards. During the junket Dizzy and Paul would face some of the all-time great black stars including future Cooperstown inductees; Satchel Page, Josh Gibson and "Cool Papa" Bell.

Dizzy knew Satchel would have been a star in the big leagues had he been allowed to play "if Satchel could join Me 'n' Paul on the Cardinals we'd wrap up the Pennant by the 4th of July and go fishin' until time to play the World Series."[13]

Josh Gibson was the greatest homerun hitter in the Negro Leagues. He is credited with 972 homeruns in his 17-year career. Josh was known as the Black Babe Ruth. However, many who saw Gibson play thought Babe Ruth should be known as the white Josh Gibson. He was elected to the hall of fame in 1972.

James Thomas "Cool Papa" Bell was the fastest man in Negro baseball. Ty Cobb said "Cool Papa" was the fastest runner who ever stole a base Satchel was impressed by Bell's speed,

"Cool Papa could pull the light switch, run across the room, hop in bed, and cover up before the light went out."[14]

Bell was so fast Olympic gold medalist and 1936 Olympic hero, Jesse Owens refused to race him. "Cool Papa" Bell played until he was 43-years-old and retired in 1946, one year before Jackie Robinson broke the Major League color-barrier. Bell had a lifetime batting average of .429 and was elected to the hall of fame in 1974.

Diz and Paul each pitched two innings and they each gave up one run. The Monarchs prevailed 7 – 0 among the spectators was Frankie Frisch, perhaps concerned for the health of his pair of aces. It was widely reported that he Ol' Flash considered the Dizzy and Daffy baseball junket an unwise venture, but Dizzy disputed that assumption.

"Why, Frank said we should go ahead." Diz related, "he said Me 'n' Paul was hot at the present time and we should get it while the gettin's good."[15]

After the game Dizzy, Paul and Frankie Frisch attended a banquet arranged to honor the Cardinal manager and his two pitching stars. Dizzy stole the show overshadowing Frisch by regaling the diners with a description of how "Me 'n' Paul tamed them Tigers in the World Series."

When Paul was called upon to speak, he shook his head and said, "I'm not qualified to make no speech. I'd rather be out on that mound with the count 3 and 2 on the batter and the bases loaded."[16]

Next stop on the Dizzy and Daffy junket was Des Moines, Iowa where the local newspaper had been running the following ad for a week;

Baseball
Dizzy and Daffy Dean
Vs
Kansas City Monarchs
Champion colored team Sat. Night Oct. 13th

Carl Duncan

8:15 p.m. Western League Park
Grandstand, $ .75   Bleachers $ .40
Chair Seats, $1.00 Box Seats, $1.25[17]

3,500 fans heeded the ad filling the stands as a police escort delivered Diz and Paul to the stadium. The weather was cold and wet as the Deans warmed up alongside a team made up of local amateurs and semi-pros, some of them soldiers from nearby Fort Des Moines. Paul was loosening up in the outfield when he slipped on the wet turf and fell on his right shoulder.

Paul was worried that he had hurt his arm so he started the game in the outfield. Diz pitched the first three innings and then joined Paul in the outfield. Paul tried to pitch but after facing only on batter he left the game complaining of soreness in his right shoulder.

Kansas City easily won the game 9 – 0. Monarchs pitcher Lefty Beverly hurled a complete game shutout. He gave up only five hits.

The Deans traveled overnight by rail to Chicago for their next game, again against the Kansas City Monarchs. Diz and Paul teamed with the semi-pro Chicago Mills at their home park, Mills Stadium on the west side of Chicago.

20,000 fans jammed Mills Stadium taxing the capacity of the park. Thousands of fans unable to get into the stadium sought high ground by nearby railroad tracks to get a view of the game. It was by far the largest crowd to ever see a game at Mills Stadium.

Paul decided to test his sore arm by starting the game on the mound. He pitched two innings, yielded three hits and one run. Diz followed Paul to the mound, worked two innings and gave up two runs on three hits. Dizzy moved to left field after he left the mound; however, Paul said his arm still hurt and went straight to the bench after his two-inning mound stint.

Dizzy marveled at the huge crowd and with dollar signs in his eyes asked, "how many cash customers do you reckon this heah place holds?"[18] Cash being the operative word. During the thirties people paid with cash, no credit cards, no checks. During each game on the tour Pat Dean joined the promoters in counting the gate receipts to make sure Diz and Paul received their correct share.

Seeing the large crowd and expecting a record payday, Diz and Paul left after the sixth inning to help Pat oversee counting the games proceeds. The sight of all that money, the Chicago Tribune reported Dizzy and Paul's share exceeded $5,000, must have seemed surreal to a pair of former itinerant cotton pickers who only a few years before earned less than a dollar for a grueling day's work.

The semi-pro Chicago Mills ended up defeating the Kansas City Monarchs 13 – 3. The Chicago defender commented "20,000 fans left well pleased. The fans didn't go to Mills stadium to see a fine exhibition of baseball, they went to see Dizzy and Daffy Dean, heroes of the St. Louis Cardinals' outfit."[19] The fans in Milwaukee, the site of their next game, were not so easy to please.

Dizzy and Paul arrived in Milwaukee for the game to be played at Borchet Stadium, home of the Milwaukee Brewers of the Western League. The crowd was sparse compared to the colossal crowd in Chicago. This disappointed Ray Doan because he had relentlessly promoted this game. Doan advertised that Dizzy and Daffy Dean would divide nine innings on the mound against the Kansas City Monarchs who would have Satchel Page pitching. What could be better? World Series heroes Dizzy and Daffy Dean opposed by the premier pitcher of the Negro Major Leagues.

Fans were understandably disappointed when Satch didn't show and Dizzy only pitched two innings. Paul did not get anywhere near the mound, again blaming his aching arm. Diz and Paul left after only five innings and irate fans stormed the box office demanding a refund, which was not forthcoming. Diz and Paul collected their share of the $3,300 gate and boarded a flight to Philadelphia.

The Milwaukee fiasco generated widespread criticism of Dizzy and Paul in particular and barnstorming in general. National League President, John Heydler, along with his American League counterpart, Will Harridge began calling for an all-out ban on barnstorming. Baseball commissioner Judge Kennesaw Mountain Landis agreed and threatened to punish Major League players who participated in the exhibitions. This was a truly hypocritical stance on the part of baseball's hierarchy as they routinely scheduled exhibition games in the regular season in order to fatten the wallets of team owners.

Leaving behind the jeers and boos of the fans in Milwaukee, the Deans eagerly anticipated a Philly payday that would rival the Chicago Bonanza. In addition to a doubleheader at Philadelphia's Shibe Park, the Dean brothers were to be paid $1,000, just for making an appearance at a softball game.

The first order of business upon arrival in Philadelphia was to have Pau's ailing arm examined by orthopedic surgeon, Dr. Van Bork. The doctor found no apparent structural damage. Van Bork warned Paul not to pitch and prescribed complete rest.

After signing autographs at the softball game and before the doubleheader at Shibe Field, Ray Doan had scheduled a visit to the historical Franklin Institute. Dr. James Barnes, director of the Institute led the Deans on a tour of the museum. Diz was not impressed. "We only got five minutes to see this place."[20] Dizzy said of the museum which visitors usually took days to go through. Diz was more interested in complaining than viewing the museum's exhibits. He told Dr. Barnes,

"You don't get much sleep doing this jumping around the country. I tried to sleep on the plane last night coming here, but my ears got all stopped up and I didn't get any rest. But this is the one time in our lives to get the dough and we're getting' while we can."[21]

"Anyway, I'm gonna try to duck that Vauderville tour, that would run me nuts. I'll stick to baseball, it's my game. Leave the stage to the actors – that's their game."[22]

While in Philadelphia Dizzy received exciting news, the Baseball Writers Association of America named him the most valuable player in the National League for 1934. Diz won in a landslide polling a total of 78, only two shy of a perfect score. Paul finished ninth in the balloting.

About this same time rumors began to circulate concerning 1933 MVP, Carl Hubbell. New York Giants manager Bill Terry was reported to have offered to trade Hubbell to the Cardinals for either of the Dean brothers. "Terry prefers Paul Dean to Dizzy because he believes Paul has two or three more pitching years in his arm than his older brother."[23]

The proposed trade made sense for the Giants. Terry was disappointed when Hubbell collapsed down the stretch in the 1934 Pennant race, whereas Diz and Paul pitched almost everyday to win the Pennant for the Cards. Hubbell harbored ill will toward the Giants because of a salary dispute. After winning the 1933 MVP award King Carl expected a salary of $25,000, however, the Giants beat him down to $18,000 in draconian negotiations. After St. Louis rejected the deal, New York management denied making the offer, not wanting to further alienate their mound star.

The Dean's busy day culminated in a doubleheader at Shibe Stadium. Diz and Paul played with a group of local semi-pros against the professional black Philadelphia Stars. The games were no contest as the negro professionals executed a twin killing.

The Deans were not much help to their teammates. Diz and Paul played the outfield in game one, both going hitless at the plate. Diz pitched a scoreless two innings in the second game while Paul again avoided the mound completely.

The 9,000 paying customers seemed somewhat satisfied with Diz and Paul's lackluster performances. Happily, there was no repeat of the riot experienced in Milwaukee.

The Deans, Diz, Pat and Paul, boarded a train and traveled to New York City. When they arrived at their Manhattan hotel the press was waiting. A reporter asked Diz about the rumored trade of Paul to the New York Giants for Carl Hubbell.

"The Cardinals won't trade Paul for Hubbell or anyone else."

The reporter persisted "would you mind hitting against Paul if he were traded?" "Boy" Diz said grinning "ah'd hit him like ah owned him."

"Hell no! you wouldn't." Paul said so violently people nearly fell out of their chairs.[24]

Dizzy told reporters "Me 'n' Paul have been on a dead run ever since we beat them Tigers and if we weren't Dizzy, we sure are in a whirlwind now."

"When this is over, I'm goin' down to Bradenton, Florida and lock every durn door in mah house. They're goin' to have to shove mah food into me through a stove pipe."[25]

The next day's game was to be played at Dexter Park in Brooklyn. Ducky Medwick, who lived in nearby New Jersey, agreed to join his Cardinal teammates and play in the exhibition game. Dizzy, Daffy and Ducky would be playing for the Brooklyn Bushwick's against the New York Black Yankees. The game was played at Dexter field in Brooklyn.

The Brooklyn Bushwicks were one of the finest semi-pro teams in the country and with the addition of three World Champions seemed sure to trounce their opponents, a mediocre negro professional team.

15,000 fans packed Dexter stadium to witness the contest. Diz pitched for the Bushwicks, Ducky patrolled left field and Paul played right field. Paul was still nursing his bum arm and when circumstances demanded a throw Paul responded with an underhanded toss.

A reporter sat with Pat Dean in the stands to get her perspective on the game. Pat said the boys were tired and looking forward to the end of the tour. "It's time I took Dizzy and Paul home to Bradenton to rest. We'll leave just as soon as they finish their vaudeville act in two weeks."[26] Pat revealed that Diz and Paul expected to make $30,000 on the tour, which they would split evenly.

Seeing Paul in right field Pat said "look at Paul out there. Isn't he the slowest, laziest gangling thing you ever saw? I swear, sometimes I think we'll have to tie him up in bailing wire to keep his arms from falling off. When the series was over, they gave Diz $500. Just for exhibiting in a window that silly pitch helmet he picked up somewhere.

Paul was amazed, he said seriously:

'Diz is someone kiddin' us about this kind of money? We ain't done nuthin' but win A couple ball games.'

"Paul, he doesn't worry about anything. I wish Dizzy had his disposition. He's burning up, on the go all the time, can't keep still a minute. Now Paul, he's the quietest, sittingest man you ever saw."[27]

On the mound Diz was burning up mad. Paul misplayed an easy flyball turning an out into a triple. To make matters worst the runner promptly stole home for the first run of the game.

Baseball was fun for Dizzy. Whether it was a World Series or exhibition game Diz found fun. However, he was also a fierce competitor who hated to lose. Dizzy was irate when Black Yankee Clint Thomas had the audacity to steal home on the Great One.

"I invited him in." said Dizzy, "I see him coming, and then when he's on his way, I fog that ball in with plenty to spare. He is out a mile, but that crooked umpire beats us. Can you imagine that? That is the first home that was ever stoled on me, and one of the Black Yankees has to do it."[28]

Me 'N' Paul

The umpire did not beat Dizzy and the Brunswicks, the Black Yankees took care of that task. Dizzy, Daffy and Ducky were held hitless by hurler Lefty "Neck" Stanley who pitched a seven-hit shutout leading the Black Yankees to a 6 – 0 whitewashing of the Brooklyn Brunswicks.

Dizzy pitched the middle three innings and played outfield for thee more. He gave up two hits, one walk and only one run, Clint Thomas' theft of home.

Promoter Ray Doan had arranged for Diz and Paul to visit Baltimore and make a promotional appearance to help raise funds for a statue of Baltimore's favorite son, Babe Ruth. Doan also scheduled a stop at St. Mary's Industrial school, a home for orphan and wayward boys where Ruth was raised.

Diz gave the assembled boys what he considered a motivational speech; "Until three weeks ago, Babe Ruth was the biggest figure in baseball," Diz declared. "Now you are looking at Dizzy Dean, the man who is walking in Babe Ruth's shoes. And if you boys, each and every one of you, work hard and have determination, you can all become great men like me."[29]

Next for the Dean brothers was a rematch with the New York Black Yankees, this time in Paterson, New Jersey. Despite the proximity to Ducky Medwick's hometown and contrary to Doan's advertising, Sullen Jersey Joe didn't show.

On a frigid Jersey night, a small crowd of less than three thousand watched Diz and Paul exact revenge on the Black Yankees. Again, Diz pitched and Paul played right field. They were backed by another semi-pro squad; "This one went by the oxymoronic name Brooklyn Farmers."[30] The Farmers beat the Black Yankees 10 – 3.

After a rare day off the Dizzy and Daffy show arrived in Cleveland for a long-anticipated duel between Satchel Paige and Dizzy Dean. Despite cold, damp weather 12,000 fans turned out to see two Champion Cards lead the semi-pro Cleveland Rosenblums against the negro professional Pittsburgh Crawfords.

The 1934 Pittsburgh Crawfords were arguable the best Negro League baseball team ever assembled. On that cold Cleveland night, the Craws fielded five future hall of famers. In addition to Satchel Paige on the mound, Josh Gibson caught, player/manager Oscar Charleston played first base, Judy Johnson held down the hot corner and Cool Papa Bell patrolled center field.

Although the Cleveland Rosenblums were semi-pro champions, reinforced by Major Leaguers Frank Doljack and Johnny Mihalec in addition to Diz and Paul, they were no match for the mighty Craws. Satch pitched six hitless innings and struck out thirteen Rosies. Diz pitched three innings, gave up one run on four hits, then played the rest of the game in the outfield with Paul. Pittsburgh won the game by a score of 4 – 1.

Diz and Satch, both accomplished clowns, entertained the shivering crowd by spoofing each other's wind-ups and other antics. After Paul singled for the Rosenblum's first hit, Diz inserted himself into the game as a pinch-runner just as he had in the World Series. This time the result was more comic than tragic. The next Craw popped up down the third base line and Diz tore out for second. Judy Johnson made the catch in shallow left field and Diz broke back for first base.

"Johnson's throw across the diamond easily doubled up Diz, but Dizzy's neat hook slide into first base won him another ovation."[31]

After the game a reporter asked Paul his impression of Satchel Paige. "That guy is something," Paul said. "He's got a hell'uve a fastball. Yes, sir, he's got a fastball."[32]

Diz was so impressed he asked Satch to show him how he gripped his fastball. Satchel gripped the ball with three fingers on top, which surprised Dizzy because most pitchers, himself included, gripped the ball with two fingers on top. Satch explained, "it's the only way I can make the pellet hop."[33] Dizzy said he might experiment with that grip in spring training.

After the game in Cleveland the Dizzy and Daffy caravan, including the Pittsburgh Crawfords, rolled along to a homecoming for Paul. The next game was held in Columbus at Red Bird Stadium, site of Paul's recent Minor League exploits. Perhaps for nostalgia's sake but probably hoping to pull in more paying customers on another cold, October Ohio night, Paul started on the mound.

Diz and Paul were playing with a team composed of local Minor Leaguers and two current Major League players, Dodger outfielder Danny Taylor and Washington Senator pitcher Bobby Kline. Paul pitched the first two innings and gave up one run on three hits. He was clearly still experiencing discomfort in his right arm.

Me 'N' Paul

Dizzy played third base and pitched the seventh and eighth innings. He also gave up only a solo run, however the star of the game was Satchel Paige. Satch pitched the first three innings for the Craws and gave up two hits and no runs. "In the third Paige pulled off one of his favorite stunts: deliberately walking the bases full then striking out the next three batters."[34]

Josh Gibson played left field instead of catcher. He hit a two-run homer a RBI single plus he stole home, thus accounting for three of the Crawfords five runs. The final score was 5 – 3, another Craw win over Diz, Paul and their cohorts.

Pittsburgh was the final stop on the Dizzy and Daffy baseball barnstorming tour. The hometown Pittsburgh Crawfords again provided the competition for Dizzy and Paul's makeshift crew. Major Leaguers George Susce, Moose Solters and Bob Garbark along with local professional players were hired to help the Deans attempt to beat the powerful Craws.

Only about 2,000 fans filed into frigid Forbes Field, many to cheer for the hometown Craws. Dizzy delighted the meager crowd by catching Satchel Paige as he warmed up. Always showboating, Diz shook his glove pantomiming how much it hurt his hand to handle Satch's fastball.

Satch and Diz pitched the first two innings for their teams. Diz actually outpitched Satchel and had his team ahead 2 – 0 after two innings. Dizzy only allowed Pittsburgh one scratch single and in his first at-bat Dizzy delivered a double driving in the second run off Satch.

After their stints on the mound both Satch and Diz stayed in the game playing in the outfield for their respective teams. With two out in the bottom of the fifth the Craws were at-bat trailing 3 – 1 when the cold, calm night was suddenly shattered by a baseball brawl. The incident was not sparked by some racial taut as might be expected in an interracial game but by and umpire's disputed call.

Crawford center fielder, Vic Harris, rapped a swinging bunt in front of home plate. Catcher George Susce promptly pounced on the ball but threw wide to first and Harris was called safe by the field umpire. Dizzy stormed in from the outfield screaming that Harris had illegally ran inside the base path causing the errant throw. Home plate umpire Jim Ahearn agreed and called Harris out.

Enraged over the overturned call, Harris, known as "Vicious Vic," in the Negro Leagues, attacked Ahearn. Both benches emptied to join the fray. Diz, never anxious to fight, tried to play peacemaker. He attempted to free George Susce from Josh Gibson's headlock. When Dizzy intervened Josh effortlessly tossed him aside without ever letting Susce loose. "Eyewitness estimates as to how far Dean traveled in the air from Gibson's one-armed heave range from five to fifteen feet."[35]

The all-out brawl continued, and eventually included the fans, "spectators leaped over the railing and into the midst of the melee."[36] Police finally arrived, order was restored, and the game continued.

The Crawfords put the game away in the eighth with four straight hits after two were out. Oscar Charleston doubled to right and came home when Josh Gibson crashed a homerun over the left field fence to deadlock the game 3 – 3. Judy Johnson tripled, and Curt Harris singled him home with what proved to be the winning run.

Umpire Ahearn wanted to press charges and have Harris jailed. The police were ready to oblige but Pittsburgh Steeler owner Art Rooney, a friend of Pittsburgh Crawford owner Gus Greenlee, used his considerable influence to keep "Vicious Vic" out of the slammer.

Paul left the pitching to Diz, Satch and others as he again avoided the mound as he had for most of the barnstorming tour. He played right field for two innings and only batted one time, so it seemed strange when he told reporters after the game. "Nothing wrong with my arm" Paul said. "I did get a few pains from pitching night baseball but listen – I know that our living depends on our arms and neither of us is going to take any long chances. I'm fine again and I want to stay that way."[37]

Paul was certainly being disingenuous about his arm problems. His arm bothered him during the entire tour, but he surely did not want Sam Breadon and Branch Rickey to suspect a sore arm before he signed his 1935 contract.

Dizzy was glad the barnstorming was over. "It's a great relief to get this thing over with. We have too much at stake, Me 'n' Paul. We've had a good time though."[38]

Paul revealed that he and Diz had offers to go on a long Vaudeville tour but would not accept. "We're gonna play one week in New York and then call it quits," Paul said. "Because we both need some rest."[39]

Me 'N' Paul

"Yeah," Diz said. "We're gonna make ourselves scarce."[40]

Broadway was ready for Dizzy and Daffy but Dizzy and Daffy were not ready for Broadway. When Diz and Paul arrived in New York City for their Vaudeville stint, publicity photos were needed. A blonde showgirl was hired to pose with Diz and Paul for the photo shoot. When Dizzy saw the provocatively dressed blonde, he balked.

"I may be Dizzy" he said, "but I ain't dizzy enough to pose for pictures with a blonde in scanties."[41]

Diz was adamant. "Hell no! nothin' doin'. I ain't gonna have baseball folks thinkin' I'm a sissy."

"Come, come" the director said. "Don't be silly."

"No sir exploded Dizzy. "I won't do it. Besides, my wife would take me to he cleaners if she saw a picture like that."

"That's right," Paul said. "Diz ain't gonna have pictures taken lookin' like one of the gigolos."

Evidently makeup was also out of the question.

"Paint is meant for the sides of barns, not for the faces of pitchers like Me 'n' Diz."[42] Paul said.

Diz and Paul's vaudeville debut came October 26th at the Roxy Theater in front of a packed house. The curtain opened to reveal Diz and Paul wearing their Cardinal uniforms and playing catch in front of a set meant to look like a big-league dugout. An announcer walked up and began to interview the boys. He asked Dizzy who did the most in winning the National League for the Cardinals. Dizzy answered, "The Giants" and the crowd laughed.

Paul said, "The Brooklyn's helped, too." This comment brought cheers.

Dizzy then explained how he managed to get hit in the head in the fourth game of the World Series.

"Wasn't nothing complicated about it." Diz said "Frisch sent me in to run for Spud and told me to use my head. I did."[43]

The announcer asked Dizzy about the riot and Medwick getting pelted with all that fruit.

"Well, if a apple a day keeps the doctor away, ol' Ducky ain't gonna be sick for the next twenty years."[44]

The act was supposed to end with Paul turning to the audience and making Schoolboy Rowe's famed query "how'mn I doing, Edna? But he forgot so the boys simply walked off the stage. The whole act only lasted about fifteen minutes.

Afterwards in their dressing room Diz allowed that "acting was easier'n fannin' Greenberg."

"Yessir, it's a plum cinch. You just stand out there for 'bout a inning and jabber away. I guess it's mighty near soft as umpirin'."[45]

Asked if he was nervous, Paul replied. "Nah, I wasn't. I felt as relaxed as I did when I was pitchin' to that Greenberg. That guy couldn't hit one of my fog balls with a paddle."[46]

After their week on Broadway Diz and Paul had one more money-making commitment before they called it a season. They headed to Long Island to film a 15-minute two-reel short subject movie for Warner Brothers. The movie was titled "Dizzy and Daffy" and co-starred Shemp Howard who later found lasting fame as one of the three stooges.

Diz and Paul pocketed $2,000 each for acting in the inane movie which mainly consisted of Shemp playing a nearly blind pitcher/manager and the Deans playing catch. When Paul was asked about the plot of the movie, he replied "I won't know what it's about until I see it."[47]

Their commitments finally finished Diz left for Bradenton, Florida, recently officially renamed Deanville. Paul headed for Arkansas to relax and enjoy his newfound celebrity status with friends and family. He soon discovered a new love interest.

Anxious to sign his two stars for the 1935 season, Sam Breadon followed Dizzy to Florida to negotiate. Paul conducted his salary negotiations with club officials by telephone, from Arkansas.

On December 5th Dizzy announced that he and Sam Breadon had come to terms on a 1935 contract. "Yep, I'm all signed, sealed and delivered to the Cardinals for next season and I'm not working for any of that coffee and cake money, either!"

"I told Sam I've got to have important dough. My asking price was $25,000. Sam offered twenty grand. We settled for a sum between those two figures; so, I guess I did all right, eh. I'm the highest paid pitcher in the business."[48]

Diz left the impression he and Breadon had met in the middle at $22,500, that was not exactly true. He actually signed for $18,500, which was still a top baseball salary in 1935.

Happily, Dizzy rhapsodized about his flourishing finances. "I'm getting round- shouldered with money," he said. "I signed a advertisin' contract for $15,000 the other day. I'm indorsin' everything from fountain pens and puppy biscuits to baby buggies and mattresses. I bought me a new automobile – and a very flashy rig it is, too. I'm gonna be a very fast man with a dollar while I'm in the chips."[49]

With Dizzy signed the Cardinal Brass turned their full attention to signing Paul who was demanding $12,500 and dating a beauty queen. Ever since Paul returned to Arkansas, he had been seeing Dorothy Sandusky, a 19-year-old local beauty contest winner. Paul had known Miss Sandusky for three years, but she said, "he only started going with me when he came back from the World Series."[50]

Evidently Paul was getting better at the love game as this romance turned out better than the ill-fated Betty Holt affair. After dating only two months Dorothy Sandusky agreed to marry Paul Dean.

The wedding was to take place in Russellville, Arkansas, Miss Sandusky's hometown, on December 21, 1934 at 5:00 p.m. The bride said "Paul wanted Dizzy to be best man, but he is in Florida and just couldn't make it here in time. We will spend our honeymoon in Mississippi and Dizzy will meet us there with his wife."[51]

Russellville was a small, rural town and could not supply the essentials necessary for a proper wedding. On the morning of the nuptials Paul drove to Fort Smith, a larger Arkansas town, in order to buy himself a new suit, a ring for his bride and get a haircut. He did not make it back to Russellville until after 8:00, consequently, he was late for his own wedding.

An unlikely marriage featuring a groom on the rebound from a failed relationship, a whirlwind two-month courtship and a spur of the moment wedding turned into a 47- year union. Paul said his marriage was "the best thing that ever happened to me."[52]

Paul and his bride honeymooned from Russellville, Arkansas to Bond, Mississippi where they met up with Dizzy and his wife, Pat. The four Deans spent Christmas with Pat's parents in Bond. After Christmas they headed to Deanville, Florida and Paul returned his focus to negotiating his 1935 baseball contract.

On December 30th Paul announced he would sign his 1935 contract with the Cardinals within a few days. Paul agreed to a salary of $6,000 and said "of course, it's no huge salary, but they've been mighty kind to Me 'n' Diz at the Cardinal office, have permitted us to make some money on the side and I'm satisfied."[53]

Paul expressed his desire to stay with St. Louis. "I hope the Cards don't sell Me or Diz. They said the New York Giants and Chicago Cubs have been after one of us for two years. I don't want to leave Frankie Frisch, but I'm goin' to play ball, no matter where they move me."[54]

CHAPTER 22

"Paul is a great pitcher and so is Dizzy, but I'm the fellow that taught them all they know"

Sportswriter, Grantland Rice caught up with Dizzy and Paul in Deanville, Florida to discuss the 1935 baseball season.

"It ought to be simple." Diz said, "St. Louis ought to win and Pittsburgh is the team we ought to have to beat. Me 'n' Paul ought to be good for fifty games."[1]

Paul made no predictions for himself, he instead praised Dizzy, "I'll fog 'em through and I'll have a better curve ball." Paul told Grantland, "but I wouldn't be surprised if Diz won thirty-five games. Honest, Mr. Rice, when Diz goes out on that mound the only thing he hasn't got is a rifle. And he don't need no rifle."[2]

Diz and Paul spent the first six weeks of 1935 enjoying themselves in the Florida sunshine. They fished with ex-teammate, Philadelphia manager Jimmy Wilson, golfed with celebrities, attended greyhound races and watched their pal heavyweight champ Max Baer box.

In late January Dizzy traveled to New York City to receive more awards for his incredible 1934 season. In addition to his National League MVP award, he was voted top athlete of 1934 and baseball writers player of the year.

By February 15th the Dean boys were ready to make some more money. They traveled to Hot Springs, Arkansas to be instructors at Ray Doan's baseball school. Along with Rogers Hornsby and Chicago Cubs pitcher Lon Warneke they would tutor young men who had ambitions to play professional baseball. The students paid to attend and some actually signed Minor League contracts.

It was not all work for Diz and Paul as Hot Springs was a famous vacation destination. Hot Springs featured not only the namesake therapeutic thermal springs but also horse racing and casino gambling.

Although gambling was illegal, local law enforcement was controlled by politicians and casino owners who brought in hordes of tourists that fed the economy. Hot Springs became a national gambling mecca which boasted dozens of casinos, the largest such operation in the United States between 1927 to 1947. "Hotels advertised the availability of prostitutes and off-track booking was available for virtually every horse race in North America."[3]

Baseball has a long history in Hot Springs. Years before Major League teams held spring training in Florida and Arizona many teams trained in Hot Springs. In 1886 the Chicago Cubs and Chicago White Sox brought their players to the resort to get them in shape for the upcoming regular season making Hot Springs the "birthplace" of spring training baseball.

200 campers showed up for Doan's baseball camp in February 1935. One of the students was very familiar to Diz and Paul. Elmer "Goober" Dean still aspired to follow his famous brothers to the Major Leagues. Despite his earlier diamond failures Elmer was still chasing the dream. However, he was not as eager to take instruction as the other students. When instructor Lon Warneke tried to give him some pointers, Elmer informed him.

"Listen Lon, you can't tell me nothin' I don't know. I'm a great pitcher just like my brothers. Look at my screw ball, better'n yours, Lon. Paul is a great pitcher and so is Dizzy, but I'm the fellow that taught them all they know."[4]

Goober did not impress scouts enough to sign a Minor League contract, however, he was able to make some money playing for the House of David, a barnstorming team Ray Doan was promoting. Elmer's last name rather than his pitching prowess secured him a place on the bearded barnstorming team. He grew a beard and was paid $250 a month to pitch baseballs which was much more than he made pitching peanuts at Buff stadium in Houston.

Diz and Paul left Doan's baseball school after two weeks and headed back to Deanville(Brarenton, Florida) where the Cardinals were to begin spring training on March 2nd. EnRoute, they received some news that upset Dizzy; Babe Ruth was coming to the National League.

By 1935 the 40-year-old Babe realized he was nearly finished as a player and he wanted to stay in baseball as a manager. Ruth wanted to manage the Yankees, but owner Jacob Ruppert supported current manager Joe McCarthy, who was a proven winner. Ruppert offered Ruth a Minor League managerial position but the Babe was not interested.

Finally, Ruppert worked out a deal with Boston Brave owner Emil Fuchs, who wanted Ruth as a gate attraction. In order to get Ruth to play another year Fuchs would make Ruth assistant manager to Skipper Bill McKechnie. Fuchs also promised the Babe he would succeed McKechnie as manager after the 1935 season.

Babe began his Major League career in Boston with the Red Sox so a homecoming to manage in Boston was agreeable to him. On February 26, 1935 the New York Yankees traded Babe to the Boston Braves of the National League.

Dizzy was upset and resented Ruth coming to the National League. "He made all his money in the American League, so why don't he stay there?" Diz queried sarcastically.

"The American League couldn't make a place for him, could they? Why don't they take care of their own players? Why come to the National League and knock a fine fellow like McKechnie out of a job? I resent Ruth coming to the National League and I think practically every player in this league will feel the same way about it."[5]

Dizzy was wrong about most other National League players resenting Ruth. Even Paul disagreed with Diz. "I welcome Babe to the National League." Paul said. "I think he will help the National League plenty and make a first division contender out of the Boston Braves."[6]

Fans and sportswriters as well as players were appalled by Dizzy's harsh words toward the Babe. "It's nothing more than sour grapes or jealousy that prompts Dizzy Dean to pop off to the effect that Babe Ruth should stay in the American League." Sports columnist Charles Johnson wrote, "up to now, Dean has been the big ballyhoo man of the National League. Now he will have to divide honors with Babe Ruth."[7]

When the flak started flying Dizzy quickly crawfished. Diz claimed he meant no disrespect to Ruth and his only concern was his friend Bill McKechnie's losing his job. Dizzy seized his first opportunity to apologize in person to the Babe.

During the first week of spring training Diz traveled from Bradenton to Tampa, Florida to see Babe's Braves play a pre-season game against the Cincinnati Reds. In the fourth inning Dizzy left his seat, went on to the field and in front of 3,500 fans apologized to the Bambino.

"It's all a mistake." Diz told The Babe. "That's okay, kid." Ruth said.

"The newspapers got me wrong." Diz explained. "I meant that it was a dirty shame that the American League let you get away."

"That's okay, kid." Babe said

"You're gonna mean money in my pocket." Said Dizzy. "Why, you're gonna draw thousands and thousands through the turnstiles."

"I hope so, kid." Said the Babe.

"Well, I just wanted to apologize." Diz continued. "I don't want no hard feeling between us."

That's okay, kid." Babe said.[8]

After finishing his public apology Diz sat on the Brave's bench as the Reds blasted Boston 12 – 1.

Other than Dizzy's antics the Card's spring training camp was mostly uneventful. The World Series Champs were returning intact except for pitcher Tex Carleton. Branch Rickey was tired of Carleton's constant bickering and his resentment of the Deans. Also, he was not durable enough to suit Frankie Frisch.

Tex was traded to the Chicago Cubs for pitcher Pat Malone, who had won 14 games in 1934. However, Malone did not help the Cards as Frisch had hoped. The ever-frugal Rickey offered Malone only $5,000, $9,000 less than he made in 1934. He refused to sign and was sold to the Yankees. Rickey planned to take up the slack with low-priced rookies.

The infield and outfield starters all returned; Bill Delancey and Spud Davis platooned at catcher. Ripper Collins played first, Frisch was at second, Leo Durocher at shortstop and Pepper Martin manned third. The starting outfield consisted of Ducky Medwick, Ernie Orsatti and Jack Rothrock. Only two positions were contested in spring training, shortstop and centerfield.

Rickey wanted increased offensive production from those two positions. Lippy Leo was a great defensive shortstop but couldn't hit his weight. Hollywood Orsatti had little power and always aggravated Rickey by holding out for more money and arriving late for spring training. Also, Orsatti and Durocher's lifestyles displeased the religious, teetotaling Rickey. Shortstop Charley Gelbert and centerfielder Terry Moore were brought in to compete against the incumbents.

Charlie Gelbert was the Cardinals starting shortstop from 1929 to 1932. St. Louis won the National League Pennant in 1930 and the World Series in 1931. Gelbert was a key member of those two Championship squads hitting close to .300 and playing flawless defense. His career was nearly ended when he shot himself in a hunting accident. Gelbert had spent the past two years rehabilitating his severely injured left leg.

"I'm confident I'm fit for fulltime Major League duty." Gelbert said as he showed unexpected stamina and ability in the Cards first spring training work-out.[9]

Terry Moore was a rookie who began his professional career in 1932. Although Moore had only three years professional experience, Rickey believed he was Major League ready. A swift, strong-armed outfielder Moore hit .328 for Columbus in 1934.

Charlie Gelbert never regained his former greatness. He did not take Durocher's job, but he did make the team as a utility infielder. Gelbert managed to hang on in the Majors for five more years with four different teams always as a utility player, never again a starter. Terry Moore had a great spring and unseated Ernie Orsatti as the starting centerfielder.

The pitching staff was the same as 1934 with the exception of the traded Tex Carleton. When Rickey sold Pat Malone, it opened up a starting spot behind Dizzy, Paul, Bill Walker and Bill Hallahan. This spot was filled by rookie Ed Heusser. Two old veterans, Jesse Haines and Dazzy Vance shouldered the relief work.

Spring training went well for Paul. He was in good shape and did not experience any arm problems. He made five appearances, pitched 27 innings, gave up 28 hits and 14 runs. His last pre-season start was an impressive complete game 6 – 3 victory over the St. Louis Browns, the Cards American League counterparts.

The St. Louis Cardinals were favorites to win the 1935 National League Pennant. Sportswriters predicted a two-team race between the Cardinals and New York Giants, with St. Louis winning. Chicago was picked third and Pittsburgh fourth. The Babe's Braves fifth followed by Brooklyn, Philadelphia and Cincinnati.

The sportswriters knew the World Champions were loaded with talent. The Cards had speed, power and superlative pitching. Frankie Frisch was afraid his Cards were becoming over-confident. Believing the press praise.

"This team must realize it cannot win this year on its reputation." Frisch said. "As a matter of fact, we were lucky last season. It will be a battle all the way for us again."[10]

The regular season for St. Louis began on April 16th in Chicago against the Cubs. In the very first inning the one player the Cards could not afford to lose went down. Cub third baseman Freddy Lindstrom smashed a line drive off Dizzy's left shin and he had to be carried from the field. Diz was taken to the hospital where x-rays showed no broken bones. He was in fine spirits after again avoiding tragedy on the diamond.

"Shucks" Diz said. "Them Cubbies ain't a-goin' to get away with knocking ol' Diz out in less than an inning. I'll be back at 'em and I'll give 'em a good trimmin'"[11]

After Diz was knocked out of the game Chicago went on to win causing the Cards to start the season 0 – 1. Still convalescing, Diz as unable to give the Cubs a "good trimmin'" In the second game of the season, however, Paul was up to the task.

4000 shivering Cub fans braved the windy, cold Chicago afternoon with hopes Paul would not last longer than Dizzy had the day before.

When the first Cub batter doubled, Paul's prospects appeared as bleak as the weather.

The leadoff Cubbie double was the last Chicago threat as Paul settled in to pitch a shutout. Ducky Medwick homered in the sixth for the only run of the games as the Cards won 1 – 0. Paul scattered eight hits walked none and struck out six.

Dizzy recovered and was ready to pitch on April 21st when the Cards invaded Forbes Field in Pittsburgh. Once again Dizzy proved his value as a drawing card. 28,000 fans turned out to watch Diz pitch. It was the largest crowd to attend a game at Forbes Field since the Pirates played in the 1927 World Series. Diz did not disappoint, he gave up only one run on 5 hits as the Cards won 6 – 1.

The Cubs came to St. Louis and again fell victim to Ducky and Daffy. Paul scattered 12 hits and Medwick drove in 4 runs as the Cards tamed the Cubs 9 – 5. Paul contributed two hits to the Card offensive onslaught as he raised his pitching record to two wins and no losses.

With the season only two weeks old Frankie Frisch started relying heavily on Diz and Paul. Between starts Frisch pitched the Deans in relief in back to back losses to the Cubs. Each were saddled with their first loss of the season. However, Diz didn't seem to mind.

"I told Frankie me 'n' Paul are ready to work out of turn – every day if he wants us to. I wanna win and nothin' would suit me better than goin' in there every other day."[12]

Paul's next start was in Cincinnati on an overcast day with intermittent rain. Paul prevailed, roasting the Reds 6 – 2 for his third win of the young season. He gave up six hits and had six strikeouts. Pepper Martin led the Cardinal batsmen going 3 for 3 with a triple and two singles.

Dizzy's last start of April was against Pittsburgh in St. Louis. 12,000 hometown fans filed into Sportsman's Park expecting Diz to easily scuttle the Pirates just as he had on April 21st in Pittsburgh, his only victory of the 1935 season. Adding to the optimism was Dizzy's mound opponent, Cy Blanton, a raw rookie.

The disappointed crowd watched as Cy Blanton channeled Cy Young as he cuffed the Cards 3 – 2. Pittsburgh pounded Dizzy for 11 hits in handing him his second loss of the 1935 season.

St. Louis finished April in fifth place with a record of 6 wins and 7 losses. Paul won all three of his starts, 50% of the Cardinal victories. His only loss was in a relief appearance.

On May 1st in Cincinnati Dizzy defeated the Reds 5 – 2. He gave up 6 hits and struck out 8 Reds. Ducky Medwick was the hitting hero as he drove in 3 of the 5 Card runs with a homer and 2 singles.

As the Cardinals traveled from city to city Diz and Paul promoted their products when they were not playing games or practicing. They made personal appearances at department stores that sold merchandise they endorsed and at theaters where their movie was playing. Dizzy had one lucrative endorsement Paul did not share.

Grape-Nuts breakfast cereal ran a series of comic strips in newspapers across America featuring Dizzy without Paul. The comic strips portrayed Dizzy in different dangerous situations where he always saved the day with his pitching prowess.

A typical comic strip had six panels and showed Dizzy performing heroic feats off the diamond. The first panel shows Dizzy sitting on a passenger train wearing a suit and tie. A young boy approaches him and says "say, you're Dizzy Dean-aren't you? Will you sign this baseball for me?" Diz replied, "I sure will, son."

In the second panel a man with a gun appeared and said "stick 'em up! An' make it fast!" Diz told the kid "give me that ball! Quick!"

The third panel showed Dizzy hurling the baseball into the bandits' face. Diz yelled "there's the fast one you called for!"

Dizzy's a hero in the fourth panel surrounded by relieved passengers. The railroad conductor says to Diz. "If it hadn't been for your "fast" thinking, he'd have robbed the express car!" Dizzy modestly replies, "shucks, that's nothing! He was set-up for a smokeball."

The commercial began in the fifth panel. The kid says to Dizzy, "gosh, Dizzy. I wish I was a fast thinker like you." Diz gives the kid advice. "Son, to think fast, you got to be wide- awake all the time, and that takes plenty of energy. I can show you one swell way to get that old energy too, if you'll have breakfast with me."

The commercial culminates in the final panel with Diz and the kid seated at a table in the dining car. Diz says, "eat grape-nuts, son, like I do.

Me 'N' Paul

It's one of the swellest energy-makers there is." The kid replies "gee, Dizzy, it tastes great, too!"[13]

In early May the Cardinals were still wallowing in fourth place. They had won only seven games of which the Dean brothers had won five. Branch Rickey's rookie pitchers were performing poorly. Wild Bill Hallahan had been useless throughout April and Bill Walker had been erratic. Even with the Deans pulling double duty the Cards rotation was unsustainable. Rickey realized he had to make a move.

With no internal options Rickey was forced to turn outside the Cardinal organization in his search for a starting pitcher. In an uncharacteristic Rickey maneuver, he paid the Philadelphia Phillies $10,000 for 32-year-old righthander Phil "Fidgety" Collins.

Phil Collins was a good pitcher on a bad team. In 1934 he won 13 games and lost 18 for the hapless Phillies. Since 1929 Collins had been one of the mainstays of the Philly pitching staff amassing a 73 – 72 won – loss record for the perpetual second division team.

Collins was elated to be going from the pitiful Phillies to the World Champion Cardinals. Also, he already had a gashouse gang worthy nickname. "Fidgety" fit nicely with Dizzy, Daffy, Ducky, Dazzy, Pepper, Ripper, Spud, The Lip and the Flash.

An eagerly anticipated sporting event took place on May 5th in Boston. Dizzy's Cards played Babe's Braves. Despite Dizzy's public apology to Ruth many fans thought bad blood still existed between the two men. Dizzy had supplanted the Bambino as the top drawing Card in sports and fans wanted to see them face each other on the field. Could the brash kid vanquish the aging superstar on the diamond as he had at the box office?

The much-publicized duel drew 30,000 fans to the stands. Diz still respected Ruth, even with the Babes' diminished skills. The old lion still had a few teeth and Dizzy was cautious. When Babe batted in the bottom of the first, Dizzy pitched carefully and finally walked him.

St. Louis broke the game open with a six-run second inning. Dizzy contributed to the scoring with a long flyball over Ruth's head that landed in the leftfield stands for a homerun.

With a six-run cushion Dizzy was braver when the Bambino batted for the second time. Dizzy grinned at Babe, turned and waved to his outfielders to back-up. Finally satisfied when the outfielders backs were almost touching the outfield fence, Dizzy climbed back on the mound and struck out the aging legend. "Babe almost broke his back swinging at Dean's steaming strikeout ball."[14]

St. Louis went on to win the game 7 – 0. Dizzy's third win was a 10-hit shut-out. Babe batted one more time in the game and grounded out. The legendary Babe Ruth's playing career was coming to a close.

Paul's next start was in Brooklyn on May 8th. Two days of inclement weather delayed the start of the series, so Paul was well-rested and ready to go. His frustration started early, in the first inning after one out Dodger shortstop Lonny Frey was issued a free pass on pitches Paul thought should have been called strikes. A flyball to Orsatti in center produced out number two. An easy grounder to Leo Durocher should have ended the inning but the usually reliable Lip threw wild to second putting Dodgers on first and third.

Although rattled by the umpire and the error Paul settled down and pitched his way out of trouble by striking out second sacker Tony Cuccinello.

After a scoreless and uneventful second frame, Paul went to pieces in the third. After right fielder Buzzy Boyle flied out Frey singled to left. Centerfielder Len Koenecke walked, again on pitches that appeared to Paul to cross the plate. First baseman Sam Leslie flied out to Orsatti, but Cuccinello walked filling the bases. Paul was fuming, wondering what he had to do to get a strike called. When leftfielder Danny Taylor walked pushing Frey across the plate Paul went berserk screaming obscenities at home plate umpire Dolly Stark, Dizzy ran to the mound to try to calm Paul down as Frankie Frisch left the dugout protesting to Stark about the strike zone. Things calmed down and the game resumed. However, when Paul's first pitch to third baseman Joe Stripp was called a ball, he threw his glove in the air and was quickly ejected from the game by umpire Stark.

St. Louis went on to lose the game in twelve innings by a score of 3 – 2. After the game Paul was still mad at the umpire Dolly Stark. "How can a fella ever win a game with them kind of calls goin' on?"[15] he wondered.

The Cardinals traveled to Philadelphia for a series with the Phillies and Dizzy received news that a little pal he considered good luck had passed away. Dizzy visited his grave under the stands at the Baker Bowl, home field of the Phillies'.

Me 'N' Paul

The tombstone read "here lies Bunny, Dizzy Dean's luck."[16]

Dizzy became very fond of Bunny, the Phillies late mascot, because he pitched a great game the first time, he met the huge white rabbit. Diz became so enamored with the luck Bunny brought him he tried in vain to buy the lucky rabbit.

As he mourned at Bunny's burial site, Dizzy lamented: "Bunny would still be living if they'd let me take care of him."[17]

Evidently Bunny's luck survived his demise as Dizzy defeated Philly in the first game of a doubleheader. Despite giving up 13 hits and 6 runs Diz and the Cards coasted to a 15 – 6 victory.

Paul started the second game attempting to make it a perfect day for the Deans. Bunny's luck did not extend to Paul. He lasted only six innings, giving up 7 hits and 4 runs, Paul absorbed the loss in the Philly 5 – 2 win.

Although night baseball had proved a success in the Minor Leagues, Major League baseball had not yet embraced the nocturnal game; consequently, most working fans could attend games only on weekends.

Sunday doubleheaders were fan favorites and drew the largest crowds of the week. Fans wanted to see the popular Deans pitch, so when possible, Frankie Frisch set up his pitching rotation to allow Diz to start one game and Paul the other.

In New York against the Giants Diz started the first game of the doubleheader and pitched well. However, shoddy Card playing drowned Dizzy. Centerfielder Terry Moore misplayed a grounder that bounded away from him and rolled to the fence allowing diminutive Giant Hughie Critz to round the bases for an inside-the-park homerun.

New York added three more runs in the seventh on Crites' second homer and four Cardinal errors. The Giants won the game 4 – 1. Perhaps Crites' two homeruns were payback for Dizzy terrorizing him with the scary black cat the year before.

St. Louis seemed determined to give away the second game also. Paul started the game by retiring the Giant lead-off batter, but Dick Bartell reached second when Ernie Orsatti dropped his easy flyball. Player/manager Bill Terry lined a single off Pepper Martin's glove leaving Giants on first and third with only one out. Mel Ott grounded to Ripper Collins who threw home trapping Bartell between third and home. Card catcher

Carl Duncan

Bill Delancey decided to run him down but lost the race. Bartell was safe at third and the bases were loaded with Giants.

It was a tough spot for Paul who should have been out of the inning, unscathed. The next New York batter hit a sacrifice fly scoring Bartell from third. That unearned run was the only score Paul allowed New York the rest of the game. St. Louis won 4 – 1 as Paul gave up seven hits walked one and struck out seven.

By mid-May Babe Ruth was occasionally productive at the plate but a liability in the field and on the bath paths. He made so many errors that some Brave pitchers refused to take the mound when Ruth was in the line-up.

In addition to his poor play Ruth's refusal to stay with the team while on the road and his huge salary further alienated his teammates. It was becoming increasingly clear he would never be able to manage the Braves and Babe knew it. The Bambino was running out of innings.

Despite his sub-par play Ruth was still a powerful gate attraction. When Boston played the Cardinals in St. Louis on May 19th the game was advertised as Dizzy Dean vs Babe Ruth. The outcome was the same as Diz and Babe's initial meeting in Boston; Dizzy's dramatics decided the game.

After holding Ruth hitless in four at-bats Diz came up in the bottom of the eighth with the bases loaded. The score was tied and there were two outs. The Great One swung helplessly at two pitches before rifling a shot to left field cleaning the bases. Diz danced home when Pepper Martin singled making the St. Louis 7 Boston 3. Dizzy held the Braves scoreless in the ninth for his fifth win of the year.

Without a doubt, Dizzy Dean was the new king of the diamond. However, Babe Ruth had one more page to add before the final chapter of his legendary career could be written. In the twilight of his playing days on May 25th in Pittsburgh, the Bambino bashed three homeruns. His third homerun, the final one of the game and of his career, went over the right field upper deck and completely left Forbes Field. The first time anyone had ever hit a ball completely out of that stadium.

Ruth was urged to make this his last game, go out in a blaze of glory, but he wanted to finish the road trip because rival teams had scheduled days to honor him. Babe played games in Cincinnati and Philadelphia before retiring on June 2nd, 1935. Ruth still wanted to manage but was never given the chance. A one-year stint as first base coach for the Brooklyn Dodgers in 1938 was his last job in baseball.

Branch Rickey believed Dizzy Dean had ushered in a new era for baseball. An era where pitching and defensive play pushed homerun hitting to the background.

"For that reason, I consider Dizzy Dean the most important player I've ever handled." Rickey said. "He is the successor to Babe Ruth as the game's no. 1 player, the game's no. 1 personality, and games no. 1 showman, and baseball has gone Dean – just as it went Ruth back in 1920."[18]

When Diz was told about Rickey's statements, he said "Jeez! Did Branch say that? Well- maybe he's right. He's a smart fella, and he's been around a long time. Guess I need to bring that up when we negotiate next year's contract."[19]

After Babe and the Braves left St. Louis the Philadelphia Phillies came to Sportsman's Park for a three-game series on May 21st Paul pitched against the Phillies and ignited a brawl that culminated with Dizzy being removed from the field by police.

The fracas began in the top of the fourth when Paul hit Phillies second sacker Lou Chiozza. Thinking the beaning was intentional, the Phillies poured on to the field after Paul. Diz led the Card charge to protect Paul and after much minor scuffling order was restored.

When Paul came to bat in the bottom of the fourth, Phillies pitcher Orville Jorgen began throwing at him. Paul managed to dodge four dusters and walked without getting hit. The Cards ended up scoring one run to take a 5 – 4 lead.

Paul did not appreciate Orville's attempted beaning and was ready to retaliate. So, when Al Todd, Dizzy's old Texas League nemesis, came to the plate in the fifth Paul plastered him with a fastball to the shoulder.

Incensed, Todd charged the mound intent on pulverizing Paul as he had Dizzy in their 1931 Texas League fight. Paul dropped his glove, raised his clinched fists, set his jaw and glared at Todd. Paul was a much better brawler than Diz and was ready to avenge Dizzy by decking big Al Todd.

Pepper Martin intercepted Todd before he reached Paul and again both benches emptied for the second melee of the game. When the fight was over Dizzy would not stop shouting insults at the Phillies and finally had to be removed from the field by stadium police. Philadelphia won the game 7 – 6 saddling Paul with the loss. He gave up 7 runs on 10 hits 3 walks and 2 hit batsmen in 6 innings of work. He struck out 4.

Dizzy was still belligerent after the game. "They can't clout us Deans on the nose and get away with it. Us Deans never forget."[20] He said.

The Phillies were still mad as well. Player/manager Jimmy Wilson, Diz and Paul's old fishing buddy, said, "It's getting so you can't get a base hit off those Deans without getting beaned your next time up. They think they can get away with anything, but, by God the Phils have declared war on them."[21]

Diz responded, "you can tell that Wilson he can kiss my ass. Them Phillies can't hurt nobody none of 'em can hit a lick."[22]

The Dodgers came to St. Louis and defeated Dizzy and the Cards 5 – 3. His record fell to 5 wins against 4 losses as Brooklyn scored 5 runs on 7 hits and 3 walks. Diz hit 1 batter and struck out 4.

Dizzy was off to a slow start and Giant player/manager Bill Terry had an explanation for his lackluster beginning to the 1935 season. Terry had some advice for Diz.

"Dizzy has too many advertising and radio men in his hair to think about pitching the way he should." Terry said. "He better pay more attention to baseball because he'll find out those advertising guys will drop him like a hot penny if he doesn't win 25 games this year."

"He needs to avoid the petty feuds that make players anxious to knock his block off. He has all the stuff to win as many games as any man in baseball, but right now he's a manager's nightmare."[23]

Of course, Dizzy thought he knew everything and the Great One was not about to take advice from an opponent.

"Nuts to Terry! Diz growled. "Let him watch out for hisself and I'll watch out for ol' Diz.

Them advertising guys don't bother me none."[24]

Bill Terry led his league leading Giants into St. Louis to face the second place Cards and Dizzy's woes continued. In one inning Diz ruined Paul's fine pitching performance.

Paul sailed into the ninth inning leading 4 – 1 having allowed only 4 hits and 2 walks while fanning five. Giant centerfielder Hank Leiber led off the ninth by laying a bunt down the third base line. Pepper pounced on the dribbler but threw the ball over Ripper's head into right field. The error sent Leiber to second. Consecutive singles scored Leiber and left runners on first and third. Paul walked the Giant pitch-hitter to load the bases. Desperate to hold the 4 – 2 lead Frankie Frisch sent Dizzy into the fray.

Bill Terry sent up a pinch-hitter to face Diz with the bases loaded. Dizzy fanned him but walked Joe Moore forcing in a run and leaving the bases loaded. Suddenly Dizzy discovered that in his haste to rescue Paul he had picked up somebody else's glove. Diz called time-out and summoned the bat boy to bring him his lucky mitt.

However, Dizzy's magic mitt failed to fell the Giants as Mark Koenig singled home two runs making the score 5 – 4. That was the final as a Card rally in the bottom of the ninth fizzled with the bases loaded. Since Paul was responsible for the three runners Dizzy inherited, he absorbed the loss.

Dizzy finally climbed back into the win column by beating Cincinnati on the last day of May. He gave up 2 runs on 7 hits and 1 walk. He struck out 9. Ducky Medwick was the Card hitting hero going 3 for 4 with 2 doubles. The 4 – 2 victory raised Dizzy's won-lost record to 6 – 4. The Cardinals finished May in second place 4.5 games behind the New York Giants.

On June 1st in Chicago Paul started the first game of a doubleheader against the Cubs. The Cubs countered with Lon Warneke, Diz and Paul's pal from Arkansas and fellow professor at Ray Doan's baseball academy.

Chicago drew first blood with a Gabby Harnett homer in the second inning. The Cards tied the game with a run in the fourth on singles by Pepper Martin, Jack Rothrock, Frankie Frisch and Ducky Medwick. St. Louis took the lead in the fifth when Terry Moore walked, Martin singled and Rothrock doubled. The Cubs deadlocked the game in the seventh on a Hack Wilson double and Harnett's RBI single. The score remained tied at two apiece through nine frames and the game headed for extra innings.

Both teams scored a single run in tenth and after the Cards failed to score in the top of the eleventh, Paul trudged to the mound for his eleventh inning of work. After one out leftfielder Augie Galan blasted a triple, putting the game winning run 90 feet from home. Frisch decided to intentionally walk two batters to load the bases and set up a potential inning ending double play.

This strategy seemed flawed because it brought to the plate future Hall of Fame slugger Gabby Harnett, who had previously driven in two of the three Cub runs with a homer and a single. However, Paul prevailed in the pressure packed situation inducing Gabby to ground into a double play, sending the game to the climatic twelfth.

Paul was the first batter in the top of the twelfth. He helped his own cause by delivering a double. Rothrock singled him to third, and when Frisch hit a short fly to center, Paul tagged up and sprinted home with the go-ahead run. Paul closed out the Cubs in the bottom of the inning to secure a 4 – 3 St. Louis victory.

After the disheartening loss, the Chicago morale sagged. They lost the second game as "Fidgety" Phil Collins gave up only a single unearned run and the Cards won 4 – 1 to complete the doubleheader sweep.

Dizzy's next start was in Pittsburgh on June 4th and he learned a hard lesson; From hero to bum can be a short ride. In one afternoon, Dizzy alienated his teammates and adoring fans.

Pittsburgh tallied four unearned runs in the third inning and Dizzy blamed his teammate's poor fielding and bad calls by the home plate umpire, Charlie Rigler. Diz stewed until the fifth inning when he blew up. St. Louis was at bat and Dizzy was riding Rigler about the strike zone when Ducky Medwick said "lay off the umpire and bear down out on the mound."[25]

"Me bear down!" Dizzy screamed. "Y'all are a bunch of lousy, no-good ballplayers who ain't good enough to be on the same field with me."[26]

Ripper Collins was fed up with Dizzy's "crazy shit" and shouted, "shut your fucking mouth or someone will shut it for you."

"You do it," Diz said "if you're man enough and not yellow."

"Don't say another word" Ducky warned. "Fuck you! I'll crack you on your Hungarian nose" screamed Dizzy, now completely out of control.[27]

No one talked to Medwick like that, not even the star pitcher. As he started for Dizzy, Paul quickly jumped up and hurried to his brother's side. Medwick grabbed a bat and shouted "keep coming both of you. I'll separate you hillbilly bastards for good."[28]

Pepper Martin and other cooler Cards intervened and prevented what could have been serious injury to players crucial to Cardinal Pennant aspirations.

Still peeved, Dizzy took the mound in the bottom of the fifth and began grooving the ball to Pirate batters. Dizzy's pitches were like batting practice and Pittsburgh easily scored four runs. Obviously, Dizzy had quit trying and even the fans and sportswriters knew.

St. Louis Post-Dispatch sports columnist Roy Stockton called it, "the most unusual and disgraceful exhibition of childish temper that I have ever seen on a baseball diamond."[29]

Frisch pulled Dizzy and the Cardinals went on to lose the game 9 – 5. Diz needed to be punished but Frisch and Branch Rickey knew they had to have Diz on the field if they were to defend St. Louis' World Championship. Therefore, they were reluctant to fine or suspend him.

Frisch read Dizzy the riot act and let him off wit ha stern warning. Frankie told reporters, "if Dizzy repeats anything like that, I will suspend him and fine him $5,000. It was an unwarranted display of temper and a most unfair thing for him to do. I do not plan any fines or disciplinary action other than the warning."[30]

Dizzy admitted he lost his temper and berated his teammates but denied he quit trying to win. "I just lost my temper" Diz said. "They (the Cardinals) said I wasn't bearing down and goodness knows I certainly was givin' all I had, and it hurt me to have them say that. Naturally I was all burned up when Rigler called that a ball, when it was a strike right through the middle and would have taken me out of the inning. But I'm going right ahead and pitch my game the best I can and that's all I can do the way I sees it. I just lost my temper and I'm sorry. I know this is a good ball club and the boys have helped me get what I have, but I just flew off my head."[31]

The Cardinals returned to St. Louis and hosted the Chicago Cubs. Paul started, pitched seven strong innings and carried a 4 – 2 lead starting the eighth. Chicago scored two runs to tie the game. Paul was pulled for a pinch-hitter and finished his day with 8 innings pitched, 4 runs on 10 hits and 3 walks. He struck out 3. The Cards rallied to win the game with a run in the bottom of the ninth. Paul did not figure in the decision having left the game with the score tied.

News of Dizzy's behavior in Pittsburgh had quickly spread to St. Louis. Fighting with teammates was bad enough but giving up in a game was unacceptable. Fans were beginning to agree with Bill Terry; Dizzy was letting business interfere with baseball. He had already lost five games, only two fewer than he lost the entire 1934 regular season, when he won 30 and lost only 7.

Dizzy's first start in St. Louis after Pittsburgh fiasco was on June 9th against the Chicago Cubs. When he came to bat in the bottom of the second Diz was booed and pelted with lemons. Dizzy dodged the lemons and responded with a sharp single to right. Boos and citrus again rained down on Diz in his second at-bat. This time Diz doubled. When Diz came to bat in the seventh he was pitching a brilliant game giving the Cubs only two runs on six hits. Diz again doubled and the boos turned to cheers. The Cards dealt the Cubs a 13 – 2 thrashing and Dizzy was once again a hometown hero.

Dizzy also earned Frankie Frisch's forgiveness. "Dizzy's the greatest pitcher in baseball when he wants to be. All he has to do is pitch and keep his mouth shut." He said.[32]

St. Louis fans may have forgiven Dizzy, but St. Louis was not the only city where Dizzy and Daffy merchandise was sold, and sales of Dizzy and Daffy products plummeted across America. Dizzy had fallen from public favor, drying up a lucrative revenue stream.

An amazing array of Dizzy and Daffy products were being marketed with Diz and Paul receiving 5% of sales. Dizzy's antics were costing the Dean Brothers big bucks. Companies and products from which Diz and Paul received royalties based on sales included:

> M. D. Dreyback Co. – Baseball caps inscribed with the emblem "Dizzy and Daffy Dean"
>
> Sackman Bros. of New York – Dizzy and Daffy Dean baseball uniforms
>
> Rice-Stix Dry Goods Co. – "Me and Paul" sweatshirts, polo shirts, neckties, Pajamas, shirts, play suits and overalls.
>
> Marx & Hass-Korrekt Co. – Dizzy and Daffy trousers and knickers for boys.
>
> A. Cohen & Sons of New York – Dizzy Dean wrist and pocket watches

Caradine Hat Co. – Paper helmets which resembled pitch helmets used in tropical Countries.

Ayling Kite Co. – Dizzy and Daffy kits.

May hosiery Mills – Dizzy and Daffy children's socks

A.G. Spaulding & Bros. – Baseball gloves and other equipment

Western tablet & Stationary Co. – Dizzy and Daffy stationery and school tablets

Super Products Co. – Dizzy and Daffy toothpaste, toothbrushes and shaving cream

Wallace Pencil Co. – Dizzy and Daffy pencils and pens.

Hall Brothers – Dizzy and Daffy greeting cards.

Hithcock Co. – Dizzy and Daffy belts and men's jewelry

Paul's next start was on June 12th in Boston. He was dominate, but sloppy Card fielding and almost no offense led to a 3 – 1 loss. A Ducky Medwick triple followed by a Ripper Collins single accounted for the lone St. Louis run. Paul shut-out Boston in every inning except the seventh when the Braves scored all three of their runs. Two singles, two sacrifices, two walks and one error gave Boston their 3 runs.

After Paul's unfortunate loss Diz beat Boston twice. Once by pitching two innings in relief and once by pitching 13 grueling innings. On June 13th Diz was called to the rescue in the eighth inning after the Braves tied the score at six apiece with none out. Diz held Boston scoreless for the final two frames and St. Louis scored twice to give Diz his 8th win of the year.

Since Dizzy had only pitched two innings, he had no problem starting the next day's second game of the Sunday doubleheader. The game turned out to be a 13-inning struggle with St. Louis finally prevailing 8 – 7. Diz gave up 12 hits, 2 walks and struck out 5 as he pushed his won – loss record to 9 – 5.

The Cardinals left Boston and traveled to New York to play the Giants. Paul started on June 17th and was quickly buried under an avalanche of Giant hits. Paul was pulled after being smashed for 11 hits and 9 runs in only 4 innings. The loss evened his record at 6 – 6, far behind his 1934 pace.

When Philadelphia player/manager Jimmy Wilson declared war on the Deans, Diz said he was not worried, "them Phillies can't hit a lick." Dizzy proved they could not hit him on June 20th in Philadelphia, holding the Phillies to 1 run on 5 hits while striking out 8. St. Louis won 3 – 1 led by Ripper Collins' two-run homer.

However, the Phillies could "hit a lick" against Paul. The next day Paul pitched and made the game a battle until the sixth inning. With the score tied at two Philadelphia pulverized Paul for 6 runs including a grand slam by Philly third baseman Johnny Vergez. Paul allowed 8 runs on 7 hits and 5 walks in only 5 2/3 innings. St. Louis lost 8 – 3.

Paul exacted a small measure of revenge two days later. The Cards were clinging to a one-run lead in the bottom of the ninth. Philadelphia had already scored 4 runs in the inning and the bases were loaded with two outs. Dean menace Al Todd came to the plate and Frankie Frisch signaled Paul in from the bullpen. With the game on the line Paul retired Todd on a pop-up to shortstop securing a 10 – 9 Card win.

Dizzy ran his record to 11 – 5 with an easy win at Ebbets Field in Brooklyn. He held the Dodgers to two runs on 8 hits and 4 walks. He fanned 5 in a 16 – 2 Card victory. Ripper Collins led the hit parade with a homerun and 5 runs batted in.

Paul's starting struggles continued the day after Dizzy's dismantling of the Dodgers. He was attempting to gain his seventh victory to match his seven defeats but failed to survive the first inning. Paul was charged with 5 runs on 4 hits and a walk. Fidgety Phil relieved Paul and picked up the win as St. Louis rallied to beat Brooklyn 12 – 7.

Paul rebounded from his dismal Dodger failure the next day. He was able to start the game since he only faced five batters the day before. Paul out-dueled Dodger hurler Van Lingle Mungo and sailed to victory on Bill Delancey's two-run homer in the eighth inning. The 6 to 4 Card win evened Paul's record at 7 wins and 7 losses. He gave up 7 hits and struck out 6.

Paul's last appearance in June was in Cincinnati against the Reds. Paul pitched six innings, gave up 9 hits and was charged with 4 runs. He left the game with a 5 – 4 lead but Bill Walker and "Fidgety" Phil Collins could not hold it and the Cards lost 8 to 6.

Diz lost to Cincinnati on the last day of June and the Cardinals found themselves in third place 8 games behind the first place New York Giants. Dizzy was pitching well with a 11 – 6 record but Paul was treading water at 7 – 7. At the end of June 1934 Dizzy's record stood at 12 – 3 while Paul had won 10 and lost only 2. Clearly Paul had problems.

Reporters asked Branch Rickey why the ballclub he assembled for 1935 was not living up to expectations. Rickey blamed pitching and the self-satisfied attitude of several players. Specific to the pitching he cited the failure of his rookie pitchers to produce, Paul Dean's failure to return to 1934 form, and the inexplicable poor performance of Bill Walker.

As for attitude Rickey said, "I don't say that all our players have become 'nigger rich', but here and there you'll find an important member of the club who has adopted a 'big shot' attitude."[33]

"Nigger rich' was not meant as a racial slur but as a descriptive term. Branch Rickey was a pious, devout man who only 12 years later would integrate Major League baseball by signing Jackie Robinson. A few days later in St. Paul, Minn. Dizzy Dean epitomized what Rickey had described as a "nigger rich" "big-shot."

After a short series in Chicago the Cards went to Minnesota for an exhibition game against the St. Paul Saints. Dizzy won his 12th game of the year in the Chicago series, however Paul was nursing an upset stomach and did not pitch.

As usual Dizzy did not want to play in an exhibition game that put no extra money in his pocket. He finally consented to make the trip after Frankie Frisch threatened to fine and suspend him. Peeved at having to make the trip, Diz sat in the dugout pouting and sulking. He finally exploded when Saint club officials and town greeters approached him and requested that he step out and take a bow.

"No, no, no" he shouted. "A thousand times no. Get away and leave me alone."[34]

The crowd did not know that Dizzy was refusing to even take a bow and they began chanting. "We want Dean! We want Dean!"[35] Still Dizzy remained along with Paul, in the corner of the dugout, refusing to even acknowledge the fans.

Finally, in the eighth inning the announcer said, "Ladies and gentlemen we're going to ask Dizzy and Paul Dean to step out of the St. Louis dugout and take a bow."[36] Again Diz and Paul snubbed the crowd by refusing to even show their faces.

When the fans realized what was happening, they started booing and jeering throughout the remainder of the game and play had to be halted until the crowd could be quieted. When the game ended Diz and Paul rushed from the field with hundreds of youngsters trailing them hoping for autographs, while the spectators continued to rain verbal abuse down upon them.

Dizzy was unrepentant, he told reporters "I didn't want to come to St. Paul in the first place. For pity's sakes, what kind of club is this Cardinal outfit to make a star like me come up here in the sticks after I pitched and beat the Cubs yesterday? No other Big-League club would make a star pitcher do such a thing. Here I am in St. Paul when I should be in St. Louis resting.[37]

At least Paul realized their behavior was unacceptable, "I'm sorry it happened," he said, "but really, I couldn't show up Dizzy. When those fans called for us to stand up, I was willing, but when Dizzy refused, I had to do what he did. And maybe Frisch is right when he talks and Me and Diz having the 'big head'. That's only natural for a young feller like me to forget myself and let success go to my head. But I'm honest about it and I'm trying to get by the best I can."[38]

Again, Frankie Frisch was disturbed and disgusted by the Dean's behavior. "It was the most disgraceful exhibition I have seen in my seventeen years in the Big Leagues," he said. "I regret that it happened, and I think it is going to hurt the Dean's popularity a great deal."[39]

But again, Frisch did nothing to punish Diz and Paul. "I do not plan to fine the Deans or take any other disciplinary measures" the manager said. "I hope they learn to behave themselves and act like Big Leaguers hereafter."[40]

Florida sports columnist Pete Norton summed up the situation best. "Dizzy Dean is the biggest puzzle in the sports world. Endowed with everything that would make him the outstanding idol of the diamond world, Dizzy seems bent on making himself the most unpopular man in the game. One thing is certain; however, Dean is assured of a job in baseball as long as he can pitch, and there is no evidence to show that the big farmer- boy has lost any of his pitching cunning."[41]

St. Louis had a three-game series with Cincinnati before the All-Star break and the Deans were seeking redemption. Dizzy's opportunity came in the first game of a Sunday doubleheader. Cincinnati loaded the bases on Card starter Jesse Haines in the fourth inning. Dizzy was called in to put out the fire and 15,000 hometown Cardinal fans greeted him with boos.

The Cards turned a 4 – 2 deficit into a 9 – 4 victory led by Dizzy's pitching, hitting, and daring baserunning. After Diz relieved Haines, the Reds were able to get only three hits off him in the remaining 5 2/3 innings. With St. Louis behind 4 – 2 Diz ignited a five-run rally in the bottom of the fifth. He led off the inning with a single, broke up a double play with a hard slide into second and finally scored on back to back sacrifice flies. The Cards went on to score 4 more runs in the inning and Dizzy coasted to his 13th victory.

Paul started the second game and turned in one of his best performances of the season. He gave up 7 hits, had 3 strikeouts and no walks. He dominated the Reds whose only run came on a solo homer. St. Louis won 5 – 1 as Paul earned his eighth victory of the year.

That doubleheader was the last games before the All-Star break. The All-Star game was traditionally the mid-point of the Major League baseball season and St. Louis was finally living up to pre-season expectations. Six wins and only one loss to start July had propelled the Cards past the Cubs into second place only six games behind the league leading New York Giants. Plenty of time left to overtake New York; If Paul regained his 1934 form and if Dizzy could at least be semi-controlled. Two very big if's, indeed.

CHAPTER 23

"Great hitters like me needs no hittin' workouts."

The third annual All-Star game took place on July 8th, 1935 in Cleveland, Ohio. The teams were selected by the previous year's Pennant winning managers, Frankie Frisch and Micky Cochrane. Frisch chose six of his Cards to play in the game. Himself, Pepper Martin, Ripper Collins, Ducky Medwick, Dizzy Dean and Strangely, Burgess Whitehead.

Whitehead was hardly a legitimate All-Star as he was not even a starter for St. Louis. He was a utility infielder who only saw action when one of the regulars needed a day off. However, Frisch admired Whitehead's slick fielding, superior intelligence (Whitehead earned University of North Carolina Phi Beta Kappa honors) and versatility.

Frisch made sure all eight National League teams were represented and said his choices were based in part upon recommendations of other managers and club owners. A seventh Card ended up in the game because

Carl Duncan

Dodger pitcher Van Lingle Mungo withdrew due to injury. Frisch selected Bill Walker to replace him.

Why would the Flash pick Bill Walker instead of Paul Dean, the Cardinal's second best pitcher? Paul would have been the obvious choice but Frisch needed a fresh arm to start the game and Paul had pitched nine grueling innings the day before the All-Star game. Also, Paul probably did not want Frankie to pick him.

The players received no compensation for playing in the All-Star game. All profits went to benevolent funds for destitute former ballplayers. As such many players considered it just another exhibition game with no extra pay. Therefore players felt they were risking injury without getting anything in return. Most would rather have the day off to rest their weary bodies for the remainder of the long, tiring season. Changes were needed to improve players enthusiasm for the game and to also make it more popular with fans.

Three main suggestions emerged to improve the game:

1) Allow fans across the country to vote on the selection of the two teams as originally done in the first two All-Star games.
2) An off-day before the game should be scheduled so more pitchers would be rested and able to perform.
3) Set aside a percentage of the gate receipts to be split among the players on the winning team.

Six Cards saw action in the 1935 All-Star game. Pepper started at third and went 1 – 4. Ducky started in left field and only had a walk to show for his four trips to the plate. Ripper was a reserve and went 0 – 1. Burgess Whitehead only saw duty as a pinch-runner. Walker pitched two innings and Diz pitched one. The Flash managed the Nationals but did not play in the game.

Bill Walker started the game for the National League and the Americans jumped on him for two runs in the first inning when Jimmy Foxx homered with Lou Gehrig aboard. The American League scored another run in the second inning off Walker and his day was done.

Dizzy entered the game in the eighth with the American League leading 4 – 1. Lusty boos were mixed with cheers as the Cardinal ace faced

Me 'N' Paul

ol' double XX Jimmy Foxx. Dizzy tried too hard to clip the corners and walked the big slugger.

After Dizzy fanned Bob Johnson, Al Simmons doubled sending Foxx to third. The next batter grounded to shortstop and Foxx broke for home but was trapped between third and home on the shortstop's throw to the catcher. Simmons meanwhile ran to third and was tagged out as Foxx came back to the same bag! Joe Cronin popped out to shortstop Arky Vaughan and Diz trudged to the dugout, saved by some truly sorry baserunning.

The American League won the game 4 – 1 leaving them undefeated in All-Star play. Bill Walker was the losing pitcher and Lefty "Goofy" Gomez was the winner. Jimmy Foxx was the hitting hero going 2 – 3 with a homerun and 3 runs batted in.

The second half of the season was shaping up favorably for St. Louis. In second place and riding a six-game winning streak, the Cards had an additional advantage. An odd scheduling quirk had St. Louis playing at home most of July and all of September.

Dizzy won his fourteenth game of the year on July 11th against Philadelphia. It was not easy, Dizzy gave up 11 hits and 3 walks but was bailed out by Ducky Medwick's two homeruns, his 10th and 11th of the year and Ernie Orsatti's 1st homer of the season. The Cards won 5 – 4 and Philly player/manager Jimmy Wilson made peace with the Deans, saying, "how can anyone stay mad at them?"[1]

Dizzy and Paul were advertised as the pitchers for a Sunday doubleheader celebrating the Cardinals 1934 World Series victory. The largest home crowd of the season – 23,000 - showed up at Sportsman's Park to enjoy the festivities and witness the hoisting of the World Championship flag. Commissioner Kenesaw Mountain Landis presented the Cardinal players with diamond rings commemorating their World Series Championship.

In the opener of the twin Bill Paul easily disposed of the Phillies 5 – 1. He gave up 7 hits and struck out 6 to notch his ninth victory of the season. Ripper Collins led the Card hitters going 2 – 4 and driving in 2 runs.

Fans were disappointed when Dizzy failed to start the second game as advertised. The temperamental star was lounging in the trainer's room instead of ascending the mound.

"My arm's tired", Diz said, "and I don't want to work when it ain't feelin' just right."[2]

Last-minute substitute Bill Walker had no problem dispatching Philadelphia, winning 10 – 1. The Cardinal victory stretched the Red Bird's victory string to 10 in a row.

At about this time numerous sources began reporting that Dizzy Dean was going to be traded to the Chicago Cubs. I.N.S sports editor, David Walsh disclosed that the trade was a done deal. He wrote that Dizzy had been traded to the Cubs for delivery sometime after the close of the 1935 season. In return the St. Louis Cardinals were to get pitcher Lon Warneke, outfielder Charley Klein and $80,000 in cash.

The tipping point was the St. Paul fiasco. Up until then Cardinal management tolerated Dizzy's antics and insubordination but as Dizzy's popularity plummeted so did his value as a gate attraction. Also, he wielded too much power.

"As matters stand, Dizzy has only to say 'Me 'N' Paul; we're goin' home, and he usually gets what he wants."[3]

St. Louis management also believed Paul would be a much better pitcher without Dizzy's undue influence.

Diz stumbled to his 15th victory in a ragged win over the Boston Braves on July 15th. He gave up 6 runs on 14 hits and was carried to victory by an unlikely power surge from Leo Durocher. Leo the Lip blasted 2 homeruns as the Cards beat the Braves 13 – 6 for their 11th straight win.

After two more Card wins over Boston, Paul took the mound attempting to sweep Boston and extend the Cardinal winning streak to 14 games. The outcome was never in doubt as St. Louis scored early and often, crushing the Braves 13 – 3. The Cardinals collected 18 hits including 2 homeruns. Paul gave up 5 hits, 1 walk and struck out 3 to secure his tenth victory of the season.

The league leading New York Giants came to St. Louis on July 22nd for a crucial series. The recent Card winning streak had cut the Giants lead to 1.5 games. In the first game of the series Wild Bill Hallahan came through slaying the Giants 8 – 5. Wild Bill's win left the Cards only a half-game behind the Giants.

The next day featured a rare Tuesday doubleheader and 31,000 fans filled Sportsman's Park to see if St. Louis could overtake the Giants. The pressure to propel St. Louis into first place fell on Paul's shoulders. Paul peeled off the pressure and pitched the Cards into the National League lead.

New York scored a single unearned run off Paul as St. Louis won the first game of the doubleheader 6 – 1. Paul gave up only 4 hits, walked 1 and struck out 12. Ducky Medwick led the Card attack with two homeruns. Paul narrowly missed the shut-out when back to back errors by Pepper Martin and Terry Moore in the seventh inning allowed the Giants to score their only run.

Dizzy was ecstatic over Paul's performance. "Everybody was askin' a short time ago what is the matter with Paul Dean, my brother. Well, I guess them Giants wish there was something the matter with him all he does is strike out 12 of them. That Dick Bartell was so mad when he fans four times, he throws his bat out toward the fence. An' he might as well throw his bat away for all the good it does him against Paul."[4]

The Cardinal's perch at the top of the National League was short-lived. In the second game of the doubleheader three errors by Pepper Martin and one by losing pitcher Bill Walker led to six Giant runs and the Cards lost 8 – 2. So, after only about two hours in second place, New York was back on top.

Only half game back Dizzy started the fourth game of the Giant series with a chance to put St. Louis back in first place. He hooked up in a pitching duel with New York ace Carl Hubbell and after six innings St. Louis led 1 – 0. Diz had only given up two hits.

In the top of the seventh Dizzy gave up a single and double putting Giants on second and third with no outs. Travis Jackson hit a hard grounder to third, Pepper Martin fielded the ball, held the runners and continuing his error binge threw the ball 15 feet over Ripper Collins' head. Both runners scored and Jackson ended up on third.

Dizzy was clearly rattled by Pepper's error and gave up a walk and two singles resulting in two more Giant runs. Diz settled down, retired the side and held New York scoreless in the two final frames. However, the damage was done, and the Cards lost the game 4 – 2.

The six-game series wrapped up with a doubleheader on Thursday July 25th. Frankie Frisch started Paul in the first game even though he had pitched nine innings on Tuesday. One day's rest was not enough, and it showed. Paul had nothing and New York slammed him for 9 hits and 3 runs in only 5 innings. St. Louis lost 3 – 1 dropping Paul's record to 11 wins and 8 losses.

The Giants continued their offensive onslaught sending Wild Bill Hallahan to the showers after only two and a half innings. New York went on to win the game 13 – 2. The Giants came into hot, dreaded Sportsman's park with a 1.5 game lead on St. Louis. They left four days later 3.5 games in front.

The Cardinal plunge continued as they finished out July losing 5 of the final 6, they played. Their only win was in the first game of a doubleheader in Pittsburgh. Diz was on the mound and pitched a good game but the outcome was in doubt until the Cards pushed across a run in the ninth to win the game, 4 – 3. Dizzy gave up 7 hits, walked two and whiffed 3.

The second game of the doubleheader was another nail-biter. The score was tied in the ninth inning when Paul was called in to replace Card starter Bill Walker. Pirates were on second and third with only one out. The first batter hit a dribbler back to Paul who nailed the runner at home for the second out. Unfortunately, Paul hit the next batter loading the bases. Paul would need to pitch carefully to the next Pirate hitter, future hall of famer, Lloyd Waner. He threw two wide ones to Waner falling behind in the count 2 – 0. When the umpire called Paul's third pitch a ball, Frankie Frisch stormed out of the dugout to question the strike zone, and Dizzy rushed to the mound to calm Paul who was visibly upset.

It did no good. Paul's next pitch was in the dirt and Waner waltzed home winning the game with a walk-off walk. The loss did not go against Paul's record as Bill Walker was responsible for the Pirate that scored the winning run.

The Cardinals concluded their July plummet by losing a memorable game on July 31st at Crosby field in Cincinnati. Frankie Frisch picked Paul to pitch in a revolutionary Major League innovation that was familiar to Paul, night baseball.

In 1935 the Cincinnati Reds were the first Major League baseball team to install lights in order to play games at night. Night baseball had been a success in the Minor Leagues for several years and Cincinnati president Larry Macphail believed the expense of installing the lights would be recouped by increased attendance. The Reds played seven-night games in the 1935 season, one against each of the National League teams.

A carnival atmosphere filled the air as fans overflowed Crosby field. Festivities included a band concert, a fireworks display and a baseball track and field meet. "Babe Herman hit the longest fungo, Bill Delancey won the 60-yard dash for Batterymen, Terry Moore won the open 60-yard race and Spud Davis was the most accurate thrower, hitting a barrel at second base twice out of three tries."[5]

At the start of the fourth inning with St. Louis winning 1 – 0, the boisterous, over- capacity crowd surged all over the field stopping play. "The crowd took possession of the dugouts, slapped players on the back and kidded them to their faces. The Cardinals had to chase small boys trying to make away with their gloves."[6]

The two policemen on duty were unable to control the rowdy fans and the game was delayed until a detail of police answered an emergency call. Some semblance of control was restored although fans remained on the field just beyond the first and third base foul lines. "There was a wall of humanity behind the plate and players had to fight their way through to get to and from Homeplate. Pop flies to right and left field were made ground-rule doubles."[7]

The contest continued to the eighth inning when the game went from strange to downright BAZAAR. Nursing a 2 – 1 lead Paul gave up an infield hit to Cincy centerfielder Sammy Byrd. Reds right fielder Goodie Goodman lifted a high fly to shallow right-center field. Frisch faded back as Terry Moore charged in from centerfield. Moore made the catch but collided with Frisch.

While the ol' Flash was being revived, a blond, buxom woman broke out of the crowd and snatched a bat. Newspapers charitably described the woman as a "nightclub entertainer." Her name was Kitty Burke and she had the fans attention as she pranced to the plate. Miss Kitty waggled her bat and her butt as she dared Paul to pitch to her.

Paul was perplexed but finally decided to play along. He tossed the ball underhanded toward the plate. Kitty swung and hit a slow roller down the first base line. Paul pounced on the ball and alertly stepped on the first base bag. Satisfied with her fifteen minutes of fame Kitty Burke disappeared back into the crowd leaving chaos in her wake.

Since the umpires allowed Kitty to bat, Frisch argued that her out should count. After much debate and delay the umpires decided to forget

Carl Duncan

Kitty's infamous at-bat and called the next Cincinnati batter to the plate as if nothing had happened.

The circus atmosphere and game delay affected Paul's concentration. Babe Herman doubled putting Reds on second and third with only one out. Bearing down Paul fanned Sunny Jim Bottomley for the second out. Lew Riggs came up and after two strikes Paul poured a pitch past him for what looked like the third strike. However, the ump called it a ball and with new life Riggs hit a pop fly that bounced into the encroaching crowd for a ground-rule double, plating two runs.

The Cards tied the game in the ninth and lost it in the tenth. However, Frisch blamed the chaotic eighth for the loss. "Umpire Stewart was afraid to call Riggs out on strikes because of that howling mob on the field."[8]

Paul pitched all ten innings giving up 4 runs on 13 hits and 2 walks. He struck out 3. The loss dropped Paul's won/loss record to 11 – 9, far worse than 1934 when his record was 12 – 4 at the same point in the season.

Strangely enough, 34 years later on that same field another woman trespassed onto the diamond while the game was in progress. IN August 1969, Morganna Roberts ran onto Crosley field not to bat, but to kiss Reds player Pete Rose. That audacious act began the career of the infamous "Kissing Bandit."

Over the next three decades the "Kissing Bandit," so called because she stole kisses, became a celebrity by interrupting sporting events to kiss the athletes. The big busted Morganna primarily targeted baseball players and she referred to her measurements (60-23-39) as Morganna's baseball stats.

Kansas City Star George Brett stole his kiss back. Three weeks after Morganna had kissed Brett during a game, he jumped on stage at a "gentleman's club" during Morganna's performance and kissed her as the crowd cheered.

There were perils associated with Morganna's pursuit of fame. She suffered various injuries leaping from the stands onto the playing field and she was hit several times by baseballs. She was arrested multiple times for trespassing and forced to defend herself in court which usually resulted in fines. Morganna was actually jailed briefly in Anaheim, California.

However, she did prevail in one trial when her attorney employed an unusual and unique defense. At a trial in Houston, Texas her lawyer used what he called the "gravity defense" to explain Morganna's unauthorized presence on the field, arguing; "This woman with a 112-pound body and 15-pound chest leaned over the rail to see a foul ball. Gravity took its toll, she fell out on to the field, and the rest is history."[9] The judge was amused and dismissed the case.

The Cards' July free-fall left them in third place 5.5 games behind league leading New York and 5 games behind second place Chicago. Dizzy's 17th victory ended the St. Louis nose-dive and ignited a winning streak.

The Cardinals got hot on August 1st in Cincinnati, both literally and figuratively. The game was played in 95-degree weather and the heat was so intense on the field Homeplate umpire Dolly Stark suffered heat exhaustion and had TO LEAVE THE GAME. Great relief pitching by Wild Bill Hallahan enabled Dizzy to escape with a 7 – 5 win. Diz gave up 5 runs on 9 hits and 4 walks in 7 innings of work.

Enroute from Cincinnati back home to St. Louis the Cardinals visited Union City, Tenn. for an exhibition game. It was the first time a Major League team played in the south during the regular season. Despite their dislike of games that paid them nothing extra, the Deans were anxious to rehabilitate their reputations after the public relations disaster in St. Paul.

Before the game Diz and Paul entertained the fans, they took infield practice, batting practice and even staged a fight to the delight of the crowd. They mingled with the fans signing autographs and when the game started Diz along with Pepper Martin announced the game over the park's amplifying system. Neither Diz nor Paul pitched.

"Undoubtedly, the Deans and not the ball game made the day a success. Any amount of money the Cardinals pay them could not be too much. They made 8,000 friends Friday."[10]

The Cardinals returned to St. Louis for a short homestand beginning with a series against the Pittsburgh Pirates. Bill Walker beat the Pirates on Saturday and on Sunday 17,000 fans crowded into Sportsman's park for a Sunday doubleheader.

Wild Bill Hallahan started the first game and was knocked out in the fifth inning when the Pirates plundered him for 3 runs. Ed Huesser relived and pitched scoreless ball until being pulled for a pinch-hitter in the bottom of the ninth with the score tied 3 – 3. Paul entered the game and held the hard-hitting Bucs scoreless in the top of the tenth. Leo the Lip gave Paul his 12th win with a walk-off single in the bottom of the inning.

Dizzy started the second game and Pittsburgh roughed him up for 8 hits and 5 runs in only 5 innings. With Pittsburgh ahead 5 – 4 Paul relieved Dizzy and pitched the 6th, 7th and 8th innings. Again, the Pirates were unable to plate a run against Paul.

In the bottom of the 8th Pepper pinch-hit for Paul, but the Cards failed to score. Bill Walker held Pittsburgh scoreless in the top of the 9th and St. Louis was down to their final three outs. The Cards needed a single run to tie and two to win.

Jack Rothrock opened with a single and was sacrificed to second. Ducky doubled him home to tie the game. Spud Davis drove Ducky home with the winning run. The hometown crowd was thrilled by St. Louis sweeping the twin Bill in dramatic fashion on walk-off singles by Duroucher and Davis. Bill Walker was credited with the win, St. Louis fourth in a row.

The doubleheader dramatics would be difficult to top, however, Diz was the man for the job. Cincinnati followed the Pirates to St. Louis and Frankie Frisch sent Bill Walker to the mound to keep the Card winning streak alive.

In the top of the first inning the Reds rocked Walker for 5 hits and 2 runs. Pop Haines assumed mound duties and pitched the second, third, fourth, fifth and sixth innings. He gave up just one run. Diz took over in the seventh with the score tied at 3-all.

Diz held the Reds hitless for four innings and when St. Louis came to bat in the bottom of the tenth the score was still 3 – 3. Dizzy walked to the plate with two on, two out and the game on the line. Diz delivered a drive into the left-field grandstand for a 3-run homerun. The circuit clout gave the Cards their third straight walk-off win and Diz his 18th victory.

In stifling 100-degree heat at Sportsman's Park, St. Louis beat Cincy 4 – 2 behind Wild Bill Hallahan. The Red Birds' sixth straight win, in torrid temperatures Pepper Martin described "as hot enough to burn the goatee off a camel,"[11] lifted St. Louis to within 4.5 games of leading New York and only one game behind second place Chicago.

Before heading to Chicago for a 3-game series the Cards traveled to Madison, Wisconsin for yet another exhibition game. No extra money for the players but owner Sam Breaden collected a guaranteed $1500 and 55% of the gate.

Diz and Paul continued to be on their best behavior they again signed autographs and took infield and batting practice. In the early innings Diz was the third base coach and Paul coached first. They did not pitch but the fans understood that would be unwise in the midst of a Pennant battle. After coaching, Diz sat in the stands hobnobbing with fans while Paul sat in the press box talking to reporters.

Paul explained his and Dizzy's opposition to exhibition games during the regular season. "The Cards seem to make them work in well, and these extra games are their business. They win having them on the schedule, but if I was running the team, I think I'd leave them out while a team was fighting for first place."[12]

When asked about his new wife, Paul said. "She's in Chicago now, and will be with me all this Eastern trip. Diz takes his wife with him every trip, and I kind of think it'd help the club if everybody did. They watch out for us, and some of us need it."[13]

He said Frankie Frisch was a fine fellow and a great manager. "He only has a few training rules. In bed by midnight, no excesses in living and a 25-cent limit in poker games."[14]

While in Madison the Cardinals gained a full game on New York because of a Giant doubleheader loss and a half-game on Chicago who lost a single game. The Cardinals embarked from Madison enroute to Chicago, the first stop on a road trip that would carry them to seven National League cities for 24 games. The Cards would return to St. Louis for the final 30 games of the season.

In Chicago Paul handcuffed the Cubs running his record to 13 – 9. He gave up only 1 run on 6 hits, walked no one and fanned 2 in the 3 – 1 Card win. Ducky Medwick led the hitters going 2 – 4 with a homerun.

Dizzy pitched the next day and Chicago handed him his 19th win with some shoddy defensive play. Cub throwing errors on consecutive plays in the third inning gave the Cards two unearned runs, their margin of victory in the 4 – 2 game. Diz scattered 10 hits, walked 1 and struck out 4.

Chicago salvaged the final game of the series. The Cubs roughed up Bill Walker and Pop Haines for a 3 – 2 win, ending the Cardinals 8-game winning streak. Before moving on to New York for a crucial 5-game series against the league-leading Giants, St. Louis played exhibition games in Battle Creek, Michigan and Rochester, New York. Another money-grab by Sam Breaden instead of a two-day rest for his weary players.

The Cards finally arrived in New York City for five games that actually counted only 3 games behind the Giants, St. Louis had a chance to climb into first place. Frankie Frisch was confident the Cards could take the series. "We'll leave the Polo Grounds in first place," predicted the Flash. "My fellows are hot and if we ever get up there nobody will drag us out."[15]

Of course, Diz was always overloaded with confidence "show me them New Your sissies! Begged Dizzy, "and I'll hogtie 'em."[16]

With St. Louis coming to the Big Apple, New York sportswriters fueled the gashouse gang image. "Those rootin' tootin' rowdies from old St. Loo – those horny-handed, hairy-eared hoodlums who'll fight, frolic or footrace for money, marbles or chalk – roared in from the west last night with blood-curdling threats that they would tear down the Polo Grounds, brick by brick, and bounce the bricks off the hapless heads of Bill Terry and his Giants."[17]

50,000 fans filled the Polo Grounds on August 13th for the first two games, a doubleheader featuring Dizzy and Daffy Dean. However, Dizzy was sick and unable to pitch. "I'm runnin' a fever of over 110 Dizzy moaned."[18]

Paul, who was celebrating his 22nd birthday, started the first game of the twin Bill. New York presented Paul with a rude surprise party, blasting him for 5 runs in only 2 innings. The icing on the cake was Giant left fielder Joe Moore's 3 run homer in the second inning. New York went on to win the game 6 – 4, gifting Paul with his 10th loss of the season.

Wild Bill Hallahan started the second game and pitched shut-out ball for 8 innings. Hallahan was also the hitting hero with a homerun, the first of his Major League career. In the ninth Wild Bill lived up to his nickname. With a 3 – 0 lead and one out he walked three straight Giants, loading the bases and putting the win in jeopardy. Frisch summoned Paul to save the game. Facing shortstop Dick Bartell, Paul's first pitch was called a ball. On the second pitch Bartell bounced into a double play, ending the game and saving the Card win.

Diz was still sick but he was already vowing revenge. "That was no way for Paul to celebrate his birthday. I'm gonna draw a bead on them Giants.

I told Frankie I would be strong enough to beat 'em if I can get this dern fever under 110."[19]

The day after the doubleheader split New York beat Bill Walker and the Cards 5 – 4, moving four games ahead in the standings. Dizzy crawled out of his sick bed to face the Giants in the fourth game of the five-game series.

Showing no ill effects of his fever Diz cut the Giants down to size inning after inning not allowing a single run. New York pitcher Hal Schumacher was just as score stingy and after eight innings the game was scoreless. Both hurlers had allowed only 3 hits.

Pepper Martin opened the ninth with a single and Jack Rothrock struck out, after bunting two fouls trying to sacrifice Pepper to second. Undeterred by Rothrock's failed attempt to put him in scoring position, Pepper swiped second. Pepper moved to third on Frisch's infield hit and scored on Medwick's sacrifice fly. It was up to the recent bed ridden Diz to hold the precarious 1 run lead.

The first two Giant hitters were future hall-of-famers Bill Terry and Mel Ott. Dizzy fanned Terry and got Ott on a pop-foul to Ripper Collins. The next Giant grounded out and Diz walked off the diamond with his 20th win, a 3-hit shutout.

Ed Heusser started on the mound for St. Louis in the final game of the series. After the Giants torched him for 2 runs in the first inning, Big Ed blanked Terry's Titans until he allowed a single run in the seventh. Although St. Louis led 6 – 3, Frisch was taking no chances, he brought Diz in to pitch the final two frames.

Diz gave up 2 hits but no runs as St. Louis won 7 – 3, loosening the Giant's grip on the National League lead. Losing three of the five games in the series left New York only 2 games ahead of St. Louis and 2.5 games ahead of the Chicago Cubs.

Next up on the last road trip of the season was a four-game series in Boston against the Braves. The Boston Braves were bleeding money, when Babe Ruth retired attendance tanked and bankruptcy loomed for Brave's owner Emil Fuchs. With the World Champion St. Louis coming to Boston, Fuchs spotted an opportunity for a cash transfusion. He devised a plan to milk more money from the Cardinals visit and greedy Sam Breaden agreed to the scheme.

The regular schedule called for single games on Sunday, Monday, Tuesday and Wednesday. However, Fuchs' plan involved some strange schedule shifting. Monday's game was moved back to Sunday in order to increase attendance by offering fans a doubleheader. That move allowed Fuchs to squeeze in an exhibition game in the middle of the four-game series. Both teams were made to travel 200 miles north for a meaningless game in Lewiston, Maine on Monday and then back to Boston for single games on Tuesday and Wednesday.

Of course, Diz was irate at yet another hated exhibition game and even Frankie Frisch, who was responsible for enforcing ownership decisions, protested the stupid schedule shift.

"This is making a joke out of a club that is fighting for the pennant." The Flash grumbled. "We're playing an unscheduled exhibition game when a day of rest would do a lot of the boys considerable good."[20]

Paul started the first game of the Sunday twin bill and battled Boston for seven tough innings. In spite of giving up 11 hits, he avoided walks and allowed only 2 runs. Paul was pulled for a pinch hitter in the eighth, but the Cards failed to score, and Boston won the game 2 – 1. The loss dropped Paul's record to 13 wins and 11 losses. After the game Paul complained about a persistent pain in his hip.

St. Louis won the second game on a dramatic unlikely homerun. In the tenth inning with the score tied and the bases loaded, Lippy Leo Durocher came to the plate. To everyone's surprise little Leo lifted a fly into the leftfield stands for a grand slam propelling the Cards to a 9 – 5 win.

With the conclusion of a long day of baseball, both teams boarded a train to Maine. Before departing Dizzy talked to reporters. He predicted a great run for me 'n' Paul in the Pennant race and took a parting shot at St. Louis Cardinal management.

"Me 'n' Paul have caught up with our loss totals of last year and I have a hunch that we are going to put on a great run and not lose another game." Then Diz grinned, saluted and said, "join the Cardinals and see the world. Next stop Lewiston, Maine."[21]

Paul did not make the trip to Maine. He had a date with doctors in Boston for examination and x-rays on his ailing hip. Dizzy wanted to stay

Me 'N' Paul

with his brother, but Paul convinced him to stay with the team and avoid dissension in the midst of the Pennant race.

6,000 fans jammed into Athletic Park in Lewiston, Maine to see the World Champion St. Louis Cardinals play the Boston Braves. Dizzy, still rehabilitating the Dizzy and Daffy brand, was on his best behavior. The game opened with Dizzy walking to the mound as the announcer introduced him to the fans. Amid cheers Dizzy demonstrated his famous wind-up by throwing several pitches across the plate. That completed his diamond duty and he disappeared into the crowd to mingle and sign autographs.

The teams played a full nine inning game with the Cards winning 8 – 3. The game featured three homeruns, two by Ducky Medwick and one by Ripper Collins. Each round-tripper earned a lucky fan a case of beer. After the game the Cards and Braves rode a train back to Boston for two games that actually counted in the standings.

Back in Boston Paul received good news from doctors. At first, he did not understand the diagnosis and finally disagreed with the findings. When told the x-rays were negative, Paul asked,

"What do you mean by negative?"[22]

The doctors explained the x-rays revealed no broken bones or injury of any kind. Paul was not convinced.

"I have stinging pain on my left side" Paul insisted. "It hurts me to walk. I'll have to take it easy working out and I won't be able to pitch in a game until next week."[23]

With Paul ailing and Dizzy scheduled to pitch the final game of the Boston series, Frisch tabbed Card Lefty Bill Walker to start the semi-final game. Diz was bored so while the Cards were talking their pre-game batting practice he ambled over and sat in the Boston dugout. Diz critiqued his teammates hitting and traded good-natured barbs with the Boston players. Finally, Brave's catcher Al Spohrer asked Dizzy,

"How come you ain't hittin' any yourself today? Even though you're not going to play, you might help your batting eye."

Diz just grinned and said, "great hitters like me needs no hittin' workouts."[24]

Dizzy went back to the St. Louis side of the field as the game started. Bill Walker carried a 6 – 3 lead going into the eighth, propelled by homers from Ducky Medwick and Jack Rothrock. The Braves ran Walker to the showers with 2 runs and Pop Haines relieved holding on for a 6 – 5 Card win.

The series wrapped up with the Cards overwhelming Boston 13 – 3. Diz won his 21st of the year allowing Boston 9 hits, 1 walk and fanning 4. He also proved he "didn't need no hittin' workout," as he went 2 – 5 at the plate and for good measure, stole a base.

St. Louis next traveled to the Big Apple for a five-game series against the Brooklyn Dodgers. The first game was rained out, but the Cards picked up a half game on New York as the Giants lost, leaving St. Louis only 2.5 games behind the league leaders.

Pennant fever infected St. Louis with fans and sportswriters rushing to board the bandwagon. Frankie Frisch firmly believed the Cards would repeat as National League Champions.

"If we return to St. Louis no more than two games out of first place, we'll positively win the Pennant." Declared the Ol' Flash. "We finish our schedule on our home grounds and I don't see how we'll be stopped. We are in a far better spot than a year ago, when we overcame a 7.5 game deficit in the final four weeks of play. Last year we were forced to make our comeback on the road, this year we finish at home."[25]

A rainout was made up with a doubleheader and St. Louis executed a twin-killing beating Brooklyn 6 – 1 and 11 – 5. Paul started the third game of the series although his hip was still bothering him.

In the third inning a 4 run Brooklyn barrage sent Paul limping from the mound favoring his left hip. In only 2 1/3 innings Paul allowed 5 runs on 7 hits and one walk. Trailing 5 – 0 Paul appeared headed for his 12th loss of the year.

St. Louis chipped away at Brooklyn's lead and going into the ninth faced only a one run deficit, with the bases loaded and two outs Ducky Medwick came through with an infield single that tied the game 7 – 7. Ripper Collins then ripped the game wide open with a double that cleared the bases and left the Cards ahead 10 – 7. Wild Bill Hallahan held the lead for the sixth consecutive Cardinal conquest.

Between games the Cards learned Chicago had beat the Giants across town at the Polo Grounds Frankie Frisch had planned to rest Paul but with a chance to wrestle first place away from the Giants he sent Paul right back at Brooklyn. It was a gutsy move considering the Dodgers had routed Paul the previous day.

Battling a bad hip and with little rest, Paul pitched the Cards into the league lead. He gave up 8 hits and fanned five beating Brooklyn 6 – 1 for his 14th win of the season. The determined Deans had defeated the Dodgers in the double-dipper pushing the Cards a half-game ahead of the New York Giants.

The Cardinals had three more cities and seven more games before returning to the friendly confines of Sportsman's Park for the final thirty games of the regular season. Perched in first place with a favorable schedule looming, Branch Rickey was cautiously optimistic, but concerned about Paul's sore hip.

"In my mind the situation is strictly up to Paul Dean." Branch said, "if he recovers and finishes as strongly as he did last year, we ought to be all right."[26]

Paul was upset about doctor's inability to diagnose his lingering hip pain. Fans were frustrated knowing Paul had to perform in the September Pennant drive. That frustration built when Sportswriters began speculating that Paul's problems might be mental.

"Paul Dean is actually talking about quitting baseball and getting back to Arkansas solitude. He has an idea that his health isn't right, and a hip injury still twinges him when he pitches, despite the statements of a whole corps of physicians that nothing is wrong with him. It may be another case of a great ball player self-driven into retirement because of imagined ailments."[27]

The Cardinals went into Philadelphia and beat the Phillies two out of three games. Diz did not make an appearance and Paul pitched one uneventful inning in relief. The Cards moved on to Pittsburgh for a short two game series. Frankie Frisch planned to scuttle the Pirates with a double dose of Deans, but Paul was still babying his bum hip, so Wild Bill Hallahan took his place.

The Pirates plundered St. Louis both games. Diz gave up 10 hits and a walk as Pittsburgh beat the Cards 5 – 1. Wild Bill and Fidgety Phil Collins fared worse as the Bucs battered them for 14 hits and 9 runs. The 9 to 3 loss left the Cards only one game ahead of New York and a game and a half in front of the hard charging Chicago Cubs.

The Cardinals limped into Cincinnati for two games before heading home for the final 30 games of the regular season. Envisioning losing endorsement dollars Dizzy implored Paul to pitch through his hip pain.

"It'll cost us $50,000 if we don't win this Pennant."[28] Dizzy warned.

Whether it was phantom pain or real pain Paul pitched through it to deal the Reds misery. 20,000 fans watched Paul beat Cincinnati with his arm and his bat. He drove in two runs and held the Reds to two runs as St. Louis won 5 – 2. The Reds managed only 7 hits and 2 walks as Paul coasted to his 15th win of the season.

Although the Cards lost to Cincinnati 4 – 3 in the final road game of the season, they remained in first place. New York was in second place one game back and Chicago trailed by a game and a half.

Pittsburgh was the first visiting team in the Cards long homestand. St. Louis beat them twice in a prolonged doubleheader. The first game went 16 innings and Paul won it in a relief role hurling three-hit shutout ball for the final seven frames while fanning five.

Dizzy started the second game and was rescued when darkness ended the game in the sixth inning just as Pirate bats began assaulting his pitches. Diz allowed 8 hits and 2 walks in the Cards 4 – 1 win.

The bottom bound Boston Braves were next to arrive at Sportsman's Park. St. Louis swept the four-game series and the Deans appeared in three of the four games, winning two and saving one.

Wild Bill Walker picked up a win in the opener as the Cards won 6 – 3. Diz went to the mound in the ninth and scalped three Braves in quick order. "Fidgety" Phil Collins benefited from a St. Louis offensive explosion as the Cards blasted the Braves 15 – 3 in the second contest.

Diz and Paul won the final two games of the series. In game three Diz relieved a faltering Wild Bill Hallahan in the seventh with Boston ahead 4 – 2. Diz put out the fire and doubled home a run in the bottom of the inning. The Cards won it with three more runs in the eighth for a final score of 6 – 4. Dizzy hurled three inning s of shut-out ball allowing only two harmless hits in three innings.

Paul pitched the final game going the distance for the winning Cards. He gave up 12 hits, walked none and struck out three in the 8 – 5 wins. The victory enabled St. Louis to stay 2.5 games ahead of the rampaging Cubs and 4 games ahead of the once mighty Giants.

Me 'N' Paul

The Dean's old pal Jimmy Wilson brought his Phillies to town for a five-game series. The Cards had won six straight games and Diz extended the streak to seven by whitewashing Philly 11 – 0 in the first game of a doubleheader. He allowed only four scratch singles and struck out nine. Dizzy also showed off his offensive skills with two run scoring singles, a stolen base and a run scored.

The Phillies jumped on Ed Heusser for four runs in the second inning of the second game bunching two errors, a walk, a single and a double to produce the runs. Four Card pitchers – Pop Haines, Wild Bill Hallahan, Bill Walker and Paul Dean – paraded to the mound after Heusser hit the showers. Walker yielded the only Philly hit the rest of the game. Paul pitched a perfect eighth and ninth, but the Cards fell 4 – 2.

Philadelphia won the third game 4 – 3 and St. Louis won the fourth conflict 4 – 2.

Frankie Frisch called on Paul to win the rubber match in order to keep Chicago in second place. The Cubs had not lost since September 4th and had closed to within one game of the Cards.

Paul was the man for the job as he limited Wilson's boys to seven blows handing Philadelphia a through thrashing to stay a game ahead of the fast-closing Cubbies. The final score; St. Louis-10, Philadelphia-2. The victory was Paul's 18th of the season bringing the total for the fraternal firm of Dean and Dean to 43, Dizzy having won 25.

The New York Giants arrived in St. Louis trailing the cards by 3.5 games and clinging to slim Pennant possibilities. Frankie Frisch planned to unleash the Deans on New York to eliminate them from the flag race.

In the initial game Diz beat King Carl Hubbell 5 – 2 for his 26th victory of the year. With that win the Deans went ahead of their 1934 pace. Diz and Paul's 1935 total of 44 victories was 4 games ahead of their mark at the same juncture of the 1934 season. Dizzy allowed 7 hits no walks and struck out 8.

The next day New York pounded Ed Heusser, Wild Bill Hallahan and Bill Walker unmercifully and led 10 – 6 going into the final frame, however, St. Louis rallied for four runs to tie the game. Anxious to eliminate New York from serious Pennant contention Frisch called on Diz to finish off the Giants, although he had pitched nine innings the previous day.

Carl Duncan

The task was too great even for the rubber-armed Dizzy. The fatal blow was not struck by Giant sluggers Bill Terry or Mel Ott but by pitcher Frank Gabler. With runners on first and second Gabler was allowed to bat in order to advance the runners with a sacrifice bunt. However, after two failed bunt attempts, he was forced to hit and delivered a double that dealt Dizzy his 9th loss of the year. Dizzy's defeat was not the day's last bad news, the relentless Cubbies won their 10th game in a row and only .004 of a percentage point from first place.

Frisch planned on pitching Paul in the next day's game to keep the Cards in first place, but his plans were dashed when Paul was felled by two fainting spells.

Paul had befriended Cardinal bat boy Kayo Brown a part-time pugilist, punch-drunk from too many jabs to the jaw. Kayo was a good kid except when he imagined he was someone else, which happened occasionally. One day when Kayo arrived at the Cardinal clubhouse he announced, "I'm Branch Rickey"[29] and preceded to fire several St. Louis players he thought had offended him.

Paul keeled over the first time while visiting Kayo in his dressing room after a preliminary bout. Kayo had been beaten badly and was bleeding profusely.

"Brown was wriggling in pain," said Dr. Richard Bullard, the physician attending Kayo. "And I think Dean's attack was mostly psychic. He said he had fainted once before when he broke an ankle."[30]

Later the same evening Paul passed out again while sitting ringside watching the main bout of the boxing match. Paul was taken to his hotel room where Cardinal team doctor, Dr. Robert Hyland, gave Paul heart stimulants. Dr. Hyland advised Frankie Frisch not to let Paul play for a few days.

"What a helluva shape that puts us in."[31] Frisch lamented.

The Old Flash was correct in his assessment, the Cards were indeed in a "helluva shape" as they lost the final two games of the Giant series and fell from first place. With Paul unavailable Diz pitched in three of the four games, winning one and losing two.

Casey Stengel brought his Dodgers to St. Louis for a five-game series, determined to keep the Cards out of first place. Paul had recovered and

Me 'N' Paul

Frisch, eager to regain the league lead, fired a Dean at the Dodgers in all five games.

In the opener Paul hooked up with Van Mingle Mungo in a classic mound duel and hits were scarce, each team tallying only four. The four Card hits produced one run, the four Dodger hits none. The 1 – 0 shut-out ran Paul's record to 19 – 11 as he fanned six and walked only one.

In a doubleheader the next day Frisch used the Dean brothers in crucial relief roles. Paul succeeded, Diz failed. In the ninth inning of the first game 'Pop' Haines was hammered from the hill and Paul was rushed to the rescue. He faced a tough situation; runners on first and second, no outs, and a two-run lead to protect. Paul faced only two Dodgers, the first fanned, the second grounded into a double play and St. Louis won 4 – 2.

In the second game St. Louis carried a one run lead going into the seventh inning. Frankie Frisch dispatched Diz to hold the slim margin, but Brooklyn battered him for three runs. The game was called on account of darkness after the Cards had scored once in the bottom of the seventh. The 8 to 7 loss was charged to Diz and dropped his record to 26 – 11.

Wild Bill Hallahan started the fourth game of the series but wilted after seven innings and Paul was beckoned for the bullpen to hold a two-run lead. He pitched two perfect innings and fanned four.

Diz regained his form in the finale beating Brooklyn 9 – 1. He scattered 6 hits, walked 2 and struck out 9. The Cards had won 4 out of 5 from Brooklyn but actually lost ground to Chicago as the Cubs refused to lose. St. Louis also lost centerfielder Terry Moore. The fleet footed flycatcher fractured his knee sliding into second.

Cincinnati came in and played the Cards three games in two days. Paul started game one but was ineffective. He was lit-up for 11 hits and 6 runs, but avoided the loss when St. Louis tied the game. Ed Heusser came in, gave up the winning runs and absorbed the loss.

The next day St. Louis swept Cincy in a doubleheader 14 – 4 and 3 – 1. Diz was masterful in the nightcap allowing only 3 hits and fanning 10.

St. Louis' fate worsened when they split a two-game series with Pittsburgh and Chicago won their 18th straight game. Neither Dean pitched, Frisch was saving his aces for the final series of the season; five games against the Chicago Cubs that would decide the 1935 National League Champion.

Carl Duncan

The Cardinals' situation was desperate but not hopeless. St. Louis would have to sweep all five games to win the Pennant outright or four out of five to gain a tie and force a play-off.

Chicago newspapers announced the Cards had two chances, slim and none. Sports columnist Frank Kearns agreed St. Louis had only two chances, however, they were not slim and none. Kearns wrote "the Cards have two chances. One is Dizzy Dean and the other is Daffy Dean."[32]

Kearns had a point, Diz and Paul had been Cubbie poison all season. Paul was especially venomous beating Chicago five times and losing only once. Dizzy was also a menace to Chicago, winning three games and losing one.

Two small town Arkansas boys drew mound duties in the opening game. Diz and Paul's pal, fellow "baseball professor" Lon Warneke from Owley, Arkansas against Daffy Dean from Lucas, Arkansas. Both were brilliant.

Paul fanned four of the first five batters he faced. The sixth hitter was 19-year-old rookie Phil Cavarretta and Paul made his only mistake of the game, he hung a high curve and Cavarretta jerked it over the right-field fence. That was the only Cub run of the contest, unfortunately for St. Louis it was the only run of the entire game. Lon shut-out the Cards on only two hits while Paul allowed seven hits, fanned seven and walked none in the 1 – 0 loss.

Chicago manager Charlie Grimm was impressed by both pitching performances. "Paul Dean pitched a magnificent game, but nobody could have beaten Lonnie today."[33]

Chicago needed one more win to clinch the National League Pennant. Rain postponed the second game of the series allowing the Cards an extra day to regroup after the backbreaking 1 – 0 loss. The game would be made-up as part of a doubleheader. Although Paul would have only one day's rest, he told Frankie Frisch he would be available for the crucial twin-bill. Sportswriter Paul Mickelson summed up the situation:

"The final hopes of the faded and worn World Champions will be the Dean brothers in today's doubleheader. Dizzy will fire all he's got in a desperate attempt to snap the Cub 19-game winning streak in the opener. If he succeeds, brother Paul, at his own request will pitch the second. Should the great Dizzy fail, it will be all over."[34]

Me 'N' Paul

The house of Cards fell, blown down by the rampaging Cubs from the Windy City. Dizzy was unable to stop the disaster, as Chicago drove the final nail in the Cardinal coffin with a 6 – 2 win that sewed up National League flag.

The Pennant race was over, so Frisch did not start Paul in the second game which Chicago won extending the Cubbie winning streak to an amazing 21 in a row. The streak ended at 21 as St. Louis won the final two games of the series.

Cub center fielder Freddie Lindstrom confirmed what many observers suspected after Dizzy was shellacked for 15 hits and 6 runs in the pivotal game. "Dizzy's fastball didn't have a thing on it. He was one tired ball pitcher."[35]

The great one himself agreed, "I ain't no alibi ball player but I didn't have my fastball or my curve, it was a bad day not to have 'em with the hair so short on the old dog's back."[36]

No one could fault the Dean boys for the Card's failure to defend the World Series crown. Dizzy appeared in 50 games winning 28 and losing 12, with an ERA of 3.04. Paul pitched in 46 games and finished with an ERA of 3.37. He won 19 games and also lost 12. Both were workhorses, Diz pitched 325 innings and Paul hurled 270 innings. Over the span of the 1934 and 1935 seasons the Dean brothers recorded 96 wins, over half of the games St. Louis won in that two-year period.

Despite pitching in 96 of the Cards 154 games, Diz and Paul were not finished pitching for the year. After advising the Cubs on how to pitch to their World Series opponents, the Detroit Tigers, Diz collected Paul and they embarked on a transcontinental barnstorming campaign.

Ray Doan, Diz and Paul's usual business partner, organized, financed and promoted the barnstorming tour. Doan again arranged games with black baseball's two top teams: the Kansas City Monarchs and the Pittsburgh Crawfords. K.C. was led by the incomparable Satchel Paige, blackball's best pitcher and perhaps the best pitcher in all of baseball. The Craws fielded a rugged line-up featuring four future hall of famers, Josh Gibson, Judy Johnson, Ray Danbridge and "Cool Papa" Bell.

Diz and Paul were accompanied on the tour by Mike Ryba, a St. Louis Cardinal rookie pitcher. Ryba was an unusually versatile player who could play any position, including catcher. The Deans and Ryba would team with local pro and semi-pro players from each city on the tour to play the black stars.

Satch and the Monarchs toured with the Dizzy trio playing exhibitions throughout Oklahoma, Kansas and Missouri. Satch and his K.C. pros won most of the games. Ray Doan marveled at Satchel's ability, "if Paige were white, he would be worth $200,000."[37]

The first part of the tour wrapped up in Kansas City. Home of the Monarchs. Cold, wet weather had plagued the barnstorming and despite the star power of Dizzy, Daffy and Satch, attendance had been disappointing.

The Pittsburgh Crawfords replaced Satch and the Monarchs as the barnstorming caravan turned Northeast for games in Ohio, Maryland, Pennsylvania and New York. Paul had to abandon the tour and hurry to St. Louis where his wife had been admitted to St. Anne hospital with an undiagnosed illness.

Dizzy continued the tour after replacing Paul with another Cardinal pitcher, rookie Jim Wilford. Attendance improved with good crowds at Shribe Park in Philadelphia and Yankee stadium in New York. However, when the tour turned south attendance dissipated. Crowds in Chattanooga, Tennessee and New Orleans, Louisiana were so sparse Dizzy refused to take the field. "I can make more money playing poker on the train."[38] he remarked.

Paul's wife recovered and he planned to rejoin the tour in Texas where games were scheduled against an American League barnstorming team led by Detroit Tigers Charlie Gehringer, Tommy Bridges and Schoolboy Rowe. The Tigers had won the 1935 World Series beating the Chicago Cubs four games to two. Ray Doan expected large crowds anxious to see Dizzy and Daffy in a rematch against Bridges and the Schoolboy.

Paul was in Texas; however, he did not join Diz to face "them pussycats" as Diz called the Tiger players. Paul was in the process of buying a farm outside of Dallas, near Garland. Dizzy preferred living in a resort town in Florida where he could fish and golf while Paul wanted to own farmland instead of "sharecropping." Dizzy was frivolous and fun-loving; Paul was hard-working and practical.

Ray Doan was furious at Paul for deserting the tour and threatened legal action. Doan reconsidered, realizing he would alienate Dizzy and also jeopardize future business deals with the Deans.

After the Texas tour Diz and his wife Pat traveled to California where Dizzy played in some exhibition games with Cardinal teammates Jack Rothrock and Ernie Orsatti. He and Pat then retired to their home in Florida to spend the winter. Paul and his wife moved to their newly purchased 80-acre Texas farm. "This will be a good investment and a place to grow some groceries,"[39] Paul said.

CHAPTER 24

"Fatten my contract or else I'll fatten hogs"

Paul enjoyed his return to farm life but realized the animals and crops required year- round care. Care he was unable to provide due to his hectic baseball schedule. Paul solved this dilemma by moving "Pa" Dean from Houston.

"My father will live on the farm and 'tend the place'"[1] Paul said.

With "Pa" living on the farm, Paul needed an off-season home for himself and wife, Dorothy. They purchased a house in a Dallas residential neighborhood a few miles from their farm. His real estate transactions complete, Paul was ready to begin negotiating his 1936 Cardinal contract, always a continuous affair.

Dizzy fired the first salvo in the annual Deans/St. Louis contract wars. He had the audacity to demand a multi-year contract. At the time one-year contracts were the norm, with few exceptions. Management preferred to base salaries on the prior year's performance, consequently players knew a sub-par year usually resulted in a salary reduction.

Dizzy journeyed to St. Louis in order to present his contractual demands to Branch Rickey in person.

"Personally, I think about $80,000 for three years will be swell. "Diz told an amazed Rickey. "Ain't I the greatest pitcher in the world? Ain't it true that with Babe Ruth gone, I'm the biggest drawing Card in baseball?"[2]

Rickey was not about to give Diz such an enormous multi-year contract and set about disparaging Dizzy. He told reporters "there will have to be a complete reversal of attitude on the part of Mr. Dean. He was not a good influence on the Cardinals last summer. He tried to run the team instead of letting Frankie Frisch do it. We don't want the team morale broken. No player is worth that. Dean has to clean up his nose or we will clean-up his uniform for somebody else."[3]

Dizzy was unfazed by Rickey's harsh words. St. Louis appeared to have the upper hand in contract negotiations since Diz would have to play for the Cards or not at all, however Dizzy had an ace in the hole. Paul had agreed to a joint hold-out and Dizzy doubted St. Louis would risk relinquishing the wins and publicity the Dizzy and Daffy duo provided.

Also, Paul seemed to have co-opted Dizzy's confidence. He told reporters his services for the upcoming season would cost the Cardinals considerably more cash.

"My contract is gonna have to be a lot bigger than it was last year," said Daffy. "They tell me I'm too young to be making so much money. Well, I'm old enough to win a danged lot of ball games for 'em."

"Last hear they told me that a young player never came to the Big Leagues and made more in two years than I did. You know what I told 'em? I told 'em they never had any Paul Deans up there before. If the Cardinals lose Me 'n' Diz they'll just have to shut the ballpark gates."[4]

Not content with mere contract drama, Dizzy created more controversy when his favorite catcher was forced to retire. Bill Delancey, Paul's best friend from their Columbus Red Bird days, contracted tuberculosis and had to abandon baseball to battle the disease.

"The Cardinals better get another catcher because I ain't pitchin' to Spud." Dizzy declared. "He cost me ball games last year and he ain't good enough to catch Me 'n' Paul."[5]

Understandably upset by Dizzy's apparent attempt to oust him from the team, Card catcher Spud Davis vowed revenge. "I'll knock Dizzy Dean's block off the minute he sets foot in the clubhouse." Diz responded, "I can throw punches as good as I throw baseballs."[6]

A mercenary element was injected into the dispute when wealthy Florida sportsman Cecil Lippard offered Diz and Spud $5,000 each to settle their differences in the ring. Why fight in private when fans would pay to see the fisticuffs, Lippard reasoned. To make the offer more enticing, Mr. Lippard offered to take only 60% of the gate receipts and let the combatants split the remaining 40%.

Always open to profitable propositions Mrs. Dizzy Dean, a shrewd businesswoman, opened negotiations and began building interest in the match.

"We're baseball players not prizefighters" said Mrs. Dean. "But my Dizzy can sure sling the mitts and although I don't know much about this fellow Davis, Diz says he's a bush leaguer and that's enough for me. So, if Dizzy can't whip him with one hand – well, we'll retire to the Minor Leagues."[7]

After hyping the potential boxing bout Mrs. Dizzy let it be known her husband wanted to play baseball not fight but if the offer could be raised to $50,000, it might be a difference maker.

Branch Rickey was appalled by the Deans behavior and sent Dizzy a scathing letter. "Your attitude toward Virgil Davis and indirectly toward Frank Frisch will not be tolerated. Such criticisms are calculated to destroy everything that makes a winning team. Your disturbing statements are disruptive and indicate no respect for our business and our ball club."

"The St. Louis baseball organization does not want you at any price unless you repent and mend your reckless ways. You should retract your statements about Mr. Davis and write the club a letter pledging your support for Mr. Frisch and be a good soldier, well- disciplined, pitching your head off regardless of whom the catcher might be."[8]

If Rickey's letter had any effect on Diz it wasn't apparent. He tooled around Florida in a yellow 12-cylinder Auburn sports sedan, visiting friends, holding court with the press and playing golf with Babe Ruth, and other cronies.

Meanwhile, Paul was in Texas buying livestock and preparing the land for spring planting on his farm. He was determined to hold out until St. Louis offered him a suitable contract.

"I'm worth a lot more than I was last season and I'm worth a lot more than they offered me. If the Cardinals don't fatten my contract, I'll stay on my farm and fatten hogs."[9]

Paul's wife, Dorothy, lamented her impending fate, from celebrity wife to farmer's wife.

"It begins to look like I'll be a milkmaid," Dorothy Dean said. "if Paul doesn't come to terms pretty soon, I guess we'll just spend a few months on our farm. Guess I'd better learn something about milking cows."[10]

Dizzy was growing anxious to "play some ball" and turned to the press to plead his case. "Last year I was paid $18,500. Rickey wants to give me the same salary. He said 'In 1934 you won 30 games and we gave you a nice raise. Last year you won 28, so we're going to give you a break. We're not going to cut your salary; we're going to pay you the same money we paid you for winning 30 games.' "Can you tie that?" Diz finished with a warning to Branch Rickey, "without Me 'n' Paul the Cards will finish in the second division."[11]

Diz and Paul were the last remaining holdouts in all of Major League baseball. They had already missed most of spring training and both sides were looking for a compromise. Dizzy dropped his demand for a multi-year contract and Paul showed some weakness when he told reporters, "I'm itching to get going but this salary business has me stopped in my tracks."[12]

Sensing an opportunity to end the stalemate, Branch Rickey offered both Deans a raise – Paul going to $12,500 and Diz from $18,500 to $22,500. Paul was ecstatic and anxious to sign. He boarded a plane in Dallas bound for Tampa, Florida. Once, in Tampa he planned to take a taxi to Bradenton to sign his contract and begin what was left of spring training. A problem developed when the cab driver wanted $12 for the fare from Tampa to Bradenton. Paul thought the fare excessive and decided to hitch-hike.

The associated press reported, "Paul Dean may know what to do with his arm when he plows that high hard one through, but his thumb was working poorly yesterday when he tried hitch-hiking."[13]

Me 'N' Paul

When all cars refused to pick him up Paul relented and paid the $12 cab fare to Bradenton. $22,500 would make Dizzy the highest paid player in the National League, but the offer was conditional. Dizzy would be required to write a letter to Branch Rickey apologizing for his comments about Spud Davis, vowing to follow Frankie Frisch's orders and pledging to avoid disruptive behavior detrimental to the St. Louis ballclub.

With the help of St. Louis sportswriter J. Roy Stockton Dizzy completed the required contrite letter. However, Stockton doubted Dizzy's sincerity saying, "a parrot might learn to recite the Lord's Prayer, but that wouldn't make it a good Christian."[14]

With Diz and Paul on board St. Louis was primed to contend for the National League crown. The pitching staff was strengthened with the addition of Roy "Tarzan" Parmelee, acquired from the New York Giants for Burgess Whitehead.

"Tarzan" had electric stuff but no idea where his pitches were headed. Casey Stengal signed Tarzan to his first professional contract while Casey was managing the Toledo Mud Hens.

Parmelee was a raw, unfinished product. Stengal had to teach him a pickoff move. The first time he tried it in a game, he hit the runner in the chest. The first baseman picked up the ball and tagged the man lying stunned on the ground. "You have it down perfect" Casey told him.[15]

Parmelee had a muscular build, 6-feet-1, 200 lbs. with broad shoulders and thick forearms. When sportswriter Jimmy Powers nicknamed him "Tarzan", Parmelee thought it was a tribute to his powerful build, but Powers told him it was because of his wildness: "Every time you pitch you seem to be out on a limb."[16]

Despite Tarzan's shortcomings Dizzy was delighted to have another live arm of the Cardinal pitching staff. He was soon predicting many wins for "Me 'n' Paul 'n' Parmelee." Rounding out the staff were returning veterans Bill Walker, Wild Bill Hallahan, and Pop Haines along with second year men Ed Heusser and Mike Ryba.

The Cardinal infield changed drastically with Leo Durocher the only constant. He remained at shortstop while Pepper Martin moved to right field replacing Jack Rothrock who retired. Charley Gelbert took over third base and rookie Stu Martin manned second base. Frankie Frisch kept his bat in the line-up by replacing either Gelbert at third or Stu Martin at second.

Johnny Mize, a big rookie from Georgia, platooned with Ripper Collins at first base. Mize batted left-handed and threw right-handed where Ripper batted right and threw left. Johnny Mize eventually replaced Ripper Collins and went on to have a hall of fame career with St. Louis.

The sad retirement of Bill Delancey left the Cards with only one catcher, Spud Davis. Delancey's spot was filled by rookie Ambrose "Bruisie" Ogrodowski. Ducky Medwick continued to star in left field and Terry Moore's terrific rookie season in center field convinced Ernie Orsatti to retire and pursue his Hollywood ambitions.

The Chicago Cubs came to St. Louis to open the 1936 regular season. Diz on the mound for St. Louis opposed by his old Arkansas buddy Lon Warneke. The Cubbies battered Dizzy for 9 runs in only 6 innings sending him to the showers. Chicago won 12 – 7.

Tarzan Parmelee outdueled Big Bill Lee winning the second game of the 3-game series 3 – 2. Paul started the rubber match and led 2 – 0 until the fifth inning when Chicago rallied for four runs. The Cubs held on for a 5 – 3 win nipping Paul for 10 hits and 4 walks. He fanned 2.

Dizzy's second start of the season was against Cincinnati and he hung on for a ragged 8 – 7 win. The Reds beat Tarzan in the second game of the series 7 – 6. Paul started the third game in search of his first victory of the season but exited in the eighth with the score knotted 5 – 5. Mike Ryba relieved and lost the game in 10 innings 8 – 6. In the no decision Paul gave up 5 runs on 9 hits, walked 2 and had no strikeouts.

Dizzy won his second game on April 26th barely besting Pittsburgh 3 – 2. Two games later Paul won his first game of the season. The New York Giants racked him for 11 hits but stranded 9 runners and Paul prevailed 3 – 2. Paul walked none and struck out 3.

The Cards caught fire in May burning up the National League with 21 wins and only 9 loses. Diz set a torrid pace winning 7 and losing only once during the month, running his record to 9 – 2. The winning spree left the Cards in first place and Diz feeling invincible.

"Them teams all look alike to ol' Diz when he's right." Dizzy said. "Guess I'll win 40 this year."[17]

Me 'N' Paul

Paul began pitching better and contributed three wins in May. On May 5th Paul started against the Boston Bees. Babe Ruth's popularity had failed to save the Boston Braves from bankruptcy and Braves owner Emil Fuchs relinquished ownership of the franchise to the National League. Before the 1936 season the National League sold the franchise. The new owners changed the name to Boston Bees and renamed the team's ballpark The Beehive.

The bees stung Paul even though he pitched his best game of the year. He allowed 5 hits, walked 3, fanned 3 and only gave up 1 run. However, St. Louis failed to score, handing Boston a 1 – 0 win.

Paul's next start resulted in another premier performance. He faced the Chicago Cubs and again allowed only one runs. This time the Cards came through with 5 runs. Paul tamed the Cubs by fanning 4, walking none and holding them to 3 hits. The 5 – 1 victory evened Paul's record at 2 wins and 2 losses.

Paul stumbled in his next start. The Boston Bees swarmed him for 8 hits and 7 runs in only five innings. However, St. Louis rallied for a 7 – 5 win saving Paul from his third loss of the young season.

After only one day's rest Frankie Frisch needed Paul in a high leverage relief role. Against the Philadelphia Phillies. Wild Bill Hallahan started the game and St. Louis quickly staked him to a three-run lead. Wild Bill failed to hold the lead giving up four runs in the third inning. Mike Ryba relieved but struggled and after six innings Philly led 6 – 4. When the Cards scored four times in the top of the seventh for an 8 – 6 lead, Frisch sent Paul in to save the game. Paul pitched three scoreless innings; the Cards scored two more runs sending St. Louis to a 11 – 6 victory.

Paul beat two Pennant contenders in his next two starts. Against the Giants in the Bronx he scattered eight hits and struck out five. He issued no walks winning the game 4 – 2. Back in St. Louis Paul beat the Chicago Cubs 2 – 1 despite allowing 10 hits and 2 walks. Beating Chicago put the Cards in first place by a half-game.

With St. Louis in first place and the Deans again carrying the Cards, Paul revealed the secret of their success.

"Smart pitching is bunk" Paul said "all you need is a strong back and a weak mind to win in this or any other league. Ol' Diz and me just fog 'em through. We don't ever pitch to spots. We just try to fog 'em through the middle with all we got."

"Frisch says to me; 'pitch this guy low and outside' but I don't pay any attention. I just try to fog 'em through and maybe the pitch is low and outside like Frisch wanted and maybe it's high and inside. I don't know. I ain't got any control. I just let 'er go and I don't care where it goes just so the hitter don't hit it."

Pop Haines was appalled. "But you got to have control." He said.

"No sir, you do not," Paul insisted. "Look at me. I don't know where the ball's going half the time. I'll let you in on something – 'Ol Diz and me, we just aim everything right down the middle and let 'er go. That high hard one and a fast curve is all that matters."

Ed Heusser tried another tactic. "You gotta admit that when begin to lose some of your stuff, you'll have to learn to pitch to spots and get some control."

"No sir," Paul replied. "I'll never learn it. I won't even try to learn to be smart. When I lose my stuff, I'll be through and no amount of smartness would save my bacon."[18]

Paul's high hard one and his fast curve failed him in his next start. On May 30th in St. Louis the Cincinnati Reds routed Paul. He was driven from the mound after only 5 1/3 innings as the Reds pounded him for 8 hits and 5 runs on their way to a 10 – 1 win.

Paul began June with a 5 – 4 win over Brooklyn he handcuffed the Dodgers for eight innings allowing only 6 hits and a single unearned run, but fell apart with one out in the ninth, he was pulled after allowing 3 runs. Paul explained his inability to record the final two outs.

"It was a hot afternoon" he said. "I was sweating as I worked. Suddenly a storm came up and blew wind against my back drying me out quickly. As a result, my muscles stiffened up and I lost my stuff. But I'll be all right in a day or so."[19]

Sadly, Paul was not "all right in a day or so." Once again with only one day's rest, Frisch sent Paul to save a game. St. Louis led Brooklyn 3 – 2 in the eighth when Paul entered the game. He quickly surrendered two runs and lost the game.

Paul was obviously ailing and was examined by St. Louis team trainer Dr. Harrison Weaver. Dr. Weaver diagnosed Paul's problem as a pulled muscle and recommended complete rest.

"It's the same kind of bad shoulder I had in the spring and fall of 1934." Paul explained "one time I was out of action for three weeks with this sort of injury."[20]

Paul thought he injured his arm when he beat Chicago in late May and aggravated the injury in later games.

"I felt a sharp pain in my arm throwing a curve against Chicago." He said. "It felt like a bee stung me on my arm. I kept on pitchin', but every once in a while, I'd get that same pain. It came on me in the Brooklyn game. I'd like to get that arm right again. Except for the soreness I'm in fine shape. When I warm up, I've got more stuff that I ever had in my life and when I get back, I think I'll really be hot."[21]

After ten days of rest Paul was ready to test his ailing arm. Frankie Frisch knew St. Louis had little chance of fending off Chicago and New York without Paul and he was anxious to get his other Dean back to work.

On June 14th Frisch started Paul against Philadelphia. He struggled in the first inning allowing a run on two walks and a single. The Cards took the lead with a 4-run outburst in their first at-bat. Paul pitched a scoreless second inning and St. Louis added 3 more runs giving Paul a 7 – 1 lead.

In the top of the third Paul yielded a walk, a double and a single which convinced Frisch Paul was not right. He sent coach Mike Gonzales to the mound to see if Paul could continue. Gonzo knew Paul as well as anyone having caught and coached Paul since their time together on the Columbus Redbirds. Paul insisted he ought to be able to hold a 6-run lead, however Gonzo was unconvinced. Dizzy rushed out of the dugout and told Paul that if his arm was bothering him – and Paul said that it was – he should not keep pitching and risk ruining the arm that was his fortune.

Paul reluctantly left the mound and the game turned into a slugfest. St. Louis finally prevailed 12 – 10 when Dizzy recorded the final three outs after Ed Heusser and Bill Walker were lit-up for 7 runs.

Paul still thought he could contribute and asked Frisch for another chance. The Flash agreed to start Paul in the first game of a doubleheader against Boston on June 17th. Before the games Pepper Martin and Paul were horsing around and started wrestling in the clubhouse. Pepper bruised his right hip and Paul twisted his aching pitching arm.

The consequences were immediate. Pepper attempted to play third but had to come out of the game. As for Paul he was raked for 8 hits and 7 runs in only 1 2/3 innings. The Bees beat the Cards 9 – 6 and Paul was charged with the loss.

Frisch was irate and announced he would take drastic steps to curb the clubhouse horseplay among his players.

"I hate to do it, but I guess I'll have to levy fines on the players who put on these wrestling matches, football games and muscle demonstrating exhibitions"[22] Frisch said.

Adding to the Card misery, Tarzan Parmelee suffered a dislocated finger on his pitching hand. In his broken English coach Mike Gonzales appraised the Card's deteriorating situation.

"He looks plenty bad," Gonzo said of the Pennant race. "pitching staff she shot to pieces. Sure, as your life. Fronck, she do his best, but she cannot pitch them game. Paul Dean and Pommellee get back so she can pitch we win maybe 10, 11 straight.

Catch first place again. But if she no can pitch, look out. See what I tole you. Maybe we have trouble stay ahead those Pirates, those Giants and maybe those Reds. He look plenty bad that Pennant race."[23]

Just how far the Cards were to travel in the National League Pennant race rested on Paul's fragile right arm. Paul and Tarzan's injuries had left the Cardinal pitching staff in shambles and Frisch was working Diz to death, using him in and out of turn starting and relieving.

Tarzan's finger would heal but Paul's prognosis was uncertain. Frankie Frisch and Branch Rickey had to know if Paul would be able to pitch for the remainder of the season. So, after 16 days of rest Frisch started Paul in the second game of a July 4th doubleheader against the Cincinnati Reds.

The rest seemed to help Paul as he pitched one-hit ball for the first three innings and as he took the mound to start the fourth St. Louis led 6 – 0. Although he survived the inning the Reds rocked Paul for three runs. The Cards added two runs in the fifth giving Paul an 8 – 3 lead. When Paul allowed a hit and a walk to the first two men, he faced in the fifth, Frisch pulled him. Cincinnati made a heroic comeback and beat the

Cards 10 – 9. Dizzy ended up absorbing the loss as he relieved in the eighth and failed to hold the lead.

The old Flash was still not ready to give up on Paul. Although he did not pitch, Paul continued to travel with the team. He ran to stay in shape and tested his arm daily hoping to throw without pain.

Finally, three weeks after the fourth of July debacle coach Gonzales reported Paul's shoulder was 'loosening up." St. Louis had a one game lead in the Pennant race when Paul last pitched and although Tarzan had returned and won two games the Cards were two games behind on July 26th when St. Louis had to play one of those dreaded exhibition games.

Frisch decided the exhibition game would be a good opportunity to test Paul's arm without risking losing ground in the tight Pennant race. After three games in Boston the Cardinals traveled to nearby Randolph, Mass to play a semi-pro shoe company team.

On July 27th the shoe company semi-pros hammered Paul for 6 hits and 4 runs in the first four innings.

"I'm no good around here," Paul said almost in tears. "I tried my best, but there's something wrong with my shoulder. I can't get anything on the ball. The shoulder hurts worse than ever now."

"I believe I may give up the game for a while, go home and forget it, and I think maybe the arm will get all right during the winter."[24]

Paul had a private meeting with Frisch to discuss his problem. "I doubt if I'll be able to pitch anymore this year, though you never can tell." Paul admitted. "My arm hurt me when I pitched against them semi-pros and I knew it was useless to carry on. I know my loss to the team means that the Cardinals will practically forfeit their chances for the Pennant.

Frisch finally realized rest would not cure Paul and decided to put the pitcher under the care of St. Louis surgeon, Dr Robert Hyland. Frisch told Paul.

"I have no doubt that your arm hurts you, but nobody seems to be able to locate the problem. All I can base my opinions on is what the club trainer tells me, and Dr. Weaver tells me you are okay and ready to pitch. Still, you say your arm is sore and I'm not the kind of a manager to doubt your word. After all, it's your arm that must be protected – for that's your career."

"I want you to return to St. Louis and see Dr. Hyland. Do everything possible to heal that arm so that you might be able to pitch later on this year. Work out every morning and again in the afternoon with the Browns. Do a lot of running and keep in shape."[25]

After examining Paul's shoulder, Dr. Hyland was optimistic. He diagnosed Paul's problem as inflammation of the sac which retains the fluid of the shoulder joint. Dr. Hyland was hopeful that Paul's shoulder would respond to treatment and he could return to mound duty within two weeks.

Paul's prognosis appeared positive, but Branch Rickey knew he needed another pitcher for the final six weeks of the Pennant drive. To that end trader Branch was able to acquire Si Johnson, a former Cincinnati Hurler.

True to his prediction, after two weeks of treatment, Dr. Hyland pronounced Paul ready to pitch. The Flash was justifiably skeptical after Paul's recent failures, therefore he used Paul in a relief role in a game that seemed hopelessly lost, St. Louis trailed Cincinnati 9 – 4 after seven innings. Paul entered the game in the eighth and retired the Reds in order.

Although Paul pitched a perfect eighth it was obvious his shoulder was still bothering him. He weakly side-armed the ball toward the plate at batting practice speed. In the ninth the Reds jumped on Paul's cripples for four hits and three runs. Cincy won 12 – 5 toppling the Cards into a tie with Chicago for first place.

The Reds left town after beating St. Louis two out of three games and the Chicago Cubs arrived at Sportsman's Park for three games to decide first place. Dizzy was deployed to dispatch the Cubs in a game that deteriorated into a donnybrook.

Before the game Chicago manager Charlie Grimm approached the Cardinal's dugout and asked why Dizzy wasn't warming up since he was scheduled to pitch. Grimm suspected Diz was unavailable for the crucial game.

Paul responded. "Oh, Dizzy's back in the clubhouse, playin' badminton or whatever you call it. Besides Charley, he don't need no warmin' up to beat you mugs."

"Better get him out here to take his lickin'," Grimm said.

Pepper piped up, "you know Charley, we jes' loaned you that Pennant last year, figurin'

Me 'N' Paul

as how's you fellas needed the money more'n we did.

Ripper reminded Grimm of the Cub failure in the 1935 World Series. "And what did you do to them Tigers? I'll tell you what. You got your butts kicked."[26]

Grimm beat a hasty retreat to his side of the diamond, since the Cards were getting the best of the good-natured ribbing.

The game started and Dizzy retired the first two Cubbies. Billy Herman was the next batter and Diz whipped a high hard one up under his chin. Ex-Card and Dean enemy Tex Carleton started screaming at Dizzy calling him among other things a yellow son-of-a-bitch. Pepper, playing third, said to Leo the Lip.

"That Carleton better keep his trap shut or Dizzy'll shut it for him."[27]

The words were barely out of Pepper's mouth when Dizzy dropped his glove and charged the Cub dugout. Tex ran toward Diz and they tore into each other. Dizzy managed to wrap his left arm around Tex's neck and began whaling away with his right fist. Caught in a perilous situation, all Tex could do was make wild, ineffective swings.

Chicago players quickly rushed to Tex's rescue and led by Paul the Cards poured into the Fray. Finally, order was restored, and umpires ejected Diz and Tex from the game. Losing Tex for the day didn't hurt Chicago since he wasn't scheduled to pitch anyway.

Unexpectedly, Cub manager Charlie Grimm petitioned umpires to allow Diz to stay in the game. Grimm reminded the umps that the huge hometown crowd (35,000) came to see Dizzy and paying customers shouldn't be disappointed. Assured Grimm didn't object and perhaps fearing a riot, umpires permitted Dizzy to continue pitching.

Play resumed, Diz recorded the third out and returned to the dugout still steaming. He stormed over to Frankie Frisch and shouted "I ain't gonna finish this game! Ain't no guy ever gonna call me the names that shoe-shine scamp called me and get away with it.

I'm going right over there and beat the hell otta him!"

Paul, Pepper and Frisch tried to calm Diz down. Paul reasoned with his brother. "Dizzy, you do the pitchin' for the family this afternoon. Let me do the fightin'. Ain't gonna hurt us none if I get throwed off the bench."

Dizzy finally simmered down. "Well, I popped him, all right. Got a coupla good licks."

Pepper smiled with relief. "Diz, you musta pulled your punches or you would have flattened him quicker'n Schmeling stopped Joe Louis."[28]

Diz went back to work, the Cards won 7 – 3 and St. Louis remained in first place. Dizzy improved his record to 19 wins and 8 losses.

Tex later admitted he purposely provoked Dizzy to get him out of the game. Tex said he thought Grimm must have lost his mind when he suggested leniency for the Card's ace.

Still unwilling to trust Paul in a regular game during the tight Pennant chase, Frisch waited for another exhibition game to test Paul's wounded wing. On August 17th Paul started against the Yankees' farm team in Akron, Ohio. Paul felt loose warming up and his fastball had some pop.

He set the Minor Leaguers down in order in the first inning, allowed a double in the second and a single in the third. In the fourth Paul was tagged for two runs on a free pass two singles and a double, finishing his day's work.

"The arm felt fine while I was warming up before the game." Paul said, "but while I was pitchin' the pain came back. I did not have the stuff I used to have. However, I intend to remain with the team, and it may be that in some time I'll be in there pitchin' regularly again."[29]

On August 24th St. Louis clung to a slim half-game lead in the National League Pennant chase. The Giants and Cubs were nipping at their heels and Frisch was out of pitching. In desperation the Flash turned to Paul Dean.

Paul's opponent was the Pittsburgh Pirates and he started strong blanking the Buccaneers in the first two innings. However, after the promising start the Bucs deep-sixed Paul scoring two runs in the third and three in the fourth. Paul was pulled with the score tied 5 – 5 having allowed 6 hits and 5 runs. Pittsburgh continued to club the Cards and won the game 17 – 5. Paul was not charged with the loss.

Paul's spirit was broken after the Pirate plundering. "I think the best thing for me to do is go home," he said with a sob. "I ain't doin' the boys any good, and they seem to know I can't win for them. Every time I try to throw a fast ball a streaking pain shoots through my shoulder."[30]

Frankie Frisch was perplexed. "I got the biggest surprise of my life when Paul got pounded the way he did," said the Card skipper. "I was in a tough way for pitchers and I figured that if he felt as good as he said he did he might come through and we'd be in a lot better shape. I really didn't have anybody else that was ready."[31]

Paul was finished for the season and so were the Cardinals. Paul applied for voluntary retirement and St. Louis agreed to pay him the remainder of his 1936 contract. He went home to Texas, hoping a full winter's rest would heal his arm. Paul finished the 1936 season with 5 wins and 5 losses.

The 17 – 6 humiliation at the hands of Pittsburgh began a six-game slide and St. Louis never regained first place, Dizzy had another excellent year. He won 24 games, lost 13 and led the National League in inning pitches.

Bill Terry's Giants won the National League crown and Chicago tied St. Louis for second place. The New York Yankees won the American League Pennant and played the New York Giants in the first subway series. The Yanks prevailed in six games led by Lou Gehrig and sensational rookie Joe DiMaggio.

The off-season was productive for the Cardinals and for Paul Dean. The Cards acquired another ace when Branch Rickey traded Ripper Collins and Tarzan Parmelee for Chicago star pitcher Lon Warneke. St. Louis Cardinal owner Sam Breaden was also dealing. He made arrangements to move the Cardinals' spring training facility from Bradenton to Daytona Beach, Florida.

Paul spent the winter working on his farm, playing golf and resting his arm. There was also a new arrival in the Paul and Dorothy Dean household. On January 19th, 1937 Dorothy gave birth to a nine-pound baby boy. He was named Paul Jerome Dean and Paul said, "he'll be a better pitcher than me and Diz put together."[32]

With another mouth to feed Paul was eager to sign his 1937 Cardinal contract. He applied for reinstatement to the active player list and informed Rickey his arm was completely healed. Paul said, "my arm never felt better, and I'm not worried about it a bit."[33]

Branch Rickey was anxious to sign Paul in order to avoid another prolonged holdout by the Deans. Dizzy was already demanding $50,000 and Rickey did not want another mutual mutiny, so he quickly boarded a train bound for Dallas. After a brief meeting at a Dallas hotel, Rickey and Paul emerged with a signed contract.

Proud Papa Paul was all smiles and unconcerned about Diz. "I don't know what Dizzy is going to do," Paul said, "but as far as I'm concerned, I'm going to report to Daytona Beach whenever they tell me to report."[34]

Rickey was pleased to have breached Dizzy's bargaining position. "If Paul is as good as he thinks he is, we won't need Dizzy at all,"[35] Rickey said.

Dizzy wanted to see his new nephew and when he arrived in Dallas reporters descended on the Deans. A photographer snapped a picture showing Dizzy, Paul and baby Paul Jerome. When the photo appeared in newspapers across America the caption read "Uncle Dizzy and daddy Daffy."[36]

Diz turned the photo op into a rant against the St. Louis Cardinals in general and Branch Rickey in particular.

"Outrageous," sputtered Dizzy, "that Rickey had the nerve to send me a contract for the same amount as last year. My wife and me laughed and sent it right back, unsigned!"

"I'll play out of baseball just as sure as I'm alive if they stop at a cent less than $50,000. I'd play cheaper than that for any other club – just to get away from Rickey and that cheap bunch.

"If I don't sign them Cardinals won't finish in the first division. Gashouse Gang my ass – a bunch of violets."[37]

Dizzy returned to his home in Bradenton to continue his holdout. Paul worked out with the Texas League Dallas Steers for a few days and then headed to the New St. Louis spring training camp in Daytona Beach.

Paul's lifelong battle with weight had began when he signed his first professional baseball contract. He soon learned cuisine superior to squirrel, rabbit, cornbread and black-eyed peas were available. Steak, seafood and rich deserts certainly trumped sharecropper's fare.

When Paul reported to spring training at Daytona Beach in 1937, he weighed a whopping 240 lbs. and there was no denying he was a gastronomical success. Paul was heavier than he had ever been and in poor shape to pitch.

"I'll need to take off about 25 lbs. to be right." Paul admitted. "All I can do is train hard and hope for the best."[38]

Paul had ample incentive to "train hard" because Branch Rickey had constructed his contract contingent on positive performance. The first week of camp produced encouraging results from Paul. He threw over a hundred pitches in intersquad games impressing both manager Frankie Frisch and captain Leo Durocher.

"From the way that he's firing that ball in there, there isn't a thing wrong with his arm."[39] Frisch said.

"His pitching movement is natural and not like it was last season when he was afraid he'd hurt his arm."[40] The Lip commented.

Paul, like the Flash and Little Leo, was encouraged by his early outings. "There was no sign of that sore spot deep in the corner of my shoulder that spoiled my pitching last summer." He said. "I believe I'll be all right if I take my time about getting in condition."[41]

The Cards played their first spring exhibition game of the 1937 season against the New York Giants in Havana, Cuba. Cuban fans were disappointed when they discovered Dizzy was absent but were placated when Paul Dean started against Carl Hubbell.

Paul and King Carl each pitched three innings. Paul allowed one unearned run on three hits while Hubbell shutout out St. Louis on one hit. The Giants went on to win 5 – 4. Paul showed fair speed on his fastball, but he was still overweight and not at his best.

When the Cardinals returned to Daytona Beach, they received some welcome news. Dizzy had ended his holdout. St. Louis gave Diz a slight raise and he capitulated.

"I'm satisfied with the salary we agreed on." Diz said. "I'm glad to get this thing ironed out so I can get out there on that baseball field where I belong."[42]

Dizzy then proceeded to predict a Pennant for St. Louis. "With two Deans, a Warneke and the rest of that good ol' Gashouse Gang, St. Louis is gonna ride herd on them Cubs, Giants, Pirates, and the rest."[43]

While Paul took his time getting in shape by running and pitching carefully, Dizzy hit the practice field "flinging aspirin tablets." Card trainer Doc Weaver marveled, "the boy's arm is like rubber. It's amazing how he can throw so hard so quickly. He can whip 'em across and never hurt his arm."[44]

Frankie Frisch continued to be cautious with Paul. During the remaining weeks of spring training Paul appeared in five games, pitched 18 innings allowing five runs on 20 hits. Paul's arm held up until the last game before returning to St. Louis. After pitching five innings against the Birmingham Barons he experienced some pain.

"I don't know what to do with the arm." He said. "Sometimes when I throw now there's a little catch or pain in the arm and at other times not."[45]

Dizzy had a good spring training with only one controversial incident. Of course, he did miss half of spring training due to his holdout and the incident was a hotel lobby brawl.

The incident took place in Tampa Florida where the Cardinals were staying after a spring game against the Cincinnati Reds. When Dizzy and his wife Patricia arrived at the hotel, Pat spotted Jack Miley of the New York Daily news and Irv Kupcinet of the Chicago Daily Times. Miley had written an unflattering article about Diz and his wife suggesting Pat wore the pants in the family and referring to Dizzy as "Mr. Patricia."

"There's that Miley" Pat exclaimed. "Go get him, Diz."[46]

Dizzy approached Miley and said, "I don't like no $125 a week man writing about me."[47]

Miley responded, "good with me, I don't like writing about bush leaguers like you and your teammates."[48]

By that time the rest of the Cardinal team had arrived surrounding Miley and his buddy Kupcinet. The Card players disliked Miley as he often referred to them in print not as the Gashouse Gang, but hoodlums. Dizzy shoved Miley and the brawl began.

Kupcinet grabbed at Dizzy and Ducky decked him with a jarring jab to the jaw. Paul punched Miley opening a gash over the writer's eye, and Diz quickly retreated from the fray. Finally, Card coach Mike Gonzales leaped in and rescued the battered sportswriters.

Still bleeding, Jack Miley shouted at Frankie Frisch. "What's the matter, Francis, can't you control those ballplayers of yours?"[49]

"No, I can't"[50] Frisch said.

Before the Cards completely dispersed, Lippy Leo who had arrived late and missed the actual fisticuffs landed a verbal punch, yelling "we're the Gashouse Gang, not Hoodlums."[51]

Strangely Kupcinet was not mad at Ducky Medwick who had punched him, but at Dizzy who started the argument but beat a hasty retreat when the brawl broke out.

"You yellow-bellied hen-pecked son-of-a-bitch, you wouldn't fight a baby," Kupcinet screamed at Dizzy. "I'll fight you anyplace, anytime, just name it."[52]

Dizzy wisely declined Irv Kupcinet's fight invitation as Irv was a former college football player who outweighed Diz by 25 lbs.

Frankie Frisch envisioned three aces in the Card rotation, Diz, Paul and Lon Warneke, so he was unwilling to give up on Paul. With that in mind Frisch started Paul in the final game before the regular season began. He had to know if he could depend on Paul.

The game was played in St. Louis against the St. Louis Browns, the Cards American League counterparts. Paul failed miserable as the Brownies bombed him for seven runs on nine hits in only 1 2/3 innings. Strangely, Paul did not blame the disastrous outing on arm pain.

"My arm felt pretty good, although they hit me," Paul said. "I want to give it a further test before doing anything about going on the retired list again."[53]

Of course, Paul's statement could have been disingenuous since his $12,500 salary would be greatly reduced if he was unable to perform.

Paul's arm misery was a mystery since examinations, x-rays and all kinds of tests failed to reveal any physical problem with the arm. Two main theories emerged to explain the phantom pain: mental and laziness.

National League president Ford Frick said. "Paul Dean is through because he has lost his confidence. He has a bad case of mental trouble."[54]

Cardinal surgeon Dr. Robert Hyland stated, "Paul has to pitch himself out of the trouble.

He needs nothing more than exercise and weight loss."[55]

Dizzy agreed with both theories. "Us Deans ain't ordinary, we don't get sore arms. Ain't nothin' wrong with Paul's arm, it's all in his head."[56]

Diz also addressed the sloth issue. "Paul's the laziest white man I know." Diz said. "Well, except for Ernie Lombardi, Cincinnati catcher, they'd make a good battery."[57]

Even Branch Rickey was perplexed. "Here's a boy who has me whipped." The Cardinal executive remarked. "I've cured the aches and ills, domestic and financial difficulties of many ball players during my time, but I'm afraid this one is too deep for the old maestro."[58]

Carl Duncan

The Paul Dean dilemma was certainly challenging for Branch Rickey. He had several options available, none particularly attractive. He could let Paul retire and rest his arm but that was tried the prior year and evidently failed. Rickey could attempt to trade Paul however the market for sore-armed pitchers was thin at best.

Rickey would prefer to send Paul to a St. Louis farm club in order to pitch his ailing arm into shape at the Minor League level, but again there was a problem. Paul would have to pass through waivers before he could be assigned to a Minor League team. A player placed on waivers could be claimed by any Major League team for $7,500. Branch Rickey was not ready to risk losing Paul, an asset once valued at $500,000, for only $7,500.

Rickey and Frankie Frisch still believed Paul's problems were mental and desperate for pitching, they decided to leave Paul on the Major League roster to begin the regular season. Although Paul truly believed his arm was injured, he agreed to keep trying to pitch. Paul knew if he retired again his salary would be drastically reduced.

Paul saw his first action of the regular season on April 24th in St. Louis against the Chicago Cubs. Frisch sent Paul to the mound at the start of the sixth inning with the Cards leading 8 – 5. Paul promptly loaded the bases allowing a single and two walks to the first three Cub batters. With the bases loaded and no outs Frisch did not trust Paul to hold the slim three-run lead. A dejected Paul left the game without recording a single out.

Four days later the Cardinals left on an extended road trip that would take them to Chicago, Boston, New York, Brooklyn, Philadelphia and Pittsburgh. Although he remained on the active roster, Paul stayed behind in St. Louis.

Paul said "I will take daily treatments from a doctor other than the club's physician and trainer. I'll spare no expense to get the soreness out of my pitching arm."[59]

Finally, Paul's persistence paid off. An examination performed at the radiology department of Washington University revealed a problem in Paul's shoulder joint. A new type of x-ray machine, known as a lamina graph, was used. The new machine was capable of taking cross-section pictures of the human body at any selected depth. The device was the first of its kind to be built in the United States.

The x-ray revealed the source of Paul's troubles, a fragment of bone chipped from the shoulder blade at the arm socket. Physicians recommended an operation to remove the loose bone chip. After consultation with Sam Breadon, Branch Rickey and Cardinal team surgeon Dr. Robert Hyland the surgery was approved.

Dr. Hyland performed the operation on May 5th at St. John's hospital in St. Louis. The operation was deemed a success. However, Dr. Hyland declined to give an opinion as to when Paul might be able to throw a baseball. The time required for Paul to recover and rehabilitate his arm was unknown. Paul left the hospital on May 13th with his arm bandaged to his side and his future uncertain.

While Paul was battling arm problems, Dizzy was busy battling opponents, umpires and league officials. On May 19th 30,000 fans filled Sportsman's Park to see the great Dizzy Dean pitch against the New York Giants "meal ticket," King Carl Hubbell. Hubbell had won 21 games in a row, the last game King Carl lost was on July 13, 1936. Diz aimed to stop that streak.

The game was what fans expected, a pitching battle. Through five innings Diz allowed only one hit and no runs. Hubbell hung a curve to Ducky Medwick in the second inning and Ducky deposited it in the leftfield bleachers for a 1 – 0 Card lead.

In the top of the sixth ex-Cardinal Burgess Whitehead singled and Hubbell sacrificed him to second. Diz went into his stretch and whipped the ball toward Homeplate. New York batter Dick Bartell flied harmlessly to Leo Durocher for the apparent second out, however umpire George Barr said Dizzy balked. He waved Whitehead to third and told Bartell he was still batting. Dizzy went ballistic, throwing his glove to the ground and screaming at Barr.

Barr informed Diz that he failed to come to a discernible stop during his stretch and therefore balked. Diz couldn't believe the call. "That's my natural way of pitchin'" Dizzy hollered, now red-faced and waving his arms. "Ain't no ump gonna tell me how to pitch."[60]

Diz finally calmed down and returned to the mound determined to protect his precarious one run lead. Given a second chance Bartell singled to tie the game. Two more Giant runs scored on hits by Lou Chiozza and

Carl Duncan

Joe Moore putting the Cards in a 3 – 1 hole. Diz finally retired the side and headed to the Cardinal dugout cursing umpire Barr and vowing revenge.

Over the next three innings Diz vented his rage on helpless New York batters. As each Giant hitter came to the plate Dizzy unleashed fastballs at their heads causing them to hit the dirt. The only two Giants to escape Dizzy's wrath were Burgess Whitehead and Carl Hubbell.

Whitehead was Dizzy's teammate on the 1934 St. Louis World Championship team, and they remained close friends. Of course, Diz was afraid to dust Hubbell since King Carl could easily retaliate with a high-hard one at Dizzy's head. In fact, New York hitters were urging Hubbell to protect them by decking Card players, but King Carl was more interested in winning his 22nd consecutive game than engaging in a beanball brawl.

Since Hubbell refused to retaliate the Giants found another way for payback. In the ninth inning New York centerfielder Jimmie Ripple bunted toward first baseman Johnny Mize forcing Diz to cover first base and enabling Ripple to run over Diz. Dizzy came up swinging and both benches emptied as the collision turned into an all-out brawl.

Police and umpires were finally able to break up the free-for-all. Initial combatants Dizzy and Ripple were allowed to stay in the game while Card catcher Mickey Owen and Giant catcher Gus Mancuso were inexplicably ejected. New York won the game 4 – 1 and afterwards in the clubhouse Dizzy was still fuming. "That wasn't no balk." Dizzy griped. "I shoulda won that game 1 – 0. We wuz robbed."[61]

American League President Ford Frick fined Dizzy and Ripple $50 each for inciting the near riot. Frick also threatened to suspend Dizzy if he deliberately threw at hitter's heads as the Giants alleged. Dizzy denied dusting Giant hitters, blaming occasional control lapses for the errant pitches.

"Hellfire" Diz said. "Even great pitchers like myself can't help being wild once in a while."[62]

Typically, Dizzy would not keep his mouth shut. It was reported that Dizzy was calling umpire Barr and President Frick liars, robbers and crooks. Also, Diz threatened to boycott the upcoming All-Star game. Frick demanded Diz sign a letter of apology for slandering league officials and throwing beanballs at the Giants or face suspension.

"I ain't done nothin'" Diz said "and I ain't signin' nothin'"[63]

Me 'N' Paul

When Frick finally realized neither the slander nor the beanball incident could be proven, he relented. Surprisingly, Diz accepted his victory graciously, saying he harbored no hard feelings toward anyone and would be honored to play in the All-Star game.

The All-star game was played on July 7th in Washington D.C. at Clark Griffith stadium. President Franklin Roosevelt threw out the first pitch and Dizzy Dean started for the National League. Dizzy was joined on the National League squad by Cardinal teammates Pepper Martin, Ducky Medwick and Johnny Mize.

Diz breezed through the first two innings shutting out the Americans on two hits and a walk while fanning two. Then came the fateful third. Diz recorded two quick outs and needed only one more to finish his day's work. Joe DiMaggio, the next batter, singled bringing up the Iron Horse, Lou Gehrig. Sweet Lou ran the count to 3 – 2 before blasting Dizzy's fastball into the stands giving the American League a 2 – 0 lead.

Earl Averill ended the inning by hitting a line-drive that bounced of Dizzy's foot to second baseman Billy Herman who threw him out. Ironically, the 1937 All-Star game would be remembered not for the legendary Lou Gehrig's mammoth homerun but for 35-year-old Earl Averill's line-drive hitting Dizzy Dean's big toe.

After the game, which the American League won 8 – 3, Diz seemed more concerned with Gehrig's Homer than his rapidly swelling big toe. "Just one more strike and I'd have had them shut out."[64] He moaned.

His toe was originally diagnosed as only bruised but x-rays revealed it was broken. Dizzy was ordered to stay home and to not put wight on his injured foot, however, after only two weeks Diz rejoined the club and told Frisch he was ready to pitch. He started against the Boston Bees on July 21st. Although he pitched a complete game and only lost 2 – 1, it was clear Diz was struggling.

Dizzy gave his version of the famous big toe injury. "Earl Averill of the Cleveland Indians, who is a very murderous hitter, is the batter. He lines the ball back at me like a shot out'n a cannon, and it cracks me on the left foot. That night I don't sleep much, and the next morning my foot is all swoll up to twicet its normal size. X-rays show my big toe is busted. I want to get back in there to help the team so two weeks after the All-Star game, I'm startin' a game in Boston with splints on my foot, and a shoe two sizes too big for me. Bein' a righthander I come down with all my weight on my left leg, and every pitch is killin' me. Pain is stabbin' clean up to my hip. Because of this, I change my natural style, and don't follow through with my body on the delivery, so's I won't have to tromp down on my hurt foot. Instead I cut a fast one loose just throwin' with my arm. As the ball left my hand, there was a loud crack in my shoulder, and my arm went numb down to my fingers. Nobody knowed it then, but ol' Diz's great arm was never goin' to be the same agin after that one pitch."[65]

Diz was pretty much useless after the All-Star game although he soldiered on until the final week of the season winning one game and losing two. Since St. Louis was eleven games out of first place, Diz did not make the last road trip of the year. He was sent home to Florida and told to rest his arm for the winter.

Paul was useless as well. After the surgery, recovery and rehab Paul's arm trouble remained a mystery. Doctors again pronounced Paul fit to pitch and again Paul was unable or unwilling to unleash his fastball. Branch Rickey believed Paul's problems were mental and tried a psychological ploy to get him to throw hard, Rickey offered Paul a wager!

"I'll let you pitch five balls to me" Rickey told Paul "and I'll catch you with my bare hands. If I drop more than one of the five, I'll give you $100. If I catch four of the five, you give me $100."[66]

Paul declined to accept the bet explaining he was not ready to throw that hard. He continued to work out daily, running, pitching batting practice and pampering his arm. Finally, early August Paul informed Frankie Frisch he was ready to test his arm in a game.

On August 12th St. Louis played the Belleville Stags in an exhibition game in Belleville, Illinois. Paul started and relied on what he once considered bunk, smart pitching. He carved up the Stags with slow curves, pinpoint control, changing speeds and pitching batters' weakness; his lethal fastball was missing, perhaps never to be found.

Optimism ran rampart through the Cardinal organization after Paul stopped the Stags with only one scratch hit in two flawless innings. The euphoria was short-lived when Paul reported arm trouble in the days following the Stag game.

"I have followed the advice of Dr. Robert Hyland and from fellow players, but without convincing myself that I am capable of pitchin' big league ball." Paul said. "I have decided that I'm not going to fool myself any longer."

"I can't explain it, but my arm jest ain't right. I can throw slow curves all right, but when I bear down with my fast one a couple of times a streaking pain shoots through my shoulder."

"I may join the club next spring, but I'm not so sure. The way I feel right now I don't think I'll ever pitch again."[67]

Branch Rickey offered to attempt to pass Paul through waivers and assign him to the Houston Buffs to help him regain his confidence at the Minor League level. However, Paul abruptly opted for voluntary retirement as he had the prior year. Paul returned to his home in Dallas intent on rehabbing his arm on his own and at his own pace.

With both Dizzy and Paul incapacitated the Cards folded and fell to fourth place, finishing fifteen games behind the Pennant winning New York Giants. Just three years removed from the 1934 Championship season, only seven of the World Series winners remained on the 1937 roster: Dizzy, Paul, Pop Haines, Frankie Frisch, Leo Durocher, Pepper Martin, and Ducky Medwick.

Of the surviving seven only Ducky Medwick excelled. Ducky was finally a full-fledged star winning the National League triple crown. He started every game of the season and batted .374 with 31 homeruns and 154 RBI's.

Injuries derailed Dizzy, Paul and Pepper. Paul only made one regular season appearance facing three batters and not recording a single out. Dizzy finished with a 13 – 7 won-loss record but was ineffective after his All-Star game injury. Pepper was plagued with many minor injuries and only started 85 games. Although Pepper had a respectable batting average of .304, he contributed only five homeruns and 38 RBI's.

Age finally overtook Frankie Frisch and Pop Haines. At age 39 the Ol' Flash managed the Cards but played in only 17 games. 43-year-old Jesse 'Pop' Haines pitched in 16 games winning three and losing three. Leo the Lip was still steady at shortstop and still couldn't hit. His batting average was a dismal .203 and he hit only three homers while driving in 47 runs.

1934 was a distant memory and the Gashouse Gang was gone forever.

CHAPTER 25

"No, we can't name him Dizzy – It sounds as if he's going to faint."

As the Great Depression continued to grip the United States, Americans turned to movies for brief relief from harsh reality. Beginning in the early 1930's animated films were a vital part of the movie-going experience. Each feature film was usually preceded by an animated cartoon. In 1937 moving picture patrons became captivated by a small black duck.

Warners' Looney Tunes was a pioneer in the rapidly-developing cartoon film industry. The Looney Tunes creative cartoon staff consisted of Fred "Tex" Avery, Isadore "Fritz" Frelend, Chuck Jones and Bob Clampet. Together they created some of the greatest cartoon stars, including Bugs Bunny, Elmer Fudd and Porky Pig.

When the cartoon Por ky's Duc k Hunt first appeared in 1937 the little black duck stole the show. In the cartoon Porky Pig went hunting but the duck always outsmarted the hapless hunter. The last scene in the cartoon featured the duck's dramatic departure. Cartoonist Bob Clampett described the creation of that final scene that made the duck a cartoon star.

"Tex Avery told me to make him exit funny. So, I had the duck cross his eyes, do a Stan Lauel jump, and then do cartwheels, and do a ballet pirouette, and bounce on his head, and so forth. Now at that time, audiences weren't accustomed to seeing a cartoon character do these things. And so, when it hit the theaters it was like an explosion. People would leave the theaters talking about this silly duck."

"We had a bit of a problem finding just the right name for him. One of the first names suggested for our duck was "Dizzy", after the famous baseball player, Dizzy Dean. But Tex said 'no, we can't name him Dizzy – It sounds as if he's going to faint.' And then we thought of Dizzy Dean's brother, who also played ball – Daffy Dean, and thus Daffy Duck was named. The name was used for the first time in the title of Tex's second Duck-Hunt cartoon, <u>Daffy Duck and Egghead</u>."[1]

Ironically, Daffy Duck became one of the most famous cartoon characters in history and Daffy Dean faded into obscurity.

Their bargaining power greatly diminished by bad arms, Diz and Paul did not hold out for better contracts in 1938. They arrived at the Cardinals 1938 spring training camp in St. Petersburg, Florida on time and in shape. No longer able to hold the Cards captive after their arm problems rendered them replaceable, the Deans meekly accepted whatever St. Louis offered.

Diz signed a contract that called for a substantial salary reduction, $7,500 less than the prior year. Paul's position was even more perilous. Since he was still on the voluntary retired list and had only contributed five wins in the last two years, Paul agreed to come to camp without a contract. He would have to prove he could still pitch before the Cardinals would offer him anything.

The Cardinals spring training camp began on March 2, 1938. Paul weighed 30 pounds less than the prior year and Frankie Frisch was anxious to see him pitch. Frisch started Paul in the Cardinals' first inters quad game and he pitched three smooth innings.

"My arm was a little stiff," Paul said, "But none of that old soreness is in there, and I worked out the stiffness after a few pitches. I Didn't have much on the ball in the game, but I believe in time the stuff I used to have will come back. One thing is certain, I'm in great shape and feel fine."[2]

Dizzy was slowed by a cold with coughing and a high fever. He finally saw his first action of the spring on March 14th against the New York Yankees. Diz pitched three innings and allowed only one hit. Paul was excited by Dizzy's impressive outing.

"Boy, wouldn't it be great if Me 'n' Diz got going good again?" said Paul. "We're gonna do it, too. That Diz is better and smarter than he ever was. I'm almost sure my arms all right, I haven't felt even a twinge so far and I've been cutting loose pretty good."[3]

After Paul's success in the inters quad game against his Cardinal teammates, Frisch was anxious to see how he fared when facing enemy batters. On a beautiful spring day in Deanville (Bradenton, Florida) Paul started against the Boston Bees. Branch Rickey was in attendance, so Paul knew he was pitching for a contract and his future.

Paul only allowed one hit over the first two innings, but it was obvious he was missing his money pitch – a blazing fastball. He survived those first two frames merely throwing slow side-arm curves and keeping the ball out of dangerous parts of the strike zone. By the third inning the Bees realized Paul was without his money ball and they made him pay. Boston butchered Paul for nine runs on nine hits.

Diz took over in the fourth, pitched four innings and gave up two runs on five hits. Boston went on to win 13 – 9. After the game Paul put on a brave face.

"I couldn't get anything on the ball," Paul said. "I was loose, and I pitched hard, but I didn't have the speed. My arm wasn't sore or stiff when I was pitchin', but it stiffened up afterwards. I'm sure that will work out the next time I throw. I'm going to keep on working and I believe in time the arm will be all right."[4]

However, Branch Rickey had a more realistic assessment. "Paul didn't show me a thing against Boston. A pitcher needs a fastball to get by in the Major Leagues and Paul lacked his old-time speed. I am afraid he is through as a member of the Cardinals."[5]

Despite the harsh words, Rickey was not ready to give up on Paul. Branch believed a stint in the Minors might resurrect Paul's career and restore his value. Paul Dean was not in high demand, so he easily passed through waivers. No team was willing to pay the $7,500 waiver price and give Paul a Major League contract.

Paul was willing to accept any contract, even a Minor League deal. Baseball still paid better than Texas black land farming. On April 5, 1938 Paul was optioned to the Houston Buffs of the Texas League, a St. Louis farm team.

"I am not through," Paul said when he reported to Houston. "I had a lot of zip on the ball in my last Florida workout and if I have that much stuff throughout the season, I think I can win."[6]

Longtime Cardinal trainer H.J. 'Doc' Weaver agreed with the decision to send Paul to Houston. He believed pitching against Minor League batters and being away from Dizzy would help Paul regain his confidence.

"Paul Dean is one of the finest specimens of pitching material it has been my pleasure to see in many years of sorting baseball ivory," Doc Weaver said. "In fact, when Paul is right, he has more on the ball than Dizzy. However, they've built Dizzy up to the sky and Paul has tried too hard to reach the peak attained by his brother. His trouble isn't in his arm, it's in his head."[7]

Back in Florida Dizzy was having a rough spring and it soon became apparent Paul was not the only Dean missing his fastball. Branch Rickey always contended it was better to trade a player too soon rather than too late, so he put Diz on the market while he still had value.

It was no secret that Dizzy was experiencing arm problems ever since his All-Star toe injury. However, many teams were still interested in the "Great One." Chicago made the best offer for Diz and on April 16, 1938 he was traded to the Cubs.

In return the Cards received pitchers Clyde "Hardrock" Shoun and Curt "Coonskin"

Davis, outfielder Tuck Stainbach plus $185,000 cash. The only baseball deal where more cash had changed hands was in 1934 when the Washington Senator owner sold his son-in-law, shortstop Joe Conin, to Boston for $250,000. Even Babe Ruth fetched only $175,000 when the Yankees bought him from Boston.

Paul weighed in on the deal, "that 185,000 smackers and a fourth of a dozen players for ol' Diz ain't bad," he said. "Us Dean boys come pretty high for a coupla sore arm fellas. But don't let 'em kid you that there's anything wrong with Dizzy's arm. It's his legs. He just hasn't rounded into shape, but he will. Me 'n' Diz ain't done yet."[8]

The sore arm issue was addressed when Rickey informed Cub owner Phil Wrigley that Diz might be damaged Goods. Wrigley was willing to accept the risk. He knew Dizzy Dean could fill the stands with paying customers even without his signature fastball. Dizzy was the most famous pitcher in baseball and even though he was no longer a St. Louis Cardinal he was still a tremendous drawing Card. Consequently, each team signed a special agreement accepting the trade no matter the physical condition of the players involved.

Dizzy exited the Cardinal clubhouse for the last time just as he had entered it for the first time – talking.

"The boys had the Pennant money sewed up, and some of it spent," Diz said. "But now that I am going to Chicago, I'll have to help them Cubbies win the money and spend it."[9]

The Cards were sorry to see Diz leave. Dizzy's partner in fun Pepper Martin was especially upset to see Diz depart.

"There goes our Pennant and World Series money," lamented Pepper. "We woulda been a cinch with Diz."

Dizzy said, "I hate to leave you boys, but I bet Mr. Wrigley will pay me $10,000 more than I'm makin' here."

"Sure he will," responded Pepper. "In chewing gum."[10]

Frankie Frisch walked up to Diz and solemnly shook his hand. Despite all the animosity between Diz and the Flash over the years, just below the surface was mutual love and respect. Frisch was genuinely sad to see the big righthander leave the Cards.

"Frankie," Diz said, "I want you to know I've enjoyed playing for you. I really have." Frisch sadly shook his head and said "Diz, I'm sorry to see you go. Be a good boy and take care of yourself."[11]

Dizzy blew into the Windy City on the winds of fame. Fans wanted to see the flamboyant flame-thrower even if he had lost some of the fire off of his fastball. The Cubs first series of the 1938 season was against the Reds in Cincinnati and each of the three Chicago newspapers sent feature writers to travel with the team to do stories on Dizzy. A photographer from a national picture magazine under the impression he was taking action shots of the great Dizzy Dean warming up was distressed when he learned he was actually filming Cub pitcher Tex Carleton, Dizzy's former Cardinal teammate.

The three-game series set attendance records for a season opening series' in Cincinnati. "The appearance of the great Dizzy Dean in the uniform of a Chicago Cub for the first time was the big drawing magnet."[12]

Dizzy started the second game of the Cincy series, pitched six innings and allowed 2 runs on 8 hits. His control was perfect as he fanned three and issued no walks. Chicago won the game 10 – 4 as Diz picked up his first win as a Cub. After the game reporters lined up to Pepper Dizzy with questions.

"I knew I was 'right' when I was warming up," Diz said. "Garbark, who was catching me, had to go over to the dugout and get a sponge for his glove to catch my fastball."[13]

Asked why he was wearing #22 on his uniform instead of the #17 he made famous as a Cardinal. Diz replied, "they gave it to me because my fast one looks like a '22' bullet as it passes the batter."[14]

In reality Dizzy's fastball was not as fast as a speeding bullet and a catcher would not need extra padding in a mitt to catch it. Diz used an assortment of curves and pinpoint control to subdue the Reds impotent offense, rarely throwing his diminished fastball. After the Cincinnati series the Cubs headed to Chicago to host St. Louis in a three-game series.

Dizzy was tabbed to start the Sunday game in order to assure maximum attendance. Diz relished the opportunity to face his former team and make Branch Rickey regret selling him. 35,000 fans packed Wrigley Field to witness the grudge game.

Dizzy clipped the Cardinals' wings with the same arsenal he used to roast the Reds, curves, cunning and control. All Dizzy did was allow no runs on four hits and two walks, he fanned one and only one Redbird reached third. He threw 96 pitches of which 61 were strikes. On offense Diz singled, walked and scored twice. Chicago won the game 5 – 0.

Buoyed by his early season success, winning two games in five days, Diz relaxed in the Cub clubhouse and talked to reporters. "Only 28 more to go," he said. "I'm good for 30 this year, just like in '34."[15]

Dizzy liked to say "it ain't braggin' if you do it."[16] This time, however the statement would have to be classified as bragging. Dizzy Dean would win only 14 more games in the remainder of his Major League career.

Dizzy's decline began in his third start of the season on April 29th against Cincinnati. He lasted only to the fourth inning citing shoulder

Me 'N' Paul

pain as the reason for his early exit. Although Diz was credited with a win four days later against Philadelphia, he left after seven innings complaining of arm pain.

Dizzy was examined by Chicago Cub team physician Dr. John F. Davis. X-rays were ordered and Dr. Davis diagnosed Dizzy's problem, inflamed shoulder muscle. Rest and rehab were prescribed to cure Dizzy's salary wing.

"There is nothing that cannot be corrected by rest and proper training thereafter,"[17] Dr. Davis concluded.

Dizzy would not return to action for over two months. While he was rehabbing Diz traveled with the Cubs and supported his teammates from the dugout. Perhaps now he realized what Paul had been experiencing. Even the invincible Deans were not immune to the epidemic of sore arms infecting Major League pitchers. In addition to the Deans other Major League pitchers plagued by arm ailments included Lefty Grove, Schoolboy Rowe, Van Lingle Mungo, King Carl Hubbell and even young phenom, Bob Feller. Each affected with varying degrees of severity.

During Dizzy's absence the Cubs floundered and by mid-July they were in fourth place 7.5 games out of first. Cub owner Phil Wrigley saw the Pennant slipping away and decided a change was needed. Manager Charlie Grimm was fired, and catcher Gabby Harnett was elevated to player/manager. Gabby turned to Dizzy to help salvage the season. Diz was ready to return to action and eager to win for his battery-mate turned manager.

Diz returned to duty on July 17th going the distance against Boston. He beat the bees 3 – 1 allowing only four hits. He repeated his winning performance six days later felling the Giants 3 – 1. New York managed only five hits off Dizzy although he still seemed incapable of delivering his signature fastball.

Dizzy's third start since his two month 'rest' resulted in disaster. In Philadelphia the Phillies shelled Dizzy for four runs in only four innings. He yielded six hits including one homerun. Worse yet, Diz said his arm hurt and he needed to see a doctor. Gabby vetoed Dizzy's request.

"I know Dizzy's arm is sore," Gabby said. "But there is no use seeing more doctors.

They all agree the only cure is rest. Still, it's been a funny case. Why, against the Giants he pitched a great game. Then in his next start against the Phillies, he didn't have a prayer."[18]

After two weeks rest, Gabby started Dizzy against the League leading Pittsburgh Pirates. The Cubs staked Diz to an early lead, he pitched well and after six innings Chicago led 7 – 1. In the seventh Pittsburgh plastered Dizzy with five hits and four runs, sending him to the showers. The Cubs piled on four more runs and held on for an 11 – 5 win. Once again Dizzy failed to go the full nine innings, however, he was credited with the win, his sixth as a Cub.

A week later Dizzy let Gabby know he was ready to give his troublesome arm another test. On August 20th Dizzy started against Pittsburgh and was shelled for 4 runs in 5 1/3 innings. This time he absorbed the loss running his record to 6 – 1 for the season.

By September 1st Chicago was 7.0 games behind the League leading Pirates and running out of games. In 1935 the Cubs made a miracle September drive winning 21 games in a row to wrest the Pennant from St. Louis. Manager Gabby Harnett knew the Cubs would need another fantastic finish to catch Pittsburgh.

Chicago's last-ditch drive started with the Cubs winning 18 of September's first 24 games. By September 26th the Cubs had clawed their way from fourth to second place only 1.5 games behind the Bucs. Dizzy only pitched in relief during the September surge never going over a few innings, but the Pirates were coming to Chicago for a three-game series that could decide the Pennant and Gabby needed his weary-armed warhorse.

Gabby tabbed Dizzy to start the first game and 42,000 Pennant-fevered fans jammed Wrigley field for the start of the crucial three game series. Dizzy shutout the hard-hitting Pirates for eight innings with sweeping curves and the occasional sub-par fastball.

Diz was nursing a 2 – 0 lead in the ninth inning with two on and two out when his old Texas League archenemy, Al Todd, came to bat. With the game and possibly the Pennant hanging in the balance, Gabby came out from behind the plate for a conference with his tiring pitcher.

Me 'N' Paul

"Diz, can't you throw any harder?" Gabby implored. "Gabby, I'm throwing twice as hard as I've ever throw'd in my life" Diz replied. "The only trouble is I can't throw fast enough no more."[19]

Gabby understood and signaled for Big Bill Lee to save the game. Cub fans appreciated Dizzy's gutsy, pressure pitching and gave him a standing ovation as he left the mound. Lee promptly unleashed a wild pitch that plated the first Pirate run, but he settled down and struck Todd out preserving Dizzy's 2 – 1 win.

After the game Cub player/coach Tony Lazzeri, a former member of the New York Yankees' legendary "murderers' row," paid tribute to Dizzy.

"That was the greatest exhibition of sheer nerve I've ever seen on a diamond." Lazzeri said. "Dizzy's arm hurt him, you can bet on that but when you have that kind of a heart, a sore arm can't stop you."[20]

Dizzy's improbable victory was Chicago's eighth in a row and cut the Pirate lead to a half game. The next day's game was even more dramatic. The game reached the bottom of the ninth with the score tied 5 – 5. With darkness descending on Wrigley field and no stadium lights the game could not go extra innings. If Chicago failed to score the game would be replayed the following day in its entirety, prior to the regularly scheduled third game of the series. Gabby Harnett knew his exhausted pitching staff would be insurmountable handicapped by a doubleheader, Chicago had to score a run or lose their best chance to catch the Bucs.

In the thickening gloom with dusk falling Gabby came to bat with two outs and the bases empty. Hope faded as he fell behind in the count no balls and two strikes. Down to his last strike Gabby struck a blow that saved the Cubs season. His clutch walk-off homerun won the game and became immortalized as the homer in the gloamin'. Gloaming meant twilight in the regional dialect and there was a popular song at the time titled <u>Roaming in the Gloaming</u>.

The dramatic victory vaulted the Cubs into the League lead and demoralized Pittsburgh. Chicago completed the series sweep with an easy 10 – 1 win and clinched the Pennant two days later in St. Louis. Dizzy and the Cubbies were going to the 1938 World Series.

Meanwhile, Paul was back in his adopted home state pitching in the Texas League, laboring to resurrect his once brilliant baseball career. Unfortunately, Paul was ineffective pitching for the Houston Buffs.

He lost four games and only won one although two of the defeats were 2 – 1 nail-biters. Paul seldom employed his fastball, relying on an assortment of slow-breaking pitches. Paul's reluctance to throw his fastball convinced the Buffalo Brass he could not be a winner for the herd. On May 31st Houston returned Paul to the Cardinals in spite of his lack of success with Houston, Paul still believed his arm was mending, he just needed time.

"My arm is still weak," Paul said, "And has to regain its strength gradually. It hasn't hurt me the few times I've cut loose with my fastball, but on the other hand, it tires quicker than it should."[21]

Paul flew to St. Louis and went through a session on the mound with Branch Rickey and Cardinal coaches observing closely. All involved in the workout were encouraged.

"Paul appeared to be freer and to have more stuff than he had in spring training,"

Rickey said. "Mike Gonzales, who caught Paul in the brief warm-up test agreed with my observations."[22]

Paul hoped his impressive audition would convince Rickey to keep him with the Cardinals, but Branch knew Paul's arm was still unproven despite the successful session. The Card G.M decided to send Paul to the St. Louis farm club in New York. Rickey assigned Paul to the Class AA Rochester Red Wings.

Paul balked at being sent to Rochester citing the cooler climate as unsuitable for his comeback. "I'd quit baseball before I'd report to Rochester," Paul said. "I've got $10,000 banked in Dallas and me and my wife can live on a dollar a day. That gives me a lot of days I don't have to play baseball."[23]

Branch Rickey knew Paul was not bluffing, unlike Dizzy, Paul did not crave the spotlight and evidently did not need baseball money. Rickey pondered his dwindling options to save his once-valuable asset. Paul agreed to continuing playing either on the St. Louis Cardinal Major League roster or a Minor League team near his home in Dallas.

Branch Rickey was unwilling to risk a Cardinal roster spot on a player with suspect skills. Rickey preferred to send Paul to the Dallas Steers but there was a problem, the Steers were a Farm team of the Chicago White Sox. Once again dealer Rickey found a way and a deal was struck.

Paul was optioned to Dallas, but he remained the property of the St. Louis Cardinals. Chicago was willing to accept the unusual arrangement; rehabbing a player for a rival Major League team, because the deal made financial sense. Paul was still a baseball celebrity and living locally made him an attractive drawing Card for the Dallas Steers. Also, if Paul regained his former brilliance, he could help propel the Steers to the Texas League Pennant.

Paul was happy to accept assignment to the Dallas Steers. He could live at home with his wife and infant son when not on team road trips. Also, he would be close to his beloved farm, and help his father oversee operations.

Paul started slowly with the Steers losing more than he won but he was gradually regaining his confidence as well as his fastball. He ended the Texas League season with 8 wins and 16 losses. However, eight of those defeats were by a margin of only one run as he received little help from his offensively challenged, bottom dwelling teammates.

"I didn't know it was possible to lose so many games by one run," Paul said. "I've got almost as much stuff on the ball as I had when I was in the Major Leagues. My curve is not quite so good, but I have control and my speed is back."[24]

St. Louis scouts agreed with Paul's assessment of his arsenal and informed Branch Rickey of Pau's progress. Rickey recalled Paul to the Cards for the final three weeks of the Major League season.

St. Louis was out of the Pennant race and Rickey wanted to access Paul's success against Major League hitters. Also, Branch was not oblivious to an obvious opportunity to fill the otherwise semi-empty stands at Sportsman's Park. With the Cubs coming to St. Louis for the last four games of the season Rickey could envision a capacity crowd eager to witness Dizzy pitted against Daffy in a pitching duel.

Paul arrived in St. Louis just in time to say good-bye to Frankie Frisch. He pitched the first game of his Cardinal comeback against the Pittsburgh Pirates and won 6 – 4. Paul went the distance allowed 12 hits but issued only one free pass. The jubilant Cardinal celebration over Paul's triumphant return to the big leagues was cut short when a somber Frankie Frisch herded the players into the Cardinal clubhouse. Frisch was moved by the situation as he announced he had been replaced as manager of the St. Louis Cardinals.

Carl Duncan

"Well fellas, the Old Flash is no longer your manager." Frisch said. "From here on, Mike Gonzales will be your boss. You fellas have been swell to me' it was a real pleasure to work with you and I wish you all the success in the world."[25]

Everyone was quiet while the distressing news sunk in. Finally, players began swearing, grumbling and voicing their resentment over the removal of the field general who turned the Cards into baseball's most colorful team – the incomparable Gashouse Gang.

Paul continued his successful comeback in his next outing by blanking the Boston Bees 4 - 0. He gave up seven hits and again showing pinpoint control, walked no one. He stumbled in his next start as Cincinnati shelled him from the mound with ten hits and three runs in five innings.

Paul would get one more start before the season ended and that start would be against the Chicago Cubs. Unfortunately, Rickey's stand-filling scenario failed to unfold. Dizzy flatly refused to participate in the proposed Dizzy/Daffy showdown.

"I won't pitch against Paul" Diz said, "and he won't pitch against me, not even if I get fined for refusing."[26]

Paul pitched the final game of the Cards season. The game was against Chicago and true to his word Diz did not oppose Paul. Since the Cubs had already clinched the Pennant and the marquee match-up of Dizzy vs. Daffy failed to materialize the stands were far from full.

Only 11,000 fans showed up to watch Paul pitch the Cards past the Cubs by a score of 7 – 5. In Paul's brief return to the Cardinals he won three games, lost one and had an ERA of 2.61. Paul explained his successful comeback.

"When I first went down to Dallas, my arm shore did hurt. Could't throw good a'tall, but I forced myself to pitch. First time it didn't work. Second time it didn't work. Third time I felt somethin' give. I thought to myself; 'well, big boy, somethin's gonna happen now, either your gonna bust the arm or she's gonna come through for you.' Fourth time I pitched I really cut loose, and you know what happened? Well the arm didn't bust, she just loosened up and I found I had my pitchin' stuff back. I wuz just scared to throw hard, but not now."[27]

With the Cardinal's season over, Paul returned to his Texas farm. Based on his recent Major League success a 1939 Card contract seemed secure. Finally, Paul's baseball future appeared bright.

The first game of the 1938 World Series took place at Wrigley Field in Chicago. The National League Champions Chicago Cubs played the American League Champion New York Yankees. The Yankees had won the World Series in 1936 and 1937. They were heavily favored for an unprecedented three-peat.

New York won the first game 3 – 1 supporting Red Ruffing with 12 routine hits off Big Bill Lee. Gabby Harnett, desperate to avoid two straight losses at Wrigley Field, turned to Dizzy. Gabby gambled that Dizzy could repeat the clutch performance he delivered against Pittsburgh in the Pennant race.

42,000 fans filled Wrigley Field to watch Diz duel Lefty "El Goofo" Gomez. Dizzy completely baffled the Bronx bombers for seven spectacular innings and the Cubs led 3 – 2. The two Yankee runs were courtesy of an egregious error by the Cubbie infield. Diz also contributed two base hits to the Cub attack while limiting New York to only three hits.

With two outs in the eighth inning, the Dizzy magic finally disappeared. Frankie "Little Wop" Crosetti solved Dizzy's "smart Pitching" and deposited one of Dizzy's slow curves into the stands for a two-run homer. As Crosetti circled the bases, Dizzy yelled at him. "You'd never have done that to me if I'd had my fastball." Frankie replied, "I know, Diz, I know."[28]

The ninth was equally cruel to Diz. Joe "Big Wop" DiMaggio matched the "Little Wop" with a two-run homerun that sent Dizzy to the showers. Diz was downtrodden after the game and apologized to his teammates. "Sorry boys, I just throwed myself out. That's the toughest game I ever lost."

"It was a great job, Dizzy." Gabby said. "Even with a bad arm you were great."[29]

As Yankee skipper Joe McCarthy savored the 6 – 3 New York win, he took time to praise Dizzy.

"That Dizzy Dean, what a heart that man has." said McCarthy. "For seven innings he made my gang look bad. Mighty bad."[30]

With a tear in her eye, Mrs. Dizzy Dean offered a poignant assessment of her husband's courageous performance. "That was the longest, most terrible game I've ever watched," she said. "That was the high and the low watching Diz in there for eight innings with nothing but a glove and a prayer. I could see the pain on Dizzy's face as he threw each ball. I knew, after that game, that he was through. It was a terrible thing to know."[31]

The Cub crushing continued as New York swept the series four games to none. New York plated 22 runs in the series while Chicago scored only 9. Yankee pitching was superb finishing with an ERA of 1.75 compared to the Cub ERA of 5.03.

Dizzy spent the winter at his home in Deanville, Florida, giving his ailing arm complete rest. The inactivity failed to heal his arm and 1939 was a miserable year for Dizzy and the Cubs. Chicago fell to fourth place and Dizzy finished with six wins and four losses. Despite Dizzy's lack of success fans still turned out to see the fading superstar.

"The fans love Dizzy not for what he did," Mrs. Dean explained, "but for what he tried so hard to do and couldn't."[32]

Perhaps sensing the end of his Major League career, Dizzy followed Paul's example and bought a farm in Texas. Dizzy and Pat Dean left Deanville and settled on a 150 acres near Paul, Dorothy, Paul Jr. and "Pa Dean. With no Deans left in Deanville the towns name reverted back to Bradenton.

Dizzy was in the Cub's starting rotation when the 1940 season began. However, after he was bombed in four of his first five starts, Dizzy decided a Minor League stint might salvage his baseball career. Diz announced he was going to the Cub's Farm Team in Tulsa, Oklahoma.

"Gonna learn to throw that ol' ball underarm" he said, "work on a new delivery."[33]

After eight Major League seasons which included four All-Star selections, four strikeout titles, four time 20-game winner, including 30 wins in 1934, a most valuable player award and a World Series Championship, Dizzy was back where he began; pitching in the Texas League.

Diz won eight and lost eight for Tulsa but despite the mediocre record Chicago recalled him in September. The Cubs were out of the Pennant race and Gabby needed to determine if Dizzy would be able to help the team in 1941. The audition was inconclusive. Dizzy finished the 1940

Me 'N' Paul

Major League season with three wins, three losses and a bloated ERA of 5.17. Turned out Gabby had no reason to worry about Chicago's 1941 season, he failed to survive the disastrous 1940 season.

The Cubs finished fifth in the National League, 25 games out of first place. Phil Wrigley replaced Gabby Harnett with Dizzy's old fishing buddy, former Philadelphia manager, Jimmy Wilson.

Dizzy retreated to his Texas farm for the winter. A winter of milking cows, slopping hogs and planting crops instead of his usual winter activities; Florida fishing, golfing and carousing with cronies.

Phil Wrigley signed Dizzy to a 1941 contract, hoping for a winning pitcher but knowing he had a gate attraction. New Chicago manager Jimmy Wilson allowed Dizzy to set his own pace during spring training and the start of the regular season. Finally, Dizzy was ready and on April 25th he started against the Pittsburgh Pirates.

The Bucs butchered Dizzy with three runs in the first inning. As he walked off the mound Dizzy finally knew what everyone suspected; the great Dean was done. Two weeks later Dizzy Dean retired from baseball. He was only 31 years old.

Phil Wrigley realized Diz could no longer pitch but believed fans would pay to see Dizzy in any capacity. The Cub owner offered Diz a job as the Cub's first-base coach. Dizzy happily accepted baseball's least demanding job. Diz described the duties associated with his new occupation. "All you do in that little box down there is tell fellas not to be caught off the bag, and you pat 'em on the back, and if they're too dumb to know if it's one or two outs, you have to tell 'em that, too."[34]

After only a month of coaching, a new business opportunity was presented to Dizzy. The offer was attractive because the skill required for the job aligned with the only talent, other than pitching, that Diz possessed, talking. The Falstaff brewing company, sponsors of St. Louis Cardinals and Browns games on radio, wanted Dizzy to join their on-air broadcast crew. The three-year $25,000 contract Falstaff offered was less than Diz earned pitching but much more than he made coaching, and since he could no longer pitch Diz decided to accept Falstaff's generous offer.

Dizzy asked his old Skipper, Frankie Frisch, for advice on how to prepare for his new profession.

Carl Duncan

"I told Dizzy to get a book and read out loud to train for radio work." Fordham educated Frisch said. "Work on your dictation grammar and try to lose your accent."[35]

Always adverse to excessive reading, Dizzy fortunately ignored Frisch's fatherly advice.

Dizzy began his sports announcing career on July 10, 1941 at Sportsman's Park in St. Louis. He provided the color commentary while Johnny O'Hara called the play-by-play action in the St. Louis Browns/New York Yankees American League game. The contest attracted a large radio audience lured by Dizzy Dean's debut and Joe DiMaggio's attempt to hit in his 49th consecutive game.

Dizzy opened his career as a sports announcer in his usual, modest fashion. "I hope I'm as good at the 'mike' as I was on the mound,"[36] Diz said.

Dizzy did not attempt to alter his personality and luckily his unorthodox announcing resonated with fans, radio audiences had never heard anyone like Dizzy Dean. His good-natured bragging, mangling of grammar and mispronouncing player's names fascinated fans. They also loved his stories; his hardscrabble childhood as an itinerant cotton-picker, his glory days with the St. Louis Cardinals when "Me 'n' Paul won 'em all and his battles with opponents, teammates, umpires, and St. Louis Cardinal management.

Dizzy's radio popularity led to National television show, the game of the week. Every Saturday during baseball season, Falstaff sponsored an important game which Dizzy and side-kick Pee Wee Reese announced. Dizzy's radio and tv earnings dwarfed the money he made playing baseball.

During Dizzy's broadcasts he introduced new words into the English language. In order to help fans decipher Dizzy's colorful comments Falstaff published the Dizzy Dean baseball dictionary. The following are some of Dizzy's definitions;

Slud: Hit the dirt.
Dead Pigeon: A guy who slud too late.
Aly Carte: Ketchin the ball with one hand.
Cunny-thumb: A pitcher that ain't got nothin' but a slow ball

<u>Bleeder</u>: A weak scratch hit that is just slow enuff so the runner can beat it out to first base.

<u>Swang</u>: This is what a guy has done after he has took a cut and missed.

<u>Pistol-Whipped</u>: A guy who is down in the dumps and sorta disjointed after losin' a close ball game.

<u>Leather-man</u>: Any ball player that is good with his glove.

<u>Wooden Indian</u>: A guy who is standin' at the plate waiting for a walk.

<u>Wish Ball</u>: A new kinda pitch for hurlers that has lost their stuff. They throw and "wish" the batter don't hit it.

<u>Belly Whopper</u>: Hittin' the dirt head first on your stummick.

<u>Gillette</u>: A fast pitch that almost grazes the batter's whiskers.

<u>Dyin' Quail</u>: A short hit over the infield that sinks like a shot bird.

<u>Fishin' Trip</u>: Swingin' at a bad pitch.

After a winter of hard work on his Texas farm, Paul reported to the Cardinals' 1939 spring training camp in excellent shape.

"I weigh 187 lbs." Paul said, "that's the lowest weight I've ever known in spring training. My arm feels all right. I can fog 'em without any kinks."[37]

Paul's optimism faded as he was mauled from the mound all spring in Florida. Finally, in the final game before the regular season began, Paul had a good outing. In the annual St. Louis City championship game. Paul allowed the St. Louis Browns only one hit in four innings. New Cardinal manager Ray Blades commented on Paul's progress.

"Paul showed me real pitching for the fist time this spring," Blades stated. "He was much better than at anytime in Florida."[38]

Unfortunately, Paul's "real pitching" failed to continue into the regular season. The Cubs clubbed Paul in his first start for 6 hits and 4 runs in only 3 2/3 innings, saddling him with a loss to start the season. By mid-August Paul had not won a single game, and his ERA was a disappointing 6.07.

On August 15th St. Louis assigned Paul to the Columbus Redbirds, back where he achieved his greatest Minor League success with a 22 – 7 record in 1933. Paul did not take the demotion well and when a reporter requested an interview, Paul refused. Pepper Martin intervened and assured Paul the reporter was writing and article about the possibility of

Carl Duncan

negroes playin in the Major Leagues, not Paul's imminent departure from the Cardinals. Paul agreed to be interviewed.

"Yes," said Paul, "I have played against a lot of negro ball players who I thought was good enough to play in the Majors. I think Satchell Paige is one of the best pitchers I ever saw, and Gibson is a mighty good catcher."

"Would you object," the reporter asked, "if a colored player were signed by the Cardinals?"

"No," Paul answered. "I would not care; all I want is my money."[39]

Paul reported to Columbus and finished the season with the Redbirds. He won two, lost two and posted a 4.25 ERA. Not a great record against a Minor League hitter, therefore Paul was surprised to learn he would be on a team's 1940 Major League baseball roster.

In the annual rule 5 draft the New York Giants selected Paul Dean. Giant manager Bill Terry wanted Paul in New York and Paul wanted a Major League paycheck.

Paul spent the entire 1940 season with the New York Giants. He had another sub-par year. Paul appeared in 27 games, won four lost four and had a decent ERA of 3.90.

As the 1940 season drew to a close the European conflict began to effect Major League baseball. Although most Americans favored neutrality, President Franklin Roosevelt knew the United States had to be prepared if America was dragged into war. On September 6, 1940 President Roosevelt signed the selective service act. Every American male between the ages of 21 and 36 was required to register for the draft.

Professional baseball players were not exempt and both Paul and Dizzy Dean were eligible to be drafted. Hugh "L.P." Mulcahy had the dubious distinction of being the first Major League baseball player drafted. "L.P." which stood for Losing Pitcher earned his nickname by losing 76 games between 1937 and 1940 for the hapless Philadelphia Phillies.

"My losing streak is over for the duration." L.P. said. "I'm on a winning team now."[40]

Paul began the 1941 season with the New York Giants and was ineffective. He pitched in only five early season games, all in relief. On May 14th New York sold Paul to Sacramento of the Pacific Coast League. The Sacramento club was managed by Paul's old Gashouse Gang teammate, Pepper Martin, and seemed a good opportunity for Paul to resurrect his

Me 'N' Paul

career, but Paul refused to report to Sacramento. He did not want to be so far away from his young family in Texas at such and uncertain time in America. Consequently, Paul was suspended from baseball.

1941 was a banner season for Major League baseball. Fans filled stadiums to watch Joe DiMaggio hit safely in 56 consecutive games, Ted Williams bat an incredible .406 and Carl Hubbell win his 300th career game. However, a catastrophic event on December 7th threatened to shutdown professional baseball.

Early Sunday morning on December 7, 1941, Japan launched a surprise aerial attack on the United States Pacific fleet anchored at Pearl Harbor, Hawaii. The unprovoked ambush sunk or damaged 18 United States warships and plunged America into World War II.

Baseball only lost about a month to World War I because the season was almost complete when baseball was cancelled on September 2, 1918 and the armistice agreement saved the following season. No one expected World War II to end anytime soon. The war raged on for four years, ultimately Franklin Roosevelt saved baseball.

"I believe that it would be best for the country to keep baseball going." The President announced. "Baseball can provide entertainment for 20 million people. Although the quality of the teams might be lowered by the greater use of older players replacing young men going into the military service, this would not dampen the popularity of baseball."[41]

Baseball would continue and Paul still wanted to play, however, he was still unwilling to play in California. Since Paul adamantly refused the Sacramento assignment, a deal was struck, and Paul was optioned to the Houston Buffs of the Texas League. Paul accepted the deal since he would be able to play ball closer to his Dallas home.

Paul had an outstanding season with Houston. He won 19 games lost only 8, pitched 239 innings and finished with a sparkling 2.05 ERA. Although Paul's excellent record was achieved against a service-thinned talent pool, it earned him another chance in the Majors. The Washington Senators bought Paul's contract but quickly traded him to the St. Louis Browns.

Paul started the 1943 season with St. Louis but was unable to repeat his Buff success with the Browns. After only two months Paul was placed on the voluntary retired list. He was not credited with any wins or losses and only appeared in five games. Paul Dean's Major League career was over.

Paul had not yet been called for military service, since he was married with children. Although he knew if the war continued, he would be drafted. Diz was still announcing baseball games and would not be drafted after failing his army physical because of a perforated ear drum.

With the draft looming Paul's wife, Dorothy, wanted to be close to her family in Arkansas. Consequently, Paul invested in a barrel-stave mill with his father-in-law and moved his family to Russellville, Arkansas. Pa and Elmer stayed in Texas to run Paul's farm.

Paul was able to keep his baseball dreams alive while barrel-making in Arkansas. The St. Louis Browns owned his contract, but Paul was able to convince them to "loan" him to Little Rock, a Minor League team in the Southern Association. The Browns believed Paul still had value and would rather have him pitching that retired.

Little Rock management accepted the deal because fans would flock to Little Rock stadium to watch Arkansas' native son pitch. Paul worked out an agreement with the team to only play in home games, so he could remain close to his wife and children. He finished the season with Little Rock, won 5 lost 2 and had an ERA of 2.84.

Paul was finally drafted. He was inducted into the United States Army in October, 1944. Again, baseball was Paul's salvation, instead of being shipped overseas to fight he was sent to California to play baseball. After basic training Paul was stationed at the Fairfield-Suisun Army base in California where he was player/manager of the base baseball team. Paul was a staff sergeant and of course had other duties, but his former star status afforded him special treatment. Many other professional baseball players volunteered for duty and saw combat during the war.

After the war Paul returned to Arkansas and pitched for Little Rock during the 1946 season. He won 2 lost 1 and had a pitiful 6.63 ERA. Paul was through as a player.

For the next few years Paul lived in Arkansas. He stayed busy with different endeavors. He ran the barrel-stave mill, managed a restaurant in Little Rock and traveled across Texas, Oklahoma and Arkansas scouting for the St. Louis Browns. In December 1948 Paul purchased the Minor

League baseball team in Clovis, New Mexico. Clovis played in the Class C west Texas-New Mexico League.

"I'll be president, general manager, manager, pitcher, and scout." Paul said. "My wife will be bookkepper."[42]

Paul sold his home and business interests in Arkansas and moved to Clovis, New Mexico. About this time Hollywood came calling. Twentieth Century-Fox paid Dizzy $100,000 for rights to his life story. Paul was offered $15,000 for the use of his name in the movie.

Paul balked, he wanted $25,000 and script approval. He was afraid the movie would not tell the true Dean story.

Paul did not get script approval and he settled for the $15,000 payment. He wanted the money to invest in another Minor League team, the Lubbock Hubbers.

The movie starred Dan Dailey as Dizzy, Joanne Dru as Pat Dean and Richard Crenna as Paul. Production was delayed when Dailey suffered a nervous breakdown.

"When this Danny fellow found out he was going to have to play me," Diz said. "He went nuts."[43]

The movie titled "The Pride of St. Louis" was completed after Dailey recovered. It premiered on April 11, 1952 and was a moderate success. Dizzy loved the movie and saw it six times. However, Paul hated "The Pride of St. Louis."

"IT stunk." Paul said. "But if they'd gotten hold of those New York and Hollywood writers and talked some sense into 'em., if they'd made the picture about the Dean Brothers – notice, I said Brothers – why, people would have stood in line to see that picture. Those New York writers always louse it up. The real story was Diz and Me, just like Diz always said."[44]

The next few years Paul owned and operated Minor League teams in Lubbock, El Paso, and Hot Springs, Arkansas. His son, Paul Jr., played high school baseball in El Paso and Hot Springs. Paul Jr. was a promising pitcher and received a baseball scholarship to Southern Methodist University (SMU) in Dallas, Texas.

Paul approved of his son's decision to attend college instead of trying professional baseball. "Pro baseball is an uncertain business," Paul said "particularly for a pitcher. You can ruin your arm on one throw. A boy just about has to have a college education these days. Me 'n' Diz never had a chance to get one."[45]

College did not suit Paul Jr. and he left SMU after his freshman year. He wanted to see if he had a future in professional baseball and signed a contract with the Milwaukee Braves organization. Unfortunately, after only two seasons in the Minor Leagues, Paul Jr. developed arm trouble and was out of baseball by 1959.

Paul was out of baseball also and spent the next several years in different business ventures. He owned service stations around Dallas, continued running his farm and operated Dizzy's carpet business in Phoenix, Arizona.

In March of 1966 Paul returned to baseball. Dr. Robert Morris hired Paul to be athletic director and baseball coach at the University of Plano, a small liberal arts college north of Dallas, Texas. Paul's first order of business was to field a baseball team for the 1967 season.

Creating an entire college baseball program in less than a year was a daunting task. Playing fields had to be built, players recruited, opponents scheduled, and equipment purchased. Paul was able to accomplish his mission and in the spring of 1967 the University of Plano Trailblazers played their first game.

CHAPTER 26

"We need Duncan out there foggin' 'em in."

I was a pitcher on Paul Dean's first University of Plano baseball team. I grew up hearing stories about Dizzy and Daffy Dean from my dad and uncles, but I had never heard of the University of Plano. Needless to say, Plano was not my first choice to continue my baseball career after high school.

My high school pitching record was marred by more losses than wins. The losses featured a disturbing number of walks, signaling a lack of control. The wins, though not numerous, were often spectacular. I once struck out 18 batters in a seven-inning high school game. Scouts said I had a Major League fastball and plus breaking pitches. I could make a baseball do anything I wanted except enter the strike-zone on a regular basis.

I was ineligible to play ball my senior year of high school because I missed the entire 9th grade. I was in a car accident and contracted osteomyelitis in my left leg. After I recovered doctors advised my parents that I should give up sports because a blow to my leg could cause a return of the disease. My mother finally gave in to my pleas and signed a release allowing me to play baseball my sophomore and junior years.

After my junior year of high school while playing summer ball I received several college baseball scholarship offers and also an opportunity to sign a professional contract with the Chicago Cubs organization. I turned down the Chicago offer because I wanted to finish high school and pursue a college baseball scholarship.

Like a lot of kids growing up in Texas, I wanted to play for the University of Texas (UT), and I was fortunate to be offered a baseball scholarship to UT. However, a poor SAT score and a depressing class rank (I ranked 499th out of 535 in my high school graduating class) sunk my UT dreams. I was advised to attend Junior College, improve my grades, and reapply to UT in two years.

I accepted a scholarship to play baseball at Paris Junior College in Paris, Texas. Sadly, my academic ineptitude followed me to Paris, and I flunked out after only one semester. Consequently, I was available when my high school teammate, Tommy Ragan, called to see if I was interested in playing ball in the spring of 1967.

I was excited to get an opportunity to play for the famous Paul Dean. I worked out for Coach Dean and he offered me a scholarship. When I informed him of my poor academic record, he assured me that would not be a problem.

A poor academic record did not preclude admittance to the University of Plano, baseball talent or money would suffice. The University of Plano was a popular destination for academically challenged young men eager to avoid the draft, which would lead to service in the Vietnam War.

The University of Plano was founded by Dr. Robert Morris. A native of New Jersey, Morris was a graduate of Fordham Law school and served in the United States Navy during World War II. After the war Morris along with Senator Joseph McCarthy became crusaders against communists.

Senator McCarthy grabbed headlines in 1950 when he alleged that communists and Soviet spies had infiltrated the United States Federal Government, Universities, the film industry and elsewhere. This was at a time in America when Cold War tensions fueled fears of communist subversion. The so called "Red Scare" led to Senate investigations of alleged communists.

Robert Morris was Chief counsel to the Senate judiciary subcommittee on internal security from 1951 to 1953, and again from 1956 to 1958. During this period Americans feared communist infiltration at every level of life. Senator McCarthy fanned the flame of that fear.

Eventually McCarthy was discredited and today "McCarthyism" is a term used to mean demagogic, reckless, and unsubstantiated accusations. Historian William Bennent wrote:

> "McCarthy addressed a real problem: disloyal elements within the U.S. Government. But his approach to this real problem was to cause untold grief to the country he claimed to love. Worst of all, McCarthy besmirched the honorable cause of anti-communism. He discredited legitimate efforts to counter Soviet subversion of American Institutions."[1]

After an unsuccessful campaign for a United States Senate seat from New Jersey in 1958, Morris moved to Texas to become President of the University of Dallas. By this time Morris was a Nationally known conservative firebrand who wrote a National syndicated newspaper column called "Around the World."

In 1962 Morris resigned from his position as President of the University of Dallas to start his own University. While plans for the new college were being finalized Morris made another foray into politics.

In 1964 Morris ran for the United States Senate from Texas. He lost in the Republican primary to George H.W. Bush. Bush lost in the general election to incumbent Ralph Yarborough, a Liberal Democrat. After his latest defeat in the political arena Morris turned his attention back to academics.

On May 8, 1964 Robert Morris obtained a charter from the state of Texas for his new college. The University of Plano was chartered as a private, coeducational, nondenominational institution. His charter secure, Morris borrowed $250,000 from Republic National Life of Dallas and purchased 700 acres of land 20 miles north of Dallas on the outskirts of Plano, Texas.

Next Morris raised $600,000 from a bond issue and began construction of classrooms, dormitories, a Student Union building, and cafeteria on the sprawling Plano campus. Morris planned to sell some of the acreage to help endow his college. The Dallas area was experiencing rapid growth and pushed residential development north to Plano increasing the value of Morris' acreage.

The University of Plano began operation in the fall of 1965. Since construction at the Plano campus was unfinished, the first classes were held in a rented building on Pearl street in downtown Dallas.

As construction neared completion at the Plano campus, Morris acquired an exotic building that became the symbol of the University of Plano.

The Federation of Malaysia built a $375,000 pavilion at the New York World's Fair. At the close of the fair Robert Morris used his influence to persuade the Malaysian Government to donate the building to the University of Plano. The building was dismantled, shipped to Plano and reconstructed at a cost of $50,000. The building contained 12,000 sq. ft. and provided the University with nine classrooms, seven administration offices, eight faculty offices and two student lounges.

The Malaysian building was very distinctive, topped with an Asian-style pagoda which served as the trademark of the University of Plano. The unique image was used on literature and advertisement for the University.

On April 2, 1966 a delegation from the Malaysian government joined Dr. Morris along with school and city officials to formally dedicate the new University. Dr. Morris used the occasion to explain his vision for the University of Plano.

"The heart and center of the University will be the Liberal Arts college, devoted as all true Universities must be, in a search for truth on a fundamental basis." Morris said. "However, the new University will be unique because it will feature a college of developmental education in addition to the College of Liberal Arts."

"The college of developmental education will be devoted to the reclamation of potentially excellent students who have dropped out of other colleges and universities for a variety of reasons other than basic capabilities.

"The developmental college will explore the causes of academic failure and attempt to remedy the problem."[2]

Dr. Morris had personal motivation for creating the college of developmental education. His son, Willie Morris, experienced learning disabilities caused by neurological problems. Intense therapy enabled Willie to eventually enroll in regular classes although he still had learning difficulties.

Morris believed there were millions of other students who were intelligent but were being denied a college education due to problems similar to Willie's. The college of developmental education would use methods developed at the institute for the achievement of human potential in Philadelphia to correct these learning disabilities.

I lost my college deferment when I flunked out at Paris. Before I could enroll at Plano and reapply for my college deferment, I was called in for my pre-draft army physical. If I passed the physical, I was in the army and baseball would have to wait.

Fortunately, when the army doctor saw my left leg, scared by three surgeries, and learned I had recovered from osteomyelitis I was classified 4-f. The doctor informed me the disease could return at any time and therefore I was unfit for military service.

I suppose I was a "potentially excellent" student since I was finally admitted to the University of Plano for the 1967 spring semester. Coach Dean fielded a decent team that spring, made up of players who had failed academically at other baseball programs.

We started slowly winning only two of our first eleven games. However, we had a strong finish winning six in a row for a final first season record of eight wins and nine losses.

I was enrolled in the college of developmental education but also took 12 hours in the liberal arts college. Sadly, I failed again. Coach Dean said I would have to sit out the fall semester, but he would try to get me back in school for the spring semester.

In January of 1968 Coach Dean arranged a meeting with Dr. Robert Morris in an attempt to get me back in school for the spring baseball season. I was nervous to be meeting the founder and President of the

University and I expected tough questions concerning my past academic failures and how I planned to correct them.

We arrived at Dr. Morris' office and found him flanked by the Dean of the Liberal Arts college and the Dean of the Developmental College, after introductions, Coach Dean said, "Dr. Morris, we need Duncan out there foggin' 'em in this spring." Dr. Morris looked at me and asked only one question.

"Are you going to do better, son?"

I stammered a "yes, sir" and I was back in school.[3]

That was the first time Coach Dean saved my college career, it would not be the last.

I never knew whether or not it was the developmental education program that reclaimed my academic career, but I had an excellent year passing 15 hours in the liberal arts college with a "B" average. Evidently, I was a prime example of how the developmental education program turned college dropouts into academic success.

The next time Coach Dean saved my college career was in the spring of 1969. The baseball program was flourishing, Coach Dean was signing high school prospects as well as Junior College players. I was maintaining a "B" average in the college of liberal arts. Everything was great until I went to a party.

I attended a University of Plano fraternity party along with two other Plano baseball players. The party was at a lake near Plano and of course alcohol was involved. We ended up in a fight with some other Plano students before the night was over.

The following Monday I was in history class when two Plano policemen came in and arrested me. I was handcuffed, taken to the City of Plano jail and charged with assault and battery. Apparently the two other baseball players were not identified as I was the only one arrested and charged.

I expected harsh treatment, dismissal from the baseball team, loss of scholarship and therefore no college education. None of that happened. Coach Dean bailed me out of jail and managed to get the charges dropped. Once again Coach Dean saved my college education and baseball career.

Paul Dean left the University of Plano after the 1969 baseball season. He returned to professional baseball accepting a job with the Tulsa Oilers. Tulsa was a St. Louis Cardinal farm team that played in the Triple A

American Association. Paul's official title was director, Tulsa Oilers baseball camp. Also, on the Oiler's payroll were Paul's Barnstorming buddy Satchel Paige and former gashouse gang hero Pepper Martin.

In the summer of 1969, I received a call from Steve Adair, who I knew from high school. When I was a senior at Hillcrest High School Steve was doing his student teaching. Steve was a recent graduate of Texas Christian University (TCU) where he played baseball, football and ran track.

Jimmy Adair, Steve's father was a baseball lifer. He played 10 years of professional baseball. All but one year in the Minor Leagues. In 1931 he played in 18 games with the Chicago Cubs. Jimmy managed in the Minors for 15 years before becoming a Major League coach. He was a coach for the Chicago White Sox (1951 – 1953) Baltimore Orioles (1957 – 1961 Houston Colt 45's/Astros (1962 – 1965). After leaving the field he became a scout. In 1970 Jimmy Adair was a scout for the Kansas City Royals.

"I heard Daffy left Plano" Steve said to me. "Who do I talk to about the baseball coaching job?"[4]

I gave him the information needed and in February 1970 Steve Adair was hired as athletic director and baseball coach at the University of Plano.

Steve Adair was young, aggressive and determined to upgrade the University of Plano baseball program. He solicited donations from local merchants and supporters of the University baseball team. His efforts resulted in an infusion of funds which he used to purchase new uniforms and equipment.

Adair also changed the name of the baseball team from Plano Trailblazers to Plano Pirates. He scheduled 40 games for the 1970 season and his father helped recruit new players.

Also, in 1970 Robert Morris again campaigned for the United States Senate seat from Texas and again he lost to George H.W. Bush in the Republican primary. Incumbent Senator Ralph Yarborough lost in the Democratic primary to Lloyd Bentsen. In the general election Bentsen defeated Bush, taking 53.5 percent of the vote.

I continued to make good grades and was scheduled to graduate after the 1971 spring semester. I planned to pursue professional baseball after I graduated. My plans were shattered when the disease that plagued me as a teenager returned, necessitating more surgery. My baseball career was over, however, I managed to graduate with the class of 1971. I was the only one in my family with a college degree, a degree I would have never obtained without Paul Dean's help.

The University of Plano survived only another five years. Most Universities have endowments, usually amassed through donations. The majority of the University of Plano's endowment funds were based on land speculation. When the Institution needed money, Dr. Morris sold off some of his 700 acres in small parcels which had appreciated in value.

The land speculation endowment plan worked well until the land boom went bust during the 1975 recession. The University underwent a series of lawsuits and land auctions until it officially closed in July of 1976. At the final auction of 20 buildings and 19 acres Dr. Morris expressed disappointment as he watched his dream die.

"It's easy to get choked up about the situation" he said. "But this is reality and I have to face it."[5]

After the demise of his University, Robert Morris returned to New Jersey. He continued to write his Nationally syndicated newspaper column and also lectured in the New York area. In 1984 Morris ran for the Senate one last time. He was defeated for the fourth time. Morris died of heart failure in 1997 at the age of 82.

Steve Adair found a soft place to land. He parlayed his success at the University of Plano (seven consecutive winning seasons and a 154 – 99 won – loss record) into a job at Southern Methodist University (SMU) in Dallas, Texas.

On July 11, 1976 Adair replaced Bob Finley as the SMU Mustangs head baseball coach. Bob Finley retired after suffering a futile 1975 season when his Mustangs won only 2 games while losing 36.

Adair was unable to revive the SMU baseball program and after the 1980 season SMU discontinued baseball. Athletic director Russ Potts dropped baseball and men's golf from SMU's intercollegiate athletic program in an effort to tighten athletic expenditures. Consequently, Steve Adair suffered the misfortune of overseeing the demise of two college baseball programs.

After 24 years in broadcasting, the final 12 years announcing "the game of the week" on television, Dizzy Dean was forced into retirement. Falstaff, Dizzy's long-time employer, no longer owned the "game of the week", the brewery was only one of several sponsors. Falstaff wanted to keep Dizzy, but the other sponsors decided to appeal to a different audience so Dizzy's contract was not renewed after the 1965 season.

Dizzy was financially secure and spent his retirement hunting, fishing, attending old- timer games, banquets and his favorite – celebrity golf tournaments. While at a celebrity golfing event in Lake Tahoe, California Dizzy complained of chest pains. He was hospitalized but left after two days without doctor's permission. Dizzy headed to Reno, Nevada for another of his favorite activities, gambling.

While having dinner with his wife in Reno, Dizzy suffered a severe heart attack. He was rushed to the hospital in critical condition. Paul was notified and hurried to Reno to be with his stricken brother. Two days later on July 17, 1974 Dizzy Dean died. He was 64 years old.

Over a thousand people traveled to Wiggins, Mississippi to attend Dizzy's funeral. The mourners included friends from all walks of life. Preachers, country singers, football coaches, politicians, businessmen, sports figures ex-teammates, merchants and farmers, people Dizzy had befriended over the years, all came to pay their final respects to the "Great One".

Paul was heartbroken. "I played second fiddle to Dizzy Dean and I'd do it again" he said. "I wish it was me instead of him because he probably enjoyed life more than I do."[6]

"I know this" Paul said "there ain't no way I'm gonna be separated from Diz for too long.

When my time comes Me 'n' Diz are gonna be back together again."[7]

After the funeral reporters asked Paul to describe Dizzy. "He was a front-runner, a natural, even when we were kids. He went out and was bold and I was glad to follow him because I got a kick out of him like everybody else."

"Diz believed in treating a fella right. We learned human beings were human beings. Diz didn't look at the color of your skin or how long your hair was. He looked at the individual. There wasn't no prejudice in Diz."

"I don't think he ever disliked anybody, but if he did, I'm gonna say five minutes was his limit."[8]

Los Angeles Times sportswriter Jim Murray wrote a poignant obituary:

"Well, we're all ten years older today. Dizzy Dean is dead and 1934 is gone forever. Another part of our youth fled. You look in the mirror and the small boy no longer smiles back at you. Just that sad old man Dizzy died the other day at the age of 11 or 12. The little boy in all of us died with him. But, for one brief shining afternoon in 1934 he brought joy to that dreary time when most needed it. If I know Diz he'll be calling God 'podner' and I hope he finds a golf course, a poker game and a slugger who's a sucker for a low outside fastball. Dizzy Dean, he might have been what baseball's all about."[9]

Paul left the Tulsa Drillers after the 1976 season. His health was deteriorating, he was overweight, and diabetic. After a mild heart attack in 1979 Paul spent most of his time in Arkansas where three of his four children lived.

On March 17, 1981, Paul died of heart failure in Springdale, Arkansas. He was survived by his wife Dorothy; two sons, Paul, Jr and Sandy; two daughters, Alma Ruth Bozeman and Dorothy Paula Patrick plus 15 grandchildren.

Dizzy always said Paul was the better pitcher and he may have been right. At age 21 Paul won 19 games including a no-hitter and also won 2 World Series games. Dizzy was still pitching in the Minor Leagues when he was 21. By the time Paul was 22 years old he had won 38 Major League games while losing 23. Dizzy's Major League record at age 22 was 19 wins and 15 losses. However, Paul never reached his potential because he was plagued with arm problems.

There is little doubt as to the cause of Paul's arm ailments, he pitched too many innings when he was so young. At age 17 when most boys are competing in high school, Paul pitched 175 innings against professional hitters. When he was a 20-year-old rookie with St. Louis Paul had already pitched 641 innings of Minor League ball plus many more Barnstorming with Dizzy.

In his first two years with St. Louis Frankie Frisch pitched Paul relentlessly. He started, relieved, pitching without proper rest, often every day. Paul was essentially finished after 1935 although he was only 22 years old. He played in the Majors for 7 more years but won only 12 more games. Paul never blamed Frisch or anyone else for his problems.

"I maybe asked for what happened to me" Paul said. "Frisch didn't cause my problems. Like Diz, I loved to pitch. I had a love and affection for the game. I had the desire. I just loved to pitch."[10]

Notes

FOREWORD

1 The Sporting News (St. Louis, Missouri) August 1, 1951 (Hereafter cited as news).
2 IBID.
3 IBID.

CHAPTER 1

1 Vince Staten, Ol' D iz – A Biography of Dizzy Dean (New York: Harper Collins, 1992) P.18 (Hereafter cited as Ol' D iz).
2 Robert Gregory, Diz – Dizzy Dean and baseball during the Great Depression (New York: Viking, 1992) P.25 (Hereafter cited as Diz).
3 J. Roy Stockton, The Gashouse Gang and a couple of other guys. (New York: A.S. Barnes, 1945) P.34 (Hereafter cited as Gang).
4 The life story of Dizzy Dean by Jack Sher. Sport Magazine (Hereafter cited as Sport).
5 Ol' D iz, P.22.
6 News, P.6.
7 Sport.
8 Conversations with Paul Dean 1967 – 1969 (Hereafter cited as Conversations).

9   Diz, P.28.
10 Dallas Morning News. (Dallas, TX) November 25, 1962 (Hereafter cited as Dallas News).

CHAPTER 2

1. Curt Smith, America's Dizzy Dean. (St. Louis: The Bethany Press, 1978) P.31 (Hereafter cited as Dizzy).
2. Diz, P.29.
3. Sport.
4. IBID.
5. Ol' D iz, P.27.
6. IBID, P.28.
7. Dallas News, March 29, 1984.
8. Sport.
9. Diz, P.36.
10. IBID, P.32.

CHAPTER 3

1. Diz, P.30.
2. IBID, P.35.
3. Ol' D iz, P.36.
4. Diz, P.35.
5. Baseball's Immortals, The story of Dizzy Dean. Hall of Fame series. (The home Plate Press, Cooperstown, N.Y. 1953) P.8.

CHAPTER 4

1. The Dizzy Dean Baseball Dictionary Falstaff Advertising Brochure.
2. Diz, P. 36.
3. Ol' Diz, P.41.
4. Lee Lowenfish, Branch Rickey – Baseb all's Fe rociou s Gent lem an (Lincoln: University of Nebraska Press, 2009) P.150.
5. IBID.

CHAPTER 5

1. Dizzy, P.24.
2. The Houston Post (Houston, TX March 18, 1930).

3 Diz, P.37.
4 Ol' D iz, P.44.
5 Diz, P.44.
6 Gang, P.38.
7 The St. Louis Star and Times (St. Louis, Missouri) August 20, 1931 (Hereafter cited as Star).
8 Diz, P. 46.
9 Longview News – Journal (Longview, TX) August, 28, 1931.
10 Conversations.

CHAPTER 6

1 The Eagle (Bryan, TX) August 9, 1930
2 Amarillo Times (Amarillo, TX) August 24, 1930.
3 The Brownsville Herald (Brownsville, TX) September 1, 1930.
4 Ol' D iz, P.55.
5 IBID.
6 BabeRuth.com. Official website of Babe Ruth.
7 Daily Capital News (Washington, D.C) August 29, 1931
8 Donald Hoenig, The October Heroes, (New York: Simon and Schuster, 1979) P.278 (Hereafter cited as Heroes)
9 Diz, P.50.
10 IBID.
11 BabeRuth.com official website of Babe Ruth.
12 Star, September 30, 1930.
13 IBID.
14 IBID.
15 IBID, October 3, 1930.
16 IBID, December 15, 1930.
17 Ol' D iz, P.59.
18 Star, December 15, 1930.

CHAPTER 7

1 Conversations.
2 Sport.
3 Diz, P. 50
4 Conversations.
5 News.
6 Dizzy, P.46.
7 Gang, P.44.

8   IBID.
9   Diz, P.54.
10 The St. Louis Post-Dispatch (St. Louis, Missouri) March 31, 1931 (Hereafter cited as Dispatch).
11 Dizzy, P.33.
12 Star, March 17, 1931.
13 Diz, P.58.
14 Star, March 17, 1931.
15 Diz, P.59.
16 Star, March 30, 1931.
17 IBID.
18 IBID.
19 Moberly Monitor (Moberly, Missouri) May 2, 1931.
20 The El Paso Herald-Post (El Paso, Texas) May 2, 1931.

CHAPTER 8

1   The busy Deans by Arthur Mann Sport Magazine, June 10, 1935.
2   News, March 26, 1931.
3   IBID.
4   Dispatch, May 5, 1931.
5   Star, May 7, 1931.
6   The Cleveland Plain Dealer (Cleveland, Ohio) May 7, 1931.
7   The Baltimore Sun (Baltimore, Maryland) November 9, 1931.
8   News, December 27, 1961.
9   The Coshocton Tribune (Coshocton, Ohio) June 2, 1931.
10 IBID.
11 The Maryville Daily Forum (Maryville, Missouri) June 22, 1931.
12 Star, June 27, 1931.
13 Dispatch, August 9, 1931.
14 The Sheboygan Press (Sheboygan, Wisconsin) September 26, 1931.

CHAPTER 9

1   Dallas News, May 18, 1931.
2   IBID.
3   Sport.
4   Diz, P.63
5   IBID.
6   Dallas News, June 16, 1931.
7   D izz y D ean : He's not so du mb! The Saturday Evening Post July 15, 1951.

8   Dallas News, July 31, 1931.
9   Diz, P.37.
10 Dallas News, March 31, 1931.
11 The Amarillo Globe-Times (Amarillo, Texas) August 7, 1931.
12 Dallas News, August 19, 1931.
13 Star, August 18, 1931.
14 Longview News-Journal (Longview, Texas) August 20, 1931.
15 Dallas News, August 30, 1931.
16 Diz, P.69.
17 Leroy "Satchel" Paige as told to Hal Lebovitz, Pit ch in' M an -Sat ch el Pa ige's Ow n St or y (Westport, CT.: Meckler Publishing, 1992) P.72.
18 Diz, P.70.
19 Corsicana semi-weekly Light (Corsicana, Texas) Sept. 22, 1931.
20 Diz, P.73.
21 Sikeston Standard (Sikeston, Missouri) October 13, 1931.
22 Arkansas Gazette (Little Rock, Arkansas) October 21, 1931.
23 Diz, P.76.

CHAPTER 10

1   Sport.
2   Ol' Diz, P.119.
3   Diz, P.91.
4   Jefferson City Post-Tribune (Jefferson City, Missouri) May 2, 1932.
5   Daniel Okrent and Steve Wulf, Baseball Anecdotes (New York: Harper and Row, 1989) P.114 (Hereafter cited as Anecdotes).
6   IBID.
7   Babe Ruth's called shot. Wikipedia.
8   IBID.
9   The Kansas City Star (Kansas City, Missouri) April 10, 1932.
10 The Evening Independent (Massillon, Ohio) April 22, 1932.
11 Moberly Monitor (Moberly, Missouri) May 10, 1932.
12 IBID.
13 Dispatch, September 24, 1932.
14 Harrisburg Telegraph (Harrisburg, Pennsylvania) September 29, 1932.
15 The Courier-Journal (Louisville, Kentucky) June 26, 1932.
16 The Evening Independent (Massillon, Ohio) July 12, 1932.
17 Jon Daly, Billy Southworth, Society for American Baseball Research (SABR) Biography project.
18 The Star Tribune (Minneapolis, Minnesota) July 21, 1932.
19 The Evening Independent (Massillon, Ohio) August 24, 1932.

20 Kansas City Star (Kansas City, Missouri) August 31, 1932.
21 The Repository (Canton, Ohio) August 31, 1932.
22 The Indianapolis Star (Indianapolis, Indiana) September 1, 1932.
23 The Jefferson City Post (Jefferson City, Missouri) September 22, 1932.

CHAPTER 11

1   Dispatch, January 15, 1932.
2   Star, January 16, 1932.
3   Dispatch, January 16, 1932.
4   Star, January 16, 1932.
5   Dispatch, January 17, 1932.
6   Star, January 18, 1932.
7   News, January 28, 1932.
8   Star, January 25, 1932.
9   IBID, February 15, 1932.
10 Dispatch, February 6, 1932.
11 Star, February 17, 1932.
12 IBID, Feb 20, 1932.
13 Jefferson City Post-Tribune (Jefferson City, Missouri) March 3, 1932.
14 Dispatch, March 2, 1932.
15 IBID, February 12, 1932.
16 IBID, March 8, 1932.
17 Tallahassee Democrat (Tallahassee, Florida) March 10, 1932.
18 Star, March 12, 1932.
19 Dispatch, March 11, 1932.
20 Star, March 26, 1932.
21 Gashouse Gang, P.24.
22 Star, May 28, 1932.
23 IBID, May 5, 1932.
24 Ol' D iz, P.79.
25 Dispatch, May 13, 1932.
26 Star, June 3, 1932.
27 IBID, June 6, 1932.
28 IBID, June 3, 1932.
29 IBID, June 15, 1932.
30 Dispatch, June 15, 1932.
31 Star, June 16, 1932.
32 Dispatch, June 15, 1932.
33 Star, June 29, 1932.
34 Dispatch, June 30, 1932.

35 Star, August 9, 1932.
36 IBID, August 25, 1932.
37 IBID.
38 Dispatch, September 24, 1932.
39 Star, September 24, 1932.

CHAPTER 12

1   The Courier-Journal (Louisville, Kentucky) March 8, 1933.
2   Mike Lynch, Art Shires, Society for American Baseball research (SABR) biography project. (Hereafter cited as Shires SABR).
3   IBID.
4   The Sandusky Register (Sandusky, Ohio) Aril 29, 1933.
5   The Courier-Journal (Louisville, Kentucky) May 18, 1933.
6   Palladium-Item (Richmond, Indiana) May 18, 1933.
7   Star Tribune (Minneapolis, Minnesota) May 24, 1933.
8   The Sheboygan Press (Sheboygan, Wisconsin) May 27, 1933.
9   The Circleville Herald (Circleville, Ohio) June 8, 1933.
10 Star, June 15, 1933.
11 The Minneapolis Star (Minneapolis, Minnesota) June 15, 1933.

CHAPTER 13

1   The Evening Independent (Massillon, Ohio) July 26, 1933.
2   The Minneapolis Star (Minneapolis, Minnesota) July 14, 1933.
3   Star, August 31, 1933.
4   The Tribune (Coshocton, Ohio) August 1, 1933.
5   The Indianapolis News (Indianapolis, Indiana) August 9, 1933.
6   The Evening News (Wilkes-Barre, Pennsylvania) August 24, 1933.
7   Salt Lake Telegram (Salt Lake City, Utah) October 9, 1933.
8   Star Tribune (Minneapolis, Minnesota) August 25, 1933.
9   The Cincinnati Enquirer (Cincinnati, Ohio) August 31, 1933.
10 Shamokin News-Dispatch (Shamokin, Pennsylvania) September 13, 1933.
11 The Minneapolis Star (Minneapolis, Minnesota) September 5, 1933.
12 Star-Tribune (Minneapolis, Minnesota) September 12, 1933.
13 The Minneapolis Star (Minneapolis, Minnesota) September 26, 1933.

CHAPTER 14

1   Dispatch, February 19, 1933.
2   IBID, March 5, 1933.

3   Diz, P.97
4   Star, April 7, 1933.
5   IBID.
6   Salt Lake Telegram (Salt Lake City, Utah) April 28, 1933.
7   Star, May 8, 1933.
8   Gerald Eskenazi, The Lip (New York: William Morrow and Company INC) 1993 P.64 (Hereafter cited as The Lip).
9   Star, May 25, 1933.
10 Ol' D iz, P.90.
11 IBID, P.91.
12 Diz, P.105.
13 The Morning Call (Allentown, Pennsylvania) July 9, 1933.
14 Star, July 10, 1933.
15 Diz, P.105
16 Dispatch, July 11, 1933.
17 Star, July 22, 1933.
18 IBID.
19 The Gashouse Gang and I, The Saturday Evening Post, July 18, 1959.
20 Star, July 25, 1933.
21 Diz, P.11.
22 Star, July 25, 1933.
23 Ol' D iz, P.93
24 The Salem News (Salem, Ohio) September 2, 1933.
25 Star, September 14, 1933.
26 Star, September 14, 1933.
27 Dispatch, September 17, 1933.
28 Salt Lake Telegram (Salt Lake City, Utah) October 5, 1933.
29 IBID, October 2, 1933.
30 Leroy (Satchel) Paige – M ayb e I'll Pit ch For ever (As told to David Lipman). (University of Nebraska Press) P.14.
31 Chuck Connors Quotes. A – Z Quotes.
32 Timothy M. Gay – Satch, Dizzy, and Rapid Roberts (New York: Simon & Schuster) 2010 P.56.
33 The Los Angeles Times (Los Angeles, California) October 16, 1933 (Hereafter cited as L.A. Times).
34 IBID, October 18, 1933.
35 IBID, October 16, 1933.
36 Star, October 26, 1933.
37 IBID.
38 The Big Springs Daily Herald (Big Springs, Texas) November 3, 1933.

39 The Marshall News Messenger (Marshall, Texas) November 5, 1933.
40 Star, December 23, 1933.

CHAPTER 15

1 Leo Durocher; Nice Guys Finish Last (New York: Simon & Schuster) 1975. (Hereafter cited as Nice Guys.
2 IBID, P.67
3 IBID.
4 Gerald Eskenazi, The Lip (New York: William Morrow and Company, INC) 1993. P.71 (Hereafter cited as The Lip).
5 Peter Golenbock, The Spirit of St. Louis (New York: Harper Collins Publishers INC.) 2000. (Hereafter cited as Spirit).
6 Star, January 18, 1934.
7 IBID, January 16, 1934.
8 IBID.
9 The New York Herald-Tribune (New York City, New York) January 25, 1934.
10 Dispatch, March 5, 1934.
11 Star, January 31, 1934.
12 Dispatch, March 5, 1934.
13 IBID, March 6, 1934.
14 IBID, March 10, 1934.
15 IBID, March 6, 1934.
16 IBID, March 12, 1934.
17 IBID.
18 Nice Guys.
19 Star, March 17, 1934.
20 Andy Sturgill, Spud Davis, Society for American Baseball Research (SABR) Biography Project.
21 IBID.
22 Spirit, P.152.
23 Cort Bitty, Ripper Collins, Society for American Baseball Research (SABR) Biography Project.
24 Spirit, P.167.
25 The Cincinnati Enquirer (Cincinnati, Ohio) April 13, 1934.
26 IBID.
27 IBID, April 17, 1934.
28 IBID.
29 Nice Guys, P.74.
30 Donald Honig, Baseball America (New York: Simon & Schuster) 1985 P.196 (Hereafter cited as America).

31 Thomas Barthel, <u>The Fierce Fun of Ducky Medwick</u> (Lanham, Maryland: Scarecrow Press, INC.) 2003 P.10 (Hereafter cited as Ducky).
32 <u>IBID</u>, P.26.
33 <u>America</u>, P.196.
34 Ernie Orsatti, Wikipedia.
35 <u>IBID</u>.
36 <u>Spirit</u>, P.160.
37 Bill Hallahan, Wikipedia.
38 Bill Walker, Wikipedia.
39 <u>IBID</u>.

CHAPTER 16

1 Bob Broeg, <u>The Pilot Light and the Gashouse Gang</u> (St. Louis, Missouri: The Bethany Press) 1980 P.132 (Hereafter cited as Pilot).
2 <u>Spirit</u>, P.172.
3 <u>Pilot</u>, P.132.
4 <u>Star</u>, April 17, 1934.
5 <u>Diz</u>, P.130.
6 <u>IBID</u>, P.131.
7 The Moberly Monitor (Moberly, Missouri) April 20, 1934.
8 The New York American (New York City, New York) April, 19, 1934.
9 <u>Diz</u>, P.132.
10 <u>IBID</u>, P.133.
11 <u>IBID</u>, P.134.
12 <u>Post</u>.
13 <u>Diz</u>, P.136.
14 <u>IBID</u>, P.138.
15 <u>IBID</u>.
16 <u>Gang</u>, P.157.
17 <u>Star</u>, May 16, 1934.
18 <u>Diz</u>, P.145.
19 The Miami News (Miami, Florida) May 19, 1934.
20 <u>Dallas News</u>, March 27, 1966.
21 <u>Star</u>, May 17, 1934.
22 <u>Diz</u>, P.149.
23 The New York Daily News (New York City, New York) May 22, 1934.
24 <u>Star</u>, May 26, 1934.
25 <u>Dispatch</u>, May 26, 1934.
26 <u>IBID</u>.
27 The Philadelphia Inquirer (Philadelphia, Pennsylvania) May 28, 1934.

28 Dispatch, May 31, 1934.
29 Star, June 1, 1934.
30 Diz, P.152.
31 Dispatch, June 2, 1934.
32 IBID, June 11, 1934.
33 IBID, June 18, 1934.
34 IBID.
35 Star, June 22, 1934.
36 The Brooklyn Eagle (Brooklyn, New York) June 23, 1934.
37 IBID.
38 The Brooklyn Times-Union (Brooklyn, New York) June 23, 1934.
39 IBID.
40 Dispatch, June 24, 1934.
41 The New York Evening Journal (New York City, New York) June 26, 1934.
42 IBID.
43 Star, July 3, 1934.
44 IBID.
45 Dispatch, July 9, 1934.
46 Ol' D iz, P.118.

CHAPTER 17

1 The Austin American Statesman (Austin, Texas) July 5, 1934.
2 Diz, P.158.
3 The New York Daily News (New York, New York) July 11, 1934.
4 The New York Sun (New York, New York) July 14, 1934.
5 The New York World-Telegram (New York, New York) July 11, 1934.
6 Ducky, P.70.
7 Diz, P.158.
8 The Star-Gazette (Elmira, New York) July 11, 1934.
9 Diz, P.161.
10 The Brooklyn Eagle (Brooklyn, New York) July 16, 1934.
11 IBID.
12 Gang, P.35.
13 Dispatch, July 22, 1934.
14 Dayton Daily News (Dayton, Ohio) July 26, 1934.
15 Dispatch, July 24, 1934.
16 The New York Times (New York, New York) July 25, 1934.
17 Dispatch, July 25, 1934.
18 IBID.
19 The New York World-Telegram (New York, New York) July 26, 1934.

20 IBID.
21 IBID.
22 The Pittsburgh Post-Gazette (Pittsburgh, Pennsylvania) July 26, 1934.
23 Dispatch, August 2, 1934.
24 IBID, August 6, 1934.
25 IBID, August 9, 1934.
26 IBID.
27 Star, August 9, 1934.
28 Diz, P.166.
29 The Austin American Statesman (Austin, Texas) August 12, 1934.
30 Diz, P.167.
31 The St. Louis Globe-Democrat (St. Louis Missouri) August 14, 1934. (Hereafter cited as Globe).
32 Star, August 15, 1934.
33 Diz, P.169
34 Dispatch, August 15, 1934.
35 IBID.

CHAPTER 18

1 The Lip, P.79.
2 Globe, August 18, 1934.
3 The Wisconsin State Journal (Madison, Wisconsin) August 21, 1934.
4 Diz, P.175.
5 Star, August 20, 1934.
6 IBID.
7 IBID.
8 Star, September 4, 1934.
9 Dispatch, September 4, 1934.
10 Star, September 4, 1934.
11 IBID.
12 Star, September 4, 1934.
13 Diz, P.132.
14 The Philadelphia Inquirer (Philadelphia, Pennsylvania) September 11, 1934.
15 The New York Times (New York City, New York) September 15, 1934.
16 The New York Herald-Tribune (New York City, New York) September 16, 1934.
17 The New York Daily News (New York City, New York) September 17, 1934.
18 The New York Post (New York City, New York) September 17, 1934.
19 The New York Times (New York City, New York) September 22, 1934.
20 Ol' D iz, P.129.
21 The Booklyn Daily Eagle (Brooklyn, New York) September 22, 1934.

22 IBID.
23 The Chicago Tribune (Chicago, Illinois) September 22, 1934.
24 The Morning News (Wilmington, Delaware) September 22, 1934.
25 The San Bernadino County Sun (San Bernadino, California) September 22, 1934.
26 Dispatch, September 22, 1934.
27 The San Bernadino County Sun (San Bernadino, California) September 22, 1934.
28 Dispatch, September 22, 1934.
29 IBID, September 23, 1934.
30 IBID.
31 The Brooklyn Daily Eagle (Brooklyn, New York) September 22, 1934.
32 IBID.
33 The Cincinnati Enquirer (Cincinnati, Ohio) September 23, 1934.
34 The New York Post (New York City, New York) September 23, 1934.
35 Dispatch, September 30, 1934.
36 Globe, September 30, 1934.
37 Brooklyn Times (Brooklyn, New York) September 30, 1934.
38 Dispatch, October 1, 1934.
39 Ducky, P.75.
40 Star, October 1, 1934.
41 IBID.
42 IBID.

CHAPTER 19

1 Charlie Gehringer, Wikipedia.
2 Lawrence S. Ritter, The Glory of Their Times (New York: McMillan and Company, INC., 1966) P.282
3 IBID.
4 IBID.
5 Hank Greenberg, Wikipedia.
6 Gregory H. Wolf, Schoolboy Rowe, Society for American Baseball Research (SABR) Biography Project.
7 Detroit Free Press (Detroit, Michigan) August 6, 1932.
8 Faye Vincent, The only game in town (New York: Simon & Schuster, 2006) P.8
9 IBID.
10 Gregory H. Wolf, General Crowder, Society for American Baseball Research (SABR) Biography Project.
11 Dispatch, October 2, 1934.
12 IBID.

CHAPTER 20

1. Dispatch, October 2, 1934.
2. New York Daily News (New York City, New York) October 3, 1934.
3. Detroit Free Press (Detroit, Michigan) October 2, 1934.
4. Damon Runyon, Wikipedia.
5. Star, October 3, 1934.
6. IBID.
7. IBID.
8. The Lip, P.83.
9. The Tampa Tribune (Tampa, Florida) October 3, 1934.
10. Ol' D iz, P.140.
11. Star-Gazette (Elmira, New York) October 2, 1934.
12. The New York Times (New York City, New York) October 2, 1934. (Hereafter cited as N.Y. Times).
13. IBID.
14. Dallas News, October 3, 1934.
15. N.Y. Times, October 3, 1934.
16. Ol' D iz, P.139.
17. The Lip, P.82.
18. The Los Angeles Times (Los Angeles, California) October 5, 1934.
19. IBID.
20. IBID.
21. Dispatch, October 4, 1934.
22. L.A. Times, October 4, 1934.
23. IBID, October 5, 1934.
24. Star, October 4, 1934.
25. Dispatch, October 6, 1934.
26. IBID.
27. IBID.
28. The New York American (New York City, New York) October 5, 1934.
29. Dispatch, October 5, 1934.
30. IBID.
31. The Detroit Free Press (Detroit, Michigan) October 6, 1934. (Hereafter cited as Detroit).
32. Chief Hogsett, Wikipedia.
33. Detroit, October 6, 1934.
34. Dispatch, October 6, 1934.
35. Star, October 6, 1934.
36. L.A. Times, October 6, 1934.

400

37 Dispatch, October 6, 1934.
38 IBID.
39 N.Y. Times, October 7, 1934.
40 L.A. Times, October 7, 1934.
41 IBID.
42 Gang, P.132.
43 Dispatch, October 7, 1934.
44 L.A. Times, October 7, 1934.
45 Star, October 8, 1934.
46 Diz, P.227.
47 Dispatch, October 8, 1934.
48 IBID.
49 Star, October 8, 1934.
50 San Bernadino County Sun (San Bernadino, California) October 8, 1934.
51 Nice Guys, P.86.
52 Diz, P.228.
53 Dispatch, October 9, 1934.
54 The Lip, P.83.
55 Chicago Daily News (Chicago, Illinois) October 9, 1934.
56 N.Y. Times, October 9, 1934.
57 IBID.
58 IBID.
59 Star, October 9, 1934.
60 N.Y. Times, October 9, 1934.
61 Star, October 9, 1934.
62 The Atlanta Constitution (Atlanta, Georgia) October 9, 1934.
63 Spirit, P.192.
64 IBID.
65 IBID.
66 The New York Sun (New York City, New York) October 9, 1934.
67 Detroit, October 9, 1934.
68 Gang, P.134.
69 Nice Guys, P.89.
70 IBID. P.90
71 Ducky, P.80.
72 Pilot, P.142.
73 The Lip, P.84.
74 Spirit, P.194.
75 Nice Guys, P.91.
76 Spirit, P.193.
77 IBID.

78 IBID.
79 The New York Sun (New York City, New York) October 10, 1934.

CHAPTER 21

1 Diz, P.239.
2 Dispatch.
3 The St. Cloud Times (St. Cloud, Minnesota) October 30, 1934.
4 The Sandusky Register (Sandusky, Ohio) October 12, 1934.
5 IBID.
6 IBID.
7 Timothy M. Gay, Satch, Dizzy, & Rapid Robert (New York: Simon & Schuster, 2010) P.78 (Hereafter cited as Rapid Robert).
8 The Moline Dispatch (Moline, Illinois) March 1, 1934.
9 N.Y. Times, October 11, 1934.
10 The Wichita Eagle (Wichita, Kansas) October 12, 1934.
11 The Philadelphia Enquirer (Philadelphia, Pennsylvania) October 12, 1934.
12 The Des Moines Tribune (Des Moines, Iowa) October 13, 1934.
13 Patricia C. McKissack and Fredrick McKissack, Jr, Black Diamond (New York: Scholastic INC. 1994) P.82 (Hereafter cited as Diamond).
14 IBID, P.63.
15 The Argus Ledger (Sioux Falls, South Dakota) October 15, 1934.
16 The Manhatten Mercury (Manhatten, Kansas) October 13, 1934.
17 The Des Moines Tribune (Des Moines, Iowa) October 14, 1934.
18 Chicago Tribune (Chicago, Illinois) October 15, 1934.
19 Rapid Robert, P.87.
20 Washington Post (Washington D.C.) October 17, 1934.
21 IBID.
22 IBID.
23 Cincinnati Enquirer (Cincinnati, Ohio) October 17, 1934.
24 N.Y. Times, October 18, 1934.
25 IBID.
26 Pottsville Republican (Pottsville, Pennsylvania) October 18, 1934.
27 IBID.
28 Brooklyn Daily Eagle (Brooklyn, New York) October 18, 1934.
29 Columbus Dispatch (Columbus, Ohio) October 21, 1934.
30 Rapid Robert, P.94.
31 IBID, P.97.
32 Cleveland Plain Dealer (Cleveland, Ohio) October 25, 1934.
33 Pittsburgh Post-Gazette (Pittsburgh, Pennsylvania) October 25, 1934.
34 Rapid Robert, P.99.

35 IBID, P.102.
36 Pittsburgh Post-Gazette (Pittsburgh, Pennsylvania) October 24, 1934.
37 IBID.
38 Washington Post (Washington D.C.) October 24, 1934.
39 IBID.
40 IBID.
41 L.A. Times, October 25, 1934.
42 IBID.
43 Chicago Tribune (Chicago, Illinois) October 27, 1934.
44 IBID.
45 Washington Post (Washington D.C.) October 27, 1934.
46 IBID.
47 Ol' D iz, P.156.
48 L.A. Times, December 6,1934.
49 IBID.
50 N.Y. Times, December 21, 1934.
51 IBID.
52 Diz, P.244.
53 N.Y. Times, December 30, 1934.
54 IBID.

CHAPTER 22

1 Dallas News, January 29, 1935.
2 IBID.
3 Hot Springs, Arkansas, Wikipedia.
4 Austin American Statesman (Austin, Texas) February 19, 1935.
5 The New York Chronicle (New York City, New York) February 27, 1935.
6 Dispatch, March 4, 1935.
7 The Minneapolis Star (Minneapolis, Minnesota) February 27, 1935.
8 The Tampa Tribune (Tampa, Florida) March 11, 1935.
9 L.A. Times, March 3, 1935.
10 Globe, March 14, 1935.
11 Star, April 17, 1935.
12 Diz, P.254.
13 Dispatch, May 1, 1935.
14 The Baltimore Sun (Baltimore, Maryland) May 6, 1935.
15 Diz, P.256.
16 Brooklyn Daily Eagle (Brooklyn, New York) May 14, 1935.
17 IBID.
18 N.Y. Times.

19 IBID, May 8, 1935.
20 The Dayton Herald (Dayton, Ohio) May 22, 1935.
21 Diz, P.256.
22 IBID.
23 Brooklyn Daily Eagle (Brooklyn, New York) May 27, 1935.
24 IBID.
25 Star, June 5, 1935.
26 Ducky, P.93.
27 IBID.
28 Ol' D iz, P.165.
29 Dispatch, June 6, 1935.
30 IBID, June 5, 1935.
31 IBID.
32 Star, June 9, 1935.
33 IBID, July 2, 1935.
34 IBID, July 5, 1935.
35 IBID.
36 IBID.
37 IBID.
38 The Minneapolis Star (Minneapolis, Minnesota) July 6, 1935.
39 Star, July 6, 1935.
40 IBID.
41 The Tampa Bay Times (Tampa Bay, Florida) July 7, 1935.

CHAPTER 23

1   Diz, P.264.
2   Dispatch, July 15, 1935.
3   N.Y. Times, July 15, 1935.
4   The Boston Globe (Boston, Massachusetts) July 24, 1935.
5   Dispatch, August 1, 1935.
6   IBID.
7   IBID.
8   IBID.
9   The Sporting News (St. Louis, Missouri) May 29, 2000.
10 The Paducah Sun-Democrat (Paducah, Kentucky) August 4, 1935.
11 Star, August 8, 1935.
12 The Capital Times (Madison, Wisconsin) August 9, 1935.
13 IBID.
14 IBID.
15 The New York Daily News (New York City, New York) August 14, 1935.

16   IBID.
17   IBID.
18   <u>Dispatch</u>, August 16, 1935.
19   The Courier (Waterloo, Iowa) August 16, 1935.
20   <u>Star</u>, August 19, 1935.
21   The Boston Globe (Boston, Massachusetts) August 19, 1935.
22   <u>Star</u>, August 20, 1935.
23   <u>IBID</u>, August 21, 1935.
24   The Boston Globe (Boston, Massachusetts) August 21, 1935.
25   IBID.
26   <u>Dispatch</u>, August 28, 1935.
27   Brooklyn Daily Eagle (Brooklyn, New York) August 30, 1935.
28   <u>Star</u>, August 31, 1935.
29   <u>Diz</u>, P.271.
30   <u>Star</u>, September 14, 1935.
31   IBID.
32   The Chicago Tribune (Chicago, Illinois) September 25, 1935.
33   <u>Diz</u>, P.276.
34   The Democrat Chronicle (Rochester, New York)
35   Ol' D iz, P.170.
36   <u>Star</u>, September 28, 1935.
37   The St. Joseph Gazette (St. Joseph, Missouri) October 7, 1935.
38   The Evening News (Chattanooga, Tennessee) October 26, 1935.
39   The Baltimore Sun (Baltimore, Maryland) January 17, 1936.

CHAPTER 24

1   The Baltimore Sun (Baltimore, Maryland) January 17, 1936.
2   Brooklyn Times Union (Brooklyn, New York) January 12, 1936.
3   Brooklyn Daily Eagle (Brooklyn, New York) January 26, 1936.
4   <u>Dispatch</u>, February 7, 1936.
5   The Atlanta Constitution (Atlanta, Georgia) March 6, 1936.
6   The Pittsburgh Press (Pittsburgh, Pennsylvania) March 6, 1936.
7   The Atlanta Constitution (Atlanta, Georgia) March 6, 1936.
8   <u>Dispatch</u>, March 16, 1936.
9   <u>Star</u>, February 15, 1936.
10   The Monitor (McAllen, Texas) March 16, 1936.
11   <u>Globe</u>, March 10, 1936.
12   <u>Star</u>, March 21, 1936.
13   The Decatur Herald (Decatur, Illinois) March 25, 1936.
14   <u>Diz</u>, P.286.

15 Warren Corbett, Roy Parmelee Society for American Baseball Research (SABR) Biography Project.
16 IBID.
17 Diz, P.287.
18 The Miami News (Miami, Florida) May 14, 1936.
19 Star, June 3, 1936.
20 IBID, June 9, 1936.
21 Dispatch, June 13, 1936.
22 Star, June 18, 1936.
23 Dispatch, June 30, 1936.
24 L.A. Times, July 28, 1936.
25 Star, July 28, 1936.
26 IBID, August 11, 1936.
27 IBID.
28 IBID.
29 Globe, August 18, 1936
30 Star, August 18, 1936.
31 IBID.
32 Dallas News, January 28, 1937.
33 Globe, January 30, 1937.
34 Dispatch, February 2, 1937.
35 IBID.
36 Dallas News, February 20, 1937.
37 IBID.
38 Globe, March 2, 1937.
39 Star, March 3, 1937.
40 IBID.
41 Globe, March 6, 1937.
42 Dispatch, March 19, 1937.
43 IBID.
44 Diz, P.314.
45 The Cincinnati Enquirer (Cincinnati, Ohio) April 15, 1937.
46 The Gazette (Cedar Rapids, OHIO) April 4, 1937.
47 IBID.
48 IBID.
49 The Brooklyn Citizen (Brooklyn, New York) April 3, 1937.
50 IBID.
51 IBID.
52 IBID.
53 Dispatch, April 18, 1937.
54 IBID, April 28, 1937.

55 Globe, April 23, 1937.
56 Diz, P.289.
57 The Journal Gazette (Chicago, Illinois) April 25, 1937.
58 Star, January 14, 1937.
59 IBID, April 29, 1937.
60 Diz, P.322.
61 Globe, May 20, 1937.
62 Diz, P.326.
63 IBID, P.329.
64 Star, July 8, 1937.
65 Ol' Diz, P.181.
66 The St. Joseph News (St. Joseph, Missouri) August 1, 1937.
67 Dallas News, August 17, 1937.

CHAPTER 25

1 An interview with Bob Clampitt. By Michael Barrier and Milton Gray (Funnyworld Revisited) michaelbarrier.com
2 Globe, March 12, 1938.
3 Lansing State Journal (Lansing, Michigan) March 21, 1938.
4 Globe, March 23, 1938.
5 Star, March 23, 1938.
6 Austin American Statesman (Austin, Texas) April 8, 1938.
7 The Harrisburg Telegraph (Harrisburg, Pennsylvania) April 24, 1938.
8 Lubbock Avalanch Journal (Lubbock, Texas).
9 The Valley Morning Star (Harlingen, Texas) April 17, 1938.
10 IBID.
11 IBID.
12 The Cincinnati Enquirer (Cincinnati, Ohio) April 21, 1938.
13 IBID.
14 IBID.
15 Globe, April 25, 1938.
16 IBID.
17 Corsicana Daily Sun (Corsicana, Texas) May 5, 1938.
18 The Boston Globe (Boston, Massachusetts) August 6, 1938.
19 Ol' D iz, P.194.
20 The Des Moines Register (Des Moines, Iowa) September 28, 1938.
21 The Greenville News (Greenville, South Carolina) May 7, 1938.
22 Globe, June 2, 1938.
23 Dispatch, June 4, 1938.
24 The Star-Gazette (Elmira, New York) August 16, 1938.

25 Star, September 12, 1938.
26 The Evening Sun (Baltimore, Maryland) September 22, 1938.
27 Star, September 9, 1938.
28 Dizzy, P.110.
29 Star, October 7, 1938.
30 IBID.
31 Sport.
32 IBID.
33 IBID.
34 Diz, P.363.
35 Pittsburgh Post-Gazette (Pittsburgh, Pennsylvania) July 18, 1941.
36 LaFayette Journal-Courier (LaFayette, Indiana) July 16, 1941.
37 The Hartford Courant (Hartford, Connecticut) March 27, 1939.
38 Star, April 17, 1939.
39 The Pittsburgh Courier (Pittsburgh, Pennsylvania) August 19, 1939.
40 Gary Bedingfield. Baseball in World War II (Baseball in Wartime, 2019)
41 IBID.
42 N.Y. Times, December 31, 1948.
43 Dizzy Dean; He's not so dumb! The Saturday Evening Post. July 14, 1951.
44 Dizzy, P.47.
45 Dallas News, July 1, 1955.

CHAPTER 26

1 William Bennet, America: The Last Best Hope, 2007.
2 Plano Daily Star-Courier (Plano, Texas) April 6, 1966.
3 Conversations.
4 IBID.
5 Plano Daily Star-Courier (Plano, Texas) April 6, 1966.
6 The Daily Oklahoman (Oklahoma City, Oklahoma) July 21, 1974.
7 Dizzy, P.48.
8 The Daily Oklahoman (Oklahoma City, Oklahoma) July 21, 1974.
9 Los Angeles Times (Los Angeles, California) July 19, 1974.
10 Dizzy, P.48.